INTERNATIONAL STUDIES ON CHRISTIAN ORIGINS

Editor
Michael Labahn

Editorial Board
Tom Holmén, Bert-Jan Lietaert Peerbolte, Loren T. Stuckenbruck, Tom T. Thatcher

Published under

LIBRARY OF NEW TESTAMENT STUDIES

476

Formerly the Journal for the Study of the New Testament Supplement series

Editor
Mark Goodacre

Editorial Board
John M. G. Barclay, Craig Blomberg, R. Alan Culpepper,
James D. G. Dunn, Craig A. Evans, Stephen Fowl, Robert Fowler,
Simon J. Gathercole, John S. Kloppenborg, Michael Labahn,
Robert Wall, Steve Walton, Robert L. Webb, Catrin H. Williams

PARADIGMS OF BEING IN CHRIST

A Study of the Epistle to the Philippians

By

Peter-Ben Smit

Bloomsbury T&T Clark
An imprint of Bloomsbury Publishing Plc

BLOOMSBURY
LONDON · NEW DELHI · NEW YORK · SYDNEY

Bloomsbury T&T Clark
An imprint of Bloomsbury Publishing Plc

Imprint previously known as T&T Clark

50 Bedford Square	1385 Broadway
London	New York
WC1B 3DP	NY 10018
UK	USA

www.bloomsbury.com

BLOOMSBURY, T&T CLARK and the Diana logo are trademarks of Bloomsbury Publishing Plc

First published 2013
Paperback edition first published 2015

© Peter-Ben Smit, 2013

Peter-Ben Smit has asserted his right under the Copyright, Designs and Patents Act, 1988, to be identified as Author of this work.

All rights reserved. No part of this publication may be reproduced or transmitted in any form or by any means, electronic or mechanical, including photocopying, recording, or any information storage or retrieval system, without prior permission in writing from the publishers.

No responsibility for loss caused to any individual or organization acting on or refraining from action as a result of the material in this publication can be accepted by Bloomsbury or the author.

Quotes from Plutarch are reprinted by permission of the publishers and the Trustees of the Loeb Classical Library from PLUTARCH: VOLUME VII, MORALIA, VOLUME II, Loeb Classical Library Volume 405, with an English translation by Phillip H. De Lacy and Benedict Einarson, pp. 12, 123, 125, 147, 148, 149, Cambridge, Mass.: Harvard University Press. Copyright © 1959 by the President and Fellows of Harvard College. Loeb Classical Library ® is a registered trademark of the President and Fellows of Harvard College.
Scripture quotations are taken from The New Revised Standard Version of the Bible, copyright © 1989 Division of Christian Education of the National Council of the Churches of Christ in the USA. Used by permission. All rights reserved.

British Library Cataloguing-in-Publication Data
A catalogue record for this book is available from the British Library.

ISBN: HB: 978-0-567-27162-4
PB: 978-0-567-66254-5

Library of Congress Cataloging-in-Publication Data
A catalog record for this book is available from the Library of Congress.

Series: The Library of New Testament Studies, volume 476

Typeset by Free Range Book Design & Production Limited

CONTENTS

Tables	vii
Abbreviations	ix
Preface	xiii

1 INTRODUCTION 1
  1.1 Purpose and Context 1
  1.2 Structure and Method of the Present Study 5
      1.2.1 The State of Research 5
      1.2.2 Paradigms in Philippians 7
  1.3 The Use of Analogies in First-Century Rhetoric 16
      1.3.1 Two Exemplary *Exempla* 28
  1.4 Rhetorical Analysis and the *Corpus Paulinum* 30
      1.4.1 Epistolography and Rhetoric 30
      1.4.2 Examples, Rhetoric, and the Rhetorical Character of Philippians 33

2 THE COMMUNICATIVE SETTING: GENRE, STRUCTURE, AIMS, AND CONTEXT OF PHILIPPIANS 37
  2.1 Introduction 37
  2.2 Philippians as a Hellenistic Letter 37
      2.2.1 Hellenistic Epistolography 37
      2.2.2 The Literary Plan of Philippians 39
      2.2.3 Time, Place, and Situation of Composition 52
      2.2.4 The Recipients in Philippi 55
  2.3 Communicative Reasons for Philippians 56
      2.3.1 Thankfulness, Well-Wishing, the Exchange of Information, and Contact 56
      2.3.2 Requests and Instructions Concerning Issues in Philippi 68
      2.3.3 Opponents and Adversaries of the Philippians and Paul: An Overview 74
      2.3.4 "Thanking" for a Gift 76

3	MODELS OF IDENTITY IN PHILIPPIANS		79
	3.1	The Christ-Paradigm (Phil. 1.27–2.18)	79
		3.1.1 Introduction	79
		3.1.2 Worthy of Christ's Gospel: Community and Unity (1.27–2.4)	80
		3.1.3 The Christ *Enkomion* (2.5-11)	85
		3.1.4 A Misfit? The Problem of Christ's Origins	94
		3.1.5 Obedience and the Glorification of the Faithful (2.12-18)	95
		3.1.6 Paul's Appeal in the Context of Philippi	105
		3.1.7 Concluding Observations	106
	3.2	Timothy and Epaphroditus as *Exempla*?	107
		3.2.1 Introduction	107
		3.2.2 Timothy	109
		3.2.3 Epaphroditus	112
		3.2.4 Timothy and Epaphroditus as Paradigms: Their Relationship to the Philippians	115
	3.3	The Paradigm of "Paul in Christ" (Phil. 3.1–4.1)	117
		3.3.1 Introduction	117
		3.3.2 Setting an Example Oneself: *Periautologia*	118
	3.4	The *Exempla* and their Aims in Phil. 3	121
		3.4.1 The Starting Point: "Dogs" in Philippi	121
		3.4.2 Excursus: Paul the Paradigm: Logical and/or Illustrative?	134
		3.4.3 Paul the Christian and Identity "in Christ"	135
		3.4.4 Excursus: Paul as a Paradigmatic Man?	144
		3.4.5 Ensuing Exhortations: Euodia and Syntyche (Phil. 4.2-3) as (Negative) Paradigms?	155
4	CONCLUSIONS		158
	4.1	*Exempla* in Philippians: Concluding Overview	158
		4.1.1 *Exempla* and the Structure of Philippians	160
	4.2	The Point of the Paradigms	160
	4.3	Embodied Identity and Relational Ecclesiology	162
	4.4	The Traditional Character of Paul's Relational Ecclesiology	163
	4.5	Paul's Authority in its Ecclesiological Context	163
Bibliography			165
Index of Authors			189
Index of References			195

TABLES

1.1:	Aristotelian Categorization of Analogies	20
1.2:	Post-Aristotelian Categorization of Analogies	20
1.3:	Post-Aristotelian 1: Distinction Based on Contents	22
1.4:	Post-Aristotelian 2: Distinction Based on Form	22
2.1:	A Comparison of a Family Letter with Philippians 4.10-20	45
2.2:	A Comparison of Philippians 1.3-11 and 4.1-10	76
3.1:	Philippian Civic Identity and Paul's Self-Presentation	125
3.2:	A Comparison of Christ and Paul in Philippians 2 and 3	139
3.3:	A Comparison of the Exaltation of Christ and Paul's Eschatological Hope	142

ABBREVIATIONS

AASF	Annales Academiae scientiarum fennicae
AB	Anchor Bible
AbhMainz	Abhandlungen der Geistes- und Sozialwissenschaftlichen Klasse, Akademie der Wissenschaften und der Literatur in Mainz
AcBib	Academia Biblica
AGJU	Arbeiten zur Geschichte des antiken Judentums und des Urchristentums
AnBib	Analecta biblica
ANRW	Aufstieg und Niedergang der Römischen Welt
APB	*Acta Patristica et Byzantina*
ASNU	Acta seminarii neotestamentici Upsaliensis
AThANT	Abhandlungen zur Theologie des Alten und Neuen Testaments
AUU	Acta Universitatis Upsaliensis
BECNT	Baker Exegetical Commentary on the New Testament
BEvTh	Beiträge zur Evangelischen Theologie
BHT	Beiträge zur historischen Theologie
BibInt	*Biblical Interpretation*
BIS	Biblical Interpretation Series
BiSe	Biblical Seminar
BN	*Biblische Notizen*
BSGRT	Bibliotheca Scriptorum Graecorum et Romanorum Teubneriana
BWANT	Beiträge zur Wissenschaft vom Alten und Neuen Testament, Stuttgart
BZ	*Biblische Zeitschrift*
BZAW	Beihefte zur Zeitschrift für die alttestamentliche Wissenschaft
BZNW	Beihefte zur Zeitschrift für die neutestamentliche Wissenschaft
CBQ	*Catholic Biblical Quarterly*
CCLP	Corpus Christianorum Lingua Patrum
CEA	Collection d'Etudes Anciennes
CEBTh	Contributions to Biblical Exegesis and Theology
CNT	Commentaire du Nouveau Testament
CollLat	Collection Latomus

ConBNT	Coniectanea biblica: New Testament Series
CP	*Classical Philology*
DJD	Discoveries in the Judean Desert
DNP	Der neue Pauly
DVfLG	*Deutsche Vierteljahresschrift für Literaturwissenschaft und Geistesgeschichte*
ESEC	Emory Studies in Early Christianity
EvTh	*Evangelische Theologie*
ExAud	*Ex Auditu*
FRLANT	Forschungen zur Religion und Literatur des Alten und Neuen Testaments
FzB	Forschung zur Bibel
GTA	Göttinger theologische Arbeiten
HBS	Herders Biblische Studien
HBT	*Horizons in Biblical Theology*
Hist.E	Historia.Einzelschriften
HNT	Handbuch zum Neuen Testament
HTKNT	Herders theologischer Kommentar zum Neuen Testament
HUT	Hermeneutische Untersuchungen zur Theologie
HWdR	Historisches Wörterbuch der Rhetorik
Hyp	Hypomnemata
ICC	International Critical Commentary
IEJ	*Israel Exploration Journal*
JBL	*Journal of Biblical Literature*
JSJSup	Journal for the Study of Judaism in the Persian, Hellenistic, and Roman Period Supplement Series
JSNT	*Journal for the Study of the New Testament*
JSNTSup	Journal for the Study of the New Testament: Supplement Series
JSPL	*Journal for the Study of Paul and His Letters*
JTC	*Journal for Theology and the Church*
JThS	*Journal of Theological Studies*
KEK	Kritisch-exegetischer Kommentar über das Neue Testament
LCL	Loeb Classical Library
LEC	Library of Early Christianity
LNSAS	Leicester-Nottingham Studies in Ancient Society
LNTS	Library of New Testament Studies
LThK	Lexikon für Theologie und Kirche
MEFR	Mélanges de l'Ecole française de Rome
NClB	New Clarendon Bible
Neot	*Neotestamentica*
NET	Neutestamentliche Entwürfe zur Theologie
NIBCNT	New International Biblical Commentary on the New Testament
NIGTC	New International Greek Testament Commentary
NKZ	*Neue kirchliche Zeitschrift*

NovT	*Novum Testamentum*
NovTSup	Novum Testamentum Supplements
NTD	Neues Testament Deutsch
NTD.E	Neues Testament Deutsch. Ergänzungsbände
NTOA	Novum Testamentum et Orbis Antiquus
NTS	*New Testament Studies*
PaP	*Past and Present*
RAC	Realenzyklopädie für Antike und Christentum
RevExp	*Review and Expositor*
RGG	Religion in Geschichte und Gegenwart
RST	Regensburger Studien zur Theologie
SBLDS	Society of Biblical Literature Dissertation Series
SBLECL	Society of Biblical Literature Early Christianity and Its Literature
SBLEJL	Society of Biblical Literature Early Judaism and Its Literature
SBLMS	Society for Biblical Literature Monograph Series
SBLRBS	Society of Biblical Literature Resources for Biblical Study
SBS	Stuttgarter Bibelstudien
SCHNT	Studia ad corpus hellenisticum Novi Testamenti
SemeiaSt	Semeia Studies
SESJ	Suomen Eksegeettisen Seuran Julkaisuja
SHAW.PH	Sitzungsberichte der Heidelberger Akademie der Wissenschaften, Philosophisch-Historische Klasse
SHC	Studies in Hellenistic Civilization
SJT	*Scottish Journal of Theology*
SMBen.BE	Serie monografica di "Benedictina" (Sezione Biblica-Ecumenica)
SNTSMS	Society for New Testament Studies Monograph Series
ST	*Studia Theologica*
StUNT	Studien zur Umwelt des Neuen Testaments
TANZ	Texte und Arbeiten zum neutestamentlichen Zeitalter
TBN	Themes in Biblical Narrative
TGr.T	Tesi Gregoriani. Serie Teologica
ThH	Theologie Historique
THKNT	Theologischer Handkommentar zum Neuen Testament
THNTC	The Two Horizons New Testament Commentary
ThR.NF	*Theologische Rundschau. Neue Folge*
ThWNT	Theologisches Wörterbuch zum Neuen Testament
ThZ	*Theologische Zeitschrift*
TICP	Travaux de l'institut Catholique de Paris
TRE	Theologische Realenzyklopädie
TTK	*Tidsskrift for Teologi og Kirke*
TynBul	*Tyndale Bulletin*
VWGT	Veröffentlichungen der Wissenschaftlichen Gesellschaft für Theologie
WBC	Word Biblical Commentary

WMANT	Wissenschaftliche Monographien zum Alten und Neuen Testament
WUNT	Wissenschaftliche Untersuchungen zum Neuen Testament
ZBK	Zürcher Bibelkommentare
Zet	Zetemata
ZNW	*Zeitschrift für die neutestamentliche Wissenschaft und die Kunde der älteren Kirche*
ZThK	*Zeitschrift für Theologie und Kirche*

Preface

This study came into existence following the discovery of serious discussion regarding the non-exemplary character of Phil. 2.5-11. This discussion surprised me. Not only did I find the view that Phil. 2.5-11 would not serve as an example highly unlikely, I also became curious as to where this view came from and how examples actually functioned in the context of first-century literature, especially in Paul's Epistle to the Philippians. I began this research in 2005, following the completion of my dissertation on eschatological meals in the New Testament at the University of Bern, Switzerland. I was able to bring it to completion while serving as an assistant professor of New Testament Studies at VU University Amsterdam.

In the course of this research, I have benefitted from the insight and support of many colleagues, for which I thank them. In the field of New Testament studies, these are especially Professors Ulrich Luz, Urs von Arx, Matthias Konradt (now Heidelberg), and Moisés Mayordomo-Marin in Bern, and Martin de Boer, Bert-Jan Lietaert Peerbolte, Arie Zwiep, and Jan Krans in Amsterdam. Furthermore, it has been a privilege to write this study as a research associate in the Department of New Testament Studies at the University of Pretoria (research project "Mission and Ethics in the New Testament and Early Christianity"). I am grateful to Professor Kobus Kok for inviting me to serve in that capacity. Interaction with systematic theologians, notably with Dr. Mattijs Ploeger, Dean of the Old Catholic Seminary (Utrecht), has proven to be very beneficial to this study as well. The latter also reflects my conviction that a continuous and conscious interaction between systematic theological (or philosophical) reflection and exegetical studies is of importance. I take this position because I think that such an interaction is hermeneutically beneficial as it helps to make explicit what would remain implicit otherwise: the interaction between a scholar's worldview and his or her interpretative work. In this respect, there is little difference between the "secular" historian of early Christianity and the "religious" student of the New Testament. Moreover, this position is much closer to the contemporary hermeneutical discourse in literary studies (e.g. comparative literature) than a position that (still) endeavors to find a supposedly "neutral" or "objective" scholarly point of view. Besides, I find it much more interesting. I am grateful to Dr. Marco de Waard, Amsterdam University College, for drawing my attention to the interdisciplinary point just mentioned. I am also grateful to the editors of the Library of New Testament Studies/the *European Seminar on Christian Origins*, notably *Privatdozent* Dr. Michael Labahn, for the inclusion of this work in their series. To Mrs. Cheryl Whittaker thanks are due for the initial proofreading of the manuscript and to Nick Fawcett for the excellent editorial services through Bloomsbury; any remaining mistakes are my own.

I am also grateful to those communities of faith and friendship that gave me a home over these past years, most recently the Old Catholic diocese of Haarlem and the Old Catholic parish of Amsterdam. I am grateful to the bishop, the Rt. Rev. Dr. Dirk J. Schoon, and to the entire community for providing an atmosphere in which devotion and critical scholarship are equally encouraged. I am also grateful to Carolin.

In line with the subject matter of this study, I sign this preface on the Feast of St. Willibrord, Apostle to the Frisians, 2012.

Peter-Ben Smit

Chapter 1

INTRODUCTION

1.1 Purpose and Context

In his letter to the Christian community in Philippi, Paul can be seen to use Christ, himself, and others, such as Timothy and Epaphroditus, as examples as part of an attempt to persuade the Philippians. Many aspects of this issue are debated, however.[1] Nevertheless, the issue has considerable implications for the interpretation of Philippians. Therefore, this topic will be taken up again, specifically by asking how the character and function of the examples (*exempla*) in Philippians can be understood. In order to do this, two main steps will be taken. First, Greco-Roman rhetorical theory and practice concerning the use of analogies and examples, in the sense of *exempla*, will be presented as a tool for understanding the rhetorical function of the examples that Paul uses. Second, in an exegesis of the relevant sections of Philippians (especially Phil. 1.27-30, 2.1-18, 2.19-31, 3.2-21, and 4.2-3), it will be asked whether Paul uses examples and, if so, what their characteristics are, how they relate to each other, and how they relate to Paul's overarching concerns in Philippians.

The study of the use of analogies in Philippians is inviting for a number of reasons. First, there has been substantial discussion about the "exemplary character" of a number of figures in Philippians, specifically Christ, Paul, Timothy, and Epaphroditus in chapters 2–3, as well as Euodia and Syntyche in chapter 4. A consensus is still lacking in this discussion. Second, the use of analogies in first-century rhetoric was ubiquitous, which makes relating this field to the study of early Christian origins, including Philippians, appealing.

---

1. From the start, it should be noted that the question of imitation is a theological powder keg. To a substantial extent, this is due to late medieval and early modern debates about grace and free will and their confessional development since the Protestant and Catholic Reformations of the sixteenth century and their multi-faceted history of reception. See for this, e.g., the remarks of Edvin Larsson, *Christus als Vorbild: eine Untersuchung zu den paulinischen Tauf- und Eikontexten*, ASNU 23 (Uppsala: Gleerup, 1962), 9–10. See also the overview of texts and scholarship concerned with the imitation of Christ in the New Testament offered by Candida Moss, *The Other Christs: Imitating Christ in Ancient Ideologies of Martyrdom* (Oxford: Oxford University Press, 2010), 21–44, as well as the observations made by David M. Stanley, "Imitation in Paul's Letters: Its Significance for His Relationship to Jesus and to His Own Christian Foundations," in P. Richardson and J. Hurd (eds.), *From Jesus to Paul* (Waterloo: Wilfrid Laurier University Press, 1984), 127–141, esp. 129. On Paul's use of himself as a model, see also the elegant (but not often cited) treatment by Ernest Best, *Paul and His Converts* (Edinburgh: T&T Clark, 1988), 1–28.

Third, interestingly, the study of the "exemplary character" of the figures mentioned above has paid relatively little attention to contemporary rhetorical theory and practice with regard to the use of analogies (see, for notes on the state of research, section 1.2.1). For this reason, there may still be much potential in relating the issue of "exemplary characters" in Philippians to precisely the use of analogies and examples in first-century rhetoric. As the fact *that* Paul uses *exempla* in Philippians has begun to receive more recognition in recent scholarship,[2] here, the focus will be specifically on *how* he uses them.

While this study focuses on the use of *exempla* in Paul's letter to the Philippians, it also touches on broader questions of Paul's understanding, or at least performance, of authority, specifically in relation to Christ and the broader community. The discussion about this has seen a number of changes in the past century.[3] Much of the research in the earlier part of the century was devoted to the study of the development of early Christian structures of authority, that is, ecclesial ministry, typically using a model that assumed a gradual shift from informally organized charismatic communities to the "early catholicism" exemplified by, most prominently, the deutero-Pauline and pastoral epistles.[4]

---

2. See, for example, the overview given by Moss, *Christs*, 21–44, noting that there is no question as to whether the imitation of Christ occurs in the New Testament—and in Philippians for that matter; see along similar lines also: Rolin A. Ramsaran, "Living and Dying, Living is Dying (Philippians 1:21): Paul's Maxim and Exemplary Argumentation in Philippians," in Anders Eriksson, Thomas H. Olbricht, and Walter Übelacker (eds.), *Rhetorical Argumentation in Biblical Texts*, Emory Studies in Early Christianity (Harrisburg: Trinity, 2002), 325–338, esp. 325–326. See with Yung Suk Kim, "'Imitators' (*Mimetai*) in 1 Cor. 4:16 and 11:1: A New Reading of Threefold Embodiment," *Horizons in Biblical Theology 33* (2011), 147–170, esp. 148–149, e.g., the following studies on Philippians and other Pauline letters, agreeing on the use of *exempla*, but disagreeing as to their function and content: Margaret M. Mitchell, *Paul and the Rhetoric of Reconciliation: An Exegetical Investigation of the Language and Composition of 1 Corinthians*, HUT 28 (Tübingen: Mohr Siebeck, 1991), Wilhelm Michaelis, "μιμέομαι," *ThWNT* 4 (1942), 661–678 (both see Paul "as a deliberative rhetorician who seeks to unify the community by an appeal to his example" [Kim, *op. cit.*, 148]). Others view Paul as promoting "colonial mimicry" or "authoritative patriarchy" (Kim's terminology), see, e.g., Joseph A. Marchal, *Hierarchy, Unity and Imitation: A Feminist Rhetorical Analysis of Power Dynamics in Paul's Letter to the Philippians*, AcBib 24 (Atlanta: Society of Biblical Literature, 2006); Sandra Hack Polaski, *Paul and the Discourse of Power* (Sheffield: Sheffield Academic Press, 1999); Elizabeth Castelli, *Imitating Paul: A Discourse of Power* (Louisville: Westminster/John Knox, 1991); Elisabeth Schüssler Fiorenza, *The Power of the Word: Scripture and the Rhetoric of Empire* (Minneapolis: Fortress, 2007), 82–109; and Antoinette C. Wire, *The Corinthian Women Prophets* (Minneapolis: Fortress, 1990), 45–47.

3. See for the following, esp., Andrew D. Clarke, *A Pauline Theology of Church Leadership*, LNTS 362 (London: T&T Clark, 2008), 11–16.

4. See, e.g., Jürgen Roloff, "Amt, Ämter, Amtsverständnis IV. Neues Testament," *TRE* 2 (1978), 508–533, and the extensive bibliography provided there, as well as idem, *Die Kirche im Neuen Testament*, NTD.E, 10 (Gottingen: Vandenhoeck & Ruprecht, 1993); see further also, David L. Bartlett, *Ministry in the New Testament* (Minneapolis: Fortress, 1993), as well as, e.g., Paula Gooder, "In Search of the Early 'Church': The New Testament and the Development of Christian Communities," in Gerald Mannion and Lewis S. Mudge (eds.), *The Routledge Companion to the Christian Church* (New York: Routledge, 2008), 9–27, and the reflections of Norbert Nagler, *Frühkatholizismus: zur Methodologie einer kritischen Debatte*, RST 43 (Bern: Lang, 1994).

A later stage of research has concentrated more on the relationship between ministerial structures that occur in the New Testament and offices as they existed in the Greco-Roman world, both in public administration and in various private associations.[5] This newer research has often also focused on the question of authority, typically in conjunction with the question of early Christian ecclesial ministry, from a critical or theological and/or hermeneutical perspective.[6] The current study interacts primarily with the latter two kinds of research on structures of authority and ministry in early Christian communities as they are reflected by Paul's letters. In doing so, it asks how Paul's use of *exempla*, of Christ, of himself, and of others plays into the understanding of Paul's performance of authority, specifically in his exchange with the early Christian community in Philippi.

Thus, this study of Paul's usage of analogies and examples in Philippians is at the same time a study in early Christian, specifically Pauline, ecclesiology. Not all aspects of the connection between these topics may be immediately obvious, however. More self-explanatory starting points for a study of ecclesiology in Philippians would, for example, be provided by the titles and functions that are mentioned in the letter's opening, Phil. 1.1, where Paul and Timothy,[7] slaves of Christ, address the "saints" in Philippi together with their "bishops"[8] and

---

5. See, e.g., Gerd Theissen, *Studien zur Soziologie des Urchristentums*, WUNT 1.19 (Tübingen: Mohr Siebeck, ²1989); Peter Lampe, *Die stadtrömischen Christen in den ersten beiden Jahrhunderten: Untersuchungen zur Sozialgeschichte*, WUNT 2.18 (Tübingen: Mohr Siebeck, ²1989); Carsten Claussen, *Versammlung, Gemeinde, Synagoge: das hellenistisch-jüdische Umfeld der frühchristlichen Gemeinden*, StUNT 27 (Göttingen: Vandenhoeck & Ruprecht, 2002); Eva Ebel, *Die Attraktivität früher christlicher Gemeinden: die Gemeinde von Korinth im Spiegel griechisch-römischer Vereine*, WUNT 2.178 (Tübingen: Mohr Siebeck, 2004); Wayne A. Meeks, *The First Urban Christians: The Social World of the Apostle Paul* (New Haven: Yale University Press, ²2003); Todd D. Still and David G. Horrell (eds.), *After the First Urban Christians: The Social-Scientific Study of Pauline Christianity* (London: T&T Clark, 2009); James Tunstead Burtchaell, *From Synagogue to Church: Public Services and Offices in the Earliest Christian Communities* (Cambridge, UK: Cambridge University Press, 1992); see also Richard S. Ascough, *Paul's Macedonian Associations*, WUNT 2.161 (Tübingen: Mohr Siebeck, 2003), esp. 110–161, as well as Ritva H. Williams, *Stewards, Prophets, Keepers of the Word: Leadership in the Early Church* (Peabody: Hendrickson, 2006). Andrew Clarke has explored this topic in *Serve the Community of the Church* (Grand Rapids: Eerdmans, 2000).

6. See, e.g., Elisabeth Schüssler Fiorenza, *In Memory of Her: A Feminist Theological Reconstruction of Christian Origins* (New York: Crossroad, ¹⁰1994), Castelli, *Imitating*, and Marchal, *Hierarchy*. See also the contributions in Amy-Jill Levine, *A Feminist Companion to Paul* (London: T&T Clark International, 2004), and further the considerations of David Seeley, *Deconstructing the New Testament*, BIS 5 (Leiden: Brill, 1994).

7. Even though it is striking that Paul continues his formulations in Phil. 1.1 in the first person singular, thus making him appear as the sole author of the letter; this agrees well with later references to Timothy in the third person (e.g. 2.19); see, e.g., F. F. Bruce, *Philippians*, NIBC (Peabody, MA: Hendrickson, 1983), 25.

"deacons." Alternatively, the question of Paul's dependence on the community in Philippi might provide a point of departure for the study of ecclesial structures presupposed by Philippians. In spite of this, the question of the occurrence and use of *exempla* touches on foundational questions of Pauline ecclesiology. The following reasons can be given for this.

First and foremost, *exempla* are expressive of the relationships that provide the fabric of early Christian communities. This applies to relationships of the Philippian community with Christ, with Paul, and with Paul's co-workers, to the relationship of members of the Philippian community with one another, and to Paul's relationship with Christ and his own co-workers.

Second, the use of *exempla* also makes visible what sources of authority and tradition a community has. Such sources (and structures) of authority and tradition include both the written and oral traditions that bears witness to the *maiores* of the community as well as the "living text" of contemporary members of the (extended) community, such as Paul and Timothy.

Third, the study of the use of *exempla*, typical as it is for deliberative rhetoric,[9] will also draw attention more clearly to the fact that what Paul does in Philippians is not just moral exhortation (paraenesis) in the narrower sense of the word,[10] but also an attempt to steer an entire community in a particular direction; in other words, his concern is an ecclesiological, not just a moral one (even if "belonging shapes behaving" and ecclesiology implies a particular ethics/morality).[11]

Therefore, *exempla* make visible both relationships in a community and the appertaining structures of authority, both of which are key questions in any study of ecclesiology. As a whole, this study will therefore also seek to make a contribution to scholarship concerned with the character of ecclesial structures, including ecclesial leadership, as it is reflected by Philippians.

---

8. See for a succinct evaluation of this term of Wilhelm Egger, *Galaterbrief. Philipperbrief. Philemonbrief*, NEB (Würzburg: Echter, 1985), 53—Egger himself was Bishop of Bozen-Brixen. This verse continues to lead to (all too) heavily confessionally informed exegesis; see, e.g., David Alan Black, "The Discourse Structure of Philippians: A Study in Textlinguistics," *NovT* 37 (1995), 16–49, esp. 23, underlining that Paul understands the "overseers" and "deacons" as "extensions of the church" and not as having a position "over it," while Wolfgang Schenk, *Die Philipperbriefe des Paulus. Kommentar* (Stuttgart: Kohlhammer, 1984), 78–82, simply removes the entire remark about church leaders, arguing that it must be a post-Pauline gloss.

9. See below, 1.4.2.

10. On the notion of paraenesis, esp. in Paul, see, e.g., Anders Klostergaard Petersen, "Paraenesis in Pauline Scholarship and in Paul—An Intricate Relationship," in James Starr and Troels Engberg-Pedersen (eds.), *Early Christian Paraenesis in Context*, BZNW 125 (Berlin: De Gruyter, 2004), 267–295, as well as in the same volume: Wiard Popkes, "Paraenesis in the New Testament: An Exercise in Conceptuality," and Troels Engberg-Pedersen, "The Concept of Paraenesis," 13–45, 47–71.

11. See, e.g., Mitchell, *Paul*, 52: "[D]eliberative speeches and letters are not moral exhortation, but rather specific situation-centered arguments for a person or a group of people to follow a particular course of action (often related to public polity)."

Introduction 5

1.2 Structure and Method of the Present Study

In order to address the questions as they have been formulated above, the following steps will be taken in this study.

First, the state of research will be surveyed, in order to outline the scholarly discussion within which this study has its place. Second, the method used in this study will be further clarified. Third, part of the theoretical framework used will be elucidated, outlining the rhetorical device of the παράδειγμα/*exemplum* and sketching its relevance for the study of Philippians in terms of rhetorical analysis. The fourth step consists of outlining the genre and structure as well as the communicative context of the epistle, and researching its aims. Fifth, the sections of Philippians that use *exempla* are studied in their literary contexts. Finally, having done all this, the whole of the study can be condensed into a number of conclusions.

This study will also include an excursus on the self-presentation of Paul as an *exemplum* from the perspective of the study of masculinity in the Greco-Roman world. While attention to the gender(ed) aspects of a text should be part of any piece of responsible exegesis, this particular excursus draws attention more specifically to the paradoxical relationship between Paul and what may be termed conventional Greco-Roman values concerning masculinity. As will be shown, on the one hand Paul's self-presentation questions many of the cultural assumptions of his day that pertained to masculinity, while on the other hand he operates fully within this matrix, presenting himself (following Christ) as a controversial but nevertheless hypermasculine figure. This deepens the understanding of Paul as an *exemplum*.

In terms of method, it may also be maintained that the basic hermeneutical premise upon which this study builds is the consideration that an appropriate historical interpretation of an ancient text should regard this text as a relic of a past process of communication within the context of a "symbolic universe" or "cultural encyclopedia" (including earlier traditions) shared by most (if not all) participants in the process.[12] Taking such a communicative situation as the hermeneutical starting point of an exegesis implies an encompassing reading of a text: it will have to be read as a whole, whereby this reading is facilitated by synchronic observations, which, in turn, are informed by diachronic considerations.

1.2.1 The State of Research

In order to provide the necessary background to the current study, here, an overview of the state of research is provided. This overview will focus on the

---

12. See, e.g., the considerations of Thomas Söding and Christian Münch, *Kleine Methodenlehre zum Neuen Testament* (Freiburg: Herder, 2005), 9–21. See also, Wilhelm Egger, *Methodenlehre zum Neuen Testament. Einführung in linguistische und historischkritische Methoden* (Freiburg: Herder, ³1993), 28–33.

study of the use of and debate about examples in Philippians. The debate about examples and their function in Paul's letters is, of course, broader and concerns, with regard to the presentation of Christ as an example, at least Rom. 6.1-11, 8.28-30; 1 Cor. 4.16, 9, 11.1, 15.44-49; 2 Cor. 3.18, 4.4; Gal. 2.19-20; Phil. 2.5-11 (3.17); and 1 Thess. 1.6, 2.14;[13] and with regard to the (self-)presentation of Paul as an example, at least 1 Cor. 4.16, 9.1-27, 11.1; Phil. 1.30, 3.17, 4.9; 1 Thess. 1.6, 2.14; and also Gal. 4.12.[14] The reason for the focus of this overview is that the discussion around this topic with regard to Philippians can be considered exemplary—in the modern sense of the word—for the discussions about this topic in Pauline literature as a whole. At the same time, it may be noted that *exempla* occur throughout early Christian literature in general.[15]

In this context, it should also be borne in mind that the term παράδειγμα enjoyed in New Testament studies considerable popularity in the wake of

---

13. This is admittedly a broad selection; e.g. Otto Merk, "Nachahmung Christi: zu ethischen Perspektiven in der paulinischen Theologie," in Helmut Merklein (ed.), *Neues Testament und Ethik* (FS Rudolf Schnackenburg; Freiburg: Herder, 1989), 172–206, esp. 172, only includes 1 Thess. 1.6, 2.24; 1 Cor. 4.16, 11.1; and Phil. 3.17 in his list. Merk also offers a helpful overview of the history of research in this respect. See for a succinct overview, Richard A. Burridge, *Imitating Jesus: An Inclusive Approach to New Testament Ethics* (Grand Rapids: Eerdmans, 2007), 144. See on 1 Cor. 8–11, Dustin W. Ellington, "Imitating Paul's Relationship to the Gospel: 1 Corinthians 8.1–11.1," *JSNT* 33 (2011), 303–315.

14. See, e.g., Willis Peters de Boer, *The Imitation of Paul* (Kampen: Kok, 1962); Brian Dodd, *Paul's Paradigmatic "I": Personal Example as Literary Strategy*, JSNTSup 177 (Sheffield: Sheffield Academic Press, 1999); Benjamin Fiore, "Paul, Exemplification, and Imitation," in J. Paul Sampley (ed.), *Paul in the Greco-Roman World: A. Handbook* (Harrisburg: Trinity, 2003), 228–257, esp. 238–245; as well as Abraham J. Malherbe, *Paul and the Popular Philosophers* (Minneapolis: Fortress, 1989), 69; Andrew D. Clarke, "'Be Imitators of Me': Paul's Model of Leadership," *TynB* 49 (1998), 329–360; Ellington, "Imitating"; and on 1 Cor. 9, see esp. Lincoln E. Galloway, *Freedom in the Gospel: Paul's Exemplum in 1 Cor 9 in Conversation with the Discourses of Epictetus and Philo*, CBETh 38 (Leuven: Peeters, 2004).

15. E.g. in Berger's work the *exemplum* occurs as follows. (1) With reference to the Roman tradition of the *exempla maiorum* (e.g. the testaments, Sir. 44–50): *exempla ad probationem* both historical (e.g. Jas. 5.17-18) and contemporary (Lk. 10.39-42). (2) *Exempla* also occur in the context of an apologetic reasoning (see Mk. 2.25-26, with an *argumentatio a minore ad maius*: Mt. 12.11, Lk. 13.15; further also: Mk. 3.24-25, and Lk. 14.5. (3) In symbuleutic texts in the context of God's own paradigmatic behavior, e.g. in terms of his care (Lk. 12.6-7, 24, 27; Mt. 6.26, 28), his punishment (2 Pet. 2.4-7; Jude 5-7; see also Sir. 16.5-15; CD 2.14–3.12; 3 Macc. 2.3-7; Test. Naft. 2.8–4.3). (4) Berger also mentions moral examples from the past (Jas. 5.11, 17-18), the catalogue of paradigms in Heb. 11; see also Philo, *Praem.* 13, and Sap. Sal. 11—for Berger these are examples of Greek (see Lysias, *Or.* 29 on Aristophanes, 45–49, and Isocrates, *Antid.* 231–235), not of OT *exempla* (see Deut. 26.5-9); further Lk. 14.32-42/Mt. 26.36-46; Lk. 22.40-46: 1 Pet. 2.21-24 with Jesus as an example, and in Acts the *exempla* in the speech of Gamaliel (Acts 5.36-37). Furthermore there are morally deterring *exempla* (Jude 11; 2 Pet. 2.15-22; Heb. 3–4 with 1 Cor. 10.1-12; see also Ps.-Philo, *Ant. Bib.* 20:3-4; Ps. 95.7-9). (5) In the context of symbuleutic texts, people are confronted with their own behavior by means of examples (see Lk. 10.13-14, 12.54-55). (6) Some texts can be seen as in close proximity to the moral *exemplum* (esp. the parable Lk. 10.29-37 and the χρεια Lk. 10.39-42). (7) Some apologetic *exempla* can also be found in Jesus' biography (see Lk. 4.25-27). See Berger, *Formgeschichte*, 28–31; further 85–86, 285–287, 331–332, 409; see also idem, *Formen und Gattungen* (Tübingen: Francke, 2005), 81-121.

Dibelius' form-critical work, though he used the term with a different interest than is used here, i.e. within the context of his analysis of the tradition of the gospel and with an eye to the emergence of *exempla* in the context of early Christian proclamation, meaning exemplary accounts that served early Christian preaching.[16]

1.2.2 Paradigms in Philippians

With regard to research on *exempla* in Philippians, three main scholarly foci can be distinguished. First, there are studies that focus specifically on the question of the exemplary character of Christ in Philippians 2. Second, there are studies that are specifically concerned with Paul's presentation of himself as an example, especially in Philippians 3. Finally, there are some studies with a broader scope. These studies will now be considered, in order to provide an overview of the state of research.

1.2.2.1 Christ the Example?
The history of interpretation of Phil. 2.5-11 has been thoroughly reviewed by Martin,[17] including an analysis of such key studies as those by Lohmeyer, Käsemann, Larsson, and Betz[18] as they have also been identified by Soon-Gu Kwon. Much of the appertaining debate in the twentieth century focused precisely on the (non-)exemplary character of this text within Philippians. Broadly speaking, exegetical preferences moved from generally assuming an "ethical" interpretation, as Martin terms it, taking Christ as the example of the appropriate way of Christian life, to preferring an interpretation in

---

16. See Martin Dibelius, *Die Formgeschichte des Evangeliums* (mit einem erweiterten Nachtrag von Gerhard Iber herausgegeben von Günter Bornkamm; Tübingen: Mohr Siebeck, 6[3]1971), 34–66. See in general also, Ruben Zimmermann, "Urchristliche Parabeln im Horizont antiken Rhetorik. Der Beitrag von Aristoteles und Quintilian zur Formbestimmung der Gleichnisse," in Linda Hauser, Ferdinand R. Prostmeier, and Christa Georg-Zöller (eds.), *Jesus als Bote des Heils. Heilsverkündigung und Heilserfarhung in frühchristlicher Zeit*, SBS 60 (FS Detlev Dormeyer; Stuttgart: Verlag Katholisches Bibelwerk, 2008), 201–225.

17. Ralph P. Martin, *A Hymn of Christ: Philippians 2:5-11 in Recent Interpretation & in the Setting of Early Christian Worship* (Downers Grove: Intervarsity, ³1997); see also Merk, "Nachahmung," 172–192, as well as Soon-Gu Kwon, *Christ as Example: The Imitatio Christ Motive in Biblical and Christian Ethics*, AUU (Uppsala: Uppsala University Press, 1998). See also Clarke, "Imitators," as well as the brief overview provided by James P. Ware, *Paul and the Mission of the Church: Philippians in Ancient Jewish Context* (Grand Rapids: Baker, 2011), 224–225.

18. See Ernst Lohmeyer, *Kyrios Jesus. Eine Untersuchung zu Phil. 2,5–11*, SHAW.PH, *Philosophisch-Historische Klasse*, 1927/28.4 (Heidelberg: Winter, 1928), and Ernst Käsemann, "Kritische Analyse von Phil 2:5–11," *ZThK* 47 (1950), 313–360; English: "Critical Analysis of Philippians 2:5–11," *JTC* 5 (1968), 45–88. References are to the German version. See further, Larsson, *Christus*, and H. Dieter Betz, *Nachfolge und Nachahmung Jesu Christi im Neuen Testament*, BHT 37 (Tübingen: Mohr, 1967).

terms of incorporation into Christ and the behavior belonging to it, denying the exemplary character of Christ. The fountainhead of most interpretations rejecting an "ethical interpretation" of Phil. 2.5-11, replacing it with what may be termed a "kerygmatic" interpretation,[19] is Lohmeyer's 1928 *Kyrios Christos*,[20] even if it was Käsemann's study of 1950 that was particularly vehement in its rejection of any such interpretation.[21] With Morgan, Käsemann's argument can be summarized as follows:

> In this hymn, the Christian community on earth takes up antiphonally what is happening in the divine court where the powers are prostrate before God's throne. It is drawn into the eschatological event and on earth witnesses to the enthronement of the Obedient one. The church does not have to say what is happening to itself. When it proclaims Christ as ruler of the world, the new world comes into view. It becomes clear that the obedient one is generating more obedient children. This is not cosmology. It is eschatology and soteriology. When the obedient one is proclaimed as world ruler, a boundary divides the old and the new world. The Christian community is now called afresh into the sphere in which it has to stand, act, and suffer. This sphere "in Christ," consists in humility and obedience, in the freedom of those who are redeemed. This hymn is thus confession, and in early Christianity confession marks the boundaries between the old and the new ages, boundaries which always threatened to get blurred in everyday life. The boundaries are maintained by explicating what it means to be "in Christ." An ethical model would not get us out of the old world. What is said here is that the world belongs to the Obedient one. He is Lord so we can be obedient. We become obedient not by imitating a model but through a word that tells us that we belong to him.[22]

With regard to this interpretative trajectory, the following can be maintained, especially with regard to the concerns of this study. First, this study concentrates on a different level than Käsemann, who paid much attention to the original meaning of the text. By contrast, here the interest is primarily in the Pauline *usage* of what is now Phil. 2.5-11, not so much in its original sense—the analysis of the meaning of a text in the context in which it is used is not exhausted by

---

19. See, e.g., Demetrius K. Williams, *Enemies of the Cross of Christ: The Terminology of the Cross and Conflict in Philippians*, JSNTSup 223 (Sheffield: Sheffield Academic Press, 2002), 68–71, for an overview of the debate using this terminology.

20. Lohmeyer, *Kyrios*. On Lohmeyer's exegesis of Phil. 2.5-11, see, e.g., Colin Brown, "Ernst Lohmeyer's *Kyrios Jesus*," in Ralph P. Martin and Brian J. Dodd (eds.), *Where Christology Began: Essays on Philippians 2* (Louisville: Westminster/John Knox, 1998), 6–42.

21. See Käsemann, "Analyse." Behind Käsemann looms the figure of Barth; see Karl Barth, *Erklärung des Philipperbriefes* (München: Kaiser, ³1936), esp. 53–62. On Käsemann's interpretation, see, e.g., Robert Morgan, "Incarnation, Myth, and Theology: Ernst Käsemann's Interpretation of Philippians 2:5–11," in Martin and Dodd (eds.), *Christology*, 43–73; for his radicalization of Lohmeyer's exegesis, see 53. See also Merk's striking thesis that being an imitator of Christ is (according to Paul) in no way related to the ethical and moral qualities of the historical Jesus; only the "Christ-event" matters. The latter Merk understands as follows: "Dieses Christusgeschehen ist im Zusammenhang der Mimesis-Aussagen zentriert auf das Daß des Gekommenseins Jesu, seine Präexistenz, Menschwerdung und das Kreuzesgeschehen" (Merk, "Nachahmung," 203).

22. Morgan, "Incarnation," 67.

establishing what it could have meant in an earlier context.[23] Second, Käsemann's theological (and hermeneutically applied) distinction between ethics on the one hand and eschatology/soteriology on the other is not followed here,[24] as, in principle, there is no clear reason why eschatology and soteriology should not be closely related to ethics. Third, different from Käsemann, this study will pay attention to contemporary rhetorical theory, which gives a more realistic starting point for the evaluation of *exempla* such as Phil. 2.5-11, thus avoiding rejecting the exemplary character of Phil. 2.5-11 on the basis of anachronistic demands on its exemplary function (i.e. by demanding full agreement between the pattern set forth in Phil. 2.5-11 and the subsequent outline of preferred behavior/career of the Christians).[25]

When returning to Martin's work and his own position, the following may be observed. First, he presents and critiques prominent nineteenth- and twentieth-century schools of interpretation: what he terms the "dogmatic view,"[26] the "kenotic theory,"[27] the "ethical example interpretation"[28] (all nineteenth century) and interpretations taking as points of departure a background in heterodox Judaism,[29] in Hellenistic thought and mythology in general,[30] in the Old Testament,[31] in specific Hellenistic examples,[32] in specific historical allusions,[33] and in a baptismal context.[34] Pointing out the strengths and weaknesses of each of these approaches, Martin is especially keen to reject an "ethical" interpretation if such an interpretation is taken to mean that Phil. 2.6-11 is used to exhort Christians to (simply) act like Christ.[35] Second, having

---

23. See below, 1.3; see also 3.1. Emphatically so, e.g., Larry W. Hurtado, "Jesus as Lordly Example in Philippians 2:5–11," in Richardson and Hurd (eds.), *Jesus*, 113–126, esp. 118–119.

24. Käsemann, "Analyse," 359.

25. See Käsemann, "Analyse," 319. The same mistake is made by Dodd, *Paul's Paradigmatic "I"*, 191, arguing that the exaltation of Christ by God in Phil. 2.9-11 is an act by God which cannot be imitated by the Philippians, which would speak against an ethical interpretation of (at least of this part of) the hymn. However, Paul's subsequent paraenesis draws on Christ's obedience first of all, only making use of an eschatological outlook to outline the destiny of the true faithful (i.e. in 1.12 and especially later in 3.2-21; see, e.g., Oakes, *Philippians*, 201–202), and, as a look at Greco-Roman thought about the use of *exempla* will show (see below, 1.3), such a one-to-one correspondence between *analogans* and *analogatum* was not even demanded. A mediating trajectory is pursued by John B. Webster, "The Imitation of Christ," *TynB* 37 (1986), 95–120, and, idem, "Christology, Imitability and Ethics," *Scottish Journal of Theology* 39 (1986), 309–326, who argues that the vision that one has of reality also determines one's attitude towards it.

26. See Martin, *Hymn*, 63–65.
27. See Martin, *Hymn*, 66–68.
28. See Martin, *Hymn*, 68–74.
29. See Martin, *Hymn*, 74–75.
30. See Martin, *Hymn*, 76–78.
31. See Martin, *Hymn*, 78.
32. See Martin, *Hymn*, 78–80.
33. See Martin, *Hymn*, 80–81.
34. See Martin, *Hymn*, 81–82.
35. The background to this is linguistic (i.e. it depends on the translation of Phil. 2.5) and in terms of content: the hymn tells one who Christ was, not what he did (see, e.g., Martin, *Hymn*, 83, and esp. 68–74, 84–88, 287–289).

studied what Phil. 2.5-11 might have meant in its original context and setting,[36] he also states how the text functions in the context of Paul's appeal: "The appeal and injunction to the Philippians are ... : become in your conduct the type of persons who, by that *kenosis*, death and exaltation of the Lord of glory, have a place in his body, the Church." Being in Christ and being loyal to him and his (kind of) lordship is thus Martin's point of departure.[37] For the rest of Philippians, this means the following: "The essence of Christ's paradigmatic actions stands out in the lineaments of the hymn, and they are exemplified in his servants like Paul, Timothy and Epaphroditus, whose lives are made conformable to his pattern of service, sacrifice and above all obedience."[38] Thus, Martin is able to integrate Phil. 2.5-11 into Paul's appeal by way of ecclesiological reasoning: belonging shapes behaving; those who are in Christ ought to live accordingly, in other words, conforming to the pattern set by the Lord. This view of things is also received by numerous other scholars.[39] While Martin argues that this is in essence not an ethical interpretation that uses Christ as an example, he still emphasizes the paradigmatic quality of Christ's actions.

In addition to this trajectory of interpretation, there has been a consistent tradition of interpreting Phil. 2.5-11 along the lines of imitation as well.[40] This scholarship is to some extent a reaction to Käsemann's position. In describing the history of research with respect to this issue, Hurtado argues that Käsemann's exegesis "was an overreaction against particular examples of 'ethical idealism' and pietism. This made it also impossible for Käsemann to do justice to the evidence of Paul's paraenetical purposes in including this passage in his letter."[41] An early example of such a reaction to Käsemann's work is

---

36. See Martin, *Hymn*, 97–283, 294–311 (Martin opts for a primarily soteriologically oriented hymn of pre-Pauline authorship from a Hellenistic setting, probably a baptismal liturgical context).
37. See Martin, *Hymn*, 291–292, quotation from 291.
38. Martin, *Hymn*, lv.
39. For an overview, see, e.g., John Reumann, *Philippians*, AB 33B (New Haven: Yale University Press, 2008), 333–339.
40. For an overview, see, e.g., Reumann, *Philippians*, 333–339. See, e.g., contributions such as Bruce, *Philippians*, 81; Moisés Silva, *Philippians*, BECNT (Grand Rapids: Baker, ²2005), 95–98; see also Troels Engberg-Pedersen, *Paul and the Stoics* (Edinburgh: T&T Clark, 2000), 109–116; John Byron, *Slavery Metaphors in Early Judaism and Pauline Christianity*, WUNT 2.162 (Tübingen: Mohr, 2003), 177–178; and Ernst R. Wendland, "Modeling the Message: The Christological Core of Philippians (2:5-11) and its Communicative Implications," *APB* 19 (2008), 350–378.
41. Hurtado, "Jesus," 126. See also the observations of Morna D. Hooker, "Philippians 2:6–11," in E. Earl Ellis and Erich Gräßer (eds.), *Jesus und Paulus* (FS Werner Georg Kümmel; Göttingen: Vandenhoeck & Ruprecht, 1975), 151–164, esp. 154: "But what is the character of this new humanity – this life in Christ? It seems to me nonsense to suggest that it is not the character of Jesus himself. It is only the dogma that the Jesus of History and the Christ of Faith belong in separate compartments that leads to the belief that the appeal to a Christian character appropriate to those who are in Christ is not linked to the pattern as seen in Jesus himself."

Larsson's study.⁴² Larsson argued, without much recourse to contemporary rhetorical theory and conventions, on the basis of keyword connections between Phil. 2.5-11 and its immediate literary surroundings, that the Christ as he is presented in this text functions as a prototype. The Philippians are to imitate this prototype, for example through their obedience; Paul is a primary specimen of such an imitation of Christ. Other examples of such reactions to Käsemann's work include Hooker,⁴³ who is followed by, e.g., Johnson,⁴⁴ as well as the work of scholars such as Fowl,⁴⁵ Fee,⁴⁶ Bockmuehl,⁴⁷ and O'Brien.⁴⁸ In this context, Park's contribution should also be mentioned, published decades after Larsson's. Focusing on the notion of "submission" in Philippians, she argues in favor of a combination of ethics and soteriology in Philippians as far as the imitation of Christ is concerned, especially with regard to his submission to God.⁴⁹ Strikingly, however, the argument generally remains at the level of linguistic considerations and does not take into account the question of *exempla* as rhetorical tools as such.⁵⁰

1.2.2.2 Paul and Other Exempla *in Philippians*
Paul also presents himself as an example in Philippians. This has attracted the attention of a number of studies, in which the precise use and importance of Paul's presentation of himself as an example is considered. Of these studies,

---

42. See Larsson, *Christus*, 230–275.
43. See Hooker, "Philippians." She does not speak of imitation of Christ, however, but of becoming conformed to him.
44. See Luke Timothy Johnson, "The Mind and Moral Discernment in Paul," in John T. Fitzgerald, Thomas H. Olbricht, and L. Michael White (eds.), *Early Christianity and Classical Culture: Comparative Studies in Honor of Abraham J. Malherbe*, NTSup 110 (Leiden: Brill, 2003), 215–236, esp. 234: "That Paul intends the Christ-hymn to be understood as exemplary is demonstrated by the way he proceeds to offer three other examples to the Philippians of a 'moral reckoning' that gives up an individual's interest for the sake of the greater good: Timothy (2:19-24), Epaphroditus (2:25-30), and Paul himself (3:1-16)."
45. Stephen E. Fowl, *The Story of Christ in the Ethics of Paul: An Analysis of the Function of the Hymnic Material in the Pauline Corpus*, JSNTSup 36 (Sheffield: JSOT Press, 1990), and idem, *Philippians*, The Two Horizons New Testament Commentary (Grand Rapids: Eerdmans, 2005), 90.
46. See Gordon D. Fee, *Paul's Letter to the Philippians*, NICNT (Grand Rapids: Eerdmans, 1995), 191–229.
47. E.g. Markus Bockmuehl, *The Epistle to the Philippians* (London: Black, 1997), 121–125, see also 228.
48. See Peter T. O'Brien, *The Epistle to the Philippians*, NIGTC (Grand Rapids: Eerdmans, 1991), 253–262.
49. M. Sydney Park, *Submission within the Godhead and the Church in the Epistle to the Philippians: An Exegetical and Theological Examination of the Concept of Submission in Philippians 2 and 3*, LNTS 361 (London: T&T Clark, 2007), esp. 10–37.
50. Partial exceptions are William S. Kurz, "Kenotic Imitation of Paul and of Christ in Philippians 2 and 3," in Fernando F. Segovia (ed.), *Discipleship in the New Testament* (Philadelphia: Fortress, 1985), 103–126, and Black, "Discourse," esp. 47; here, Black provides a statement about the use of *exempla* in the letter, but does not further elaborate this.

Dodd's in particular provided a helpful overview of the research until 1999,[51] which will not be repeated here. The main interpretative issues that have come to the surface in the discussion include most prominently the issue of Paul's understanding of authority in relation to his presentation of himself as an example.[52] Thus, with regard to the question of the imitation of Paul, the questions at stake seems to be the following. What is the point of Paul's call(s) upon others to imitate him? How does this relate to the believers' relations to Christ and to one another? What is the goal of this exhortation to imitate Paul?[53] Dodd himself asserts that "the imitation of Paul can and should be understood both as a pedagogical technique and as an implied assertion of authority as a summons to conform to the pattern set by Paul as the regulative model."[54] Because it brings out a number of issues that will have to be addressed later on in this study as well, it is worthwhile to briefly present Dodd's treatment of Paul's example of himself in Philippians here.[55] Dodd's general conclusion runs as follows:

> Paul's use of self-characterization in Philippians combines persuasive artistry, polemics and paraenesis. In Philippians 3, it has been maintained, Paul presents his renunciation of Jewish credentials against those who were flouting theirs, probably promoting circumcision. The rhetoric of his paradigmatic "I" is shaped by his polemical purpose ... Thus, Paul's Jewish self-presentation is with the express purpose of exemplifying his renunciation of these qualities because of Christ ... When he presents himself as a model, he knows that another option exists

---

51. See Dodd, *Paul's Paradigmatic "I"*, 18–29, drawing especially on De Boer, *Imitation*. See also Peter Oakes, *Philippians: From People to Letter*, SNTSMon 110 (Cambridge, UK: Cambridge University Press, 2001), 121–128.

52. See for a particularly outspoken perspective, Castelli, *Imitating*, 89–117, esp. 116: "Paul's discourse of mimesis uses rhetoric to rationalize and shore up a particular set of social relations or power relations within the early Christian movement. His use of the notion of mimesis, with all of its nuances, reinforces both Paul's own privileged position and the power relations of the early Christian communities as somehow 'natural.' That is to say, the hierarchy of power is in tune with a much larger and more self–evident structure which incorporates both the earthly community and the divine order. Participating in the mimetic relationship with Paul, the early communities are to be rewarded with salvation. Resisting the mimetic relationship, by contrast, has dire consequences." Castelli refers specifically to 1 Thess. 1.6-7, 2.4; Phil. 3.17; 1 Cor. 4.16, 11.1; and Gal. 4.12. See for a more mediating position, Stanley, "Imitation," 141: "They are intended to point to a reality transcending merely human exemplarity, moral influence, or external simulation. Nor can Pauline imitation be reduced to obedience to the apostle's authority. Paul's singular use of imitation and example is the result of his radical insight into the gospel as the communication of God's saving power in Christ and his total awareness of human impotence vis-à-vis that divine power. In urging the imitation of himself upon his own Christian foundations, he endeavors to lead them to share his own experience of man's need to rely with full confidence on the divine power graciously offered through 'his gospel.'"

53. See Dodd, *Paul's Paradigmatic "I"*, 29.

54. Dodd, *Paul's Paradigmatic "I"*, 29.

55. See Dodd, *Paul's Paradigmatic "I"*, 171–172.

for his readers, thus his use of self-characterization is at once paradigmatic and polemical.[56]

However, Dodd also notes a problem with respect to Paul's paradigmatic use of himself in Philippians, as he indicates that there are three issues which stand in the way of "full identification of Paul's model of imitation."[57] These are the following: some of Paul's self-references are "inimitable," of which a prime example is Paul's "hyper-Jewish" identity in Phil. 3.4b-6; then, there are too many references to things that lay in the past or that are unknown to the present-day reader of Paul's work, such as other examples (see, e.g., Phil. 3.17), or things Paul has taught in the past.[58] Further on in his study,[59] Dodd also argues against Paul's paradigmatic function in Philippians in terms of him representing Christ to the Philippians by being a "Christ-Type"[60] for the Philippians. He does so on the basis of the following observations. He first argues that Paul's "paradigmatic self-presentation" in Phil. 3 includes: (a) self-renunciation of confidence "in the flesh"; (b) confidence "in Christ"; (c) proper eschatological reserve; (d) encouragement to press on; (e) the regulative teacher to be obeyed; and (f) one who has contentment from trusting prayer.[61] As Christ does not exemplify any of these characteristics in Philippians, Paul cannot possibly be an *exemplum* that is modeled on Christ. Dodd does allow that "Paul's paradigmatic 'I' exemplifies the soteriological significance of life 'in Christ'," but not that "Paul presents himself as an imitator of Christ in Philippians."[62] Finally, it should be noted here that Dodd restricts his theoretical reflections on the use of *exempla* in the first person to considerations about *mimesis*,[63] without addressing the broader question of *exempla* and more precisely that of *periautologia*, as this study will do, thereby aiming at a more

---

56. Dodd, *Paul's Paradigmatic "I"*, 194–195. This resonates well with his general conclusions about Paul's use of himself as an *exemplum*: "[I]t is very apparent that Paul's references to himself are by no means informed by a uniform strategy. Sometimes Paul literally portrays himself or his past to underline his calling and authority, while at other times his 'I' takes on a rhetorical flair and rather is meant as 'you'. In places Paul's self-references engage the pastoral situation faced, while in other places his self-characterizations may have more to do with generally held social requirements surrounding self-discussion. ... [I]t is misleading to conceive of Paul's self-presentations in his letters as 'autobiography', since this suggests that the purpose of his self-presentation is merely to express himself and the details of his life. Rather, his self-characterizations are highly selective, serving as antidotes for the particular rhetorical situation by seeking both to undermine his opposition and to provide a clear model for his readers" (idem, *op. cit.*, 171).
57. Dodd, *Paul's Paradigmatic "I"*, 182.
58. Dodd, *Paul's Paradigmatic "I"*, 182–183; the problem is that Dodd seems to want a perfect reader to fully comprehend Paul's statements in Philippians; however, neither today, nor in the past, has such a reader existed, yet the letter still seems able to communicate.
59. Dodd, *Paul's Paradigmatic "I"*, 193–194.
60. So L. Gregory Bloomquist, *The Function of Suffering in Philippians*, JSNTSup 78 (Sheffield: JSOT, 1993), 168.
61. Dodd, *Paul's Paradigmatic "I"*, 193.
62. Dodd, *Paul's Paradigmatic "I"*, 194.
63. See Dodd, *Paul's Paradigmatic "I"*, 16–18.

specific localization of *exempla* in the first person (singular) within the context of Hellenistic rhetoric.[64]

Another significant study has been published by Fowl, who studies Phil. 2.5-11 in the context of a study on the "function of the hymnic material in the Pauline corpus."[65] His particular vantage point is that of the use of the notion of "exemplars" as it has been developed by T. S. Kuhn.[66] An "exemplar" is "a concrete formulation or experiment which is recognized and shared by all scientists."[67] Strangely, Fowl seems to be unfamiliar with the notions of the *exemplum* or the παράδειγμα, or the like, even if they would have had the distinct advantage of being rhetorical concepts contemporary with Paul.[68]

In addition, an article by O'Brien should be mentioned here, as he argues in general that Paul makes use of "godly models" in Philippians throughout; his contribution is especially noticeable as he also identifies Phil. 2.17 as an *exemplum*.[69] This argument also occurs in his commentary of 1991, where he further defends the thesis that Phil. 2.19-30 "also has a paraenetical purpose by pointing to [Timothy and Epaphroditus] as models of a selfless attitude that Paul wants the community to follow."[70] He only demonstrates this thesis indirectly, however, noting at the end of his discussion of Phil. 2.19-30 that, where Paul is willing to sacrifice himself, Timothy serves the gospel unselfishly and shows a genuine concern for the Philippians, and Epaphroditus' dedication to his mission nearly cost him his life.[71]

A further study that is of importance here is Bianchini's *L'Elogio di sé in Cristo* of 2006,[72] in which the author proceeds to analyze Phil. 3.1–4.1 from the perspective of precisely *periautological exempla*. Noting that there are difficulties with reading Phil. 3.1–4.1 as one coherent unit from the perspective of rhetorical analysis,[73] Bianchini nevertheless offers an interpretation along these lines by reading this part of Philippians as consisting of (sandwiched) positive and negative examples, the positive one consisting of Paul's *periautological exemplum*[74]—Bianchini draws on contemporary rhetorical theory in order to

---

64. See below, 3.3.2.
65. Fowl, *Story*.
66. Fowl, *Story*, 92–95, referring specifically to T. S. Kuhn, *The Structure of Scientific Revolutions* (Chicago: University of Chicago Press, ²1970).
67. Fowl, *Story*, 93.
68. Park's critique of Fowl (*Submission*, 26–31) on the basis of his understanding of "vindication" seems to be beside the point: if, as Fowl suggests, Christians have to endure shame during their earthly sojourn, the participation in heavenly glory is a vindication indeed.
69. See Peter T. O'Brien, "The Gospel and Godly Models in Philippians," in M. J. Wilins and T. Paige (eds.), *Worship, Theology and Ministry in the Early Church: Essays in Honor of Ralph P. Martin*, JSNTSup 87 (Sheffield: JSOT Press, 1992), 273–284, esp. 280; it remains difficult to see why this should indeed be the case, however.
70. O'Brien, *Epistle*, 315, see also 443.
71. O'Brien, *Epistle*, 344.
72. Francesco Bianchini, *L'Elogio di sé in Cristo. L'utilizzo della* περιαυτολογία *nel contexto di Filippesi 3,1–4,1* AB 164 (Rome: Pontificio Istituto Biblico, 2006).
73. See Bianchini, *L'Elogio*, 8–26.
74. See Bianchini, *L'Elogio*, 53–137.

analyze the *exempla* in Phil. 3.1–4.1[75]—and the negative one consisting of Paul's description of the "dogs."[76] In a conclusion that is akin to the findings of this study, Bianchini summarizes his findings as follows: "L'autoelogio paolino, fondato sull'elogio di Cristo, si resolve in un'esortazione, rivolta a tutti i credenti, a fare come l'Apostolo della propria vita una lode di Cristo, ripercorrendo un itinerario di conformazione alla sua morte e risurrezione."[77] While this study will benefit from the insights of Bianchini, it will move beyond them by interacting more extensively with Greco-Roman theory about *exempla*, specifically of the *periautological* kind, and by providing a more encompassing discussion of all *exempla* in Philippians, not just the ones in chapter 3.[78]

Also of significance for the research undertaken here is Bittasi's study.[79] Bittasi indeed notes that models of identity are of significance in Philippians, but then proceeds to interpret this without much reference to contemporary rhetorical or epistolary theory. Instead, he relies heavily on the (presumably chiastic) structure of Philippians. This approach leads him to the thesis that Phil. 2.19-30 is the letter's actual core statement, thus presenting Timothy and Epaphroditus as the central *exempla* of the letter.[80] Bittasi arrives at his conclusion by arguing that Paul makes his point by using two examples of φρονεῖν as one should ἐν Χριστῷ, i.e. Phil. 2.1-18 (centering on Christ) and 3.2-16 (centering on Paul), but above all by means of the *exemplum* that can be found at the center of the letter, namely that of Timothy and Epaphroditus (Phil. 2.19-30), "men of communion" who are in their lives guided by "being in Christ," in other words, by φρονεῖν what was in Christ and hence becoming *exempla ad imitandum*. This structure of Philippians points to its core: the *exemplum* of Timothy and Epaphroditus. So far, Bittasi's thesis. As a main criticism of this position, in the course of this study an alternative view of the relationship between, in particular, the Christ *exemplum* and the subsequent information about Timothy and Epaphroditus will be provided. Furthermore it may be noted that chiastic patterns in letters are not commonplace, which should make one suspicious of a proposal like Bittasi's, and, more importantly, Paul himself does not seem to give more weight to the *exemplum* of Timothy and Epaphroditus than to either Christ's *exemplum*, or his own example.

Furthermore, Sandnes, in his study of bellies and bodies in the Pauline epistles, briefly touches on the theory of *exempla*, though mainly in its Aristotelian variant without paying attention to the development of the theory and praxis of the use of *exempla* following Aristotle. Even so, he also quotes

75. See Bianchini, *L'Elogio*, 55–61.
76. See Bianchini, *L'Elogio*, 139–198.
77. Bianchini, *L'Elogio*, 272: "The Pauline self-praise, based on the praise of Christ, results in an exhortation, addressed to all the faithful, calling upon them to turn their own lives into a song of praise of Christ, returning to an itinerary of conformation to his death and resurrection" (author's translation).
78. Bianchini's discussion of Phil. 2 remains relatively brief; see idem, *L'Elogio*, 230–245, most of which is concerned with the relationship between the *exempla* in Phil. 2 and 3. This lack of attention to *periautological* rhetoric also applies to Ellington, "Imitating."
79. Stefano Bittasi, *Gli esempi necessari per discernere: il significato argomentativo della struttura della lettera di Paolo ai Filippesi*, AnBib 153 (Rome: Pontificio Istituto Biblico, 2003).
80. See also Wendland, "Modelling," for a similar, but more modest argument.

a dictum from the *Rhetorica ad Alexandrum* ("examples are actions that have occurred previously and are similar to, or opposite of, those which we are now discussing"—*Rhet. Al.* 8:1) to give a definition of *exempla*.[81] In addition, Park's study merits attention here again, given that she also offers an interpretation of Paul, Timothy, and Epaphroditus, as well as Euodia and Syntyche, as *exempla*, especially with regard to the question of submission, on which she focuses,[82] taking issue with Castelli's "Foucaultian" interpretation of the same topic.[83] Further, Engberg-Pedersen identifies Paul's role as one of modeling Christ to the Philippians without much argument.[84] He is largely in agreement with Patte, who argues that Paul is an example in Philippians because of his Christ experience; in other words, the way being in Christ has shaped his life.[85] Like Engberg-Pedersen, Debanné also operates mainly on the assumption of paradigms in Philippians in his discussion of enthymemes in Philippians.[86] The latter also applies to Bittasi[87] and Hellerman.[88]

Thus, with the partial exception of Bittasi, of the more recent studies of Philippians, none engages Greco-Roman theories of παραδείγματα or *exempla* at much length, even if the use of these rhetorical tools is often assumed. In this respect, the present study will fill the gap in the study of Philippians.

1.3 The Use of Analogies in First-Century Rhetoric

In Pauline scholarship, the topic of *mimesis* or imitation has been given considerable attention, especially given the fact that the topic occurs most prominently in the Pauline letters among the New Testament writings.[89] *Mimesis* is often acknowledged as one of the popular philosophical tools of which Paul makes use when presenting himself and his views, specifically with an eye to educating his audience (παιδεία),[90] or with an eye to convincing his audience

---

81. Karl Olav Sandnes, *Belly and Body in the Pauline Epistles*, SNTSMon 120 (Cambridge, UK: Cambridge University Press, 2002), 139–140, here 140.
82. Park, *Submission*, 38–79.
83. See Park, *Submission*, 94–116.
84. Engberg-Pedersen, *Paul*, 91.
85. Daniel Patte, *Paul's Faith and the Power of the Gospel: A Structural Introduction to the Pauline Letters* (Philadelphia: Fortress, 1983), 172–175.
86. Marc J. Debanné, *Enthymemes in the Letters of Paul*, LNTS 303 (London: T&T Clark, 2006), 102–103.
87. Bianchini, *L'Elogio*.
88. Joseph H. Hellerman, *Reconstructing Honor in Roman Philippi: Carmen Christi as Cursus Pudorum*, SNTSMon 132 (Cambridge, UK: Cambridge University Press, 2005), 2: "after the analogy of Jesus."
89. See, e.g., Clarke, "Imitators," 329–330. Clarke's argument (350) that Paul's injunctions to imitate him are not part of a power play are not followed here; certainly Paul exercises some power over the Philippians by urging them to follow his own example.
90. See, e.g., De Boer, *Imitation*, 1–13, 24–28; Bert-Jan Lietaert Peerbolte, "Paul and the Practice of παιδεία," in Riewerd Buitenwerf, Harm W. Hollander, and Johannes Tromp (eds.),

and substantiating his argument. This has been acknowledged both in Pauline studies and in New Testament studies in general.[91] This is in line with an earlier observation that there is an emerging agreement as to the existence of *exempla* in Paul's letters.[92] For this reason, the focus can now be on the question of their use and function.

The use of analogies, such as the *exemplum* or παράδειγμα[93] (sometimes also used as general designations for such analogies) enjoyed a long tradition and virtually ubiquitous popularity within Greek, Hellenistic, and Greco-Roman rhetorical traditions.[94] Fundamentally, as Morgan puts it, *exempla* were "sayings and doings of famous men and women of the past as examples to be imitated or avoided."[95] *Exempla* could be used in a variety of different arguments, but, especially in later phases of its development, were especially popular within moral or ethical literature, where suggestive examples were used in order to move the audience or readership in a certain direction.[96] The audience is invited to draw (its inductive) conclusions on the basis of an analogy presented by means of an *exemplum*.

Known already to Plato, the παράδειγμα was integrated into rhetorical theory more firmly by Aristotle, who described it as a rhetorical device suitable for all

---

Jesus, Paul, and Early Christianity, NTSup 130 (Leiden: Brill, 2008), 261–280; Susan Eastman, "Imitating Christ Imitating Us: Paul's Educational Project in Philippians," in J. Ross Wagner, C. Kavin Rowe, and C. Katherine Grieb (eds.), *The Word Leaps the Gap: Essays on Scripture and Theology in Honor of Richard B. Hays* (Grand Rapids: Eerdmans, 2008), 427–450, esp. 430–434, 448–50, as well as in the same volume, E. P. Sanders, "Did Paul's Theology Develop?", 325–347, esp. 343–347.

91. See with regard to this, e.g., Malherbe, *Philosophers*, 51–58, 69–71, 74, as well as with regard to popular philosophy and the New Testament in general, idem, "*Hellenistic Moralists* and the New Testament," *ANRW* II.26.1 (1992), 267–333, and with regard to Paul, Stanley E. Porter, "Paul of Tarsus and His Letters," in idem (ed.), *Handbook of Classical Rhetoric in the Hellenistic Period 330 B.C. – A.D. 400* (Leiden: Brill, 1997), 533–585, esp. 570–576.

92. See above, section 1.

93. See esp. Martin Paul Schittko, *Analogien als Argumentationstyp. Vom Paradeigma zur Similitudo*, Hypomnemata 144 (Göttingen: Vandenhoeck & Ruprecht, 2003); Peter von Moos, *Geschichte als Topik. Das rhetorische Exemplum von der Antike zur Neuzeit und die* historiae *im "Policraticus" Johanns von Salisbury*, Ordo 2 (Hildesheim: Olms, 1988), esp. 48–113; and Fiore, "Paul," as well as idem, *The Function of the Personal Example in the Socratic and Pastoral Epistles*, AnBib 105 (Rome: Biblical Institute, 1986). See in general also, Bice Mortara Garavelli, *Manuale di retorica* (Milano: Bompiani, [7]2003), 23, 73, 76, 251, and Heinrich Lausberg, *Elemente der literarischen Rhetorik* (Ismaning: Hueber, [10]1990), para. 404. See also Zimmermann, "Parabeln."

94. In agreement with two of Schittko's four theses: "1. daß die antiken Theoretiker darin übereinstimmen, auf Ähnlichkeitserkenntnis basierende rhetorische Mittel als einen eigenen Argumentationstypus zu betrachten. 2. daß die einzelnen Theoretiker aber, was den Inhalt, die Form, die Funktion und Wirkungsweise dieser Mittel angeht, durchaus unterschiedliche Ansichten haben" (Schittko, *Analogien*, 16).

95. Teresa Morgan, *Popular Morality in the Early Roman Empire* (Cambridge, UK: Cambridge University Press, 2007), 122.

96. See, e.g., Malherbe, *Philosophers*, 51.

rhetorical genres, and by the *Rhetorica ad Alexandrum*. Subsequently, it was developed by various Hellenistic and Greco-Roman thinkers, as is reflected in the *Rhetorica ad Herrenium* as well as in the works of Cicero and Quintilian.⁹⁷ Naturally, the appertaining theory has changed in the course of these centuries. Taking Aristotle's considerations as a starting point, the following sketch will help to appreciate this development and with it the significance of this rhetorical device in first-century (CE) culture, thus providing the matrix within which Paul's use of examples and analogies can be interpreted. The contributions of Cicero and Quintilian are of special significance in this respect, as their work brackets the rhetorical theory relevant to the first century CE.⁹⁸

Central to Aristotle's dealing with analogies is his distinction between and according treatment of logically valid analogies; in other words, those contributing to a demonstration of proof, which are termed παραδείγματα and discussed in his treatment of demonstration of proof (πίστις),⁹⁹ and ornamental analogies, which are termed εἰκών and belong to his treatment of style (λέξις). The way in which this first kind of an Aristotelian παράδειγμα proves a point is best explained through the following example:¹⁰⁰

> We have an example when the major extreme is shown to be applicable to the middle term by means of a term similar to the third. It must be known both that the middle term applies to the third and that the first applies to the term similar to the third. E.g. let A be "bad," B "to make war on neighbours," C "Athens against Thebes" and D "Thebes against Phocis." Then if we require to prove that war against Thebes is bad, we must be satisfied that war against neighbours is bad. Evidence of this can be drawn from similar examples, e.g., that war by Thebes against Phocis is bad, and war against Thebes is against neighbours, it is evident that war against Thebes is bad. Now it is evident that B applies to C and D (for they are both examples of making war on neighbours), and to A to D (since the war against Phocis did Thebes no good); but that A applies to B will be proven by means of D. The same method will obtain supposing that our conviction that the middle term is related to the extreme is drawn from more than one similar term. Thus it is evident that an example represents the relation, not of part to whole or of whole to part, but of one part to another, where both are subordinate to the same general term, and one of them is known. It differs from induction in that the latter, as we saw, shows from an examination of all the individual cases that the <major> extreme applies to the middle, and does not connect the conclusion with the <minor> extreme; whereas the example does not use all the individual cases for its proof. (Aristotle, *Prior Analytics* 24 [= 68b.38–69a.19])

---

97. See Schittko, *Analogien*, 57–145.
98. For this discussion, see Schittko, 114–145.
99. See, e.g., Schittko, *Analogien*, 25–32.
100. Translation: Hugh Tredennick (ed. and trans.), *Aristotle: Prior Analytics*; LCL (Cambridge, MA: Harvard University Press, 1967). See Schittko, *Analogien*, 27, Moisés Mayordomo-Marín, *Argumentiert Paulus logisch? Eine Analyse auf dem Hintergrund antiker Logik*, WUNT 1.188 (Tübingen: Mohr Siebeck, 2005), 70–71.

Schittko summarizes the Aristotelian point of view as follows: "Die paradeigmatische Argumentation erscheint … wie eine Argumentation vom einzelnen mit einem 'Umweg über das Allgemeine.'"[101] He illustrates this with a diagram:

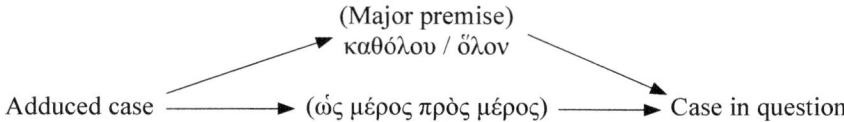

This means that the παράδειγμα differs from (other) enthymemes because the major premise is gained through an example,[102] and from an ἐπαγωγή because it does not appeal to all comparable cases and does not include a syllogism either.[103]

As indicated, in Aristotle's thought the use of analogies also plays a role of importance in the field of style (λέξις).[104] The aim of the use of this second kind of analogies, i.e. what Aristotle calls "metaphor" and "image" (μεταφορά or εἰκών), was not so much to persuade the audience by means of a logical argument, but rather to move it by means of an illustration; in other words, through πρὸ ὀμμάτων ποιεῖν. This distinction is of importance as such, but also of relevance in view of the later development of the theory and use of παραδείγματα. Important is not only the different function of the μεταφορά or εἰκών, but also that this kind of illustration drew on a wider range of imagery (including the *res naturae*) than the παράδειγμα, which was (typically) restricted to the field of human *res gestae* in Aristotelian rhetorical theory.[105] Schittko has schematized these Aristotelian distinctions as follows:[106]

---

101. See Schittko, *Analogien*, 27, as well as Mayordomo-Marín, *Paulus*, esp. 70; further also, 135, 137.
102. The enthymeme can be best understood as a truncated syllogism, i.e. a proof that follows the logic of a syllogism, but does not give the reader all the constituent parts, for example leaving out one of the premises or even the conclusion. The reader has to infer the parts that are missing. See, e.g., James C. Raymond, "Enthymemes, Examples, and Rhetorical Method," in Robert J. Connors, Lisa S. Ede, and Andrea A. Lunsford (eds.), *Essays in Classical Rhetoric and Modern Discourse* (Carbondale: Southern Illinois University Press, 1984), 140–151. On enthymemes in Paul, see Debanné, *Enthymemes, passim*.
103. The ἐπαγωγή is another of induction, of which Aristotle gives a definition in *Top.* 105a, regarding it as an argument moving from the specific to the general. See Schittko, *Analogien*, 27–28.
104. See for this, e.g., Schittko, *Analogien*, 39–42.
105. See Schittko, *Analogien*, 39–42, Fiore, "Paul," 229.
106. Schittko, *Analogien*, 159; see also 25–45. See also Fiore, "Paul," 229.

Table 1.1: **Aristotelian Categorization of Analogies**

Terminology	παράδειγμα			μεταφορά
	Historical examples	Fables	Fictional accounts	εἰκών
Function	logical proof			style (ornamentative)
Mode of operation	rational			through illustration

In addition, in the (roughly contemporary) *Rhetorica ad Alexandrum*, a broader definition of the παράδειγμα is found, namely one that considers them as concerning "actions that have occurred previously and are similar to, or the opposite of, those which we are now discussing."[107] Here, the distinction between examples that prove and those that illustrate is much less clear-cut. Furthermore, the *Rhet. Al.* underlines the importance of using recent examples because of their proximity to the audience, and allows the use of material taken from other sources than historical events as part of a παράδειγμα.[108]

In post-Aristotelian rhetorical theory,[109] as it is for example reflected in the *Rhetorica ad Herrenium* and Cicero's *De Inventione*, some shifts take place.[110] Most significantly, the Aristotelian distinctions between παράδειγμα (logical proof) and εἰκών (illustration), and their assignment to the discussions of πίστις and λέξις respectively, fades (see *De Inv.*) or disappears entirely (*Rhet. Herr.*).[111] This leads to a situation that can be visualized by comparing the following chart, provided by Schittko,[112] with the above chart of the Aristotelian approach:[113]

Table 1.2: **Post-Aristotelian Categorization of Analogies**

Terminology	Similitudo (in a broad sense)		
	Exemplum	Imago	Similitudo (in a narrower sense)
Function	proof		style (ornamentative)
Kind of proof	logical		illustrative

107. *Rhet. Al.* 8:1.
108. *Rhet. Al.* 32:1–5.
109. Between the Aristotelian era and that of the first century, there is little evidence of further development of the theory of the παράδειγμα. See Fiore, "Paul," 231.
110. See for this and the following the brief presentation in Schittko, *Analogien*, 159–160.
111. See Schittko, *Analogien*, 159.
112. Schittko, *Analogien*, 159.
113. For this distinction, see, e.g., Schittko, *Analogien*, 70–72, 160.

In this table, it is of significance that there are few clear-cut and strict distinctions in the second column. In other words, while the notion of *similitudo* can be used to describe all kinds of analogies and comparisons, three somewhat more distinct terms were also used to describe subtypes of the *similitudo* (*exemplum*, *imago*, and again *similitudo*, but now in a narrower sense). These various kinds of analogies could function both as proof and as stylistic ornament (two functions that were not always easy to distinguish between) and operated along the lines of both logic and illustration. This is a substantial change *vis-à-vis* earlier thought on the subject, especially as it is reflected in the work of Aristotle, where proof and style were clearly distinguished and different kinds of analogies were assigned to different parts of rhetorical theory. In the first century, these distinctions had faded; Quintilian's attempts to revive them are but one more witness to this.[114] The following quotation from the *Rhetorica ad Herennium* 4.45:59 illustrates this situation well:[115]

> Comparison is a manner of speech that carries over an element of likeness from one thing to a different thing. This is used to embellish or prove or clarify or vivify. Furthermore, corresponding to these four aims, it has four forms of presentation: contrast, negation, detailed parallel, abridged comparison. To each single aim in the use of comparison we shall adapt the corresponding form of presentation.

Generally speaking, therefore, in post-Aristotelian rhetorical theory Aristotle's two kinds of analogies are now taken together and discussed under the broader heading of *similitudo* or *comparabile*.[116] As a consequence of this, "illustrative" analogies (*imagines*) can now also be found in discussions about demonstrations of proof or probability, even though this kind of analogy does not aim at a rational (or logical) reasoning, but rather at influencing the audience emotionally in order to move it in the desired direction.[117] These examples prove something through demonstration, not by means of logical argument.[118] Indeed, examples and analogies begin to function more and more by virtue of the *auctoritas* of the material that they use, rather than by virtue of the "fit" they provide between the subject under discussion and the *res gestae* to which they refer.[119] This development coincides with the emergence of the *exemplum* (that is, *exemplum virtutis*) as a prominent device in moralistic literature.[120] Thus, the rhetorical use of logical analogies that employ examples is more or less embedded into or subordinated to a broader area of rhetorical strategies of persuasion that also employ analogies. For the analysis of *exempla* in

---

114. For this aspect of Quintilian's work, see, e.g., Schittko, *Analogien*, 143–144, 159.
115. Theodor Nüßlein (ed. and trans.), *Rhetorica ad Herennium* (Düsseldorf: Artemis & Winkler, ²1998), 292.
116. See for this, Schittko, *Analogien*, 159
117. See, e.g., Schittko, *Analogien*, 159.
118. See Mitchell, *Paul*, 42–43; also Williams, *Enemies*, 103.
119. See Schittko, *Analogien*, 159.
120. See esp. the extensive study by Morgan, *Morality*, esp. 122–159.

Philippians, these observations are of significance, as this development means that it is likely that here the same broader approach to *exempla* would be used. This shift in post-Aristotelian rhetorical theory may, again with Schittko,[121] indeed be accounted for by referring to the dominance of the λέξις (style) over πίστις (proof) in later times.

To be sure, distinctions between various kinds of comparisons and analogies continued to be made in rhetorical theory. However, the criterion for distinguishing various types of analogies ceased to be the logical characteristics of a comparison. In post-Aristotelian theory, much was made, for example, of the content of the analogies; e.g. *res gestae* were seen to provide a different sort of analogy (*exempla*) than comparisons that drew on examples taken from nature (*similitudo* in the narrower sense and *imago*). Similarly, the precise linguistic form of the comparison became a distinguishing mark. Logical(ly valid) reasoning could be part of a comparison, but this was not a necessity.[122] Schittko has again helpfully mapped the situation with regard to this:

Table 1.3: **Post-Aristotelian 1: Distinction Based on Contents**

Terminology	Similitudo (in the broader sense)	
	Exemplum/παράδειγμα	Similitudo/παραβολή/Imago
Content	Res (ut) Gestae	Res/Natura

Table 1.4: **Post-Aristotelian 2: Distinction Based on Form**

Terminology 1	Similitudo (in the broader sense)				
Linguistic Form	Double-sided ("normal")		Single (brevior similitudo)		
	Separata (often *exemplum*)	Conexa (sic... ut, often similitudo)	Antono-masia	Allegory	Metaphor
Terminology 2	Similitudo/Exemplum		Exemplum		Similitudo

Having thus outlined the use of analogies in first-century Greco-Roman rhetoric, it should be noted as well that the use of predominantly Latin terminology here should not obscure the fact that what has been said about analogies also reflects what was happening in Greek rhetoric at the same time. Notably, the *exemplum*, as it has been discussed here, has a counterpart in

---

121. See Schittko, *Analogien*, 160.
122. See Schittko, *Analogien*, 164: in the table presented there, παράδειγμα and *exemplum* are equated on the basis of their content (*res gestae*), while it becomes clear too that the same *res gestae* can also be part of logically valid comparisons, here termed *similitudo*.

the Greek *chreia*, common as it was to the primary, secondary, and rhetorical education in a Greco-Roman context,[123] as, e.g., Morgan has noted, using the terms *chreia* and *exemplum* synonymously.[124] This means that there can be a close relationship between the way in which an author such as Plutarch used examples and analogies[125] and what Paul of Tarsus did in his writings.

In addition to what has been outlined so far, some further aspects of the use of analogies, specifically as they figure under the heading of *exempla* and are related to their functioning and social setting, should be considered.

To begin with, an understanding of *exempla* (and many more of the *similitudines* used in first-century rhetoric) as "cultural symbols,"[126] drawing on insights from sociology and cultural studies, may be helpful.[127] Studies employing this notion seek to explain how and why analogies operated that were not strictly logical in character, but still contributed to the advancing of an argument. From this

---

123. See, e.g., the editions by Ronald F. Hock and Edward O'Neil (eds.), *The Chreia in Ancient Rhetoric: The Progymnasmata* (Atlanta: Scholars, 1986); Hock and O'Neil (eds.), *The Chreia and Ancient Rhetoric: Classroom Exercises*, Writings from the Greco-Roman World (Atlanta: SBL, 2002); and on their place in the curriculum, see, e.g., Teresa Morgan, *Literate Education in the Hellenistic and Roman Worlds* (Cambridge, UK: Cambridge University Press, 1998).

124. See esp., Morgan, *Morality*, 5: "An exemplary story (*chreia* in Greek, *exemplum* in Latin) is the short, pithy account of a saying or action of a famous man (or less often, woman)." Some significant work is also being done on Paul's use of the *chreia*: see, e.g., Anders Eriksson, *Tradition as Rhetorical Proof: Pauline Argumentation in 1 Corinthians*, CBNTS 29 (Stockholm: Almqvist & Wiksell, 1998); Samuel Byrskog, "The Early Church as a Narrative Fellowship: An Exploratory Study of the Performance of the *Chreia*," *Tidsskrift for Teologi og Kirke* 78 (2007), 207–226; and Fiore, "Paul."

125. See further, e.g., Frederick E. Brenk, "Setting a Good Exemplum: Case Studies in the Moralia, the Lives as Case Studies," in A. G. Nikolaidis (ed.), *The Unity of Plutarch's Work: "Moralia" Themes in the "Lives", Features of the "Lives" in the "Moralia"* (Berlin: De Gruyter, 2008), 237–254, esp. 241. See, e.g., Berger, *Formen*, 84–86, and idem, *Formgeschichte*, 28–31, 80–93, and on 76, with special reference to *exempla maiorum*. See with regard to the Gospels, Burridge, *Imitating*, 28–29, 73–78 (including rabbinic literature).

126. See esp., Michael Stemmler, "*Auctoritas exempli*. Zur Wechselwirkung von kanonisierten Vergangenheitsbildern und gesellschaftlicher Gegenwart in der spätrepublikanischen Rhetorik," in Bernhard Linke and Michael Stemmler (eds.), *Mos Maiorum. Untersuchung zu den Formen der Identitätsstiftung und Stabilisierung der römischen Republik*, Historia—Einzelschriften 141 (Stuttgart: Steiner, 2000), 141–205; idem, "Institutionalisierte Geschichte. Zur Stabilisierungsleistung und Symbolizität historischer Beispiele in der Redekultur der römischen Republik," in Gert Melville (ed.), *Institutionalität und Symbolisierung. Verstetigungen kultureller Ordnungsmuster in Vergangenheit und Gegenwart* (Cologne: Böhlau, 2001), 219–240; and in the same volume, Andreas Haltenhoff, "Institutionalisierte Geschichten. Wesen und Wirken des literarischen *Exemplum* im alten Rom," 213–217; see further also the considerations of Morgan, *Morality*, 1–10, as well as Stefan Rebenich, "Historical Prose," in Porter (ed.), *Handbook*, 265–337, and in the same volume, Ruth Webb, "Poetry," 339–369.

127. See Stemmler, "*Auctoritas*," 142–143 and esp. 159. See esp. Peter L. Berger and Thomas Luckmann, *Die gesellschaftliche Konstruktion der Wirklichkeit. Eine Theorie der Wissenssoziologie* (Frankfurt: Fischer, ⁵1997), 36, 38–40, 56–98, 102–103, and Jan Assmann, *Das kulturelle Gedächtnis. Schrift, Erinnerung und politische Identität in frühen Hochkulturen* (München: Beck, ⁴2002), 34–48.

perspective, Stemmler described what takes place in Cicero's use of the Roman history:

> Die römische Geschichte wird bei Cicero zu einem Gemälde, zu einem Zeichensystem, das aus Farben, Linien und Formen ein Gesamtbild darstellt, ein Abbild von eben der ideellen *res Romana*, dem Wesen der römischen Gesellschaft, die als Ursache für den bisherigen Erfolg Roms angesehen wird. Hier findet die römische Republik ... einen Angel- und Ruhepunkt, eine Quelle der Selbstvergewisserung und Geborgenheit.[128]

In this way, history and memory provide a source for the creation and sustaining of identity, which also applied to emerging early Christian identity.[129] With these considerations, the difference between "logical" and "affective" analogies can also be reformulated:

> [Die logischen *Exempla*] dienen der rationalen Erfassung und der Argumentation; sie sind somit im Wesentlichen funktional. [Die symbolischen *Exempla*] hingegen erzeugen durch ihre *auctoritas* eine nicht-rationale Form der Normativität; sie transzendieren quasi das konkret geschilderte Fallbeispiel durch die persönliche Autorität des Protagonisten.[130]

This kind of "symbolic" *exemplum* has a number of characteristics that will be outlined briefly here. First, the (positive and negative) examples taken from, for example, the quarry provided by the history of the *res romana/ publica*, possess a persuasive quality: *auctoritas*. It may seem that "Greek" and "Roman" theoreticians disagree here,[131] but the boundaries between them are rather porous in practice.[132] Second, a main condition for the validity of such

---

128. Stemmler, "*Auctoritas*," 142: "In the work of Cicero, Roman history becomes a painting, a semiotic system, that produces, by means of colors, lines, and forms, an overall picture, an image indeed of the ideal *res Romana*, the essence of Roman society, which can be considered to be the reason for the success of Rome so far. Here, the Roman republic ... finds its pivot, a source of self-reassurance and shelter" (author's translation). See for this emphasis also, e.g., Tonio Hölscher, "Die Alten vor Augen. Politische Denkmäler und öffentliches Gedächtnis im republikanischen Rom," in Melville (ed.), *Institutionalität*, 183–211. See also the very well-documented study by Matthew B. Roller, "Exemplarity in Roman Culture: The Cases of Horatius Cocles and Cloelia," *Classical Philology* 99 (2004), 1–56.

129. See, e.g., the considerations of Judith M. Lieu, *Christian Identity in the Jewish and Graeco-Roman World* (Oxford: Oxford University Press, 2004), 62–97.

130. Stemmler, "*Auctoritas*," 159: "[The logical *Exempla*] serve rational assessment and argumentation; they are, therefore, essentially functional. [The symbolic *Exempla*] on the other hand evoke a non-rational form of normativity through their *auctoritas*; they transcend, as it were, the concrete example through the personal authority of the protagonist" (author's translation).

131. As indeed argued by Stemmler, "*Auctoritas*," 150.

132. See, e.g., Morgan, *Morality*, 122–129. Morgan's findings largely agree with those of Françoise Frazier, *Histoire et morale dans les* Vies Parallèles *de Plutarque*, Collection d'Études Anciennes 124 (Paris: Les belles lettres, 1996), esp. 275–281. It is true, however, that for Aristotle *auctoritas* played no role of importance at all, while comparability (ὅμοιον πρὸς ὅμοιον) and the degree of recognition a παράδειγμα could expect were of decisive importance. See Aristotle, *Rhet.* 1.2:19, 2.20:2; see also Stemmler, "*Auctoritas*," 151.

analogies, which are always rooted in the past (however recent) or even in the present, is the idea that events and situations from the past can have analogies in the present or future. Closely related to this is the demand that an *exemplum* should be *verum*. In other words, it should not be "false" (*falsum*). This is best understood as referring to authenticity or veracity, not historicity in the modern sense of the word.[133] Third, it is significant to see from where a symbolical *exemplum* derives its *auctoritas*:

> Die autoritative Kraft der *exempla* basiert auf dem charismatischen und zugleich doch auch meritokratischen Nimbus, der einer historischen Persönlichkeit anhaftet und die der Redner in der aktuellen Redesituation für sich geltend macht. Der Redner verkörpert geradezu die historische Persönlichkeit, die er mit der Assoziationskraft des *Exemplum* evoziert. Das *Exemplum* bietet also die Gelegenheit, die maßgebliche Autorität der Vorfahren für sich ins Feld zu führen, wobei gerade durch die Addition von *exempla* in der Rede der Eindruck entstanden sein mag, daß hier die Repräsentanten und Produzenten des *mos maiorum* angetreten seien, um die *veteres mores et maiorum instituta* durch ihren Einsatz zu retten, und daß die Reihe dieser Repräsentanten unmittelbar in die gegenwärtige Situation münde, für die man selbst die Verantwortung trage und in der man sich der Vorfahren als würdig erweisen müsse.[134]

Fourth, an *exemplum* (i.e. the *illustrans*) should have some degree of comparability with the matter under discussion (i.e. the *illustrandum*).[135] This was a matter discussed extensively, especially in earlier Greek rhetorical theory; its significance in Roman and, later, Greek rhetorical theory declined inversely proportionally to the increase in the significance of the concept of *auctoritas* (see above). The detailed (earlier) Greek discussions and evaluations of the use of examples and analogies give way to a much more allusive and associative way of dealing with *exempla*, whose validity now depends on their *auctoritas*

---

133. For a discussion of examples taken from history and from fables, see, e.g., Stemmler, "*Auctoritas*," 151–152; Aristotle, *Rhet.* 2.20:2, *Rhet. Herr.* 4:57; and Quintilian, *Inst. Orat.* 12.2:22.

134. Stemmler, "*Auctoritas*," 161: "The authoritative power of the *exempla* is based on the charismatic and at the same time also meritocratic nimbus that had become attached to a historical personality and that was claimed by a speaker for himself in the context of an actual speech. The speaker even embodies the historical personality that he evokes by means of the associative power of the *exemplum*. The *exemplum* offers the opportunity to claim the definitive authority of the ancestors, in the case of which through the addition of *exempla* in a speech the impression may have arisen that the representatives and the creators of the *mos maiorum* had appeared, in order to save the *veteres mores et maiorum instituta* through their entrance, and that the line of these representatives issued immediately in the present situation, for which one carried the responsibility oneself and in which one had to prove oneself worthy of the ancestors" (author's translation). See the similar arguments by Williams, *Enemies*, 103, and Mitchell, *Paul*, 45.

135. See for this terminology, e.g., Kristoffel Demoen, "A Paradigm for the Analysis of Paradigms: The Rhetorical *Exemplum* in Ancient and Imperial Greek Theory," *Rhetorica* 15 (1997), 125–155, esp. 126–127. See also idem, *Pagan and Biblical Exempla in Gregory Nazianzen: A Study in Rhetoric and Hermeneutics*, CCLP 2 (Turnhout: Brepols, 1996), 35–56, for an earlier version of the same argument.

rather than on their comparability.[136] Nevertheless, an *exemplum* should be "appropriate," but this seems to connote primarily the necessity of using the right measure in choosing an *exemplum*: it should neither have too much *pathos* for the occasion, nor carry too little *auctoritas* to persuade the audience.[137] Fifth, the latter can be further specified by turning to the remarkable similarity between the function these symbolical *exempla* have and the function ascribed to myths in Platonic thought.[138] Given that symbolic *exempla* can be effective because of their illustrative clarity and vividness ("Anschaulichkeit") and speak to the emotions of the audience, they can strengthen, supplement, and even replace a rational or logical argument, convincing the audience where (mere) logic, for whatever reason, fails to do so.[139] Sixth, one significant (practical) prerequisite for *exempla* to be able to do their work is that they are known to the audience; in other words, that the audience will be able to identify with them. This can be illustrated by the following quotation from Plutarch *De Laude Ipsius* (*Mor.* 544E–F):

> Therefore in the Spartan choruses the old men sing: "Time was when we were valiant youths," the boys sing: "So we shall be, and braver far," and the young men: "So now we are: you need but look." Here the legislator acted well and like a statesman in proposing to the young examples [παραδείγματα] close at hand and taken from their own people, employing as spokesmen the very men whose actions were to be their model.[140]

From this quotation it becomes clear that the best *exempla* were close at hand, hence allowing a certain kind of immediacy, based on a shared tradition, and on members of the same group. Seventh, and as indicated above, this emphasis

---

136. See Stemmler, "*Auctoritas*," 151–154; see on 152–153: "Es läßt sich also bisher festhalten, daß die römische Rhetoriktheorie ein für die griechische Lehre ganz wesentliches und nachdrücklich formuliertes Merkmal des Beispiels stark eingeschränkt, ja beinahe aufhebt. Die beim griechischen παράδειγμα nicht zu übersehende Forderung der Analogie vom historischen Fall einerseits und dem, was in der Rede gezeigt werden soll, andererseits wird in der römischen Theorie nirgends explizit aufgegriffen, sondern kann allenfalls aufgrund ihrer kontextuellen Einbettung in ein theoretisches System, das wiederum griechisch sein mag, bedingt rekonstruiert werden. Das Schweigen der römischen Theoretiker ist signifikant. Geht man davon aus, daß die Analogiebedingung für das *exemplum* als unpassend empfunden wurde, so bietet sich als Konsequenz die These an, daß das Beispiel in der römischen Rede eine stark assoziative Funktion übernahm. Diese Annahme findet ein weiteres Argument in dem Befund, daß der Begriff der *auctoritas* ein Merkmal der *exempla* ist, das auf der Grundlage einer spezifisch römischen Sichtweise autonom in die Theorie eingebracht wurde, ohne sich von den griechischen Vorgaben einengen zu lassen."
See also further below on cultural symbols, and also the examples noted by Mitchell, *Paul*, 42–43: Isocrates, *Or.* 5:111, 113–114, 6:82, 7:84, 8:36–37, 143, *Ep.* 2:5; Dio Chrysostomos, *Or.* 37:23, 41:9–10; Demosthenes, *Or.* 15:35; Plato, *Ep.* 7:336C.
137. See Stemmler, "*Auctoritas*," 166–167.
138. See Stemmler, "*Auctoritas*," 161–163. See also the literature mentioned there.
139. See Stemmler, "*Auctoritas*," 161–162.
140. Phillip H. de Lacy and Benedict Einarson (trans. and ed.), *Plutarch's Moralia* VII LCL 405 (Cambridge, MA: Harvard University Press, 1968), 148.

on the affective ("seductive")[141] symbolical and/or historical *exempla* and their *auctoritas* leads to a tension within Roman rhetorical theory itself: whereas the kind of *exemplum* just described is often preferred, the other "logical" kind of *exemplum* is not given up; both remain, standing next to each other in a more or less unreconciled way.[142]

Against this background, the aspect of the meaning of a tradition (e.g. an *exemplum*) that is used in an analogy should also be considered. In German scholarship, a pair of terms is used with respect to that which has considerable heuristic potential, namely: *Eigenbedeutung* (the meaning of something *per se*) and *Ernstbedeutung* (the meaning of something in a particular setting). Demoen,[143] following Lausberg,[144] understands this pair of terms as follows: "These terms refer to the hermeneutical aspects of the *exemplum*. The *exemplum* reveals a semantic double layer: the quoted history (the *illustrans*) has a meaning in itself (the *Eigenbedeutung*) and a semantic intention within the context (the *Ernstbedeutung*)."[145]

The significance of this distinction is twofold. First, it clarifies how an *exemplum* functions semantically and thus also on what basis it could be challenged (either by challenging the correctness of the assumed *Eigenbedeutung*, or by doubting the appropriateness of the intended *Ernstbedeutung*).[146] Second, this terminology strongly suggests that in order to work out how an *exemplum* is intended, it is more useful to begin with a look at the *Ernstbedeutung* than at the *Eigenbedeutung*, as the latter has (often) little to do with the intended rhetorical function of a particular *exemplum*. The importance of this observation is increased if it is taken into account that one particular *exemplum* (as they were readily available in collections)[147] could be applied to a large number of different situations.[148]

All of this can be further discussed by presenting some "exemplary" uses of analogies, by a contemporary Greco-Roman author, Plutarch, and by the (near-) contemporary Fourth Book of Maccabees.

---

141. So, Jean-Michel David, "Majorum Exempla sequi: l'exemplum historique dans les discours judiciaires de Cicéron," in Jacques Berlioz and Jean-Michel David (eds.), *Rhétorique et histoire. L'exemplum et le modèle de comportement dans le discours antique et médiéval*, Mélanges de l'Ecole française de Rome 92:1 (Rome: École française, 1980), 67–86, esp. 71: "L'*exemplum* n'est donc pas qu'un moyen de preuve par comparaison. Il est aussi l'instant d'une émotion séductrice."
142. See Stemmler, "*Auctoritas*," 155–156. See for an overview, also, D. H. Berry and Malcolm Heath, "Oratory and Declamation," in Porter (ed.), *Handbook*, 394–420.
143. See Demoen, "*Exemplum*," 127.
144. See Heinrich Lausberg, *Handbuch der literarischen Rhetorik: eine Grundlegung der Literaturwissenschaft* (Stuttgart: Steiner, ⁴2008), § 421.
145. See Demoen, "*Exemplum*," 127.
146. See Demoen, "*Exemplum*," 137.
147. See, e.g., Morgan, *Morality*, 122–126, with emphasis on both the Greek and Roman character of the use of *exempla*.
148. See, e.g., Morgan, *Morality*, 127.

1.3.1 Two Exemplary Exempla

That the use of *exempla* as has just been discussed was ubiquitous in first-century literature may be illustrated by pointing to two representative examples.

First, Plutarch, a cultural hybrid as he was,[149] presents a significant example of the use of the (symbolic) *exemplum*.[150] Following Duff, Plutarch's prosopography in the *Vitae Parallelae* has a double purpose:

> First, one should come to an understanding of the character of the subject. ... Secondly, and more importantly, Plutarch thought that a knowledge of the character of the great men of the past should lead the reader in his own life to imitate the good and abhor the bad; the study of the past was – or at least should be – a morally improving activity.[151]

In short, the various lives discussed by Plutarch constitute *exempla*. In order to illustrate Plutarch's way of working here, it is useful, however, to turn to an example from Plutarch's non-biographical work, given that it addresses an issue that will be of relevance for the analysis of Phil. 3 as well. In *De Laude Ipsius* (*Mor.* 539A–547F), Plutarch discusses the subject of *periautologia*, i.e. self-praise, with the help of *exempla*.[152] The following two instances demonstrate this.

> In the first place self-praise goes unresented if you are defending your good name or answering a charge, as Pericles was when he said: "Yet I, with whom you are angry, yield to none, I believe in devising needful measures and laying them before you; and I love my country and cannot be bought." For not only is there nothing puffed up, vainglorious, or proud in taking a high tone about oneself at such a moment, but it displays as well a lofty spirit and greatness of character, which by refusing to be humbled humbles and overpowers envy. For men no longer think fit even to pass judgment on such as these, but exult and rejoice and catch the inspiration of the swelling speech, when it is well-founded and true. The facts confirm this. Thus when the generals were tried on the charge that they had not returned home at once on the expiration of their term as Boeotarchs, but had invaded Laconia and handled the Messenian affair, the Thebans came near to condemning Pelopidas, who truckled to them and entreated mercy; but when Epameinodas expatiated on the glory of his acts and said in conclusion that he was ready to die if they would admit that he had founded Messenê, ravaged Laconia, and united Arcadia against their will, they did not even wait to take up the vote against him, but with admiration for the man, commingled with delight and laughter broke up the meeting. (*Mor.* 540C–E)[153]

---

149. Plutarch was born in Boeotia and was a recipient of Roman citizenship, but he considered himself a Greek nevertheless, devoting, e.g., his *Vitae Parallelae* to an intercultural enterprise.
150. See, e.g., Morgan, *Morality*, 124; see also Frazier, *Histoire, passim*.
151. Tim Duff, *Plutarch's Lives: Exploring Virtue and Vice* (Oxford: Clarendon, 1999), 49–50. See also the preceding discussion of Plutarch's programmatic statements in this respect, Duff, *op. cit.*, 13–49.
152. See Duff, *Lives*, 49–51. See on *periautologia* below, in the section on Phil. 3.1-21, 3.3.2.
153. De Lacy and Einarson (ed. and trans.), *Moralia*, 120–125.

Here, Plutarch introduces Pericles and Epameinodas as authoritative examples to make his point: self-praise is justified when one has to answer a charge, especially one *ad hominem*. However, he also goes beyond this in *Mor.* 544D–E:

> It is not enough, however, to praise ourselves without giving offence and arousing envy; there should be some use and advantage in it as well, that we may appear not merely to be intent on praise, but to have some further end in view. Consider first, then, whether a man might praise himself to exhort his hearers and inspire them with emulation and ambition, as Nestor by recounting his own exploits and battles incited Patroclus and roused the nine champions to offer themselves for the single combat. For exhortation that includes action as well as argument and presents the speaker's own example (παράδειγμα) and challenge is endued with life: it arouses and spurs the hearer, and not only awakens his ardour and fixes his purpose, but also affords him hope that the end can be attained and is possible ... Here [at Sparta] the legislator acted well and like a statesman in proposing to the young examples close at hand and taken from their own people, employing as spokesmen the very men whose actions were to be their model.[154]

It will be clear that Plutarch's way of arguing is fairly far away from Aristotle's demands on a logically valid *exemplum*: rather than proving logically that self-praise is justified, Plutarch demonstrates that admirable men from the past have praised themselves in certain situations and therefore this should be regarded as appropriate. This differs significantly from the Aristotelian example given earlier.[155] In order to be convinced by Plutarch's example, it is only necessary to acknowledge that Pericles and Epameinondas were great men, worthy of imitation. Logic does not play a role here. Thus, this first *exemplum* shows the way a symbolic *exemplum* works: it not only presents Plutarch as an *exemplum*, but within it Pericles and Epameinondas use their own heroic deeds as *exempla virtutis*, achieving acquittal of all charges leveled against them.

The second example shows a different picture. A good example of an exhortative *exemplum* that seems to remain close to the Aristotelian tradition is found in 4 Macc. 16.16-25,[156] where the exhortative speech of the mother of the seven martyrs (to be) to her sons is recounted:

> "My children, noble is the struggle, and since you have been summoned to it to bear witness for our nation, fight zealously for our ancestral Law. Shameful were it indeed that this old man (sc. Eliezer) should endure agonies for piety's sake, while you young men were terrified of torments. Remember that it is for God's sake you were given a share in the world and the benefit of life, and accordingly you owe it to God to endure all hardship for his sake, for whom our father Abraham ventured boldly to sacrifice his son Isaac, the father of our nation; and Isaac, seeing his father's hand, with knife in it, fall down against him, did not flinch. Daniel also, the righteous one, was thrown to the lions, and Hananiah and Azariah and Mishael were cast into the fiery furnace,

---

154. De Lacy and Einarson (ed. and trans.), *Moralia*, 146–149.
155. See above, 1.3.
156. See in Hellenistic Jewish tradition further also the testamentary literature and the praise of the forefathers in Sir. 44–50. See, e.g., Berger, *Formgeschichte*, 84.

and all endured for the sake of God. Therefore, you who have the same faith in God must not be dismayed. For it would be unreasonable for you who know true religion not to withstand hardships." With these words the mother of the seven exhorted each one and persuaded them to die rather than transgress the commandment of God, and they knew full well themselves that those who die for the sake of God live unto God, as do Abraham and Isaac and Jacob and all the patriarchs.[157]

In this case, different from Plutarch, the *exempla* referred to (Eleazar, Abraham, Isaac, Jacob, Daniel, Hananiah, Azariah, and Mishael) are not constitutive for the actual argument put forward in these verses.[158] Rather, they are only (moving and exhorting) illustrations of the mother's thesis (i.e. her first line). The latter's compelling character derives much rather from an argument (i.e.: "Remember ... his sake"). Thus, according to Aristotle's observations for the suitability of *exempla* in rhetorical praxis, this is an illustrative rather than a logical *exemplum*.

With these two examples, together with the (logical) Aristotelian example quoted earlier,[159] much of the scope of the possible uses of the *exempla* in Greco-Roman rhetorical praxis, within which Paul's writings should be located, has been covered. Because of the way in which analogies were used in first-century literature, a working assumption of this study is that in Pauline literature, such techniques are used according to common first-century conventions, which also means that they are not likely to follow a strictly logical way of proving something. Nevertheless, in a few cases it will be attempted to formalize Pauline analogies and examples according to Aristotelian criteria for logical validity.

1.4 Rhetorical Analysis and the Corpus Paulinum

1.4.1 Epistolography and Rhetoric

Some clarifications about the relationship between epistolography and rhetorical theory should be made at this point in order to avoid confusion about their use in this study, without, however, wishing to rehearse the history of research over the past thirty years.[160] Paul writes his letters not only to uphold

---

157. Trans. H. Anderson, "4 Maccabees," in James H. Charlesworth (ed.), *The Old Testament Pseudepigrapha* II (London: Darton Longman and Todd, 1985), 531–564, esp. 561–562.
158. Verse 17: "Remember that it is for God's sake you were given a share in the world and the benefit of life, and accordingly you owe it to God to endure all hardship for his sake." This can be regarded as a valid argument on its own that needs no further elaboration.
159. See above, 1.3.
160. See for an overview, e.g., Carl Joachim Classen, *Rhetorical Criticism of the New Testament*, WUNT 1.128 (Tübingen: Mohr Siebeck, 2000), esp. 1–17, as well as idem, "St. Paul's Epistles and Ancient Greek and Roman Rhetoric," in Stanley E. Porter and Thomas H. Olbricht (eds.), *Rhetoric and the New Testament: Essays from the 1992 Heidelberg Conference*, JSNTSup 90 (Sheffield: Sheffield Academic Press, 1993), 264–291, esp. 265–280, and further, Christine Gerber, *Paulus und seine "Kinder". Studien zur Beziehungsmetaphorik der paulinischen Briefe*, BZNW 136 (Berlin: De Gruyter, 2005), 48–51, and the literature mentioned there.

his relationship with the various churches he was associated with, but also to direct these churches. This brings Paul to use within his letters various types of argumentation, which can be analyzed on the basis of an understanding of contemporary rhetorical theory and practice. At the same time, it should be taken into account that letters are to be regarded as distinct from speeches, as their communicative role is different: whereas speeches are intended to be delivered to a live audience, letters were intended precisely to cross the spatial gap between sender and addressee(s), partially making up for their absence from one another and attempting to uphold a relationship through letter writing.[161] However, it may be expected that in letters, especially in those that outline an argument or make a plea, patterns and strategies of persuasion occur that function much as they occur in speeches.[162] Thus, even if rhetorical aspects remain of importance, the fact of the different communicative settings and functions of speeches and letters warns against reading letters as speeches with an epistolary framework attached to them.[163] This would also go against contemporary rhetorical and epistolary theory.[164] Addressing this situation, Klauck has formulated a helpful *via media*.[165]

---

161. As is generally acknowledged, this is one of the most important functions of ancient letters. For an overview, see, e.g., Gerber, *Paulus*, 56–60, 67–69, who also rightly argues that the apostolic absence is not a typically Pauline motif.

162. See, e.g., Hans-Josef Klauck, *Ancient Letters and the New Testament: A Guide to Context and Exegesis* (Waco, Baylor: 2006), 266; Classen, *Criticism*, 1–17; Jeffrey T. Reed, "The Epistle," in Porter (ed.), *Handbook*, 171–193, esp. 171; idem, *A Discourse Analysis of Philippians: Method and Rhetoric in the Debate over Literary Integrity*, JSNTSup 136 (Sheffield: Sheffield Academic Press, 1997), 160–163; and esp. Peter Bürgel, "Der Privatbrief. Entwurf eines heuristischen Modells," *Deutsche Vierteljahrsschrift für Literaturwissenschaft und Geistesgeschichte* 50 (1976), 281–297, esp. 285. For Ben Witherington III, *Friendship and Finances in Philippi: The Letter of Paul to the Philippians*, The New Testament in Context (Valley Forge: Trinity, 1994), 14–15, the fact that letters function in some ways like speeches suffices to analyze them using a rhetorical framework. For a different view, see, e.g., Stanley E. Porter, "Paul as Epistolographer *and* Rhetorician?", in idem, Dennis L. Stamps (eds.), *The Rhetorical Interpretation of Scripture: Essays from the 1996 Malibu Conference*, JSNTSup 180 (Sheffield: Sheffield Academic Press, 1999), 222–248.

163. Even if such letters existed, see in the New Testament, e.g., 1 John, 1 Peter and, to a certain extent, Hebrews. The question of the precise rhetorical character of letters is an old one, given that the topic has been discussed from (at least) the Hellenistic era until modern New Testament scholarship; see, e.g., Reed, "Epistle," 171–172, who also gives a number of examples of so-called "rhetorical epistles" (186–190).

164. See, e.g., Reed, *Discourse*, 453–454. See esp., also, Stanley E. Porter, "The Theoretical Justification for Application of Rhetorical Categories to Pauline Epistolary Literature," in Reed and Olbricht (eds.), *Rhetoric*, 100–122.

165. Hans-Josef Klauck, *Die antike Briefliteratur und das Neue Testament*, UTB (Paderborn: Schönigh, 1998), 179; see also, idem, *Letters*, 208–211, where the same is said, albeit less poignantly. Ralph Brucker, *Christushymnen oder epideiktische Passagen? Studien zum Stilwechsel im Neuen Testament und seiner Umwelt*, FRLANT 176 (Göttingen: Vandenhoeck & Ruprecht, 1997), esp. 253–258, puts forth a different argument, arguing with Hermann Probst, *Paulus und der Brief: Die Rhetorik des antiken Briefes als Form der paulinischen Korintherkorrespondenz (1 Kor 8–10)*, WUNT 2.45 (Tübingen: Mohr Siebeck, 1991), 55–107, that letters were indeed patterned after speeches, even as a rule (254).

Thus, while regarding a letter as a letter by paying due attention to its communicative setting and composition, rhetorical analysis will be used here in order to understand parts of the strategy of persuasion employed within a letter, assuming that Paul follows, at the very least in a mimetic way, contemporary rhetorical conventions and strategies. This also means that one does not have to assume that Paul was a fully trained rhetorician, meticulously composing his speeches and arguments according to a textbook of rhetoric,[166] but only to acknowledge that Paul argued within the context of a society that knew and used particular rhetorical strategies and that he was probably familiar with some of them, applying them throughout his letters, and thus also arguing in a way that was accessible to his readers.[167] In line with this, it will be assumed that Paul used within his letters a variety of rhetorical tactics, especially as he may have expected that his letters—often aiming at persuasion, guidance, and offering praise or blame—would be read out in public.[168] In other words, letters should be analyzed in terms of epistolary conventions as far as their macrostructure is concerned,[169] while allowing for rhetorical elements at levels below this, as

166. For this reason, the argument as it has been put forward by R. Dean Anderson, Jr., *Ancient Rhetorical Theory and Paul*, CBETh 18 (Kampen: Kok, 1996), *passim*, that Paul's letters have little to do with contemporary rhetoric will not be followed here. See the review by Margaret M. Mitchell in *CBQ* 60 (1998), 356–358. What speaks strongly against a strict distinction between letters and rhetoric is, also, that some of the most significant ancient treatises on epistolography find themselves within the context of larger works on rhetoric. This holds true of, e.g., Demetrius (*De Eloq.* 223–225) and C. Iulius Victor (*Ars rhet.* 26–27), whereas pseudo-Libanius (ἐπιστολιμαῖοι χαρακτῆρες) and pseudo-Demetrius (τύποι ἐπιστολικοί) wrote treatises solely on the topic of letter writing.

167. The view taken here comes close to that of Klauck: "One question that continues to be raised concerns the education level of our New Testament letter writers. Did Paul, the writer to the Hebrews, and the rest of the New Testament authors learn the rules of rhetoric in school, so that they will have applied them self-consciously in their writing? We can most nearly answer this question in the affirmative for the author of Hebrews, otherwise we must register our reservations. That Greco-Roman rhetoric was used in Diaspora Judaism is beyond doubt in the light of the indisputable examples of 4 Maccabees ... and Philo of Alexandria. But Paul and the authors of the Catholic Epistles lag somewhat behind this education level. Yet this does not make recourse to classical rhetoric useless. The New Testament letter writers could have taken over some of the rhetorical features of their letters more subconsciously by imitation, through their confronting texts and a culture bearing a rhetorical stamp, and with the purpose of arguing persuasively in their own rhetorical situation" (*Letters*, 226). See also Classen, "Epistles," 290–291. Similarly also, Jeffrey T. Reed, "Using Ancient Rhetorical Categories to Interpret Paul's Letters: A Question of Genre," in Porter and Olbricht (eds.), *Rhetoric*, 294–324, esp. 324, as well as Witherington, *Friendship*, 14–15. See, e.g., the position taken by Reed, "Epistle," 174–175, as well as, e.g., Williams, *Enemies*, 78, 90. See in general, also, Zimmermann, "Parabeln," 221–222. Thus, this study takes a mediating position between the outright rejection of rhetorical categories by Anderson, *Theory*, and the reading of Philippians in rhetorical terms principally, as has been spearheaded by Duane F. Watson, "A Rhetorical Analysis of Philippians and its Implications for the Unity Question," *NovT* 30 (1988), 57–88.

168. See for some observations, e.g., Witherington, *Friendship*, 6–7.

169. These considerations come close to Reed's conclusions with regard to Philippians: "In summary, a *few* epistolary formulas found in the three spatial locations of letters (opening, body, closing), share *some* similarity with the four principal parts of rhetorical arrangement (*exordium*,

Introduction 33

well as for some functional overlap between epistolary elements and rhetorical tools. At this point, it should be added, in preparation for the next section, that specifically the deliberative "species" (or "genus") of rhetoric (as distinguished from juridical and epideictic "species") was most frequently used in letters.[170]

1.4.2 Examples, Rhetoric, and the Rhetorical Character of Philippians

With regard to the specific focus of this study it should be noted that *exempla* tended to be associated with one of the three main modes of rhetoric in particular, even if it could be used in all three,[171] namely with deliberative rhetoric,[172] which aimed at persuading an audience to (not) follow a particular course.[173] As Mitchell has it, "The deliberative proof by example functions with an implicit

---

narratio, confirmatio, peroratio). But the slight similarity is only functional, not formal. In other words, there is no inherent formal relationship between the basic theory of epistolary structure and the technical teaching about rhetorical arrangement. The similarities may be explained by the fact that language is often used pragmatically in different genres to do the same thing. More importantly, the epistolary theorists and letter writers say nothing explicit about structuring letters according to a rhetorical arrangement" (Reed, *Discourse*, 450). See also his general statement of this approach to letters in idem, "Epistle," 174–175; see further also Fee, *Philippians*, 16. These considerations also speak against viewing Philippians as a whole as an extended diatribe—after all, it remains a letter. At the same time, this does not exclude the possibilities of elements of a diatribe appearing in Philippians given that the letter's aim suits this particular literary form too. Schoon-Janssen has identified the following elements in Philippians that would agree with the use of a diatribe in Philippians: images from family life (Phil. 2.22), the juridical life (Phil. 1.8), from the world of sports (Phil. 3.13-14), a play on words (Phil. 3.2), a comparison (Phil. 2.22), a paradox that reverses values formerly held (Phil. 2.17), an ironical passage, in which the opponent is ridiculed (Phil. 3.2), the expression of a wish (Phil. 3.11) and the very typical expression τί γάρ in Phil. 1.18); these all occur once in Philippians. Elements that are typical of the diatribe and that occur more often in Philippians are: antitheses (Phil. 1.15, 16-17, 21, 23-24, 29; 2.8-9, 15, 17, 21, 27; 3.2-3, 7, 8, 9; 4.11, 12), turns of phrase using the imperative (Phil. 1.27; 2.2, 3, 12, 14, 18, 29; 3.1-2, 17; 4.1, 4-6, 8-9), and objections and rejections (Phil. 3.4-6; 4.10-13, 16-17). See Johannes Schoon-Janssen, *Umstrittene "Apologien" in den Paulusbriefen. Studien zur rhetorischen Situation des 1. Thessalonicherbriefes, des Galaterbriefes und des Philipperbriefes*, GTA 45 (Göttingen: Vandenhoeck & Ruprecht, 1991), 143–144. Schoon-Janssen follows Rudolf Bultmann, *Der Stil der paulinischen Predigt und die kynisch-stoische Predigt*, FRLANT 13 (Göttingen: Vandenhoeck & Ruprecht, 1984 [1910]), 88–105.

170. See, e.g., Mitchell, *Paul*, 20–23, esp. 21–23, for historical evidence that does not need to be reproduced here.

171. The three kinds of ancient rhetoric were, at least since Aristotle's definition of them in *Rhet.* 3.1:5: judicial, epideictic, and deliberative. The first mode of rhetoric was used mainly for defense and accusation, the second is concerned with delivering praise and blame, and the third with dissuasion and persuasion. See, e.g., Williams, *Enemies*, 98.

172. See Mitchell, *Paul*, 14, 23, and Williams, *Enemies*, 99. See also and esp., Brucker, *Christushymnen*, 290–292.

173. See, e.g., Aristotle, *Rhet.* 1.3:5, Quintilian, *Inst.* 3.8:6. See Williams, *Enemies*, 100, and esp. Mitchell, *Paul*, 24, 39–42.

or even explicit appeal to imitate the illustrious example (or avoid the negative example)."[174]

Without wishing to turn letters into speeches, it should be noted that Philippians has some other characteristics besides the use of *exempla* which suggest that its rhetorical mode is (most) akin to that of deliberative rhetoric.[175] This observation, in turn, makes the occurrence of *exempla* in Philippians both more plausible and more fitting[176]—the case made in this study, however, does not rest on such a tentative rhetorical categorization of Philippians. Further characteristics of deliberative rhetoric that are related to Philippians include the following.

First, deliberative rhetoric is characterized by an orientation towards the future as far as the subject of deliberation is concerned. Given that deliberative rhetoric attempts to address a future course of events and actions, this orientation is perspicuous.[177] In accordance with this, the addressees of a deliberative argument also have a specific role to play: as different from being a judge (κριτής) of the past as in judicial rhetoric or from being a spectator (θεωρός) as in epideictic rhetoric, in deliberative rhetoric the addressees are to be the judges of what is to come. In Philippians, a letter in which Paul attempts to influence the future behavior of this early Christian community to a very considerable extent, an explicit orientation towards the future can be found in, e.g., Phil. 1.10, 28; 2.16; 3.12-14, 20-21.[178] Assuming, as do rhetorical theorists, that one "divines and judges" the future on the basis of the past,[179] it becomes perspicuous how examples (i.e. *exempla*), which are per definition taken from the past (however recent),[180] fit into the deliberative *species* of rhetoric very smoothly.[181] An orator would typically use authoritative examples from the past, both positive ones

---

174. Mitchell, *Paul*, 42.
175. As Reed, "Epistle," 172–176, helpfully observes, some caution should be exercised, however, given that there were only three types (*species*) of rhetoric available (judicial, epideictic, deliberative) and, depending on the handbook that one goes by, between about twenty and forty types of letters. Also Debanné, *Enthymemes*, 95, sees Philippians as approximating to the deliberative *species*.
176. See the similar argument of Mitchell, *Paul*, 42, for 1 Corinthians.
177. See, e.g., Aristotle, *Rhet.* 1.3:4, 3.13:2, Quintilian, *Inst.* 3.8:10–11, as well as the discussion by Mitchell, *Paul*, 24–25, who is followed by, e.g., Williams, *Enemies*, 99–100.
178. See, e.g., Williams, *Enemies*, 100. Also the various admonitions in Phil. 1.27; 2.2-5, 12-18; 4.2-3, 4-6, 8-9 are oriented towards future courses of action, just as the various discussions of the behavior of Timothy (Phil. 2.19-24) and Epaphroditus (Phil. 2.25-30) are concerned with the future.
179. See, e.g., Mitchell, *Paul*, 39–41, Williams, *Enemies*, 102, Witherington, *Friendship*, 57–58. See also, Aristotle, *Rhet.* 1.9:40, 3.17:5; and Andocides, *Or.* 3:2, *Rhet. Al.* 8:1–2, 32:1–2; Demosthenes, *Proemia* 42:2; Aristides, *Or.* 24:23; Cicero, *De Or.* 2:335; Quintilian, *Inst.* 3.8:36–66, 5.11:6–8.
180. Even examples from the present were an option. See, e.g., Mitchell, *Paul*, 40, and esp. *Rhet. Al.* 8:1–2, Apsines, *Ars Rhet.* 1:373; the closer an *exemplum* was, both in time and space, to the case at hand, the better; see, e.g., Democrites, *Or.* 3:23, Isocrates, *Or.* 5:113, Dio Cassius, *Hist. Rom.* 52.9:4, and in letters: Socrates, *Ep.* 5:21–22, 28:10.
181. In fact, epideictic elements (e.g. the implied praise of Christ in Phil. 2.5-11, Paul's praise of Timothy and Epaphroditus as well as of himself in the remainder of ch. 2 and in ch. 3) are all parts of overarching deliberative sections. See, e.g., Karl-Wilhelm Niebuhr, *Heidenapostel aus Israel*.

and negative ones,¹⁸² urging his audience to act or not act as these examples had done. While one cannot argue that a particular writing is (mainly) deliberative in character because it uses *exempla*, their occurrence certainly points in this direction, especially when considering the function of *exempla*/παραδείγματα in deliberative rhetoric: to substantiate something by referring to an example and by pointing out the similarities between a past situation and a current situation in need of a solution.¹⁸³ Furthermore, it may be noted here that specifically in deliberative rhetoric, the character (ἦθος) of the speaker itself was of paramount importance.¹⁸⁴ Even if the issue of *periautologia* as such will be addressed more extensively elsewhere in this study,¹⁸⁵ here it should be emphasized that the person of the speaker was always of importance, whether drawn upon explicitly or not,¹⁸⁶ and functioned as a living *exemplum* to be (trusted and) imitated.¹⁸⁷ It seems that these insights provide a helpful backdrop for the interpretation of the use of *exempla* in Philippians.

Second, deliberative rhetoric is characterized by the usage of a particular sort of appeals, especially such that point out the more advantageous of multiple options (τὸ συμφέρον, i.e. *utilitas*).¹⁸⁸ This is at the same time the goal of deliberative rhetoric. Judicial rhetoric and epideictic rhetoric have different goals, namely proving that something is (not) the case and convincing the audience that someone should (not) be praised or blamed.¹⁸⁹ In order to achieve one's aim of persuading the audience to choose the most advantageous option, one will have to convince it that a particular option is indeed to be preferred over another one (see, e.g., Phil. 2.1-4, 12-18; 3.17-20).¹⁹⁰ Part of this same way of arguing is to play off (minor) short-term advantages against (major)

Die jüdische Identität des Paulus nach ihrer Darstellung in seinen Briefen, WUNT 1.62 (Tübingen: Mohr Siebeck, 1992), 80. See also Williams, *Enemies*, 100. From the epideictic character of Phil. 2.5-11 it does not follow that it would be plausible most closely to associate Philippians as a whole with epideictic rhetoric; see, however, Claudio Basevi and Juan Chapa, "Philippians 2.6–11: The Rhetorical Function of a Pauline 'Hymn'," in Porter and Olbricht (eds.), *Rhetoric*, 338–356.

182. See Mitchell, *Paul*, 40–41; Williams, *Enemies*, 102.

183. See, e.g., Mitchell, *Paul*, 42. Among rhetorical theorists, see Aristotle, *Rhet.* 3.17:5, Quintilian, *Inst.* 3.8:24.

184. See, e.g., Aristotle, *Rhet.* 1.2:3–4; see also, e.g., Quintilian, *Inst.* 3.8:13, and the discussion by Mitchell, *Paul*, 45–46.

185. See below, 3.3.2.

186. See for examples, e.g., Abraham J. Malherbe, *Moral Exhortation: A Greco–Roman Sourcebook*, LEC 4 (Philadelphia: Westminster, 1986), 135–136; esp., e.g., Demosthenes, *Ep.* 1:10; see also Mitchell, *Paul*, 45–46; Williams, *Enemies*, 103–104.

187. See Williams, *Enemies*, 104, and the literature referred to there. This was also a standard component of rabbinic tradition; see, e.g., Birger Gerhardsson, *Memory and Manuscript: Oral Tradition and Written Transmission in Rabbinic Judaism and Early Christianity* (Lund: Almquist & Wiksell, 1961), esp. 184, as well as, e.g., Kathy Ehrensperger, *Paul and the Dynamics of Power: Communication and Interaction in the Early Christ-Movement*, LNTS 325 (London: T&T Clark, 2007), 140–141.

188. The terms used in Greek and Latin rhetorical manuals, see, e.g., Mitchell, *Paul*, 25–32; Williams, *Enemies*, 100.

189. See, e.g., Reed, "Epistle," 172.

190. See, e.g., Aristotle, *Rhet.* 1.6:1 and the discussion by Williams, *Enemies*, 101.

long-term advantages (see, e.g., Phil. 2.12, 16; 3.17-20).[191] Third, there are particular subjects that are particularly appropriate for deliberation (and not judicial or epideictic rhetorical strategies).[192] The general well-being of a community is particularly prominent among such subjects.[193] Among rhetorical theorists, there seems to be considerable and long-standing agreement about this. Aristotle's position was still held by many in the first century; he noted as suitable subjects for deliberative rhetoric: "Ways and means, war and peace, the defense of the country, imports and exports, legislation" (*Rhet.* 1.4:7). To the second topic, "war and peace," also the topic of concord (*concordia*/ὁμόνοια) belonged, which was defined as the "opposite of factionalism."[194] With regard to Paul's literary heritage, Mitchell has argued convincingly that it would be appropriate to read 1 Corinthians as a deliberative letter focusing on the question of *concordia*. Given the importance of the topic of unity in Philippians, it may well be possible to relate Paul's argument(s) in Philippians to the same kind of deliberative argument; pointers to this are Paul's use of the notion of living as citizens worthy of the gospel (Phil. 1.27), the safety of the πόλις (Phil. 3.1b), and the character of the real commonwealth of the Christians (Phil. 3.21).[195] Having made these observations, it is now possible to turn to introductory considerations with regard to Philippians itself.

---

191. See, e.g., Quintilian, *Inst.* 3.8:34–35 and the discussion by Williams, *Enemies*, 101.
192. See, e.g., Mitchell, *Paul*, 60–64. Similarly, Cynthia Briggs Kittredge, *Community and Authority: The Rhetoric of Obedience in the Pauline Tradition* (Harrisburg: Trinity, 1998), 94–96.
193. See, e.g., Mitchell, *Paul*, 23; see also, Williams, *Enemies*, 99.
194. Mitchell, *Paul*, 61.
195. See for this, e.g., Witherington, *Friendship*, 12–13; Williams, *Enemies*, 104–110.

Chapter 2

THE COMMUNICATIVE SETTING:
GENRE, STRUCTURE, AIMS, AND CONTEXT OF PHILIPPIANS

2.1 Introduction

This section clarifies the historical and communicative setting of Philippians. It provides the necessary context for the further interpretation of the letter, especially with regard to the analysis of Paul's use of examples. Therefore, the genre of Philippians as a letter and with that (the problems of) its literary plan, some of its main themes, and its place and time of composition, will have to be addressed here. As the former three matters are, for the research undertaken here, of more significance than the latter two (place and time), attention will be divided accordingly.

2.2 Philippians as a Hellenistic Letter

2.2.1 Hellenistic Epistolography

Without being able to discuss the entire field of Hellenistic epistolography here,[1] the subject will have to be addressed on its own nevertheless,[2] thus moving beyond the discussion of the relationship between rhetoric and epistolography offered earlier.[3] In the introduction to his anthology of Greek and Latin letters, Trapp gives the following definition of letters, which may serve as a starting point for the discussion of epistolography here as well:

> A letter is a written message from one person (or set of people) to another, requiring to be set down in a tangible medium, which is itself to be physically conveyed from sender(s) to recipient(s). Formally, it is a piece of writing that is overtly addressed from sender(s) to recipient(s), by the use at the beginning and end of one of a limited set of conventional formulae or salutations ... which specify both parties to the transaction. One might also add ... that the need for a letter as a medium of communication normally arises because the two parties are physically distant ... from

---

1. What cannot be dealt with here are the (physical and political) circumstances under which letters were produced. See on this, John L. White, *Light from Ancient Letters* (Philadelphia: Fortress, 1986), 3–20.
2. For overviews of the field, see, e.g., Gerber, *Paulus*, 51–54.
3. See above, 1.4.1.

each other, and so unable to communicate by unmediated voice or gesture; and that a letter is normally expected to be of relatively limited length.[4]

This definition is helpful, as it both describes the communicative situation in which letters are used[5] and restricts the characteristics of a letter to two elements: a relatively short size and a few formal aspects.[6] This enables one to identify a large group of writings as letters, while also acknowledging the wide variety of forms and contents associated with letters.[7] It also means to take into account that ancient epistolary handbooks do not so much help to classify letters as such, but rather aid the reader to work out which social situations can be addressed in letters and what the appropriate style and tone for any given situation is by providing examples for this.[8] This notwithstanding, it is possible

---

4. Michael Trapp (ed.), *Greek and Latin Letters: An Anthology with Translation* (Cambridge, UK: Cambridge University Press, 2003), 1.
5. See also the narrower outline of Eve-Marie Becker, *Schreiben und Verstehen: paulinische Briefhermeneutik im Zweiten Korintherbrief*, NET 4 (Tübingen: Francke, 2002), 32–33, claiming that letters fulfill the functions of continuing the conversation with an absent person, replacing the absence of this person, and furthering friendship. Even though the third aspect does occur very often, however, it is probably too specific to be included in a general formal definition of letters, as seems to be indicated by White, *Light*, 218, who notes that letters should secure "maintenance of contact, the communication of information, and the statement of request or command." Also the triad παρουσία, ὁμιλία, and φιλοφρόνησις, as referred to by Becker, *op. cit.*, 33 and as presented by Klauck, *Briefliteratur*, 153, following Heikki Koskenniemi, *Studien zur Idee und Phraseologie des griechischen Briefes bis 400 n.Chr*, AASF B.102:2 (Helsinki: Finnish Academy, 1956) and Klaus Thraede, *Grundzüge griechisch-römischer Brieftopik*, Zet 48 (München: Beck, 1970), refers to a more personal kind of letter already, unless φιλοφρόνησις is understood in a very general sense, referring to the strengthening of all kinds of relationships possible.
6. On which, see further, Trapp (ed.), *Letters*, 34–38; the subject does not need to be discussed at length here.
7. Trapp, *Letters*, 1. This can be conveniently illustrated by drawing attention to the large numbers of letter types identified by Greco-Roman epistolographists as well as to the particular focus of their theorizing, which has not so much the formulary opening and closing of a letter in view, but much more its "body," which is "not mere information to be communicated, but rather a medium through which a person performs an action or a social transaction with someone from whom he or she is physically separated" (Stanley K. Stowers, "Social Typification and the Classification of Ancient Letters," in Jacob Neusner, Peder Borgen, Ernest S. Frerichs, and Richard A. Horsley [eds.], *The Social World of Formative Christianity and Judaism: Essays in Tribute to Howard Clark Kee* [Philadelphia: Fortress, 1988], 78–90, 85). For two of the main epistolographical treatises, see the work of pseudo-Demetrius, listing 21 different types of letters, and the treatise on epistolary theory transmitted in a work attributed to both Proclus and Libanius, which lists 41 different types of letters. See, e.g., Trapp (ed.), *Letters*, 38–46, and Klauck, *Briefliteratur*, 157–164.
8. See Klauck, *Briefliteratur*, 163, with Stowers, "Typification," 86: "The types in the handbooks give a sample, in the barest outline, of form and language that is appropriate to the logic of the social code in a particular instance." The following examples, omitting both opening and closing, may illustrate this. Ps.-Demetrius provides for the "blaming type" the following muster: "Since time has not yet permitted you to return thanks for the favors you have received, (your failure to do so) is not the reason why I supposed it well not to mention what you have

to develop an epistolary pattern or model on which every author can be imagined to vary.⁹ These observations are useful for the interpretation of Philippians to the extent that they provide insight into the general communicative situation in which this letter stands and thus of what may be expected from it—and what not. This will be returned to below, especially in view of proposals to classify Philippians as a "letter of friendship."¹⁰

2.2.2 The Literary Plan of Philippians

Taking the above into account, together with the earlier considerations about epistolography and rhetoric,¹¹ any proposal regarding the literary structure of Philippians should both consider typically epistolary elements and be open to a variety of sections and aspects of the letter that may well be identified with the help of rhetorical categories. In view of the occasional nature of an average letter, probably with the exception of so-called "literary letters" (e.g. Seneca's *Epistulae morales*, "letters" like Hebrews or 1 John, or for that matter also Revelation), it seems to be preferable from the perspective of Greco-Roman epistolary theory and practice to assume that Philippians is not so much a literary piece of art with a clear architecture, but rather has a fairly loose structure. This does not mean, however, that it is useless or impossible to structure Philippians. Rather, it suggests that not too much importance should be attached to the structure of a letter and that not too much should be

---

received. And yet you will (continue to) be annoyed with us, and impute words (to us). We do, then, blame you for having such a disposition, and we blame ourselves for not knowing that you are such a man" (τύποι ἐπιστολικοί, 4:5–11). Pseudo-Libanius provides for the same kind of letter the following text: "You did not act well when you wronged those who did good to you. For by insulting your benefactors, you provided an example of evil to others" (ἐποστολιμαῖοι χαρακτῆρες, 15:17–16:1, 22:4–6). Texts taken from Abraham J. Malherbe, *Ancient Epistolary Theorists* (Atlanta, Scholars Press, 1988), 31, 71.

9. See for example, also, Klauck, *Briefliteratur*, 52. Klauck discerns the following elements as parts of a typical letter (*op. cit.*, 54). First, he distinguishes three main parts, i.e. opening, body, and closing. These are each subdivided into multiple subsections. The opening of the letter can consist of a prescript with the name of the sender (*superscriptio*) and the receiver (*adscriptio*), a greeting (*salutatio*), the letter's introduction (including a wish for the recipient's well-being, a thanksgiving, remembrances, intercessions, and expressions of joy). The body of the letter can consist of an opening, further remembrances and expressions of joy, and further information (appeals, directions, admonitions, and recommendations), requests (in various places), and various clichés (standard formulas), as well as admonitions, and information concerning traveling and visiting plans. The end of the letter may contain an epilogue with concluding admonitions, a reflection upon the act of writing, an expression of the wish to visit in person, and a postscript with greetings, as well as greetings to be passed on, requested greetings, well-wishing, sometimes a note on having written the letter oneself or on its authenticity, and the letter's date.

10. For considerations about such a proposal, see, e.g., Fowl, *Philippians*, 8–9; see also 2.2.2.2.

11. See above, 1.4.1.

expected from attempts at structuring a letter. In this way the present proposal is critical of the approaches of, for example, Wick,[12] Bittasi,[13] Davis,[14] Black,[15] and, more recently, Heil,[16] and, while following the lead of, e.g., Watson and Brucker,[17] comes closer to the more hybrid results of, e.g., Holloway[18] and Reed.[19] In order to outline the position taken here, first an overview of the epistolary structure will be given, after which a discussion of its various elements in terms of epistolary conventions is offered.[20]

With these considerations in mind, the plan of Philippians can be described as follows as far as its epistolary macrostructure is concerned:[21] Address and greeting (1.1-2), thanksgiving and prayer (1.3-11), disclosure (1.12-26), commendations and petitions (1.27–4.1), final petitions (4.2-9), expression of

---

12. See Peter Wick, *Der Philipperbrief: Der formale Aufbau des Briefs als Schlüssel zum Verständnis seines Inhalts*, BWANT 135 (Stuttgart: Kohlhammer, 1994), esp. the overview on 203–209. Wick argued that Philippians should be seen as a large chiasm with Phil. 2.5-11 at its center. See, e.g., the diagrams in Wick, *op. cit.*, 61–63, and the critical remarks in the review by Richard S. Ascough, *JBL* 114 (1995), 750–752.

13. See Bittasi, *Esempi*, esp. 210.

14. See Casey Wayne Davis, *Oral Biblical Criticism: The Influence of the Principle of Orality on the Literary Structure of Paul's Epistle to the Philippians*, JSNTSup 172 (Sheffield: Sheffield Academic Press, 1999), esp. 159–161; Davis also suggests that Phil. 2.19-30 is the center of a concentric structure of Philippians, which, however, seems unlikely in view of the (linear) progression of the letter and the weight of other passages.

15. See Black, "Discourse."

16. See John Paul Heil, *Philippians: Let Us Rejoice in Being Conformed to Christ*, Early Christianity and Its Literature 3 (Atlanta: Society of Biblical Literature, 2010), and the two reviews published in the *Review of Biblical Literature*: Todd D. Still, review of John Paul Heil, *Philippians: Let Us Rejoice in Being Conformed to Christ* (http://www.bookreviews.org) (2012) and Peter-Ben Smit, Review of John Paul Heil, *Philippians: Let Us Rejoice in Being Conformed to Christ* (http://www.bookreviews.org) (2012). A main point of criticism concerns the use of a "macro-chiasm" to structure Philippians. See on this topic, also, Stanley E. Porter and Jeffrey T. Reed, "Philippians as a Macro-Chiasm and Its Exegetical Significance," *NTS* 44 (1998), 213–231; the latter contribution reacts critically to Boyd Luther and Michelle V. Lee, "Philippians as Chiasmus: Key to the Structure, Unity and Theme Questions," *NTS* 41 (1995), 89–101.

17. See Brucker, *Christushymnen*, 292–300, and also Watson, "Analysis." See also the brief commentary by Witherington, *Friendship*, that follows a similar outline.

18. See Paul A. Holloway, *Consolation in Philippians: Philosophical Sources and Rhetorical Strategy*, SNTS.MS 112 (Cambridge, UK: Cambridge University Press, 2001), 7–33.

19. See Reed, *Discourse*, 178–254, for his considerations; naturally, this does not imply a return to the judgment of Adolf Deissmann, *Paul: A Study in Social and Religious History* (trans. W. E. Wilson; London: Hodder & Stoughton, ²1927), 14, who stated that Paul produced his letters "mostly without any careful arrangement, unconstrainedly passing from one thing to the other, indeed often jumping."

20. For a survey of proposals with regard to this, see Duane F. Watson, "A Reexamination of the Epistolary Analysis Underpinning the Arguments for the Composite Nature of Philippians," in Fitzgerald, Olbricht, and White (eds.), *Christianity*, 157–177, esp. 159–160.

21. For an outline of elements pertaining to this, see Klauck, *Letters*, 9–42, esp. the table on 42.

joy for the receipt of a gift (4.10-20), closing greetings (4.21-22), and closing wish for grace (4.23).²² This approximates to Reed's proposal, but differs from it as well because of the integration of Phil. 3.1–4.1 into the epistolary framework. The reasons for doing so will be discussed subsequently. When following the common tripartite "opening," "body," and "closure" subdivision of ancient letters, Phil. 1.1-11 and Phil. 4.21-23 agree with the opening and closing sections of other such letters, which would leave Phil. 1.12–4.20 as the "body" of the letter.²³

When turning to clearly identifiable epistolary elements in some more detail, the following may be noted.²⁴ First, the letter's opening (Phil. 1.1-2), including the identification of the sender, the addressee, and the greeting, is commonly seen as a relatively extensive and in some respects adapted, but nevertheless recognizable Greco-Roman epistolary opening.²⁵ Second, there is also a wide-ranging agreement that Phil. 4.21-23 constitutes a good example of a common closing of a letter, including greetings (Phil. 4.21-22) and a ("Christianized") wish for the Philippians' well-being (Phil. 4.23).²⁶ Third, Phil. 1.3-11 is often regarded as a more or less typical "thanksgiving" section, which occurred more often than not, though most of the time in a much shorter fashion, in Hellenistic (and Jewish) letters. As was already indicated, this leaves Phil. 1.12–4.9 as the "body" of the letter,²⁷ which is also precisely the place where trouble begins, as relating the body of Philippians to other parts of common Greco-Roman letters has proven to be difficult for a number of reasons. Specifically, Phil. 3.1 and Phil. 4.10-20 give rise to problems.²⁸ This situation leads not only to theories about the compilation of Philippians out of multiple letters, but also to the question as to what one may expect from the "body" of a letter in terms of its structure and contents. Taking up the latter question, Alexander has shown that it is still well possible to relate the body of Philippians to literary patterns also found in what she terms "family letters," i.e. letters with the primary purpose of reassuring the recipient(s) of their senders' well-being and of requesting information about the well-being of the recipients in return. As Alexander observes:

---

22. See Reed, *Discourse*, 289; see also Klauck, *Letters*, 317–320.
23. See, e.g., Reed, *Discourse*, 289. Here, Phil. 4.10-20 is taken as part of the "body" as well, as the thank-you note at this place is too problematic to be considered part of a common closing of a letter.
24. See for the following, esp., Loveday Alexander, "Hellenistic Letter-Forms and the Structure of Philippians," *JSNT* 37 (1989), 87–101.
25. See, e.g., Alexander, "Letter-Forms," 88, stating that there is scholarly agreement on this matter.
26. See, e.g., Alexander, "Letter-Forms," 88.
27. The "disclosure" and the final petitions identified above are also part of the letter's body.
28. See for this, e.g., Alexander, "Letter-Forms," 88–89.

[A] significant feature [of these letters] is the lack of a clear "body", if by that we mean a "business" section framed by, and clearly separable from, the exchange of family greetings and news. Put another way, the whole point of these letters—their real "business"—*is* the exchange of news between the sender and his family.[29]

Reading Philippians in these terms, while noting that these family letters could very well include directions as well,[30] helps to illuminate both its communicative setting and (part of) its aims, as well as helping to make sense of the pattern it follows. In more detail, Alexander's argument runs as follows. First, she shows how a pattern also discernible in a number of so-called "family letters" can be found in Philippians as well.[31] This concerns the following elements, some of which have been touched upon already: (1) address and greeting (Phil. 1.1-2);[32] (2) prayer for the recipients (Phil. 1.3-11);[33] (3) reassurance about the sender (Phil. 1.12-26);[34] (4) requests for reassurance about the recipients (Phil 1.27–2.18);[35] (5) information about the movements of intermediaries (Phil. 2.19-30);[36] (6) exchange of greetings with third parties (Phil. 4.21-22);[37] and (7) a closing wish for health (Phil. 4.23).[38] While this has clarified somewhat what may be expected from the "body" of

---

29. Alexander, "Letter-Forms," 93; see also White, *Light*, 197, Koskenniemi, *Studien*, 107.
30. See, e.g., the family correspondences as published by White, *Light*, 95–99, 106–108.
31. See the considerations of Alexander on the basis of White, *Light*, letters 102–105 in "Letter-Forms," 90–93. See also the considerations of Watson, "A Reexamination."
32. Following the common form "x to y χαίρειν," see, e.g., White, *Light*, 196. For comments on the Pauline adaptation of this form, see above.
33. See, e.g., White, *Light*, letters 103B:5–6, 7–8, 104A:4–5, as well as Alexander, "Letter-Forms," 91–92.
34. See White, *Light*, letters 103A:6–10, 24, 104A:5–6, 11–12, 22–23, 105:48. The formula in Phil. 1.12: γινώσκειν δὲ ὑμᾶς βούλομαι indicates this as the "main information-bearing focus" of the letter (Alexander, "Letter-Forms," 92, 94; see White, *op. cit.*, 207, n. 85, and compare no. 102:2).
35. See White, *Light*, letters 103:11–14, 104A:12–14, 105:4–11; see also Alexander, "Letter-Forms," 92–93.
36. See White, *Light*, letters 102:8–9, 103A:21–22, 103B:7–9, 104A:5–6, 14, 16, 105:5–8, 12–17, 35–37. Of significance for Philippians are notes such as the one that appears in letter 105:35–37, indicating that the transport of this letter was effected by somebody who happened to travel in a certain direction. Letter writing had much to do with taking advantage of these coincidences.
37. See White, *Light*, letters 103A:18, 20, 25, 103B:14–21, 104A:16–19, 105:40–46, as well as Alexander, "Letter-Forms," 93. With Alexander, it may be noted that it is indeed striking how much space the exchange of greetings takes up in these (relatively short) letters.
38. Alexander, "Letter-Forms," 94.
39. These two issues are two of the four core issues determining the discussion about the integrity of Philippians as they have been identified by Reed, *Discourse*, 152; see also Williams, *Enemies*, 50, Williams himself remains largely undecided (54), but decides to opt

a letter somewhat further, it has still left out discussion of the (problematic) sections 3.1–4.9 and 4.10-20,[39] which have given rise to various proposals for viewing Philippians as a secondary composition out of multiple earlier letters.[40] As the unity of the letter is also defended on the basis of epistolary conventions, this question must be addressed here now too.[41]

When turning to Phil. 3.1–4.9, significant problems arise as early as Phil. 3.1.[42] First, there are two questions concerning the formulations that Paul uses. (A) If Paul meant something like "finally" with τὸ λοιπὸν in Phil. 3.1 and intended χαίρετε as a concluding greeting, then the verse constitutes a considerable oddity in the midst of the letter. However, neither of these interpretations seems to be the only convincing one: τὸ λοιπὸν can very well

---

for viewing Philippians as a unity on the basis of the various interrelated themes and verbal parallels in Philippians. Implicitly, his third (lexical parallels within these sections and the rest of Philippians) and fourth (the question of genre) issues are also addressed in the course of this paragraph.

40. See the helpful table of the various proposals (from 1803 till 1995) presented by Reed, *Discourse*, 146–149, as well as his general overview on 124–152, for which see also Veronica Koperski, "The Early History of the Dissection of Philippians," *JThS* 44 (1993), 599–603. See for a critical overview of the pertinent arguments and positions further: e.g. O'Brien, *Epistle*, 10–18, Holloway, *Consolation*, 7–33, as well as a ditto overview by Williams, *Enemies*, 42–50. See also Reumann, *Philippians*, 8–16, and Michael Byrnes, *Conformation to the Death of Christ and the Hope of Resurrection: An Exegetico-Theological Study of 2 Corinthians 4,7–15 and Philippians 3,7–11* (Roma: Pontificia Università Gregoriana, 2003), 147–164, and Horst Balz, "Philipperbrief," *TRE* 26 (1996), 504–513, esp. 507. These studies concern themselves mostly with internal evidence; as far as external evidence is concerned see the overview provided by Reed, *op. cit.*, 143–145. Philippians commonly appears as one letter in second-century canons (Marcion, the Muratorian fragment, as well as in the Old Latin tradition and in the Peshitta), and Polycarp's reference to ἐπιστολὰς may be a reference to the "injunctions" of one letter, while he may also have thought of both the Thessalonian and Philippian correspondence (as they are both Macedonian). Alternatively he may have used a plural because of Paul's reference to earlier support by the Philippians in Phil. 4.16. Finally, the plural as such only shows that Polycarp knew of other (now lost) letters, which need not surprise us (the same is the case with the Corinthian correspondence, see 2 Cor. 2.4, 7, 8). However, already Marcion is not aware of any further letter(s). Also the text of the reference to multiple letters may be corrupt, which might also apply to the reference to two letters to the Philippians in the *Catalogus Sinaiticus* (dittography, parablepsis). Furthermore, the letter to the Laodiceans omits (i.e. does not quote from or allude to) parts of all sections of Philippians, not merely from later additions, and possibly even cites from Phil. 3.2 in verse 13.

41. See, e.g., Reed, *Discourse*, 152, as well as his extensive own argument (including a reflection on the relevance of such questions), in idem, *op. cit.*, 401–418, for a strong argument in favor of the letter's literary unity. See also Brucker, *Christushymnen*, 280–290.

42. The proposal set forth by Jeffrey T. Reed, "Philippians 3:1 and the Epistolary Hesitation Formulas: The Literary Integrity of Philippians, Again," *JBL* 115 (1996), 63–90, which is based on epistolary hesitation formulas, is intriguing, but builds on too many low probabilities regarding exceptions to various grammatical and syntactical rules to make it viable. For a recent listing of reasons why one could see a literary seam at Phil. 3, see Angela Standhartinger, "'Join in imitating me' (Philippians 3.17): Towards an Interpretation of Philippians 3," *NTS* 54 (2008), 417–435, esp. 418.

mean "furthermore" and is indeed used in this sense in letters.⁴³ (B) There are no clear parallels for the use of χαίρετε in the concluding formula of a letter with the meaning "greetings." Naturally, χαίρειν (and sometimes χαῖρε or χαίροις) is used in this sense,⁴⁴ but only at the beginning of a letter—never at its end.⁴⁵ Reading χαίρετε as a resumption of the theme of joy, which pervades Philippians as a whole, may therefore be the preferable solution.⁴⁶ On top of this, recent research has identified so many agreements between the contents of Philippians 2 and 3 that any arguments on the basis of a thematic shift have ceased to be compelling.⁴⁷ Therefore, the pattern of the "family letter" (which also applies to many other letters) still seems to be an attractive option for structuring Philippians. This is, however, not to say that the section Phil. 3.1-21 is not a problem in terms of this pattern, as it certainly constitutes an exception to a regular letter's common course.⁴⁸ However, this need not be a problem: due to their sheer length (with the exception of Philemon) and, for this reason, the likelihood that they will be addressing more than one issue, it may be expected that there will be no single category of letters that fits the Pauline epistles like a glove.

With Phil. 4.10-20 the problems are of a different kind. First, the question arises whether Paul writes his letter (primarily) in response to a gift that he has received from the Philippians. If this is assumed as the main reason for Paul's writing of the letter, or as one reason among others, it remains curious that he expresses his gratefulness so late in the letter. A possibly illuminating parallel is found in a letter from a young soldier to his mother (POxy XII 1481).⁴⁹

---

43. See J. G. Winter, "In the Service of Rome: Letters from the Michigan Papyri," *Classical Philology* 22 (1927), 237–256, esp. 245, referring to P. Mich. 191, line 8 of 18; see also BGU III.846, line 10 of 24. See Alexander, "Letter-Forms," 96–97. For an argument in favor of this expression's announcement of the ending of an epistle, see, e.g., Schenk, *Philipperbriefe*, 242–243, as well as Reumann, *Philippians*, 452–459, noting that the expression changed its meaning from "finally" to "now" when the redacted version of Philippians was created.

44. See Francis Xavier J. Exler, *The Form of the Ancient Greek Letter: A Study in Greek Epistolography* (Washington, D.C.: Catholic University of America Press, 1923), 35–36, 67–68; see further, Alexander, "Letter-Forms," 97.

45. See Exler, *Form*, 69–77; see further, Alexander, "Letter-Forms," 97.

46. See Alexander, "Letter-Forms," 97.

47. See the observations below on Paul and Christ, 3.4.3.2.

48. One may also argue in favor of the unity of Philippians, understanding the harsh transition in Phil. 3.1-2 as an expression of a pause in dictating the letter, during which Paul received new and disconcerting information about the Philippian community. See Ulrich B. Müller, *Der Brief des Paulus an die Philipper*, ThHKNT 11.1 (Leipzig: Evangelische Verlagsanstalt, ²2002), 10–12.

49. See White, *Light*, 101; see further, Alexander, "Letter-Forms," 97–98.

Table 2.1: **A Comparison of a Family Letter with Philippians 4.10-20**

POxy XII 1481	Phil. 4.10-20
Theonas to his mother and lady, Tetheus, very many greetings. I want you to know that the reason I have not sent you a letter for such a long time is because I am in camp and not on account of illness; so that you do not worry yourself (about me). I was very grieved when I learned that you had heard (about me), for I did not fall seriously ill. And I blame the one who told you. Do not trouble yourself to send me anything. *I received the presents from Herakleides. My brother, Dionytas, brought the present to me and I received your letter.* I give thanks to (the gods) ... continually ... *Postscript*: do not burden yourself to send anything to me.	[10] You have revived your concern for me; indeed, you were concerned for me, but had no opportunity to show it. [11] Not that I am referring to being in need; for I have learned to be content with whatever I have. [12] I know what it is to have little, and I know what it is to have plenty. In any and all circumstances I have learned the secret of being well-fed and of going hungry, of having plenty and of being in need. [13] I can do all things through him who strengthens me. [14] In any case, it was kind of you to share my distress. [15] You Philippians indeed know that in the early days of the gospel, when I left Macedonia, no church shared with me in the matter of giving and receiving, except you alone. [16] For even when I was in Thessalonica, you sent me help for my needs more than once. [17] Not that I seek the gift, but I seek the profit that accumulates to your account. [18] I have been paid in full and have more than enough; I am fully satisfied, now that I have received from Epaphroditus the gifts you sent, a fragrant offering, a sacrifice acceptable and pleasing to God. [19] And my God will fully satisfy every need of yours according to his riches in glory in Christ Jesus. [20] To our God and Father be glory forever and ever. Amen.

Even though Paul and the young soldier probably have different reasons for doing so, both place the thanks for the received gift(s) at the end of their letter; both also seem to suggest that, even though the gifts are appreciated, there is no real need for them—at least the recipient does not wish to show such need. For Paul this reaches a high in his statement that οὐχ ὅτι ἐπιζητῶ τὸ δόμα, ἀλλὰ ἐπιζητῶ τὸν καρπὸν τὸν πλεονάζοντα εἰς λόγον ὑμῶν (Phil. 4.17). This shows, at the very least, that it is apparently possible to vary the prominence of a thank-you note by placing the thanks either at the beginning or at the end of a (family) letter.

Furthermore, it has been argued that the expression of joy in Phil. 4.10 suggests that this was the beginning of the body of an originally independent letter, now truncated and incorporated into Philippians. For a variety of reasons, this does not seem to be tenable anymore. With Dahl and White, it may be argued that expressions of joy can belong to both the opening and closing of a letter, not just to its beginning.[50] Furthermore, drawing on Koskenniemi's

---

50. See White, *Light*, 201.

insight that "the expression of joy is the normal accompaniment to the receipt of a letter."[51] Alexander has concluded that the place of an expression of joy depends on the place in a letter in which the acknowledgment of the receipt of a gift is made.[52]

These considerations, which draw on considerable support from others,[53] render theories viewing Philippians as a composite letter superfluous. Simultaneously, they also provide a starting point for the further analysis of parts of Philippians. Given that not all will be convinced by this, it should additionally be borne in mind that Philippians, in the form in which it presents itself now, wishes to be read as a whole, specifically as one unified letter from Paul. This also needs to be taken into account, at least in a final exegesis of the letter.[54] To this, it should be added that postulating multiple letters also implies postulating multiple contexts and fairly detailed knowledge about the correspondence between Paul and the Philippians; knowledge that seems hard to arrive at.

2.2.2.1 A Note on Expressions of Joy in Philippians
Even if it should be acknowledged that Philippians will probably never read entirely smoothly, it is still appropriate to draw attention to the fact that Paul's famous exhortations to rejoice in Phil. 2.18, 3.1, and 4.4 are all placed at junctures where Paul changes the topic: from exhortation to the recommendations of Timothy and Epaphroditus in Phil. 2.18-19, from these recommendations to his *periautological* argument in Phil. 3.2-21, and from the latter to further recommendations in Phil. 4.4. Furthermore, Phil. 4.1 also contains a reference to joy in the context of a transition.[55] In addition, in Phil. 4.10 the shift to the "thank-you note" is marked by a reference to Paul's joy, and Phil. 2.17 can be taken together with Phil. 2.18 as far as its transitory function is concerned. Further instances of joy in Phil. 1.4, 25 and 2.2, 29 do not clearly mark transitions, even if Phil. 1.25, 2.2 and 2.29 are placed close towards junctures.

These observations might contribute in two ways to the exegesis of Philippians. First, the question as to what exactly the expressions of joy are doing in Philippians receives a further dimension, namely one related to the structure of Philippians. Second, with regard to the structure and unity of Philippians, it may be an indication that Paul (or, when assuming a composite letter, whoever is responsible for Philippians in its final shape) was aware of the various rough transitions and took care to mark them, presumably in order to indicate continuity in the context of (apparent) discontinuities.

51. Alexander, "Letter-Forms," 98. See Koskenniemi, *Studien*, 177.
52. See Alexander, "Letter-Forms," 98.
53. See, e.g., Dodd, *Paul's Paradigmatic "I"*, 172–174 and the literature referred to there.
54. See Müller, *Brief*, 8–9.
55. See also, e.g., Terence Y. Mullins, "Formulas in New Testament Epistles," *JBL* 91 (1972), 386–388, White, *Light*, 77–78, and Watson, "Reexamination," 162.

2.2.2.2 Philippians and Epistolary Genres

Having discussed Philippians from the perspective of epistolary conventions, one question, namely that of the letter's epistolary genre, has not been fully addressed yet, as only some considerations about the pattern of family letters were given.[56] This should be done here, as it might be heuristically helpful to relate Philippians to one particular genre of letters. Various proposals have been made in this respect and it seems sometimes, at least to some, that hardly any agreement has been reached beyond agreeing that Philippians is a letter.[57] As Reed has provided an overview of these various proposals, this does not need to be repeated here.[58] However, some types of letters seem to be particularly illuminating for the study of Philippians and will be considered now.

First, especially given its length and its directive function, Philippians is like contemporary administrative letters, to which Paul would have had ready access, for example through inscriptions.[59] Such letters would typically be sent by superiors to inferiors in order to convey orders and/or directions.

Second, given the often personal character and tone of his letters in general and Philippians in particular,[60] Philippians should also be related to the conventions and functions of correspondence between family and friends, as it is an aim of many contemporary letters to uphold a friendly relationship between sender(s) and recipient(s).[61] Beyond this, a specific genre of Hellenistic letters dealing with friendship can be identified. As far as the general contours and aims of this genre are concerned, a useful starting point can be found in the following observation of Trapp, who not only lists "creating and sustaining friendships"[62] as the third main area of concern in ancient letters (the other two are the distance between sender and recipient and the [in]adequacy of a letter to overcome it),[63] but also notes with regard to letters of friendship as well as of other letters, that "[L]etters exist in order to establish and conduct relationships between senders and recipients. In this role they are constantly liable to become involved in games of etiquette and power."[64]

---

56. For an overview of proposals, see, e.g., Reed, *Discourse*, 168–178.
57. See, e.g., Reed, *Discourse*, 155: "Suffice it to say that scholars agree that Paul's letters are letters – end of story."
58. See Reed, *Discourse*, 154–178.
59. See Reed, *Discourse*, 177; also Tobin, "Discussion," 50. A striking example is the "Letter of Claudius to the Alexandrians," *Sel. Pap.* 6.1912 (41 CE); given that Paul's letters were often intended as circulars (see, e.g., Gal. 1.1; see also Col. 4.16), this provides another parallel with administrative letters: see, e.g., Josephus, *Ant.* 11:3, *Vit.* 245; P. Oxy. 1409 (278 CE).
60. Exegesis has long recognized this; see, e.g., Barth, *Erklärung*, 1, referring to this as the common point of view.
61. See, e.g., Trapp, *Letters*, 40.
62. Trapp, *Letters*, 40.
63. See Trapp, *Letters*, 38–40.
64. Trapp, *Letters*, 41. Trapp's collection includes a number of eloquent examples of this (see esp. nos. 41, 55). The analogies with Philippians are obvious. Williams, *Enemies*, 78–82, concurs and provides an overview of elements of tension and conflict in Philippians.

This observation is also helpful because it gives an impression of how the connection between letters, rhetoric, and especially exhortation may be conceived: they are all part of a shared game of power. In this context, it ought to be stressed that the rhetoric of friendship can very well aim at convincing and exhorting the addressees. This comes as no surprise, due to the characteristics of the ancient discourse on friendship (φιλία/amicitia). As Stowers puts it: "Ancient friendship has very little in common with the modern institution of private or personal friendship. Indeed, the ancient institution of friendship encompassed both politics and business,"[65] while many aspects of ancient friendship were also related to concepts and images associated with the military.[66] Philippians does indeed contain a substantial amount of *topoi* that are (also) related to the discourse on φιλοφρόνησις, such as the exchange of news and information, the topic of absence and presence, the yearning for the recipients and the ideal of being together, the emphasis on being of "one heart and mind,"[67] as well as the thanksgiving (Phil. 1.3-11), the request for information about the recipients (Phil. 1.27), the promise of remembrance (Phil. 1.39), and the mutually imparted joy (Phil. 2.18-29; 4.1).[68] The notion of friendship is helpful by way of comparison,[69] but as

---

65. Stanley K. Stowers, "Friends and Enemies in the Politics of Heaven," in Jouette M. Bassler, *Pauline Theology. Vol. 1: Thessalonians, Philippians, Galatians, Philemon* (Minneapolis: Fortress, 1991), 105–121, esp. 109. See further also, e.g., Thomas Späth, "Männerfreundschaften—politische Freundschaften? Männerbeziehungen in der römischen Aristokratie," in Walter Erhart and Britta Herrmann (eds.), *Wann ist der Mann ein Mann? Zur Geschichte der Männlichkeit* (Stuttgart: Metzler, 1997), 192–211. On the general background, see, e.g., E. Badian, "Amicitia," *DNP* 1 (1996), 590–591, and H.-J. Gehrke and B. von Reibnitz, "Freundschaft," *DNP* 4 (1998), 669–674. For the New Testament, see, e.g., M. Theobald, "Freundschaft I. Griechisch-hellenistisch und NT," *LThK* 4 (³1995), 132–133, and Alan C. Mitchell, "'Greet the Friends by Name': New Testament Evidence for the Greco-Roman *Topos* on Friendship," in John T. Fitzgerald (ed.), *Greco-Roman Perspectives on Friendship*, SBL Resources for Biblical Study 34 (Atlanta: Scholars Press, 1997), 225–262, esp. 226–236. On Philippians and friendship, see esp. G. Walter Hansen, "Transformation of Relationships: Partnership, Citizenship, and Friendship in Philippi," in Amy M. Donaldson and Timothy B. Sailors (eds.), *New Testament Greek and Exegesis: Essays in Honor of Gerald F. Hawthorne* (Grand Rapids: Eerdmans, 2003), 181–204, esp. 198–204.
66. See for an exploration of this topic, Marchal, *Hierarchy*, 23–72.
67. See, e.g., Schenk, *Philipperbriefe*, 65. For a fuller overview, see, e.g., John T. Fitzgerald, "Philippians in the Light of Some Ancient Discussions of Friendship," in idem (ed.), *Friendship, Flattery, and Frankness of Speech*, NTSup 82 (Leiden: Brill, 1996), 141–160, and Ken L. Berry, "Friendship Language in Philippians 4:10–20," in Fitzgerald (ed.), *Friendship*, 107–124. For a critical, but nevertheless sympathetic review of the value of this perspective for the interpretation of Philippians, see esp. Reumann, *Philippians*, 678–685, 688; critical are also, e.g., Müller, *Brief*, 25–26, and Nikolaus Walter, "Der Brief an die Philipper," in Nikolaus Walter, Eckhart Reinmuth, and Peter Lampe, *Die Briefe an die Philipper, Thessalonicher und an Philemon*, NTD 8.2 (Göttingen: Vandenhoeck & Ruprecht, 1998), 11–101, esp. 20–21.
68. See, e.g., Gerber, *Paulus*, 240.
69. See for an overview of scholarship that sees Philippians as a letter of friendship: Ware, *Paul*, 163–165.

Bormann[70] and Reumann, for example, state,[71] it should be maintained that it does not provide a perfect fit in all respects.

Furthermore, as has been indicated already, Alexander has argued that Philippians is similar to contemporary "family letters,"[72] in spite of the fact that it is much longer and covers much more ground that an average family letter.[73] Alexander accounts for this as follows, doing justice to both the pattern discernible in Philippians and its unusual development: "[T]hat simple message of reassurance, prompted perhaps by the practical need to take advantage of Epaphroditus' return, is developed by Paul at successively deeper levels, not as a logical argument but following a natural train of thought suggested, at least in part, by the normal conventionalities of the family letter."[74] The "deeper levels" Alexander refers to are, among others, the more argumentative sections of Philippians, in which Paul uses the exchange of information to express his concerns simultaneously, as is every now and then also the case in family letters, be it on a much more moderate scale.[75]

Third, the hortatory character of Philippians (and Paul's other letters), gives a reason to relate them to the letters written by Hellenistic moralists. One reason for this is the proximity of letters using *exempla* to paraenetical letters, identified by pseudo-Libanius as the παραινετική ἐπιστολή. He offers the following outline of it: "My good friend, always be a follower of virtuous men. For it is better for the follower of good men to enjoy a good reputation than following the bad to be shamed by all."[76] As Sterling recognizes, this means that the paraenetical letter existed as a form of its own, that exhortation was closely connected to the imitation of examples, that public reputation was of the essence, and that style and form were interrelated. Furthermore, "The function of such a letter is not to teach anything new, that would be advice; rather, it is

---

70. See Lukas Bormann, *Philippi: Stadt und Christengemeinde zur Zeit des Paulus*, NTSup 78 (Leiden: Brill, 1995), 164–170: the fact that Philippians regulates the relationship between an individual and a group, not between two equal men, speaks against reading Philippians as a letter of friendship *per se*. He suggests the model of a patron–client relationship, which is probably heuristically helpful, esp. in view of Phil. 4.10-20. Why this suggestion does not explain anything, as Gerber, *Paulus*, 240, states, is unclear to the present author—Gerber, *op. cit.*, 241, argues that Paul views the material support he receives from the Philippians in Phil. 4.10-20 as mutual exchange, but fails to note that Paul ends up "on top" as far as the exchange of gifts is concerned. See also for similar considerations, Briggs Kittredge, *Community*, 96–98.

71. See Reumann, *Philippians*, 678–685, 688.

72. See Alexander, "Letter-Forms."

73. See the examples cited by Alexander, "Letter-Forms," 91, and those provided by White, *Light*, 102–105.

74. Alexander, "Letter-Forms," 100.

75. See further, White, e.g. letters 95–99, and, further, the analysis on 204–211.

76. Trans. Gregory E. Sterling, "Hellenistic Philosophy and the New Testament," in Stanley E. Porter (ed.), *Handbook to the Exegesis of the New Testament* (Leiden: Brill, 2002), 313–358, esp. 325.

to reinforce what the hearers already know but have not incorporated into their lives fully."[77]

Fourth, somewhat in analogy to the paraenetical letters just mentioned, Philippians may also be seen in the context of Jewish Diaspora letters, such as James.[78] Taatz, followed by others, has argued that the Pauline letters stand not only within a tradition of Hellenistic letter writing generally speaking, but also within a more specifically Jewish tradition of the government of communities in the Diaspora by means of letters—a tradition that is, as such, part of a larger body of Jewish letters.[79] She argues a strong case, explaining both the function and, in particular, part of the content of Paul's letters,[80] to which also the proximity of certain characteristics of Pauline letters to Jewish "liturgical" and epistolary conventions should be counted, specifically concerning elements such as the use of "hymns," confessional formulas, appeals to Scripture, and doxological formulations.[81] In spite of her argument, however, Philippians will not be treated as "typically Jewish" here. The reason for this is the proximity of Jewish epistolary conventions to the overarching tradition of Hellenistic epistolography,[82] which also included

---

77. Sterling, "Philosophy," 325.
78. See, e.g., Karl-Wilhelm Niebuhr, "Der Jakobusbrief im Licht frühjüdischer Diasporabriefe," *NTS* 44 (1998), 420–443, for a reflection on James in the light of early Jewish diaspora letters, to which James shows a considerable proximity; for a similar argument, see also, Donald J. Verseput, "Genre and Story: The Community Setting of the Epistle of James," *CBQ* 62 (2000), 96–110, esp. 99–104.
79. See for an overview, Klauck, *Briefliteratur*, 181–226.
80. See Irene Taatz, *Frühjüdische Briefe. Die paulinischen Brief im Rahmen der offiziellen religiösen Briefe des Frühjudentums*, NTOA 16 (Göttingen: Vandenhoeck & Ruprecht, 1991); see esp. her conclusions, 110–114. Taatz draws on the following letters to substantiate her argument: introductory letters (2 Macc. 1.1–2.18, together with related letters in 1 Macc. 5.10-13; 8.22-28; 10.18-20, 25b-45; 11.30-37; 12.6-18, 20-23; 13.36-40; 14.20-23; 15.2-9; 16-21; 2 Macc. 9.19-27; 11.16-21, 22-26, 27, 33, 34-38; Ezra 4.11b-16, 17b-22; 5.7b-17; 7.12-26; Dan. 3.31–4.15; 6.26-28), prophetic letters (Jer. 29; Ep. Jer.; 2 Bar. 78–86; 4 Bar. 6.19-25), a number of letters from rabbinic literature, as well as some letters found in Elephantine (as published by Arthur E. Cowley [ed. and trans.], *Aramaic Papyri of the Fifth Century B.C.* [Oxford: Oxford University Press, 1923], 21, 27, 30–31), and finally letters from the era of Bar Kochba (see P. Benoit, J. T. Milik, and R. de Vaux, *Les grottes de Murabba'at*, DJD II [Oxford: Clarendon, 1961], Nos. 42–28, and Yigael Yadin, "Expedition D," *IEJ* 11 [1961], 36–52). See for the documentation, Taatz, *op. cit.*, 13–17. See also Manabu Tsjuji, *Glaube zwischen Vollkommenheit und Verweltlichung. Eine Untersuchung zur literarischen Gestalt und inhaltlichen Kohärenz des Jakobusbriefes*, WUNT 2.93 (Tübingen: Mohr Siebeck, 1997), 18–20.
81. See Reed, *Discourse*, 178; also Wick, *Philipperbrief*, 101, makes a very similar proposal, namely that the traditions on which Paul could draw were: the Hellenistic friendship letter, the family letters, the paraenetical letter and the early Jewish diaspora letter. See also John L. White, "Saint Paul and the Apostolic Letter Tradition," *CBQ* 45 (1983), 433–444, esp. 436.
82. In spite of Taatz's general argument, her conclusion that "die inhaltliche Konzeption der fühjüdischen Briefe ... als Pastoralschreiben mit Betonung der Fürbitte, mit Paränese und direkter Anweisung und Übermittlung von Trotz und Hoffnung" agrees with the "inhaltliche Konzeption

other "encyclical" letters with a cybernetic purpose.[83] Simultaneously, it must be acknowledged that the unusual length of the Pauline epistles (with the exception of Philemon) as well as their function, may well be explained against this background of the Diaspora letters. In view of all of this and also given Paul's identity as someone inhabiting the Hellenistic world, communicating with many non-Jews—especially the probably largely "Gentile" congregation in Philippians—one is probably best advised not to classify Paul's letters immediately as "Jewish" but rather to allow them to be what they (probably) are: hybrids of two epistolary traditions,[84] serving a purpose similar to early Jewish cybernetic letters.[85]

Fifth, Holloway takes the situation of Paul, that is, his imprisonment, as the starting point for his interpretation of Philippians as a letter of consolation.[86] This should be considered briefly here as well. While there are doubtless elements of consolation in Philippians (see, e.g., Phil. 1.12-26), it is questionable whether Holloway's use of the genre "letter of consolation" is really distinct enough from the genre that is often favored in scholarly literature: Philippians as a letter of friendship. In fact, Holloway takes his starting point in Seneca's *Ad Helviam matrem*, which, however, as Seneca (*Ad Helv.* 1:3) and Holloway both note,[87] is rather exceptional in character.

Recognizing that Philippians probably does not fit one category of letters like a glove, and that, precisely because it is a (long) letter, it may well serve multiple purposes,[88] the following observations may be made when

---

der paulinischen Briefe" (*Briefe*, 113) would also apply to a comparison of Paul's letters with non-Jewish Greco-Roman letters; for example the family letters that Alexander, "Letter-Forms," has drawn on.

83. See, e.g., Klauck, *Briefliteratur*, 71–93, 121–146; see also, e.g., Abraham J. Malherbe, *Paul and the Thessalonians: The Philosophic Tradition of Pastoral Care* (Philadelphia: Fortress, 1987).

84. See, e.g., Taatz, *Briefe*, 112.

85. Gerber, *Paulus*, 54–56, argues that there is a fundamental difference (55) between early Jewish diaspora letters and Paul's epistles, given that Paul writes to communities that he was instrumental in founding in order to discuss issues arising after his departure and with an interest in maintaining contact while writing from a position of authority, and that the Jewish diaspora letters were addressed to a broader audience and did not addresses new communities, but the diaspora, which was in need of further teaching. Furthermore, the latter constitutes a kind of revelatory literature, unlike the Pauline letters. However, even only listing these issues makes clear that the differences are smaller than they seem. Paul does not only write to communities that he founded (Romans is a clear exception); the letters coming from Jerusalem certainly also claim authority, Paul also teaches, even on the basis of revelation, and maintaining contact was an aim of both sorts of literature.

86. Holloway, *Consolation*; see esp. 161–164 for his concluding argument.

87. See Holloway, *Consolation*, 55–83, esp. 62, for his full considerations considering the genre of a consolatory letter. For a substantial critique see Alan C. Mitchell's review of Holloway's book in *Journal of Religion* 83 (2003), 435–436.

88. See, e.g., Reed, *Discourse*, 178.

attempting to bring these backgrounds together into one term. First, Byron's description of what he calls "letters of friendly moral exhortation" may be noted: "The letter of friendly moral exhortation was typically used among friends or between superiors and inferiors in order to persuade readers towards one action while dissuading them from another."[89] In turn, this comes close to Reed's classification of Philippians as a "personal hortatory letter."[90] This means that in terms of its genre, Philippians is a letter, its function (or, as Reed calls it, "activity type") is exhortation (i.e. deliberative with paraenetical elements), and its style is personal. This makes Philippians come close both to letters such as Diaspora letters and to letters of friendship (and, as was noted earlier, family letters), without easily fitting into one of these categories completely.[91]

2.2.3 Time, Place, and Situation of Composition

Even though the issues discussed in this section do not touch upon the subject matter of this study directly, they do so indirectly, as views regarding time and place of the writing of this letter decide much about the historical context within which the letter is placed and interpreted. The discussion here will be brief and aims at outlining the position favored in this study, mainly based on a profile of Paul's situation as it emerges from Philippians. In this context, it should also be acknowledged that not only the context of the genesis of the letter should play a role in the process of its interpretation, but also the context of its recipients.[92] First, however, attention has to be turned to the description of Paul's situation in Philippians. Among other things, Paul writes Philippians with the intention of informing the Philippians about his whereabouts and his fate, though unfortunately he does not give many precise details. Hence, there is little scholarly agreement with respect to the place and time of the composition of Philippians. In view of this situation, it is probably wisest not to assume a precise time and place for the composition of the letter, but rather

---

89. Byron, *Metaphors*, 171; see also Stanley K. Stowers, *Letter Writing in Greco-Roman Antiquity*, LEC 5 (Philadelphia: Westminster, 1986), 94.

90. Reed, *Discourse*, 291. This comes close to the considerations of Niebuhr, *Heidenapostel*, 82–83, concerning the genre of Phil. 3.1–4.1, noting the closeness to the *genus deliberativum*. See also O'Brien, *Epistle*, 35–38, noting multiple purposes in Philippians, including the strengthening of friendship and exhortation. See further Bockmuehl, *Philippians*, 32–40, who adopts an eclectic approach that comes close to the one chosen here. Fee, *Philippians*, 46, prefers "hortatory letter of friendship." The view taken here seems consonant with Engberg-Pedersen's concept of Philippians as a letter of *paraklesis* (*Paul*, 105–109).

91. It is also possible to view Philippians (and all Pauline letters with the exception of Philemon) as representing a unique genre, as, e.g., R. Russell, "Pauline Letter Structure in Philippians," *JETS* 25 (1982), 295–306, argues.

92. See below, 2.2.4.

to work with a profile of Paul's situation. This profile may be sketched as follows:[93]

1. Paul is imprisoned in a larger city,[94] with contact with the imperial administration.[95]
2. His situation has been life-threatening,[96] though there is hope that he will be a free man soon again.[97] It is not necessary, however, that the imprisonment lasted during his entire stay in the (unidentified) city.
3. His stay, probably including court proceedings and the like, may well have taken up a significant amount of time (see also the movements related to Epaphroditus).[98]

---

93. See the concise compilation of Raymond E. Brown, *An Introduction to the New Testament* (New York: Doubleday, 1997), 493–494, and also Holloway, *Consolation*, 41–43, as well as Williams, *Enemies*, 94–97. See also, e.g., Johan S. Vos, "Phil 1,12–26 und die Rhetorik des Erfolges," in Georgios Galitis, Joachim Gnilka, Lars Hartman, Vasile Mihoc, Benoît Standaert, and Johan S. Vos, *Per me il vivere è Cristo (Filippesi 1,1–3,21)*, SMBen.BE (Sezione Biblico-Ecumenica) 14 (Rome: Benedictina, 2001), 53–87, esp. 53–54.

94. The theme of his imprisonment is taken up a few times in Philippians, both as part of factual information about Paul's whereabouts (see esp. Phil. 1.7; see also 1.17 and 3.25) and also in its theological interpretation (see Phil. 1.13–14; see in general also 1.20-26, 3.10). Paul's thanksgiving for the support of the Philippians (Phil. 4.10-20) may also be related to his imprisonment.

95. The (considerable) size of the city can be deduced from the fact that it contained a praetorium (Phil. 1.13) and imperial officials (Phil. 4.22). The contact with the imperial administration seems to have been twofold: This administration was probably responsible for holding Paul prisoner, but Paul also preached among the officials (1.13-14) and some of them have converted (Phil. 1.12, 4.22). The presence of a praetorium, however, does not tell one in which city Paul is. Many buildings in many cities could be described with this term. See for evidence, e.g., Martin Dibelius, *An die Thessalonicher I II. An die Philipper*, HNT 11 (Tübingen: Mohr Siebeck, 1937), 65–66; and cf. Mt. 27.27; Mk. 15.16; Jn. 18.28, 33, 19.9. See more recently, also, Müller, *Brief*, 52.

96. This seems to be indicated by Phil. 1.20-24, if Paul's considerations are, as may well be assumed on the basis of his general contextual approach to matters theological, indeed grounded in his own experiences and not merely an academic matter.

97. See Phil. 2.24. Paul's ability to come to Philippi presupposes that he can travel around freely again.

98. Brown, *Introduction*, 493–494, lists the following elements: "1. News reaches the Philippians of Paul's imprisonment; 2. They send Epaphroditus with a gift (4.15), but staying with Paul, he became ill, even to the point of death (2.26, 30); 3. News reached the Philippians of Epaphroditus' illness; 4. Epaphroditus heard that this news distressed the Philippians; 5. Paul had sent or is now sending Epaphroditus back to Philippi (2.25-20); 6. Paul hopes to send Timothy soon (2.19-23), and indeed to come himself (2.24)." Even though Udo Schnelle, *Einleitung in das Neue Testament* (Göttingen: Vandenhoeck & Ruprecht, ⁶2007), 153–154, is right in warning against underestimating mobility in the Mediterranean world, he himself seems to come down on the other side by assuming not only a traveling speed of some 37 kilometers a day, but also ideal traveling conditions that would have allowed travelers to travel substantially faster than this.

4. Timothy was with Paul, as was Epaphroditus, and Paul was in contact with many other Christians.[99]
5. Paul experiences competition from other early Christian missionaries, both in the city of his imprisonment[100] and in Philippi.[101]

This profile suits all three or four locations that have been suggested for the composition of Philippians: Jerusalem/Caesarea, Ephesus, and Rome.[102] A plausible case may especially be made for Ephesus.[103] This location is close enough to Philippi for an intensive exchange of persons and information. Furthermore, a not-unproblematic stay in that city (sometime in 54–56 CE) is covered by both Acts 19 and 1 Cor. 15.32.[104] At the same time, it suffers from none of the disadvantages of the other proposals, especially with regard to the distance to Philippi and the moment in Paul's biography. For example, Paul states in Philippians that he wishes to come to Philippi soon (Phil. 2.24). This makes it highly unlikely that Paul was in Rome, given that his intended goal after Rome was Spain, not Macedonia. If Ephesus is the place of the composition of Philippians, this also determines the time of its composition, which would be around 55 CE.[105] As indicated, however, this matter will not

99. See esp. the greetings in Phil. 4.21-22.
100. See Phil. 1.15-18, as well as the discussion by, e.g., Fowl, *Philippians*, 43, following O'Brien, *Epistle*, 105. The situation of Paul, its consequences, background, and the function of its description in his letter, are discussed thoroughly by Christfried Böttrich, "Verkündigung aus Neid und Rivalität? Beobachtungen zu Phil 1,1," *ZNW* 95 (2006), 84–101.
101. See esp. Phil. 3.2-21. Paul is apparently well informed about the Philippian community.
102. See for a concise overview, e.g., Reumann, *Philippians*, 13–14; in the course of the past century, the majority of exegetes has moved from supporting Rome (see, e.g., Barth, *Erklärung*, 11) to supporting Ephesus as the place of the penning of Philippians (and/or its constituent parts; see, e.g., Reumann, ibid.). A recent argument in favor of authorship in Rome is offered by O'Brien, *Epistle*, 19–26, as well as by Bockmuehl, *Epistle*, 25–32, and Fee, *Philippians*, 34–37.
103. See, e.g., the concise and convincing arguments of Peter Pilhofer, "Philippi," *RGG* 6 (⁴2003), 1274–1275, following the lead of Adolf Deissmann, "Zur ephesinischen Gefangenschaft des Apostels Paulus," in W. H. Buckler and W. M. Calder (eds.), *Anatolian Studies Presented to Sir William Mitchell Ramsay* (Manchester: Manchester University Press, 1923), 121–127, whose arguments are also followed by Gerhard Barth, *Der Brief an die Philipper*, ZBK (Zürich: TVZ, 1979), 8–10; see further, esp., Frank S. Thielman, "Ephesus and the Literary Setting of Philippians," in Donaldson and Sailors (eds.), *Greek*, 205–223, and also Schenk, *Philipperbriefe*, 338, Müller, *Brief*, 15–21, Klauck, *Briefliteratur*, 240, as well as Ulrich B. Müller, "Der Brief aus Ephesus. Zeitliche Plazierung und theologische Einordnung des Philipperbriefes im Rahmen der Paulusbriefe," in Ulrich Mell and Ulrich B. Müller (eds.), *Das Urchristentum in seiner literarischen Geschichte*, BZNW 100 (FS Jürgen Becker; Berlin: De Gruyter, 1999), 155–171.
104. Although no imprisonment is mentioned there, it should also be taken into account that many imprisonments of Paul have gone unrecorded; see 2 Cor. 6.5, 11.23, written before the imprisonments in Jerusalem/Caesarea and Rome.
105. See, e.g., Müller, *Brief*, 22; similarly, e.g., also Walter, "Brief," 16–17. See also the discussion by Reumann, *Philippians*, 6–8.

2.2.4 The Recipients in Philippi

As a Roman colony,[106] Philippi was a city of its own in a number of ways. Most importantly, it was a very Roman city.[107] Even if only for this reason, it is important to take note of the kind of recipients the letter was addressed to.[108] The city had been founded as a Roman *colonia* in 42 BCE, only to be refounded 11 years later under the name *Colonia Iulia Augusta Philippensis*,[109] designated for veterans of Augustus' wars against Cassius and Brutus (defeated by Augustus at Philippi) and against Mark Anthony and Cleopatra. The "little Rome"[110] that came into existence in this way had the legal status of a city in Italy. While "Romanitas" was the dominating factor in the city,[111] the city reflected many elements found throughout the Roman empire, such as a largely Hellenistic culture, including a broad spectrum of religious life,[112] within which, as would be expected, the imperial cult occupied a prominent place.[113]

---

106. Though with a longer history of settlement; see, e.g., Hellerman, *Honor*, 64–67.

107. See, e.g., the concise statements regarding this by Peter Pilhofer, *Philippi. Band 1: Die erste christliche Gemeinde Europas*, WUNT 1.87 (Tübingen: Mohr Siebeck, 1995), 92. See also Mikael Kellbe, *Paul between Synagogue and State: Christians, Jews, and Civic Authorities in 1 Thessalonians, Romans, and Philippians* (Stockholm: Almqvist & Wiksell, 2001), 212–219, and, e.g., Walter, "Brief," 11–12, Reumann, *Philippians*, 3–4. Pilhofer's work remains a standard work on Philippi, together with Bormann, *Philippi*, and Charalambos Bakirtzis and Helmut Koester (eds.), *Philippi at the Time of Paul and After his Death* (Harrisburg: Trinity, 1998). For a profile of Greco-Roman cities in general, see Craig S. de Vos, *Church and Community Conflicts: The Relationships of the Thessalonian, Corinthian, and Philippian Churches with Their Wider Civic Communities*, SBLDiss 168 (Atlanta: SBL, 1999), 27–119; his sketch of Philippi can be found on 234–250.

108. This aspect is underlined by, e.g., Peter Oakes, "Jason and Penelope Hear Philippians 1.1–11," in Christopher Rowland and Crispin H. T. Fletcher-Louis (eds.), *Understanding, Studying and Reading: New Testament Essays in Honour of John Ashton*, JSNTSup 153 (Sheffield: Sheffield Academic Press, 1998), 155–164.

109. On the topography, see, e.g., Pilhofer, *Philippi*, 52–77.

110. See with regard to the ethnic make-up of the city, Pilhofer (*Philippi*, 85–92), who has identified a substantial Thracian, Greek, and Roman presence. The Roman part of the population was the largest.

111. See, e.g., Reumann, *Philippians*, 3, and further, e.g., Müller, *Brief*, 1–4.

112. See the overview provided by Pilhofer, *Philippi*, 92–113.

113. See, e.g., Reumann, *Philippians*, 3–4; see also Bormann, *Philippi*, 66–67. But the imperial cult was not necessarily the dominant cult; see the critical remarks of Pilhofer, *Philippi*, 47–48.

Strikingly, little evidence of substantial Jewish presence in Philippi has been found (in spite of Acts 16).[114]

Even though the present study is not primarily concerned with the possible reception of Philippians in Philippi, it may well be assumed that Paul was aware of the character of the city—he seems to be very attached to the Philippian community and to know it well—and would take its specific character into account in his writing. This means that the meaning of some of the concepts and images he uses may well be read from a very "Roman" point of view. In this respect, not only should notions such as "commonwealth" (or "citizenship") be considered, but so also should notions of honor and shame, especially concerning their social role and their bestowal (or infliction).[115]

2.3 Communicative Reasons for Philippians

No letter is written without a reason. These reasons can differ greatly, however. They may include, as Alexander has noted, the exchange of greetings, good wishes, and information about the health and whereabouts of senders and recipients as such. This is no different in Philippians, though there is much more to the letter than just this. In the following the most significant of these aspects will be considered, relating the "family" or "friendship" parts of the letter to its "argument" in other sections.[116]

2.3.1 Thankfulness, Well-Wishing, the Exchange of Information, and Contact

As in most non-literary and non-administrative correspondence, mutual well-wishing and the exchange of information, primarily as a means of upholding a relationship,[117] constitute a significant part of Philippians. In this context, attention may be drawn to a number of features of the letter especially, as they fulfill communicative functions also found in contemporary letters: the introduction and the greetings, expressions of thanksgiving, gratefulness and well-wishing, as well as references to the (long-standing) relationship between the sender and the recipient of a letter, and finally the exchange of information about the author of a letter and his future plans (especially with regard to the recipients).

---

114. See, e.g., Pilhofer, *Philippi*, 231–234, as well as Reumann, *Philippians*, 4, Mikael Kellbe, "The Sociological Factors Behind Philippians 3.1–11 and the Conflict at Philippi," *JSNT* 55 (1994), 97–121, and idem, *Paul*, 220–223.
115. See, e.g., Hellerman, *Honor*, 3–109, for an extensive overview of the role honor (specifically the *cursus honorum*) played in Roman Philippi. See similarly, Pilhofer, *Philippi*, 142–146.
116. For the topics that are identified below, see also the list provided by Reumann, *Philippians*, 77.
117. See above, 2.1., 2.2.

2.3.1.1 Introduction and Greetings

The setting of the communicative scene takes place, at least initially, in the epistolary prescript and salutation. Contemporary letters commonly use very short versions of both. Paul remains within this framework,[118] but he also elaborates upon it.[119] Strikingly, Paul introduces himself and Timothy on a par[120] and as δοῦλοι Χριστοῦ 'Ιησοῦ (Phil. 1.1).[121] This self-designation can be regarded both as a recognizable use of the (self-)description of devotees of YHWH in the LXX and in early Jewish writers,[122] and as highly controversial in terms of Greco-Roman social values.[123] Even though the number of surviving Pauline epistles might be too small to develop statistics about prescripts and salutations, it is striking that this expression occurs on its own only in Philippians in the Pauline letters. It seems plausible that Paul has not chosen to make this exception without a reason, a reason which may well come to the surface in the letter's body, specifically in the section around Phil. 2.5-11 (Phil. 1.27–2.18),[124] in the section containing the *exemplum* of Paul (Phil. 3.2-21),[125] and in the further description of Timothy's qualities (Phil. 2.19-24).[126] The expression may also be a commentary on Paul's situation

---

118. Compared with the prescripts of, e.g., Romans and Galatians, the prescript of Philippians is remarkably short; see, e.g., Barth, *Brief*, 13.

119. See on the mixed Hellenistic-Jewish character of Paul's formulations: Taatz, *Briefe*, 113, with reference to 2 Bar. 78.2 for the use of ἔλεος καὶ εἰρήνη and to the introductory letters to 2 Maccabees for the use of χαίρειν in order to translate and/or replace שלום. Of importance is also her note on Paul's use of χάρις, which sounds familiar to "χαίρειν" (Taatz, *Briefe*, 112). See also the overview offered by Reumann, *Philippians*, 64–68, 89–92.

120. Why Timothy occurs so prominently here is a matter of speculation, see, e.g., Barth, *Brief*, 13–14. He is most likely not the co-author, given that Paul writes the remainder of the letter in the first person singular and introduces Timothy in the third person singular in Phil. 2.19-24. More likely is the option that Timothy is mentioned because he is a co-founder of the community in Philippians; see Müller, *Brief*, 32, Walter, "Brief," 31–32.

121. See Byron, *Metaphors*, 150.

122. See, e.g., in the LXX, 2 Sam. 11.9, 11, 13; 1 Kgs. 1.33; 2 Kgs. 18.24; Ezra 5.11; Neh. 10.30; Isa. 42.19; Da$^{th.}$ 3.93, 6.21, 9.11 (δοῦλοι του θεοῦ); Jdt. 11.4 (δοῦλοι του κυρίου). See for an overview, Byron, *Metaphors*, 22–29, 47–58. For further occurrences in the *Corpus Paulinum*, see esp. Rom. 6.16-17, 19-20; 1 Cor. 7.21-23; Eph. 6.5-6, 8; and see Rom. 1.1; 2 Cor. 4.5; Gal. 4.1-7. See, with Byron, *Metaphors*, 33–34; also the work of Philo. In Philo's work, the "language of enslavement" can be found in the context of the relationship of humanity and God (see, e.g., *Mut.* 46:4), the control (passionate) vices can exercise over people (see, e.g., *Somn.* 2.51:5, *Prob.* 17), and in the context of religious (liturgical) service (see, e.g., *Post.* 182, *Sobr.* 126, 131). Philo has outlined his own concept of freedom most extensively in *Prob*. Also Josephus uses the language of slavery in a religious context; see, e.g., *Ant.* 5:39, 8:198, 11:90, 101; *B.J.* 3:354 (individuals as "slaves of God"), *Ant.* 7:367, 11:70, 101 (priests), *Ant.* 8:257; *B.J.* 7:323 (Israel). See Byron, *op. cit.*, 31–33. Finally, the Testaments of the Twelve Patriarchs should be mentioned, where enslavement is also mentioned in a religious and ethical context; see, with Byron, *op. cit.*, 30–31, e.g.: Test. Jud. 15.2; Test. Ash. 3.2. The result of this enslavement is the impossibility of obeying God (see Test. Jud. 18.6; Test. Jos. 7.8). See also 4 Macc. 13.2, and Ep. Arist. 256.

123. See, e.g., Witherington, *Friendship*, 47–49.

124. See below, 3.1.

125. On which, see below, 3.4.

126. On which, see below, 3.2.2.

(i.e. his imprisonment), as in Phlm. 1, indicating that, whatever the situation, Paul is the slave of Christ, not of those who hold him in captivity.[127] These circumstances might also explain why Paul does not use the title "apostle" here.[128]

The references made to the Philippians, such as "saints in Christ" (Phil. 1.1) are in general unremarkable,[129] as is the rest of the greeting. More striking is the explicit reference to ἐπίσκοποι and διάκονοι,[130] which has caused and still causes all kinds of controversies, especially when the verse is taken as a witness to the development of early Christian church order.[131] This, however,

---

127. See, e.g., Gerber, *Paulus*, 148–149, 244–245. Thus, this is probably the most controversial title of Paul: following a tradition common to the Old Testament/Hebrew Bible, he, who calls himself a slave to Christ and is a slave in the eyes of society, is in fact using a *nom de gueux*, designating a particularly honorable position in the eyes of God (and presumably in the eyes of the people of God); see idem, *op. cit.*, 151, as well as Müller, *Brief*, 33.

128. Another reason might be the particularly intimate relationship between the Philippians and Paul (and Timothy), but given the fact that Paul employs his authority at considerable length elsewhere in the letter, this argument (as preferred by, e.g., Barth, *Erklärung*, 2) might not be convincing in the end.

129. See for similar designations calling the addressees "saints": Rom. 1.7; 1 Cor. 1.2; 2 Cor. 1.1; but not Galatians, 1 Thessalonians, or Philemon. The holiness indicated here is derivative, i.e. it derives from God's holiness (so, e.g., Barth, *Brief*, 14, as well as Reumann, *Philippians*, 58–59, and, with characteristic emphasis, Barth, *Erklärung*, 2: "'Heilige' Menschen sind unheilige Menschen, die aber als solche von Gott ausgesondert, in Anspruch und Beschlag genommen sind für seine Herrschaft, für seinen Gebrauch, für sich, der heilig ist." Paul, however, did not necessarily wrestle with the question of how "eine empirische Volksgemeinschaft" can be "Gottes heilige Volk"; see idem, *op. cit.*, ibid.). While the notion of "saints" may well be eschatologically connoted in the sense of the holy remnant (see, e.g., Isa. 4.3; 62.12; Ezek. 37.28; see similarly, e.g., Acts 9.13, 32; Heb. 13.24; Rev. 14.12), it does not need to be this for the reason given by Barth; see rather Müller, *Brief*, 33–34.

130. Barth, *Brief*, 15–16 makes the fruitful suggestion that these officers should not be considered as deacons in the later sense of the word, i.e. with a specific responsibility for the poor and needy (as intended in Acts 6.1-7, though the deacons ordained there never engage visibly in any works of charity, but are mainly depicted as preaching), but rather in the sense of 1 Cor. 3.5; 2 Cor. 3.8, 6.4, 11.23; Rom. 12.7; texts that suggest that διακονία was associated with teaching primarily. However, Barth's proposal can be further differentiated. As Gerber, *Paulus*, 119–141, has argued, Paul uses the two self-designations ἀπόστολος and διάκονος in two distinct ways: "Die Bezeichnung διάκονος weist auf eine bis zu vierstellige Relation zwischen Auftraggeber, -nehmer, Aufgabe und dem von der Aufgabe Begünstigten, konkret also etwa die Übermittlung einer Botschaft. Impliziert, z.T. auch expliziert ist, dass die Initiative für das Handeln des διάκονος Paulus bei Gott liegt, er also nicht im eigenen Interesse agiert. Ἀπόστολος lenkt den Blick auf die Initiation des Geschehens und so auf die Legitimität des Gesandten aufgrund einer besonderen Christuserfahrung."

131. For an overview, see, e.g., Reumann, *Philippians*, 62–64. Pilhofer, *Philippi*, 140–147 (following a tradition that includes Barth, *Erklärung*, 3–4), makes the fruitful proposal that the officeholders of the Philippian community, specifically the "bishops," should be seen in analogy to those of (cultic) associations in Philippi, specifically to the office of *procurator*. See for a comparison with a variety of secular and religious offices also, e.g., Dibelius, *Philipper*, 60–61; Ascough, *Associations*, 129–139; and Reumann, *Philippians*, 62–64.This background speaks

is not the place to elaborate upon this aspect of the verse. Rather, it should be noted that Paul apparently attempts to address the Philippian community appropriately by making special reference to its office bearers.[132] No specific "bishop" or "deacon" is identified in Philippians, however, and while it might be speculated that the three individuals named in Phil. 4.2-3 would be office bearers of some kind, this is not necessary.[133] Notably, Paul's use of the first person plural when referring to "our Father" (1.2) expresses a significant bond between Paul, Timothy, and the Philippians.

The greetings,[134] which give the author of a letter the opportunity to let the voices of a larger group of people be heard (see 4.21) and to address people by name when writing to a larger group of them, are in Philippians relatively short and general (Phil. 4.21-22; see the longer list in Rom. 16).[135] Notably, they include an unusual note on the members of the imperial household (Phil. 4.22).[136]

---

against suggestions (see, e.g., Barth, *Brief*, 15–16) that the structure of the early Christian communities addressed by Paul was not much developed: if structures were adapted from other associations, such structures could have been in place relatively early. The "bishops" in Philippians could therefore be seen against the same background as the officers mentioned in, e.g., Rom. 12.8, 1 Cor. 12.28 and 1 Thess. 5.12. This makes conjectures such as the one that Schenk, *Philipperbriefe*, 78–82, proposes, arguing that the reference to the officers is a post-Pauline gloss, superfluous. Why a "Verwalter" is something completely different from someone exercising an institutionalized ministry, as Müller, *Brief*, 34, has it, is unclear.

132. Along these lines, e.g., Dibelius, *Philipper*, 61; see also the view of Walter, "Brief," 31.

133. Is the debate between Euodia and Syntyche the first recorded debate between two female ἐπίσκοποι? The text is in principle open to this interpretation. However, as no person is addressed directly or identified personally as either "bishop" or "deacon," and as it also remains unclear what these officeholders do, it is difficult to move beyond establishing that there are obviously the leading officers of the community in Philippi and that there are at least two sorts of officers. For an informed speculation, see, e.g., Lars Hartman, "Overseers and Servants – For What? Philippians 1:1–11 as Read with Regard to the Implied Readers of Philippians," in Galitis, Gnilka, Hartman, Mihoc, Standaert, and Vos, *Vivere*, 13–51 (including summaries of discussions and responses).

134. These largely agree with Hellenistic conventions; whether Paul wrote these greetings with his own hand as he had done for Galatians (see Gal. 6.11), 1 Corinthians (see 1 Cor. 16.21) and Romans (see Rom. 16.22) is unclear.

135. See further the following instances in the New Testament: 1 Cor. 11.19-24 and 2 Cor. 13.12 (even shorter than in Philippians); Gal. 1.18 contains only a concluding benediction, as does Eph. 6.23; Col. 4.18 contains a short greeting, as does 1 Thess. 5.26; similarly 2 Thess. 3.17 and 1 Tim. 6.21 contain only a benediction, while 2 Tim. 4.19-21 contains a longer greeting, whereas Tit. 3.14 is very short again; while Philemon contains, despite its shortness, relatively extensive greetings in vv. 23-24; Heb. 13.24 contains very general greetings again; James contains none at all; 1 Pet. 5.13 contains cryptic greetings; 2 Peter none at all; 1 John again none; 2 Jn. 1.13 contains very general greetings, as does 3 Jn. 15; whereas they are lacking in Jude; Revelation, technically speaking also a letter (see Rev. 1.11), contains no greetings but has a concluding valediction (Rev. 22.21).

136. This is not necessarily an indication that the letter was written in Rome; the imperial household that is indicated with οἱ ἐκ τῆς Καίσαρος οἰκίας (Phil. 4.22) encompassed all slaves and freedmen of the emperor, including those in Ephesus, for example. See, e.g., Barth, *Brief*, 80.

2.3.1.2 Thanksgiving, Gratefulness and Well-Wishing

The first part of Philippians after prescript and salutation (Phil. 1.1-2) consists of a long thanksgiving of Paul to God[137] because of his communion with the Philippians (Phil. 1.3-8) and of a prayer on their behalf (Phil. 1.9-11).[138] In the course of this, Paul also mentions his gratefulness for the support of the Philippians (1.5; see also 1.7).[139] Another section expressing Paul's gratefulness (oddly) comes at the very end of the letter (Phil. 4.10-20). All of these elements can be integrated into common epistolary patterns;[140] all of them are also related to the purposes of Philippians.

The thanksgiving in Phil. 1.3-8 follows a common pattern.[141] It largely leaves out the delicate issue of the gift (but see 1.5) and it underlines in solemn language the intimate relationship of Paul with the Philippian Christian community[142] and their "partnership in the gospel,"[143] or "for the gospel,"[144]

---

137. At least formally, as Fowl, *Philippians*, 21, notes, the addressees of Paul's written thanksgiving were of course also the Philippians.

138. See, e.g., Müller, *Brief*, 38, for this structure; verses 7-8 have a transitory function between 1-6 and 9-11, and the two sections of Phil. 1.3-11 are concluded with references to the day of Christ.

139. See for a more metaphysical interpretation, e.g. Barth, *Brief*, 21. Müller, *Brief*, 51, entertains the possibility that the Philippians provided the financial means to bribe Paul's prison guards to allow him more privileges, a common practice; see also the earlier contribution by Wilhelm Michaelis, "Die Gefangenschaftsbriefe des Paulus und antike Gefangenenbriefe," *NKZ* 36 (1925), 586–595, esp. 594.

140. See, e.g., Müller, *Brief*, 37; this section of Philippians agrees with the opening section of Hellenistic letters and can therefore be termed proemium. As far as the thanksgiving is concerned, see esp. Jeffrey T. Reed, "Are Paul's Thanksgivings 'Epistolary'?", *JSNT* 61 (1996), 87–99.

141. Consisting of an introduction such as εὐχαριστῶ τῷ θεῷ μου (as in Phil. 1.3; see further Rom. 1.8, 1 Cor. 1.4, 1 Thess. 1.2, Phlm. 4), a reference to the permanent remembering of one another (especially before God; see, besides Phil. 1.3, 7, further: Rom. 1.9, 1 Thess. 1.2, Phlm. 4), an indication of the reason for thankfulness (see also Phil. 1.5; cf. Rom. 1.8, 1 Cor. 1.4-5, 1 Thess. 1.3-4, Phlm. 5), and an indication of the theme or main concern of the letter. See, e.g., Barth, *Brief*, 17; Gerber, *Paulus*, 64–65; Müller, *Brief*, 37–38; and Walter, "Brief," 34–35.

142. Rom. 1.8-9 contains a short and very general thanksgiving for the faith of the Romans; in 1 Cor. 1.4-8 the thanksgiving is for the charisms the Corinthians have received; in 2 Cor. 1.3-6 the thanksgiving remains very impersonal and does not touch on the issue of communion, but rather sticks to the theme of suffering and comfort. Strikingly, Galatians has no thanksgiving whatsoever, 1 Thess. 1.2a only mentions the fact of thanksgiving in the prayers of Paul, Silvanus and Timothy, though the reason for these prayers is mentioned in the subsequent verses, which, in fact, constitute a thanksgiving that continues until 3.13; see for a further thanksgiving, Phlm. 4-7. For comparative observations, noting also the particular cordiality of this section of Philippians, see, e.g., Barth, *Brief*, 17–20, Müller, *Brief*, 39–40.

143. An enterprise with business-like aspects undergirded by common interests; see below, 3.1.5.5. See also, e.g., Hansen, "Transformation," 182–189. Many interpretations take the reference to κοινωνία εἰς τὸ εὐαγγέλιον (Phil. 1.5) as participation in the gospel; see, e.g., Barth, *Brief*, 18–19.

144. See for this, e.g., James P. Ware, *The Mission of the Church in Paul's Letter to the Philippians in the Context of Ancient Judaism*, NTSup 120 (Leiden: Brill, 2005), 166–167; see further 168–171; the concrete shape of this partnership probably included the support mentioned in Phil. 1.5 and 4.10-20.

specifically during Paul's imprisonment and trial,[145] thus setting the tone for much of what is to come and sketching a positive picture of the relationship.[146] Even if it is not apparent here yet, this stress on (long-standing) fellowship will appear to be a precondition for the (effective) use of *exempla* later on in the letter, as they only function within a shared tradition.[147]

Although prayer has already been mentioned in Phil. 1.3, where it is related to thanksgiving, the actual petitions of this prayer are only mentioned in Phil. 1.9-11. As it would have been perfectly acceptable to mention only prayer,[148] the fact that Paul has decided to explicate his individual petitions is of significance. Indeed, the two main elements of Paul's prayer, petitions concerning brotherly love and growth in discernment, may well be seen to reflect two main concerns of the whole letter: the unity of the community (Phil. 1.27–2.18) and indeed faithfulness to "true doctrine" (Phil. 3.2-21). The unity of the Philippians may also be underlined by Paul's prayer for *all* Philippians (Phil. 1.4, 8),[149] while the fellowship between Paul and the Philippians is emphasized by this section as a whole.[150] Phil. 1.9-11 constitutes in this context, also, somewhat of an interpretative obstacle, as it is the climax of Paul's prayers for the Philippians, but it does not state precisely what the Philippians should discern so that they may be pure and blameless at the day of Christ (Phil. 1.10).[151] Proleptically, the solution, which derives from the exegesis of other parts of Philippians, may already be stated here: what the Philippians will need to discern is that the cross belongs to the "career" of a Christian, in other words, that suffering is part of the picture,[152] and that the orientation of (earthy) existence "in Christ" is eschatological (see Phil. 1.10b-11).[153] This content, however, is still open in Phil. 1.9-11. This note on

---

145. See Phil. 1.7, on which, see, e.g., Müller, *Brief*, 43–44.
146. Brucker, *Christushymnen*, 301–302, plausibly identifies elements of Phil. 1.3-11 as epideictic.
147. See above, 1.3.1.
148. See, e.g., White, *Light*, 200. In Rom. 1.9-10, Paul only mentions his future coming to Rome as the object of his prayers; 1 Corinthians does not contain a prayer in this place at all, nor does 2 Corinthians, neither does Galatians; 1 Thess. 1.2 only mentions prayers again, as is the case in Phlm. 4.
149. So, e.g., Williams, *Enemies*, 108; see also Black, "Discourse," 29. While Heil, *Philippians*, 39–40, is right in noting that Paul refers frequently to the encompassing nature of things (every prayer, always; for all), only the last of these references may have significance for the unity of the Philippians as a major concern of Paul in this letter.
150. Presumably, this discernment is related to growing in ἀγάπη (verse 9), which adds a Christian touch to vocabulary that is otherwise shared with contemporary popular philosophy For this emphasis, see, e.g., Heil, *Philippians*, 43, 48, Williams, *Enemies*, 108; see also Black, "Discourse," 29, with emphasis on the alliteration found in verses 3-8.
151. See, e.g., Müller, *Brief*, 45–46.
152. See below, esp. 4.2. This comes close to, e.g., the view of Heil, *Philippians*, 1–4, esp. 2.
153. See, e.g., Müller, *Brief*, 46. This section of Philippians presents ethical perfection as leading towards an eschatological goal.

discernment at the beginning of the letter probably also fits the proximity of Philippians to the rhetorical *genus deliberativum* well.[154]

Thus, functioning as a *captatio benevolentiae* (in the looser sense of the term),[155] and as a common part of a letter, the introductory thanksgiving and prayer contribute much to preparing the reader for the rest of the letter both strategically (rhetorically) and thematically.[156] Rhetorically it could be compared to a speech's *exordium* that sets the scene and prepares for the *propositio*.[157]

Finally, the instances of well-wishing that occur in Philippians, specifically in Phil. 4.23 and to some extent also in the greeting in 1.2,[158] and which are part of the standard repertoire of Hellenistic letters,[159] should be mentioned here. However, they do not need to be commented upon specifically, apart from noting that they remain within the usual Pauline parameters and that, by agreeing with the expectations that a recipient might have of a letter, they contribute to a smooth and friendly kind of communication.

2.3.1.3 Paul and the Philippians: Past, Present, and Future

Paul's emphasis on his close relationship with the Christian community in Philippi, unique in the *Corpus Paulinum*,[160] is not without reason. As is also indicated by Acts 16.9-40, the Christian community in Philippi is a Pauline foundation. This seems to be implied by Phil. 1.5 as well (ἀπὸ τῆς πρώτης ἡμέρας ἄχρι τοῦ νῦν).[161] Since those days, there has been a continuing fellowship of prayer (Phil. 1.3-4)[162] and partnership "in the good news" (Phil. 1.5). This partnership also included material support of the Philippians for Paul (see in particular Phil. 4.10-20 as well as 1.5).[163] This fellowship and partnership also leads to a longing to see each other[164] and the exchange of letters and emissaries

---

154. See, e.g., the considerations of Schenk, *Philipperbriefe*, 112–123, on the *genus deliberativum*; see above, 1.4.2.

155. See, e.g., Egger, *Philipperbrief*, 54. This should not be taken to mean that the thanksgiving at the beginning of the letter is a *captatio benevolentiae*, as they occur in speeches. See for the *captatio benevolentiae* at this point, e.g. Gerber, *Paulus*, 64, as well as Schenk, *Philipperbriefe*, 101–104, and Reumann, *Philippians*, 149, concerning verse 3. Williams, *Enemies*, 109, describes these verses as an *exordium*.

156. See similarly, e.g., Müller, *Brief*, 47: "V. 9–11 weisen deutlichen auf den paränetischen Hauptteil 1,27–2,18 voraus."

157. See, e.g., Witherington, *Friendship*, 35.

158. See, e.g., Reumann, *Philippians*, 740–741.

159. See, e.g., Gerber, *Paulus*, 65–66.

160. See for a representative overview, e.g. Walter, "Brief," 12–14; see also Reumann, *Philippians*, 5–6.

161. See, e.g., Holloway, *Consolation*, 43–44.

162. On which see, e.g., Gerber, *Paulus*, 64–65, 72–74.

163. See, e.g., Holloway, *Consolation*, 44–45. This support also indicates that the Philippians had a considerable interest in Paul's mission. Fowl, *Philippians*, 22–23, nuances rightly that what is in view in Phil. 1.5 might be more encompassing than what is mentioned in Phil. 4.10-20.

164. See, e.g., Gerber, *Paulus*, 72.

in the current situation of physical separation.[165] At least, this is the picture Paul presents at the beginning of his letter, probably assuming that the Philippians will be able to identify with it.[166] This state of affairs also establishes Paul as a figure of considerable status for the Philippian community, as one of its *maiores*, so to speak. In fact, the communion between Paul and the Philippians as it had been established in the past will serve as a basis for Paul's further explorations in Philippians.[167]

2.3.1.4 The Exchange of Information

As the exchange of information is central to letters of all possible kinds, including letters of friendship and in family letters, some attention should be paid to this aspect of Philippians as well. From the start, however, it should be underlined that the way information is presented contributes simultaneously to the rhetorical aims pursued by a letter. This will be illustrated by discussing the two parts of Philippians that contribute the most to the exchange of information: 1.12-26 and 2.19-30.

2.3.1.4.1 Paul's Situation (1.12-26)

At this point it is not of so much importance to evaluate Paul's actual situation at the moment of composition of Philippians from an historical point of view, as to consider its presentation in Philippians.[168] Paul's description, namely, probably aims both at conveying information about his own well-being (and requesting the same about the well-being of his correspondents), and at recommending the author to his audience.[169] As became clear above,[170] Paul provides significant pieces of information about himself at a position in his letter where it may be expected (in Phil. 1.13-26, after the introductory formula in Phil. 1.12). What may have been expected on the basis of contemporary letters is indeed the case in this section:[171] Paul attempts to assure the Philippians of his well-being despite his imprisonment and the possibly mortal danger that he is in,[172] while simultaneously drawing attention to the fact that his imprisonment is because of Christ,[173] and that it has encouraged others to proclaim the gospel

---

165. Letters relativize one's absence; see, e.g., Gerber, *Paulus*, 69–72.
166. See, e.g., Holloway, *Consolation*, 87–92.
167. See also, e.g., Williams, *Enemies*, 109.
168. For this line of thought, see, e.g., Joachim Gnilka, *Der Philipperbrief*, HThK.NT (Freiburg: Herder, 1968), 55.
169. See, e.g., Müller, *Brief*, 48, "briefliche Selbstempfehlung."
170. See above, 2.3.1.1–4.
171. See, e.g., White, *Light*, letters 102–105, and most other letters included in this volume.
172. See, e.g., Phil. 1.20, 2.17; see also the remarks by, e.g., Barth, *Brief*, 20, and Walter, "Brief," 14–15.
173. See Müller, *Brief*, 49, "die tiefere, nämlich theologische Bedeutung seiner persönlichen Gefangenschaft."

as well,[174] albeit that some do so out of envy.[175] The Philippians may have expected to hear otherwise due to Paul's imprisonment. He, however, well aware of his less-than-rosy situation, aims to convince the Philippians that, in reality, he is a successful missionary (1.12-16). Thus, Paul rehabilitates himself and presents himself as an authoritative and successful agent of the Gospel.[176] It is in this way that he establishes himself as a person who is indeed in the position to exhort and teach the Philippians. As has been indicated earlier and will be argued more extensively later,[177] the ambiguity surrounding Paul's acknowledgment of the Philippians' support suits this self-portrayal. Furthermore, Paul's description of the true state of affairs concerning himself may also have consoled the Philippians in their worries about Paul.[178] Phil. 1.19-26 continues Paul's description and evaluation of his own situation, specifically with regard to his future and to his wish for deliverance (σωτηρία) through the prayers of the Philippians and the workings of the Spirit (v. 19).[179] This deliverance can have two shapes: death and being with Christ, or life and working for Christ as well as coming to the Philippians.[180] This somewhat paradoxical

---

174. See, e.g., Barth, *Brief*, 25–26. For a study that underlines the importance of proclamation in Paul's thinking with special emphasis on this portion of Philippians, see James A. Smith, *Marks of an Apostle: Deconstruction, Philippians, and Problematizing Pauline Theology*, Semeia Studies 53 (Atlanta: Society of Biblical Literature, 2005). Similarly, Ware, *Paul*, who is unaware of Smith's study, places much emphasis on the importance of proclamation in Philippians. Still, I would argue that proclamation is but one aspect of the Christ-like identity that Paul exhorts the Philippians to embody.

175. With, e.g., Barth, *Brief*, 27, it is not likely that the people mentioned in the verses 15a, 17 are the same as those mentioned in verse 14. What this "envy" (or for that matter any of the invectives used in verse 17) means precisely is open to speculation (see Barth, *op. cit.*, 27–28; see also the refreshingly irenic considerations of Barth, *Erklärung*, 22–24); at any rate it may have to do with some sort of competition for the imprisoned Paul, whose position may well have been questioned due to his imprisonment. Similarly, Müller, *Brief*, 52–56; the theological position of these people is not questioned by Paul; so also, e.g., Walter, "Brief," 40.

176. See on this, e.g., Vos, "Rhetorik." Morna D. Hooker, "Philippians: Phantom Opponents and the Real Source of Conflict," in Ismo Dunderberg, Christopher Tuckett, and Kari Syreeni (eds.), *Fair Play: Diversity and Conflict in Early Christianity*, NTSup 103 (Leiden: Brill, 2002), 377–395, esp. 386, rightly terms this section of Philippians an "apologia." See also Marchal, *Hierarchy*, 13.

177. See below, 2.3.4.

178. See, e.g., the observations of Holloway, *Consolation*, 45–47.

179. In Phil. 1.19, Paul echoes Job 13.16LXX: ἀποβήσεται εἰς σωτηρίαν; Paul may well have understood his situation *vis-à-vis* God in analogy to that of Job, specifically in terms of dependence on God. See Barth, *Brief*, 29. Thus, Paul uses Job here as a paradigm (see, e.g., Ware, *Paul*, 203). The notion of "deliverance" is eschatologically connoted; see, e.g., Müller, *Brief*, 57.

180. Both could also be seen as expressions of Paul's obedience to Christ, which he emphasizes from Phil. 2.12 onwards; however, this is not noted explicitly at this point in Philippians. As Barth, *Brief*, 29, notes, Paul is sure that there will be σωτηρία for him, in whatever form. Ware, *Mission*, 208–209, argues that Paul assumes that his defense in court will be so effective that he will be delivered from prison alive.

situation can be understood by looking at both the "career" of a Christian that Paul outlines in Philippians (through suffering to glory) and the renewed consideration of both "suffering" and "glory" that result from it. While being exalted with Christ[181] is ostensibly the more attractive option,[182] remaining "in the flesh" (verse 22) would mean further fruitful work on behalf of Christ, which would also be an expression of Christ's lordship and would thus glorify Christ.[183] At any cost, Paul wishes to avoid being shamed and thus shaming the cause of the gospel.[184] The σύγκρισις that Paul uses here to present his (seemingly) surprising conclusion is a good example of its kind, and thematically prepares Paul's exhortations in Philippians to endure and even identify with suffering (see, e.g., Phil. 1.29-30, 3.17, 4.9).[185] This includes the orientation of Paul away from his own interests towards the interests of the Philippians in the midst of his suffering: even though his considerations begin with an emphasis on himself and the more attractive option for him,[186]

---

181. As throughout Philippians, Paul operates here with a notion of immediate glorification in the hour of one's death (Phil. 1.23), which may differ from other Pauline statements about eschatology, e.g. those in 1 Thess. 4.13-18 and 1 Cor. 15.52. As Barth, *Brief*, 33–35, argues, it is important to resist attempts to harmonize Paul's thought in this matter and to pay attention primarily to what he wishes to say using one or another eschatological image to outline the significance of faith and hope in Christ; Barth largely follows Dibelius, *Philipper*, 68–70. See further, also, Müller, *Brief*, 63–70, and Walter, "Brief," 43–44. See similarly, though with an emphasis on Paul's notion of resurrection and transformation at the *parousia*, Matthias Konradt, *Gericht und Gemeinde. Eine Studie zur Bedeutung und Funktion von Gerichtsaussagen im Rahmen der paulinischen Ekklesiologie und Ethik im 1 Thess und 1 Kor*, BZNW 117 (Berlin: De Gruyter, 2003), 478–480. For an argument for a more explicit harmonization with other Pauline statements on the same, see, e.g., Schenk, *Philipperbriefe*, 154–158. Reumann, *Philippians*, 252–253, opts for a vaguely defined and described intermediate state in Phil. 1.23. The argument of Stefan Schreiber, "Paulus im 'Zwischenzustand': Phil 1.23 und die Ambivalenz des Sterbens als Provokation," *NTS* 49 (2003), 336–359, is insightful as it presents early Jewish texts considering the immediate post-moral state of martyrs and patriarchs.

182. Whether this concept is understood by considering it from a Hellenistic philosophical or early Jewish perspective seems to matter little. See Nijay K. Gupta, "'I Will Not Be Put to Shame': Paul, the Philippians, and the Honourable Wish for Death," *Neotest* 42 (2008), 253–267 (with emphasis on Jewish traditions), and for a brief consideration of Greek and Hellenistic notions of the attractiveness of death, see, e.g., Müller, *Brief*, 60.

183. E.g. as a faithful witness; see, e.g., Barth, *Brief*, 30, 32. See also the remark by Müller, *Brief*, 58,"die Welt wird an dem Schicksal des Apostels erkennen müssen, 'daß Christus der Herr ist'" (quoting Dibelius, *Philipper*, 55).

184. See, e.g., Müller, *Brief*, 57–58; the echo of passages from the Old Testament such as Pss. 21.6LXX, 24.2–3.20LXX, 68.7LXX, 118.31, 80, 116LXX points to the fact that the shame that the faithful incurs also amounts to God's abandoning of the faithful. Ware, *Mission*, 204–206, argues that Paul does not want to become ashamed of the gospel.

185. See for these observations, Samuel Vollenweider, "Die Waagschalen von Leben und Tod: Zum antiken Hintergrund von Phil 1,21–26," *ZNW* 85 (1994), 93–115, esp. 101. In agreement with him and his identification of Paul's pattern of thought as a σύγκρισις, see Reumann, *Philippians*, 235–237. See also, e.g., Dodd, *Paul's Paradigmatic "I"*, 177–178.

186. See the position of ἐμοί in Phil. 1.21 and the subsequent reflection on his personal preference in verses 22–23.

he then decides against it,[187] opting for suffering in order to sustain (his communion with) the Philippians.[188] This choice stresses both Paul's orientation towards the well-being of the Philippians and his adherence to notions of honor and shame that were (at least at first sight) at odds with conventional Greco-Roman values.[189] In fact, as Simmons puts it, here also "Paul serves as a living paradigm modeling total consecration to the cause of Christ."[190] Phil. 1.30 also connects Paul's struggles and those of the Philippians explicitly.[191] In fact, a strong case can be made for the interpretation of the entirety of Phil. 1.12-26 as having a paradigmatic function in Philippians. Ware has recently made a plausible case for this.[192] To begin with, in 1.12-18a, the courageous Christians around Paul at the place of his imprisonment may be seen as embodiments of an attitude that Paul calls for. Further, Paul's remarks about himself in 1.18b-26 can be read in a similar way, as was just argued. With regard to Phil. 1.12-18a, the following may be observed. First, the fearlessness of the Christians around Paul at the place of his imprisonment is lauded in 1.14 (τολμᾶν ἀφόβως τὸν λόγον λαλεῖν), while Paul exhorts the Philippians in 1.28 to take precisely such an attitude (μὴ πτυρόμενοι ἐν μηδενὶ ὑπὸ τῶν ἀντικειμένων). In 1.15, reference is made to εὐδοκία; a

---

187. Whether this means deciding against suicide must remain open here; this question is secondary in any case for the interpretation of these verses; see for a summary, e.g., Reumann, *Philippians*, 237–238. See for the case in favor of Paul's consideration of suicide, esp. Arthur J. Droge, "*Mori Lucrum*: Paul and Ancient Theories of Suicide," *NovT* 30 (1988), 263–286; further also, James L. Jaquette, "A Not-so-Noble Death: Figured Speech, Friendship and Suicide in Philippians 1:21–26," *Neotest* 28 (1994), 177–192; N. Clayton Croy, "'To Die is Gain' (Philippians 1:19–26): Does Paul Contemplate Suicide?", *JBL* 122 (2003), 517–531; Lukas Bormann, "Reflexionen über Sterben und Tod bei Paulus," in Friedrich Wilhelm Horn (ed.), *Das Ende des Paulus: Historische, theologische und literaturgeschichtliche Aspekte*, BZNW 106 (Berlin: De Gruyter, 2001), 307–330, esp. 319–321. See also, Peter-Ben Smit, "War Paulus suizidal? Ein psychiatrisch-exegetischer Aufriss," forthcoming in *Biblische Notizen*.
188. James L. Jaquette, "Life and Death, *Adiaphora*, and Paul's Rhetorical Strategies," *NovT* 38 (1996), 30–54, argues on the background of Stoic convictions that within the realm of *adiaphora*, preferable options could be discerned (even if they were morally neutral) and that Paul, by opting for the stance that expressed the least self-interest, was able here to provide "the Philippians with a model of love determining action on which to pattern their own." It would be interesting to read these verses through the lens of Roman *pietas*. *Pietas* could also lead to setting aside personal interests for the sake of the state. See, e.g., Richard Alston, "Arms and the Man: Soldiers, Masculinity and Power in Republican and Imperial Rome," in Lin Foxhall and John Salmon (eds.) *When Men were Men: Masculinity, Power, and Identity in Classical Antiquity* (London: Routledge, 1998), 205–223, esp. 213.
189. With respect to this passage, see, e.g., Witherington, *Friendship*, 47–49.
190. William A. Simmons, "Divine Sovereignty and Existential Anxiety in Paul: Soliloquy and Self-Disclosure in Philippians," in T. L. Cross and E. B. Powery (eds.), *The Spirit and the Mind* (Lanham: University Press of America, 2000), 119–129, esp. 123.
191. See, e.g., Williams, *Enemies*, 120, and Walter, "Brief," 45.
192. Hence, see for this and the following, especially Ware, *Paul*, 184–223. Not all of Ware's connections are of the same strength, however. Still, enough remains to make a strong case.

term that returns in 2.13. The note on ἀγάπη in 1.16 returns in 2.1-2. In 1.17, ἐριθεία occurs, which will return in 2.3 (obviously, this would constitute a negative *exemplum*); the same is true for ἁγνῶς in the same verse and ἁγνά in 4.8.

In this way, Paul not only introduces himself and his situation in Phil. 1.14-26, but also sets the tone for much of what will come. Both the Christians around him and he himself may well fulfill a paradigmatic function.[193]

2.3.1.4.2 Recommending Timothy and Epaphroditus (2.19-30)

A second significant part of Philippians that conveys information is Phil. 2.19-30. This time, it is not so much Paul's own (traveling) plans that are of central significance,[194] but rather those of others, as he informs the Philippians about the whereabouts of his two companions, Timothy and Epaphroditus. Their (possible) paradigmatic significance within Philippians will be discussed below;[195] here, the focus should be on the kind of information conveyed by the references to them first. While doing this, it should be kept in mind that conveying information takes place not only for its own sake, but also to provoke a certain reaction to it. In the case of Timothy and Epaphroditus, Paul without doubt seeks to provoke a positive reaction on the part of the Philippians with regard to both the two men and, by association, himself.

The main information Paul conveys is that he hopes to send Timothy to Philippi (Phil. 2.19), and that he has also been forced to send Epaphroditus back to Philippi (Phil. 2.25). As there are many examples of letters which restrict the information given about the traveling plans of their authors and others to the barest outline, using epistolary clichés, Paul could well have stopped here. That he does not do so suits the more elaborate character of his writings in general and simultaneously invites the speculation that Paul has more in view than merely passing on information. In fact, Paul goes on to communicate that Timothy is both a very faithful collaborator (Phil. 2.20, 22) and very favorably disposed towards the Philippians (Phil. 2.19, 21), before repeating his intention to send this very person (τοῦτον μὲν οὖν ἐλπίζω πέμψαι, Phil. 2.23) as soon as he has worked out his own situation. The rhetorical effects of this additional information will be elaborated upon later.[196]

As far as Epaphroditus is concerned, the information that Paul gives the Philippians mainly concerns his illness and near-death, presumably while and because of ministering to Paul (Phil. 2.27-30), because of his knowledge of

---

193. See also Ware, *Paul*, 202.
194. Traveling plans are a standard topic of Hellenistic letters in general as well as of Pauline epistles; see, e.g., Gerber, *Paulus*, 74, for an overview; see esp. Rom. 15.28; 1 Cor. 4.18-21, 16.5-8; and 2 Cor. 12.14.
195. See 3.2.
196. See below, 3.2.2.

their concern about this (Phil. 2.26). He does not, however, give any details beyond noting that his collaborator survived a near-mortal illness (Phil. 2.26, 30). By providing this information, Paul probably responds to concerns voiced by the Philippians. As the sending of Epaphroditus does not depend so much on Paul's needs as on Epaphroditus' needs, Paul can promise to send him as soon as possible (σπουδαιοτέρως, Phil. 2.28).

By dwelling upon all this, Paul both provides information about his two co-workers and in doing so underlines the relationships between him, his co-workers, and the Philippians. That this presentation of Timothy and Epaphroditus also contributes to Paul's deliberative interest in Philippians will be argued later in this study.[197]

2.3.2 Requests and Instructions Concerning Issues in Philippi

Apart from exchanging information and underlining their good mutual relationship—the elements of Philippians that come closest to family letters—Paul also touches quite extensively upon a number of issues regarding which he instructs the Philippians. The sections of Philippians in which Paul provides guidance are among the lengthiest ones of the letter and among the parts of Philippians that are the most dissimilar from contemporary letters, especially in terms of their length. Formally, however, they do resemble instructions given in contemporary letters, which cover virtually all subjects imaginable, ranging from the management of a farm to abandoning a child.[198] Some particular issues about which Paul gives instructions can be isolated and should be enumerated and introduced here, so as to provide a background for the discussion of the precise use of *exempla* in the remainder of this study.

2.3.2.1 Suffering
The issue of suffering in Philippians is of considerable importance and has led to substantial discussion.[199] With Wolter, it may be maintained that Paul makes his suffering and that of the communities that he is concerned with plausible as part of identity in Christ by relating it closely to Christ's suffering and by viewing it as one of the elements that creates and shapes fellowship in the gospel.[200] In Philippians, the notion of suffering is first mentioned in Paul's self-presentation, in which he has to account for his sufferings because of the gospel (1.7, 12-18) and it permeates the letter

---

197. See below, 3.2.
198. See White, *Light*, letters 82–85, and idem, *op. cit.*, letter 72.
199. Dodd, *Paul's Paradigmatic "I"*, 177; see esp. Bloomquist, *Function*, 18–69, for an overview of the discussion, and see further, Williams, *Enemies*, 71–78.
200. Michael Wolter, "Der Apostel und seine Gemeinden als Teilhaber am Leidensgeschick Jesu Christi: Beobachtungen zur paulinischen Leidenstheologie," *NTS* 36 (1990), 535–557, esp. 556–557.

afterwards.²⁰¹ In fact, it can be said that everyone in the letter seems to suffer for the gospel, or at least to be involved in the ἀγών for it.²⁰² Interpretations of the importance of this theme have been varied.²⁰³ In a discussion of the subject, Dodd singled out two plausible solutions. The first is that difficulties about the issue of suffering arose from the point of view of Paul's "radical Jewish Christian"²⁰⁴ opponents in or around Philippi,²⁰⁵ as they surface elsewhere in the letter (esp. in ch. 3). The second option is that Paul's (and others') suffering was problematized from quite a different point of view, that of theological triumphalism proceeding from a thoroughly realized understanding of eschatology.²⁰⁶ Though Dodd acknowledges that "it is entirely inferential,"²⁰⁷ he nevertheless accepts Koester's suggestion "that Paul and the Philippians were confronting triumphalist proponents of a too-strongly realized eschatology for whom suffering was incompatible with their

201. See Phil. 1.7, 12-18, 21-26; 2.8, 17, 25-30; 3.10, 18; 4.11-14.
202. With the possible exception of Timothy, though his identity is so closely bound up with Paul's that it is hardly a significant exception. See Dodd, *Paul's Paradigmatic "I"*, 178. The same argument could be made for Clement in Phil. 4.3. On the ἀγών in general, see, e.g., Uta Poplutz, *Athlet des Evangeliums: eine motivgeschichtliche Studie zur Wettkampfmetaphorik bei Paulus*, HBS 43 (Freiburg: Herder, 2004), *passim*, and Martin Brändl, *Der Agon bei Paulus: Herkunft und Profil paulinischer Agonmetaphorik*, WUNT 2.222 (Tübingen: Mohr Siebeck, 2006), *passim*. Paul's lively use of metaphors drawn from the area of sports has led Rainer Metzner, "Paulus und der Wettkampf: Die Rolle des Sports in Leben und Verkündigung des Apostels (1 Kor 9.24–7; Phil 3.12–16)," *NTS* 46 (2000), 565–583, to suspect that Paul was personally acquainted with athletics and, when writing to Philippi, used this experience as well as the four-yearly games at Ephesus as a source of inspiration (576). While Metzner's argument that Paul must have been acquainted with sport is plausible, it should be added that he may have written with the sporting scene in Philippi in mind as well (a *palaestra* was built in the second century and it is hard to imagine that no sport events took place in the city before that).
203. Bloomquist, *Function*, 18–70.
204. For this terminology, see Lukas Vischer, Ulrich Luz, and Christian Link, *Ökumene im Neuen Testament und heute* (Göttingen: Vandenhoeck & Ruprecht, ²2009), 90: "in der heutigen Forschung heißen sie [sc. the opponents of Paul in Galatia]—wiederum abwertend—oft 'Judaisten'. Wir möchten diese negative sprachliche Etikettierung durch denjenigen, die sich in der Geschichte durchgesetzt haben, nicht mitmachen und sprechen darum neutral von 'radikalen Judenchristen'." At this point, it should be noted, in order to avoid the pitfall of (unintentional) anti-Judaism on these pages, that the following evaluation of Paul's relationship with Judaism, precisely also concerning his "conversion" as he comments on it in Phil. 3, is generally shared here; e.g., Niebuhr, *Heidenapostel*, 111–112: "Stellt Paul ... auch seinen Wandel vom exemplarischen Vertreter jüdischen Lebens zum Apostel Jesu Christi als radikale Kehrtwendung dar, so beurteilt er diese Wende doch nicht als Abkehr von den Inhalten jüdischen Gottesglaubens und Heilsverständnisses. Aus der Perspektive seines eschatologischen Verkündigungsauftrages sieht er im Gegenteil gerade in dieser Wende einen Ausdruck des heilschaffenden Handelns des Gottes Israels, der sein Volk erwählt hat, ihm durch die Verkündigung der Propheten auch die Heiden einschließendes heil verheißen hat und dieses Heil jetzt im Christusgeschehen anbrechen läßt."
205. Dodd, *Paul's Paradigmatic "I"*, 178–179.
206. Dodd, *Paul's Paradigmatic "I"*, 179–180. Along these lines see also Davorin Peterlin, *Paul's Letter to the Philippians in the Light of Disunity in the Church*, NTSup 79 (Leiden: Brill, 1995), 31–51, *et passim*.
207. Dodd, *Paul's Paradigmatic "I"*, 179.

'presentation of the believer's life in terms of triumphalism and present glory.' At all costs suffering and persecution must be avoided."[208]

However true it is that Paul employs the "already/not yet" figure of thought a number of times in Philippians, emphasizing especially the "not yet" nature of Christian existence on earth and its orientation towards heavenly vindication and glory—to be reached through the struggle (ἀγών) and its inherent suffering[209]—it is nevertheless not necessary to follow the inference of Dodd and others that (one of) the front(s) Paul has to face in the Philippian community is one of an all-too-realized eschatology. If the proposal that the argument problematizing Paul's suffering came from more "radical Jewish Christian" opponents makes sense, there is no need to look for further groups for whom this would be problematic. Put differently, the issue of suffering could have been problematized by anybody,[210] given that it ran counter to conventional anthropological views in the Greco-Roman world;[211] but since it also suits the profile of a more "radical Jewish Christian" group, there is no need to look for further groups of opponents. The precise nature of these "radical Jewish Christian" opponents and their role for the Philippian community will be considered below (2.3.2.3). Here, however, it may be remarked already that besides theological reasons, a social reason may also have made it attractive for early Christian communities to adopt identity markers of Judaism.[212] Given that early Christians (who were no longer identifiable as members of the Jewish community—or were no longer seen as part of it by the community itself) ran a higher risk than Jews that were also recognized as such[213] of being accused of being un-Roman,[214] operating in such a way

208. Dodd, *Paul's Paradigmatic "I"*, 189; quotation within Dodd's quotation from Martin, *Philippians*, 34.
209. See also below, 3.1, esp. 3.1.5.2.
210. This also follows from Dodd's conclusions (*Paul's Paradigmatic "I"*, 180); he argues that both "radical Jewish Christians" and those adhering to an all-too-fully-realized eschatology would have had theological reasons to oppose Paul's integration of suffering into their concept of Christian life.
211. See below, 3.4.4, where the issue of Paul's (and others') controversial masculinity is discussed. Similarly, e.g., Walter, "Brief," 48–49, who rightly notes that the notion of suffering for God was as such available in early Judaism as well.
212. See, e.g., Niebuhr, *Heidenapostel*, 96–97; see in this respect also the argument of Kellbe, "Factors," which is substantially repeated in idem, *Paul*, 231–278, on the attractivity of the opponents' position; see esp. 261–267. Similarly also, De Vos, *Church*, 265–275.
213. This notwithstanding considerable anti-Judaism in the Hellenistic world; see, e.g., the overview of ethnographic treatises on Judaism given by René Bloch, *Antike Vorstellungen vom Judentum: Der Judenexkurs des Tacitus im Rahmen der griechisch-römischen Ethnographie*, Historia-Einzelschriften 160 (Stuttgart: Franz Steiner, 2002), 176–185. Müller, *Brief*, 76, for example, rightly notes that "gentile" converts to both Judaism and Christianity—to the extent that they could be clearly distinguished—had to face considerable resistance, as is well expressed in the considerations of Tacitus, *His.* 5:5. On the status of Judaism in the Roman Empire, see further, e.g., Mikael Tellbe, *Paul between Synagogue and State: Christians, Jews, and Civic Authorities in 1 Thessalonians, Romans, and Philippians*, ConBNT 34 (Stockholm: Almqvist & Wiksell, 2001), 24–79; E. Mary Smallwood, *The Jews Under Roman Rule: From Pompey to Diocletian. A Study in Political Relations* (Leiden: Brill, 2001) and idem, *The Reluctant Parting: How the New Testament's Jewish Writers Created a Christian Book* (San Francisco: HarperSanFrancisco, 2005).

that identification with Judaism remained possible for outsiders would have brought social advantages (such as a reduced chance of marginalization, and/ or persecution).[215]

2.3.2.2 Unity

Unity is of paramount importance in Philippians.[216] Beginning in Phil. 1.27-28, admonitions to stand together follow one upon another. The admonition that begins in Phil. 1.27-28 continues in Phil. 2.1-4; the meek (and "altruistic", v. 4) attitude towards one another that is advocated there (Phil. 2.3) is substantiated by what follows in Phil. 2.5-11.[217] Also, the presentation of Timothy and Epaphroditus contains elements that point to the importance of the theme of unity.[218] Phil. 3 has, according to the view taken here, in the first place to do with an outside threat to the Philippian community, but Paul's formidable appeal to the Philippians not to align themselves with the "dogs" is in itself also an attempt to retain communion between himself and the Philippians. A direct appeal to unity appears again in Phil. 4.1-3, where one pair of quarreling members of the Philippian community is named, Euodia and Syntyche, who are "known to us because they did not agree."[219] The content of their disagreement, serious enough for Paul to mention it and hence probably potentially threatening the life of the community (of which these two women are likely to have been senior members),[220] is not stated explicitly, however, and it is probably beyond the scope of exegetical reconstruction to narrow it down in any precise way.[221]

---

214. See, e.g., Pilhofer, *Philippi*, 135–136.
215. A similar case may be found in Gal. 6.12. See, e.g., Barth, *Brief*, 67. See also, Niebuhr, *Heidenapostel*, 96: "die Konflikte des Paulus in jüdischen Diasporagemeinden könnten auf einen innersynagogalen Differenzierungsprozeß hindeuten, in dessen Verlauf die paulinischen Christengemeinden als eigenständige Gruppierungen im Gegenüber zu den nichtchristlichen Gemeinden auch nach außen hin als von der Synagoge unterschiedene Gruppen erschienen, [dies] verschärfte ihre rechtliche und politische Lage."
216. See, e.g., the forceful argument of Black, "Discourse," 17 (*et passim*); see further also, O'Brien, *Philippians*, 38–39.
217. See especially the forceful argument of Troels Engberg-Pedersen, "Radical Altruism in Philippians 2:4," in Fitzgerald, Olbricht, and White (eds.), *Christianity*, 197–214.
218. See below, 3.2.
219. Nils A. Dahl, "Euodia and Syntyche and Paul's Letter to the Philippians," in L. Michael White and O. Larry Yarbrough (eds.), *The Social World of the First Christians: Essays in Honor of Wayne A. Meeks* (Minneapolis: Fortress, 1995), 3–15, esp. 3. The precise identity of the two women is not known; for an overview of more and less well-educated guesses, see, e.g., Reumann, *Philippians*, 625–628.
220. See, e.g., Dahl, "Euodia," 4.6, as well as Barth, *Brief*, 71.
221. So, e.g., Barth, *Brief*, 71. Dodd, *Paul's Paradigmatic "I"*, 175, claims that it has to do with the problem of suffering, but it is hard to see how to substantiate this suggestion. For a host of further opinions, see, e.g., Reumann, *Philippians*, 625–628.

2.3.2.3 "Dogs"

Here, the identity of those people that Paul refers polemically to as "dogs"[222] in Phil. 3.2 should be considered briefly, in terms of both their stance and their activities. Paul's reaction to them will be discussed more fully later.[223]

First, a plausible interpretation of the activities that the "dogs" employed can be found in a more technical meaning of the word ἐργάτης, which had acquired the sense of "missionary" in early Christian literature.[224] When this meaning is also applied to the use of the noun in Phil. 3.2, then what one encounters in Phil. 3 may well be a group of itinerant early Christian missionaries that competes with Paul.[225] Early Christianity was a highly pluriform phenomenon, which also applied to so-called "Pauline communities,"[226] and "missionaries" traveling from one community to the other can therefore easily be imagined.

Second, the precise religious identity of the group of people upon which Paul descends in Phil. 3 is a matter of debate. Because it depends on a "mirror-reading" of the passages involved, the question is methodologically complicated.[227] Most often, it is described as a group that regards more elements of Jewish (ritual) Torah as binding for all Christians than Paul accepted.[228] It is also the one clearly identifiable group that is related to the issue of disunity in Philippians. Whether this group was Jewish *sensu stricto*,[229] or not, or whether one has to

---

222. On the historical and conceptual background, see esp. Stefan Schreiber, "Cavete Canes! Zur wachsenden Ausgrenzungsvalenz einer neutestamentlichen Metapher," *BZ* 45 (2001), 170–192, esp. 187–189 on Phil. 3.2, with conclusions that are largely in agreement with the position taken here.

223. See below, 3.4.

224. See, e.g., Mt. 9.37-38/Lk. 10.2, Mt. 10.10/Lk. 10.7, Lk. 13.27, 2 Cor. 11.13, 1 Tim. 5.18, 2 Tim. 2.15, and *Did.* 13.2. For a discussion, see, e.g., Fowl, *Story*, 99, Holloway, *Consolation*, 134, Williams, *Enemies*, 157–158, Niebuhr, *Heidenapostel*, 88–89, Barth, *Brief*, 56, and Reumann, *Philippians*, 472.

225. See, e.g., Fowl, *Story*, 99.

226. A term that may lead one to imagine that early Christian communities were more monolithic and less diverse than they actually were. See, e.g., David Horrell, "Pauline Churches or Early Christian Churches? Unity, Disagreement, and the Eucharist," in Anatoly Alexeev, Christos Karakolis, and Ulrich Luz (eds.), *Einheit der Kirche im Neuen Testament: dritte europäische orthodox-westliche Exegetenkonferenz in Sankt Petersburg, 24.–31. August 2005*, WUNT 1.218 (Tübingen: Mohr Siebeck, 2008), 185–203.

227. See, e.g., Bianchini, *L'Elegio*, 182–186; for caution regarding mirror-reading, see also, e.g., Niebuhr, *Heidenapostel*, 88, and the extensive account, demonstrating both the necessity and the inherent difficulties of this method with regard to Galatians provided by John M. G. Barclay, "Mirror-Reading a Polemical Letter: Galatians as a Test Case," *JSNT* 31 (1987), 73–93. See in general also Klaus Berger, "Die impliziten Gegner. Zur Methode der Erschließung von 'Gegnern' in neutestamentlichen Texten," in Dieter Lührmann and Georg Strecker (eds.), *Kirche* (FS Günther Bornkamm; Tübingen: Mohr, 1980), 373–400, as well as Vos, "Rhetorik," 54–55. The problems involved in mirror-reading, however, are not such that it becomes plausible that Phil. 3.2-21 does not deal with specific opponents at all and is a deutero-Pauline text with a very general character, as Darrel J. Doughty, "Citizens of Heaven: Philippians 3.2-21," *NTS* 41 (1995), 102–122, argues.

228. See, e.g., Dodd, *Paul's Paradigmatic "I"*, 175–176.

229. So, e.g., Dibelius, *Philipper*, 86, but he is open to both options; see also, Schoon-Janssen, *"Apologien"*, 128. Walter, "Brief," 74, for example, opts for Jews (or Jewish Christians that are called Jews as well).

do with a "radical Jewish Christian" "circumcision-party,"²³⁰ may well be an anachronistic question—in many ways, one is dealing with alternative early Jewish identities in this period. Still, from a modern perspective the description "radical Jewish Christians" probably fits best.²³¹ Quite in spite of this, however, the possibility remains that Paul placed groups that viewed circumcision as necessary for integration into the people of God on a par with Israel in as far as it does not recognize the Christ-event in its true significance. The danger that this "radical Jewish Christian" group poses is, according to Paul, precisely the one to which Israel has (largely) succumbed: not to recognize the true significance of the Christ-event, that is, achieving a right standing before God through the cross of Christ, apart from ethnic, religious, or social status and identity. Given that this group probably consists of competing missionaries and that Paul writes to warn the Philippians against them, it seems likely that this group was not in the Philippian community yet, but might be expected to try to get into it soon.²³²

Apart from the question of the identity of the group addressed in Phil. 3, the precise issues at stake will have to remain relatively unclear as well,²³³ though if the terms of abuse used in Phil. 3.2 are only a little precise, circumcision was probably a predominant issue.²³⁴ The pejorative use of the word "dog"²³⁵ that Paul applies to his adversaries was in early Judaism not uncommon for Gentiles,²³⁶ and the fact that precisely the term "dog" was also used to refer to eunuchs makes it highly likely that here a similar issue is in view. The hyperbolic insult leveled at Paul's competitors is also reminiscent of similar rhetoric in Gal. 5.12.²³⁷ Certainly when taking into account the use the LXX

---

230. See, e.g., Williams, *Enemies*, 221, and O'Brien, *Epistle*, 26–35. Many authors assume that the persons in view are "outsiders" to the Philippian community; see, e.g., Peterlin, *Philippians*, 98–99.
231. See also the observations of Dodd, *Paul's Paradigmatic "I"*, 175.
232. See, e.g., the convincing argument of Niebuhr, *Heidenapostel*, 81; also Dibelius, *Philipper*, 87, argued already that the "dogs" are not in the Philippian community.
233. See, e.g., also the cautious stance of Bianchini, *L'Elegio*, 187–194.
234. See, e.g., Dodd, *Paul's Paradigmatic "I"*, 174, Barth, *Brief*, 56, and Niebuhr, *Heidenapostel*, 88 (noting that this is the only thing that one can be reasonably sure about regarding the opponents).
235. This point does not need to be belabored here: dogs were held in negative regard throughout the Greco-Roman world; see, e.g., Reumann, *Philippians*, 460–461.
236. See Dodd, *Paul's Paradigmatic "I"*, 175; see, e.g., Mt. 15.21-28 par., as well as Ps. 22.16, 20; Isa. 50.10-11; 1 En. 89.41-50.
237. See, e.g., Walter, "Brief," 74–75. As Holloway, *Consolation*, 133, notes, Paul remains very eloquent while uttering his invective against his opponents, using the stylistic means of anaphora, assonance, paronomasia, parsicolon, and chiasm. See also Niebuhr, *Heidenapostel*, 90, who draws attention to a number of further agreements between Galatians and this section of Philippians: Gal. 6.13-14: ἐν ... σαρκὶ καυχήσωνται, καυχᾶσθαι ... ἐν τῷ σταυρῷ—Phil. 3.3: καυχώμενοι ἐν Χριστῷ Ἰησοῦ; Gal. 2.19: Χριστῷ συνεσταύρωμαι—Phil. 3.20: συμμορφιζόμενος τῷ θανάτῳ αὐτοῦ; Gal. 2.16: οὐ δικαιοῦται ... ἐξ ἔργων νόμου ἐὰν μὴ διὰ πίστεως—Phil. 3.9: μὴ ἔχων ἐμὴν δικαιοσύνην τὴν ἐκ νόμου ἀλλὰ τὴν διὰ πίστεως; Gal. 2.17: εὑρέθημεν—Phil. 3.9: εὑρεθῶ; ἀπεκδεχόμεθα in Gal. 5.5 and Phil. 3.20.

makes of κοιλία and αἰσχύνη as euphemisms for the male reproductive organ, this option becomes attractive.[238] Thus, Paul uses a pejorative commonly reserved for Gentiles, i.e. those outside the people of God, in order to attack his "radical Jewish Christian" opponents.[239] This would well suit the background to Paul's use of this particular insult: the question of the identity of the people of God.[240] This is a more likely interpretation than viewing the reference to the "belly" as an attack on the this-worldly attitude of Paul's opponents.[241]

2.3.3 Opponents and Adversaries of the Philippians and Paul: An Overview

In the light of the above, it is helpful to provide a brief overview of the various opponents of Paul (and the Philippians) as they are presupposed by this study.[242] This should serve as an orientation, rather than as an exhaustive discussion of this virtually inexhaustible subject.[243]

First, there are those who imprisoned Paul, most likely the authorities in Ephesus.[244]

Second, the group of intra-Christian troublemakers that Paul mentions in Phil. 1.15, 17 should be noted. They preach Christ out of envy, rivalry, and partisanship in Paul's immediate context, but do not seem to play a role of much importance anymore in the rest of Philippians. They compete with Paul and seem to take advantage of his suffering, specifically of his imprisonment.

---

238. See, e.g., Chris Mearns, "The Identity of Paul's Opponents at Philippi," *NTS* 33 (1987), 194–204, esp. 198–200. Other options abound, however; see, e.g., for a succinct overview, Dibelius, *Philipper*, 93.
239. See Martin, *Philippians*, 125, Dodd, *Paul's Paradigmatic "I"*, 175; and, critical of the idea, Niebuhr, *Heidenapostel*, 89.
240. See on this, e.g., James D. G. Dunn, "One Church – Many Churches," in Alexeev, Karakolis, and Luz (eds.), *Einheit*, 3–33; see, e.g., also, Dibelius, *Philipper*, 87.
241. See the convincing argument of Sandnes, *Body*, 136–164, emphasizing that the literary context needs to provide the interpretation of the otherwise unclear notion of "belly-worship" here. For an interpretation along the lines of a "libertine" attitude, see, e.g., Walter Schmithals, *Paul and the Gnostics* (Nashville: Abingdon, 1972), 109, and Martin, *Philippians*, 145–146. Patristic authors prefer a reference to dietary regulations, which Sandnes, *op. cit.*, 145–146, shows to be unlikely (Jewish sources accused those neglecting dietary regulations of being belly-oriented, not vice versa), but which is followed by, e.g., Helmut Koester, "The Purpose of the Polemic of a Pauline Fragment," *NTS* 8 (1962), 317–332; John J. Gunther, *St. Paul's Opponents and Their Background: A Study of Apocalyptic and Jewish Sectarian Teachings*, NTSup 35 (Leiden: Brill, 1973), 98; Kurz, "Kenotic," 116; and Dodd, *Paul's Paradigmatic "I"*, 176.
242. See, e.g., Veronica Koperski, *The Knowledge of Christ Jesus My Lord: The High Christology of Philippians 3:7–11*, CBETh 16 (Kampen: Kok, 1996), 113.
243. See Dodd, *Paul's Paradigmatic "I"*, 174, referring to a list of 18 different interpretations for Paul's opponents in Philippians, as well as the overview of the discussion by Williams, *Enemies*, 54–60, with special reference to the 15 interpretative options for Paul's opponents in Phil. 3 that have been listed by Gunther, *Opponents*, 2. Williams' own proposal, largely in agreement with what is said here, can be found in idem, *op. cit.*, 155–159.
244. On considerations about the place of composition of Philippians, see above, 2.2.3.

In Paul's view they even intend to increase his predicament. These people may well be those Paul has in mind when he commends Timothy in Phil. 2.21, stating that (unlike Timothy) οἱ πάντες γὰρ τὰ ἑαυτῶν ζητοῦσιν, οὐ τὰ 'Ιησοῦ Χριστοῦ, even if this is not necessary.

Third, ἀντικείμενοι appear in Phil. 1.28. They are in Philippi, located outside of the community, given that the community is called upon to stand strong against them (Phil. 1.27).[245] Given the comments on their (future) destruction in Phil. 1.28, these opponents may well be Philippian (civil) officials that caused problems for the community.[246] Paul interprets the oppression or at least difficulties implied by Phil. 1.28 as a sign of the upcoming destruction of the opponents of the Philippian community.[247] That this group is the same as the one addressed in Phil. 3 is unlikely given the parallel drawn between Paul's situation in his prison and that of the Philippians (1.30).[248]

Fourth, there are those mentioned in Phil. 3.2 and, intermingled with Paul's own *exemplum*, throughout chapter 3.[249] As was indicated above,[250] this "radical Jewish Christian" group is probably not in Philippi yet, but constitutes a potential threat. In Phil. 3, only one group of opponents (or competitors) is in view, not two or three.[251] It is unlikely that the "perfected" in verse 15 should be seen as a separate group of opponents,[252] given that τέλειοι in verse 15 refers back to τετελείωμαι in verse 12 and that τοῦτο in verse 15 must refer back to the entire previous argumentation. Therefore, it is the most plausible that Paul addresses the entire Philippian community here, in a way that is akin to 1 Cor. 2.6, 14.20 (see Rom. 12.2). Additionally, those referred to in verse 18, the "enemies of the cross," do not need to be seen as a separate group either,[253] but may well be seen as a further description of one and the same group, again referred to as a negative example for the Philippians.[254]

Thus, a certain parallel exists between the situation of the Philippians and that of Paul, as is made explicit in Phil. 1.29-30.[255] Both are suffering because of outside pressure. In all likelihood, both also have to cope with disagreement

---

245. So also, e.g., Kellbe, *Paul*, 233.
246. See, e.g., convincingly, De Vos, *Church*, 261–265. Though some caution is appropriate, see the considerations of Barth, *Brief*, 38.
247. Following Hawthorne, Fowl argues that the suffering of the Philippians is a sign with two possible interpretations: a sign of the Philippians' destruction (from the point of view of their opponents) or of their salvation (from Paul's point of view). See Stephen E. Fowl, "Philippians 1:28b, One More Time," in Donaldson and Sailors (eds.), *Greek*, 167–179, esp. 178–179.
248. Different, e.g., is Niebuhr, *Heidenapostel*, 90.
249. For a succint overview of options, see Ware, *Paul*, 197.
250. See below, 2.3.2.3.
251. With, e.g., Barth, *Brief*, 69.
252. For this and the following, see, e.g., Niebuhr, *Heidenapostel*, 85–86, 91.
253. See, e.g., Dodd, *Paul's Paradigmatic "I"*, 181.
254. For this and the following, see, e.g., Barth, *Brief*, 66–67; Niebuhr, *Heidenapostel*, 89–90; Schenk, *Philipperbriefe*, 284–285, 291; diff., e.g., Gnilka, *Philipperbrief*, 204–205.
255. See, e.g., Barth, *Brief*, 37; see also Klauck, *Briefliteratur*, 240.

over this suffering. In the place of his imprisonment, Paul has to cope with competing missionaries, who, taking advantage of his situation, preach the gospel out of envy and seek to increase his suffering, while, in Philippi, the Philippians probably have to deal with pressure from local authorities as well as with people offering an alternative to Paul's gospel. Paul underlines the analogy between his situation and that of the Philippians and, in doing so, invites the Philippians to identify with him.

2.3.4 "Thanking" for a Gift

A further reason for the writing of Philippians is in all likelihood the communication of both the reception of and thanks for a gift that Paul received from the Philippians. This should be considered at this point.

Following what seem to be concluding hortatory remarks in 4.1-9, where Paul returns both to the question of unity (Phil. 4.2-7) and to the issue of retaining Paul's teaching (Phil. 4.8-9),[256] Paul adds a "thank-you note" in Phil. 4.10-20, commenting on a gift that he had received from the Philippians and that he had only hinted at briefly in Phil. 1.5, even if Phil. 4.1-10 is semantically connected to Paul's thanksgiving in Phil. 1.3-11:[257]

Table 2.2: **A Comparison of Philippians 1.3-11 and 4.1-10**

Phil. 1.3-11	Phil. 4.10-20
Εὐχαριστῶ τῷ θεῷ μου ... μετὰ χαρᾶς (Phil. 1.3-4)	Ἐχάρην δὲ ἐν κυρίῳ (Phil. 4.10)
ἐπὶ τῇ κοινωνίᾳ ὑμῶν (Phil. 1.5) συγκοινωνούς μου τῆς χάριτος (Phil. 1.7)	συγκοινωνήσαντες (Phil. 4.14) ἐκοινώνησεν (Phil. 4.15)
τοῦτο φρονεῖν ὑπὲρ πάντων ὑμῶν (Phil. 1.7)	τὸ ὑπὲρ ἐμοῦ φρονεῖν (Phil. 4.10)

By thanking the Philippians for the gift, Paul takes up a theme that occurs frequently in Greco-Roman letters. However, he does so relatively late in his letter, as has already been noticed. Letters were often accompanied by gifts or were sent in response to gifts. Gifts also expressed the structure of

---

256. The reference to ἃ καὶ ἐμάθετε καὶ παρελάβετε καὶ ἠκούσατε καὶ εἴδετε ἐν ἐμοί, ταῦτα πράσσετε can well be read as referring back not only to Paul's actual presence among the Philippians, but also as pointing forward to his *periautological exemplum* in Phil. 3.2-21. See, e.g., Dodd, *Paul's Paradigmatic "I"*, 182.
257. See Müller, *Brief*, 47.

a relationship, which in the Greco-Roman world often consisted of donors and recipients, or patrons and clients.[258] The relationship between Paul and the Christian community in Philippi is no exception in this respect.[259] The material support that Paul received from the Philippians brings him into an awkward situation. Has he, the "patron" of the community (in terms of the proclamation of the gospel), become its client (in terms of material support)?[260] In a manner not unlike his rhetorical strategy concerning the return of Onesimus in his letter to Philemon, Paul is able to turn the tables on his epistolary counterparts in Philippians. In order to avoid finding himself at the "bottom" of the hierarchy of his relationship with the Philippians,[261] Paul argues[262] that by providing the Philippians with an opportunity to give him material support—a rare privilege to begin with (see Phil. 4.10, 15); Paul underlines this special relationship, possibly to avoid insulting the Philippians[263]—he has in fact given a gift to them: the gift of having the opportunity to add to their heavenly account (Phil. 4.17-19). This, Paul argues, is his main concern regarding the gifts of the Philippians (Phil. 4.17),[264] given that he is, in fact, utterly autonomous himself,[265] unaffected by affluence or hardship (Phil. 4.11-13).[266] At the same time, Paul adds to his (laudatory) statements about the gift a repetition of one of his main themes

---

258. For an overview of the social background, see, e.g., G. W. Peterman, *Paul's Gift from Philippi: Conventions of Gift-Exchange and Christian Giving*, SNTSMon 92 (Cambridge, UK: Cambridge University Press, 1997), esp. 1–89, as well as the excellent analysis by Martin Ebner, *Leidenslisten und Apostelbrief. Untersuchungen zu Form, Motivik und Funktion der Peristasenkataloge bei Paulus*, FzB 66 (Würzburg: Echter, 1991), 331–364.

259. See, e.g., Ascough, *Associations*, 149–157, for a cogent description.

260. For an overview of Hellenistic conventions concerning gifts, see, e.g., Bormann, *Philippi*, 161–205. Peterman, *Gift*, 157–160, argues that questions of hierarchy are not in view, but only questions of partnership; the one, however, does not exclude the other, and early Christian communities did contain forms of hierarchy.

261. This would, despite the argument set forth by Reumann, *Philippians*, 686–687, not conflict with a friendly relationship: even friendships could (and often were) hierarchical.

262. Given the relatively self-contained nature of Phil. 4.10-20 as well as its clearly argumentative character, rhetorical analysis of this part of Philippians as such is helpful; for a proposal, see, e.g., A. H. Snyman, "Persuasion in Philippians 4.1–20," in Porter and Olbricht (eds.), *Rhetoric*, 325–337.

263. See, e.g., Holloway, *Consolation*, 159, who notes that Seneca—in this respect probably representative of sentiments current in first-century society in general—noted in *De benef.* 2.24:2-3 that a response to a gift which indicated that the gift was not really needed would be regarded as offensive.

264. See, e.g., Holloway, *Consolation*, 159.

265. This autonomy is a qualified one: it rests upon God giving Paul the strength to be autonomous; see Phil. 4.13 and the discussion by Holloway, *Consolation*, 158. This ideal was also found in contemporary philosophical schools; for emphasis on the Stoic background, see Engberg-Pedersen, *Paul*, 101.

266. Compared to Paul's initial statement of joy over the gift in Phil. 4.10, verses 11-13 constitute a so-called "correctio," which allows a speaker (or in this case, author) to state something and to take it back partially. See, e.g., Holloway, *Consolation*, 157.

in Philippians: by giving him the gift, the Philippians have shared in his suffering (Phil. 4.14: ἐποιήσατε συγκοινωνήσαντές μου τῇ θλίψει). Thus, what is an occasion for writing a letter, the receipt of a gift, simultaneously provides an opportunity for Paul to describe, towards the end of his letter, the (real) state of affairs regarding his relationship with the community in Philippi.[267] At this point, it may also be remarked that viewing Phil. 4.10-20 as part of the *peroratio* of the entire letter becomes somewhat problematic against this background: the obvious correction of a misunderstanding (at the cost of the position of the Philippians) is hardly likely to evoke the (positive) *pathos* that needed to be evoked by a *peroratio*.[268]

---

267. As far as the relationship of this episode to life in Philippi is concerned, Pilhofer's considerations are of interest, as they relate the "do ut des" principle at work in Phil. 4.10-20 to the life of various associations in Philippi. See for a wealth of material, Pilhofer, *Philippi*, 147–152; through "do ut des," honor was sought through investments as well as rendered through investments; both could work both ways: i.e. by rendering someone honor one could present oneself as a benefactor, while the one receiving honor this way would be indeed honored. Specifically, Pilhofer argues that many of these associations had the task of rendering honor to their benefactors; given that the Philippians, probably organized in a way akin to these associations, were seeking the honors not of an earthly "commonwealth" anymore, but of one that is heavenly, their financial investments needed to be redirected: "Als Christ investiert man nicht in den Brunnen am Forum und nicht in den Tempel der Silvanusfreunde (*sc. um sich irdische Ehre zu erwerben oder jemandem solche zu erweisen*). Die dafür sonst verwendeten Mittel sind frei und können ἀξίως τοῦ εὐαγγελίου verwendet werden, so insbesondere zur Unterstützung des Paulus" (idem, *op. cit.*, 152). One may wonder, however, precisely also with respect to this claim of Pilhofer: did the Philippians really stop being a "typical" association, or did they view Paul as their new benefactor? It may well be that the Christian community in Philippi continued to function as an association, albeit with a focus not on civil honors, but on benefaction bestowed on them by Christ through Paul as his earthly agent and with honors (in terms of support) given to Paul (and hence added to the Philippians' heavenly account).

268. See, e.g., Witherington, *Friendship*, 110–111, and Brucker, *Christushymnen*, 299.

Chapter 3

MODELS OF IDENTITY IN PHILIPPIANS

3.1 The Christ-Paradigm (Phil. 1.27–2.18)

3.1.1 Introduction

Whereas the place of Phil. 1.27–2.18 within the whole of Philippians has already been discussed when considering the overall plan of Philippians,[1] here some attention should be given to the way in which this section itself may be structured,[2] especially rhetorically, as this decides much about the way it is to be interpreted.

To begin with, Phil. 1.27-30 may be seen as a first section of this pericope and can, with regard to its function, be described as the "thesis statement" of the letter,[3] in rhetorical terms the *propositio*,[4] indicating the core of what is to follow.[5] Phil. 1.27 itself also constitutes the beginning of a more exhortative section of Philippians,[6] belonging to the body of the letter, following on from the prescript, salutation, thanksgiving, and prayer, and the disclosure

---

1. See above, 2.2.2.
2. See, e.g., Müller, *Brief*, 73.
3. Concerning the relationship between rhetoric and epistolography, see above, 1.4.2.1.
4. See, e.g., Williams, *Enemies*, 114; see also Kellbe, *Paul*, 232, O'Brien, "Gospel," 277, Black, "Discourse," 33–35, 44. We must bear in mind the caution expressed by Reed, "Epistle," 181, who notes that letters often address more than one theme; indeed the subject of the gift that the Philippians gave to Paul (see prominently addressed in Phil. 4.10-20) has little to do with the subject of the internal unity of the Philippian community. Petrus J. Gräbe, "'... as citizens of heaven live in a manner worthy of the gospel of Christ'," in Jan G. van der Watt (ed.), *Identity, Ethics, and Ethos in the New Testament*, BZNW 141 (Berlin: De Gruyter, 2006), 289–302, esp. 289, also views Phil. 1.27 as the core statement of the letter, but without reference to rhetorical theory.
5. For the following, see, e.g., Williams, *Enemies*, 109; here, however, a more cautious stance is taken concerning the relationship between rhetoric and epistolography. See also Reed, "Epistle," 181, who notes that this section "serves to generate a positive relationship of trust and compliance between the speaker and the listener ..." Reed also sees an analogy in terms of their function between the opening section of many epistles and the *exordium* of speeches. For a critical review, see, e.g., Reumann, *Philippians*, 142–143, who rightly notes that not all topics addressed in Philippians are mentioned in its (supposed) *exordium*.
6. Therefore it should be taken with Phil. 2.1-18; see, e.g., Fowl, *Story*, 77; diff., e.g., Bittasi, *Esempi*, 53. On the transitory function of Phil. 1.27-30, see, e.g., Peterlin, *Letter*, 55–59.

(about Paul's condition) in Phil. 1.12-26.[7] In Phil. 1.27, Paul introduces a first exhortation, to live (πολιτεύομαι) in a manner worthy of the gospel of Christ, while he also links back to the preceding self-disclosure: the preceding issue of Paul's absence is explicitly addressed when Paul indicates that his exhortation is valid both in his absence and in his presence.[8] This agrees well with the placement of μόνον at the beginning of the verse, as it indicates a continuing line of thought and places emphasis on what will follow, i.e. the exhortation to live (πολιτεύομαι) in a manner worthy of the gospel of Christ.

If Phil. 1.27-30 can be described as fulfilling the function of the *propositio* (together with a very brief *narratio*)[9] of the rhetorical line of thought of Philippians, then much of what follows in Phil. 2 can be likened to a *probatio*, in which reasons, specifically examples, are adduced to convince the audience to accept what was set forth in the *propositio*.[10] When following this consideration, it may be observed that Phil. 2.1-4 restates many of the themes of Phil. 1.27-30 in a conditional sentence,[11] while also taking up notions addressed earlier in Phil. 1.[12]

3.1.2 Worthy of Christ's Gospel: Community and Unity (1.27–2.4)

Here, a few further observations should be made on the section of Philippians that leads into the *enkomion* in Phil. 2.5-11. The goal of these observations is to clarify what is at stake precisely.

Concerning Phil. 1.27, beginning with μόνον, which indicates both a continuing train of thought and that a matter of central concern, in this case living worthily as a citizen (πολιτεύομαι),[13] will be mentioned,[14] the following may be maintained. First, it may be noted that the verb πολιτεύομαι points to the realm of civic concerns, an impression that is strengthened by the fact

---

7. See, e.g., Fowl, *Story*, 78. It is striking that, in contrast to the preceding section, from now on nothing more is disclosed about Paul, but the Philippian community is called upon to conduct its life in a particular way (see verses 27–30).
8. See Müller, *Brief*, 72.
9. So, e.g., emphatically, Brucker, *Christushymnen*, 304–305.
10. See, e.g., Reumann, *Philippians*, 277–278.
11. See, e.g., Williams, *Enemies*, 120, and Duane F. Watson, "The Integration of Epistolary and Rhetorical Analysis of Philippians," in Stanley E. Porter and Thomas H. Olbricht (eds.), *Rhetorical Analysis of Scripture*, JSNTSup 146 (Sheffield: Sheffield Academic Press, 1997), 398–426, esp. 418.
12. See, e.g., Williams, *Enemies*, 123.
13. Otherwise only in Acts 23.1; see, e.g., Pilhofer, *Philippi*, 136, n. 6. For considerations regarding its meaning, see, e.g., Williams, *Enemies*, 115. Reumann, *Philippians*, 275, offers the appealing translation "exercise citizenship." The use of this verb is striking; in analogous cases Paul uses περιπατέω; see the discussion by Pilhofer, *Philippi*, 136, and see esp. Rom. 6.4, 8.4, 13.13, 14.15; 1 Cor. 3.13, 7.17; 2 Cor. 4.2, 5.7, 10.2-3, 12.18; Gal. 5.16; Phil. 3.17-18. This does not mean, as Dibelius, *Philipper*, 70, argued, that the meaning of the more common verb needs to be read into the less common one; rather, as Pilhofer does, one should ask what could have moved Paul to use an alternative expression here. Similarly also, Müller, *Brief*, 74–75.
14. See, e.g., Müller, *Brief*, 74, for analogous uses of μόνον: see, e.g., Gal. 1.23, 2.10, 3.2, 5.13.

that the turn of phrase ἀξίως τοῦ εὐαγγελίου τοῦ Χριστοῦ points in the same direction, given that one could also be "worthy of the city" and the like in Philippi.[15] Taking the gospel as the measure for worthy citizenship is striking,[16] given that it is an inner-Christian criterion that was otherwise acknowledged by no one,[17] and could be controversial politically.[18] In fact, by using the notion of "citizenship," which reappears in Phil. 3.20, Paul may have phrased things in a way that takes the Philippian context into account: the Philippians lived in a city in which many enjoyed Roman citizenship.[19] Hence, it is possible that Paul paints the obligations of heavenly citizenship on the canvas of the notion of Roman citizenship.[20] At the same time, the notions of worthiness and steadfastness may also have appealed to the Philippians, many of whom were veterans, because of their association with military ideals and virtues.[21]

Paul's appeal in Phil. 1.27-28a, or, rather, his summing up of what sort of news he would like to receive about the faithful "citizens" of Philippi,[22] mentions first standing together in one spirit and then, as a consequence of this, being of one mind and fighting together for the faith in the gospel, irrespective of Paul's absence or presence. This note on Paul's presence and absence also highlights the importance of the apostle's personal—and paradigmatic—embodiment of identity in Christ.[23] To this Paul adds, as the negative side of the same coin:

15. For supporting evidence, see Pilhofer, *Philippi*, 136–137. See also, e.g., Walter, "Brief," 45, following Pilhofer.
16. For this argument, see, e.g., Kellbe, *Paul*, 239–243; see along similar lines also the argument of Robin Scroggs, "Paul the Prisoner: Political Asceticism in the Letter to the Philippians," in Leif E. Vaage and Vincent L. Wimbush (eds.), *Asceticism and the New Testament* (London: Routledge, 1999), 187–208, esp. 193–201. See also Paul's notion of citizenship in Phil. 3.20.
17. Certainly not by the authorities in Philippi; see, e.g., Pilhofer, *Philippi*, 137.
18. For the relevance of this approach, see esp. Angela Standhartinger, "Die paulinische Theologie im Spannungsfeld römisch-imperialer Machtpolitik. Eine neue Perspektive auf Paulus, kritisch geprüft anhand des Philipperbriefs," in Friedrich Schweitzer (ed.), *Religion, Politik und Gewalt*, VWGT 29 (Gütersloh: Gütersloher Verlagshaus, 2006), 364–382.
19. An alternative option would be to view the references to citizenship here and in Phil. 3.20 as standing in contrast to *collegia* in Philippi; see, e.g., Wendy J. Cotter, "Our *Politeuma* is in Heaven: The Meaning of Philippians 3:17–21," in Bradley H. McLean (ed.), *Origins and Method: Towards a New Understanding of Judaism and Christianity*, JSNTSup 86 (Sheffield: JSOT Press, 1993), 92–104, esp. 103–104.
20. See, e.g., Williams, *Enemies*, 115–117. See similarly, Dirk Schinkel, "'Unsere Bürgerschaft befindet sich im Himmel' (Phil 3,20): ein biblisches Motiv und seine Entwicklung im frühen Christentum," *BN* 133 (2007), 79–97, esp. 81–83. These observations speak against the otherwise cogently argued case of Ernest C. Miller, Jr., "Πολιτεύεσθε in Philippians 1.27: Some Philological and Thematic Observations," *JSNT* 15 (1982), 86–96, who contends that the verb in question has principally a background in the LXX. This may well be as far as Paul is concerned, but assuming that Paul considers his audience, in Philippi the local political context will have determined the verb's meaning and connotations for the readers of Philippians to a large extent.
21. See Reumann, *Philippians*, 280–281. See also De Vos, *Church*, 277–279.
22. For this and the following, see, e.g., Müller, *Brief*, 75.
23. This emphasis has analogies in philosophical texts and is related both to the *mimesis* of the teacher by the pupil and to the importance of the personal embodiment of a particular teaching by the teacher. See, e.g., Ware, *Paul*, 242; cf. Seneca, *Ep.* 11:8–10, 25:5–6; Lucian, *Nig.* 6–7; as well as 1 Thess. 3.6-8.

not allowing oneself to be distracted or to be intimidated into backing away by any adversaries—here presumably Philippian authorities are in view.[24] While Paul's reference to standing strong or even "in phalanx" for their struggle for the gospel may echo military ideals,[25] the imagery also evokes the idea of an outside enemy or of the experience of pressure from the outside,[26] even if it is not stated explicitly here.[27]

All of this is substantiated by the statements made in Phil. 1.28b-30. In verse 28b,[28] Paul notes that all that happens is a sign of the (upcoming divine and eschatological) destruction of the adversaries and of the (equally divine and eschatological) deliverance of the Philippians.[29] The latter is explicated in verses 29-30 (ὅτι continues the line of thought). In these verses, Paul argues that it has been granted to the Philippians not only to believe in Christ, but also to suffer for him, which reinterprets the suffering that the Philippians have to endure (verse 29). In this way, Paul also gives a reason for showing the conduct he calls for in verses 27-28: he describes suffering for Christ as a gift beyond the gift of faith (verse 29) and presents it as an expression of remaining faithful to Christ. This argument (verse 29) is further substantiated by a very brief *exemplum*. Using formulations that literally place his own example before the eyes of the Philippians,[30] Paul states in Phil. 1.29-30 that the Philippians have to deal with the same struggle (or battle)[31] as he had and still has, thus suggesting an analogy between their situations.[32] In as far as the Philippians recognized Paul as being both close to them and as a figure of some authority, this *exemplum* indeed substantiates and makes attractive what Paul had just argued in verses 27-29.[33] Paul seems to assume a position of some authority *vis-à-vis* the Philippian community on the basis of the long-standing relationship

---

24. On the various opponents in Philippians, see above, 2.3.2; see also Müller, *Brief*, 75–76, who rightly notes that the Jewish community in Philippi was probably much too small to be a force of political importance. Similarly, Walter, "Brief," 46, as well as, e.g., Reumann, *Philippians*, 278–279, who provides a helpful overview of interpretative options. For a different view, see Gnilka, *Philipperbrief*, 99–100.
25. See, e.g., Krentz, "Language," 120–124; De Vos, *Church*, 277–279.
26. See, e.g., Fowl, *Story*, 78–79.
27. See, e.g., Fowl, *Story*, 85–86, and see above, 2.3.1.4.
28. Barth, *Brief*, 36–37, notes rightly that, like in Gal. 5.25, here imperative and indicative stand in such a relationship to one another that the indicative substantiates the imperative. See also Schenk, *Philipperbriefe*, 169–171.
29. See, e.g., Müller, *Brief*, 76–77.
30. On *exempla* in the first person, see below, 3.4.2. Here specifically Phil. 1.30b gives the impression that Paul wishes to illustrate something: οἷον εἴδετε ἐν ἐμοὶ καὶ νῦν ἀκούετε ἐν ἐμοί. For this and the following, see also Ramsaran, "Living," and Black, "Discourse."
31. Edgar M. Krentz, "Military Language and Metaphors in Philippians," in McLean (ed.), *Origins*, 105–127, esp. 112, makes the plausible suggestion that Paul's terminology of struggling in Philippians should be seen in the context of Philippi as a military (i.e. veterans') colony.
32. See, e.g., Barth, *Brief*, 37.
33. See, e.g., Engberg-Pedersen, *Paul*, 83, 106.

between the Philippian community and himself, in which he functions as one of the *maiores* of the community.

While Paul's apparent defense of suffering might seem to run counter to much Hellenistic religious and philosophical sentiment,[34] it is of importance to note that Paul presents his view from the perspective of the common concept of the ἀγών that he and the Philippians share (verse 30; see also 27). The true ἀγών consists of remaining faithful to Christ, which may involve considerable suffering. As was already noted, in this context, Paul presents himself as a brief *exemplum* by stating that the Philippians undergo the same ἀγών (discussed in Phil. 1.27-29) as they have witnessed in him and about which they now hear (Phil. 1.30; Paul presents his own struggle in 1.12-26).[35] Whereas the theme of the ἀγών is done with for this section in verse 30,[36] the topic of unity is taken up and elaborated upon subsequently: Paul paraenetically returns to this subject in Phil. 2.1-4.[37]

Phil. 2.1-4 constitutes a new section of Phil. 1.27–2.4. It begins with a fourfold invocation in Phil. 2.1,[38] where the repetitive εἴ τι(ς) in Phil. 2.1 sets the verses apart from Phil. 1.30, from which it nevertheless follows (note: εἴ τις οὖν).[39] The focus of Phil. 2.1-4 is the internal unity of the community—in Phil. 1.27-30 the focus was more on standing together against an outside threat.[40] The four items mentioned in Phil. 2.1 (the last one through a *hendiadys*) are all phenomena that contribute to a life in community, specifically to communal life "in Christ."[41] Of course, internal unity is also of importance for being able to stand firm against outside aggressors.[42] Verse 1 prepares for the wish that Paul utters in verses 2-4, in a long ἵνα-clause that is initiated by and concretized in the imperative πληρώσατε in Phil. 2.2a. Paul's wish consists of a call for unity that is all the more urgent because of its repetitive character.[43] At the same time, Paul identifies the Philippians as a source of joy for himself. In doing so, he positions himself as a close relation of the Philippians (i.e. as a friend).[44] This

---

34. See, e.g., Müller, *Brief*, 77–78.
35. See, e.g., Reumann, *Philippians*, 295, and, rightly noting that an analogous interpretation of suffering can also be found in 2 Macc. 13.14, and 4 Macc. 11.20, 15.29, 16.16, 19, 25, and 17.11-16, Müller, *Brief*, 78–80.
36. It recurs in 2.16 and especially in Phil. 3.12-16.
37. Especially through the use of the imperative πληρώσατε in Phil. 2.2. See, e.g., Bittasi, *Esempi*, 54.
38. On the style, see, e.g., Brucker, *Christushymnen*, 305–307, as well as Barth, *Brief*, 39, largely following Dibelius, *Philipper*, 71. Similarly, Müller, *Brief*, 81.
39. See, e.g., the detailed observations of Schenk, *Philipperbriefe*, 173–178, as well as the discussion by Witherington, *Friendship*, 60–61, drawing the attention to the connecting function of οὖν in Phil. 2.1.
40. See, e.g., Walter, "Brief," 51. See in general also the argument of Oakes, *Philippians*, 84–102.
41. See, e.g., Müller, *Brief*, 81–83.
42. For alternative considerations, see, e.g., Müller, *Brief*, 87–88.
43. See, e.g., Müller, *Brief*, 84.
44. See, e.g., Reumann, *Philippians*, 323.

emphasis on the friendly relationship between Paul and the Philippians may also add to the effect of Paul's appeal.[45]

While Paul covers the positive side of his appeal in verse 2 (τὸ αὐτὸ φρονῆτε, τὴν αὐτὴν ἀγάπην ἔχοντες, σύμψυχοι, τὸ ἕν φρονοῦντες), in Phil. 2.3-4 he unfolds his exhortation further by outlining the attitudes that the Philippians are to avoid: ἐριθεία and κενοδοξία. The latter is a term commonly used to (negatively) describe someone with too high an opinion of themselves;[46] the former expression means something like "selfishness."[47] The negative presentation of these two concepts is unsurprising, which is not, however, the case for the subsequent recommendation of ταπεινοφροσύνη, which describes a lowly attitude that was not held in high regard in Hellenistic society in general.[48] In the final part of the exhortation, Paul calls upon the Philippians to behave as follows: μὴ τὰ ἑαυτῶν ἕκαστος σκοποῦντες ἀλλὰ [καὶ] τὰ ἑτέρων ἕκαστοι. All of this is summarized well by Dahl:

> Having admonished the addressees to be of one mind, Paul spells out what this implies: to share the same love and, being inwardly united (σύμψυχοι), to have one concern and goal in mind (τὸ ἕν φρονοῦντες, 2:2). He further proceeds to adduce attitudes that will either hinder or promote unity among Christians: selfishness (ἐριθεία) and empty conceit (κενοδοξία) in contrast to the humble attitude (ταπεινοφροσύνη), in which one regards others higher than oneself.[49]

As will become clear from its subsequent discussion, Phil. 2.1-4 leads neatly into the *exemplum* that follows. Both Phil. 2.1-4 and the *enkomion* in 2.5-11 address and promote an alternative way of life (i.e. life in Christ) and they agree in this respect in terms of a general questioning of contemporary social values along the same lines in Philippians.[50] For example, if both parts of the composite ταπεινοφροσύνη are considered, it echoes both what the Philippians are called to do—that is, to think the same (Phil. 2.2) and specifically to think "that in Christ" (Phil. 2.5)—and what Christ does in the *enkomion*—that is, to humble himself (Phil. 2.8).[51] Humility appears as a precondition for mutuality and thus community, one of Paul's main concerns in Philippians. Furthermore,

---

45. See, e.g., Reumann, *Philippians*, 323; Heil, *Philippians*, 82–83.
46. For its Pauline usage, see, e.g., Gal. 5.15.
47. On this and some of the linguistic background, see, e.g., Müller, *Brief*, 84.
48. See, e.g., Witherington, *Friendship*, 63; Williams, *Enemies*, 125; Müller, *Brief*, 85–86, Reumann, *Philippians*, 327–328. In the Old Testament/Hebrew Bible this notion was held in honor; see, e.g., Pss. 10.17-18, 25.18, 31.7; Prov. 3.34, 11.2, 15.33; Job 5.11-19, which also applied to the community of Qumran; see, e.g., 1 QS 2.24, 4.3, 5.24-25. See also, however, the positive connotation of ταπεινός in Socratic and cynic philosophy, as discussed by Hans Dieter Betz, *Der Apostel Paulus und die sokratische Tradition: Eine exegetische Untersuchung zu seiner "Apologie" 2 Korinther 10–13*, BHT 45 (Tübingen: Mohr Siebeck, 1972), 45–57.
49. Dahl, "Euodia," 10.
50. See, e.g., Byron, *Metaphors*, 172–173; Williams, *Enemies*, 124; Fee, *Philippians*, 186–187.
51. See similarly, e.g., Müller, *Brief*, 113; Brucker, *Christushymnen*, 207.

the call to disregard one's own interests, mentioned in Phil. 2.4, also agrees with the attitude represented by Christ in Phil. 2.6.[52]

Thus, by the end of Phil. 2.1-4 Paul has not only restated the most important themes that were introduced explicitly in Phil. 1.27-30 (suffering belongs to Christian existence; the appropriate response is to stand together in mutual support with a humble attitude towards one another),[53] but he has also prepared for their further substantiation in the following *enkomion*.[54]

3.1.3 The Christ Enkomion (2.5-11)

3.1.3.1 The Social Location and the Origin of Phil. 2.5-11

In spite of the fact that this study does not touch on the original meaning of Phil. 2.5-11 (*Eigenbedeutung*) primarily, but concentrates on the significance of the *enkomion* in its present context (*Ernstbedeutung*), it is nevertheless the case that the use of the *enkomion* as an *exemplum* may also shed some light on the *enkomion*'s social location and on its origins.

First, Paul's use of the *enkomion* as an *exemplum* increases the probability of it being known to him as well as to the Philippians. This is suggested by the way *exempla* function: those employing them give directions for the present situation or present an argument with regard to a future situation by drawing on a shared past/tradition that is recognized by both the author and his/her audience. Showing the present in the light of a shared tradition is the heart of an *exemplum*. This strongly suggests that both Paul and the Philippians were familiar with Phil 2.5-11.[55] This might also point to a place different than Philippi or Ephesus for the composition of Phil. 2.5-11; where exactly, then, must remain open, but Antioch, as the place of Paul's catechesis, might be an option.[56]

Second, Pauline authorship of the *enkomion* is also rendered unlikely by its use as an example, if "authorship" means that he has composed it for this specific situation, as it would not allow Paul to use the text as a tradition known to both the Philippians and himself anymore. More importantly, the (merely) partial fit between the παράδειγμα and the situation in which it is used also strongly suggests that this is an appeal to shared but not entirely fitting tradition. This is in the best tradition of the use of *exempla* as cultural symbols. Furthermore, some of the *enkomion*'s theological aspects (e.g. the absence of Jesus' death "pro nobis" and its emphasis on his obedient death

---

52. See, e.g., Reumann, *Philippians*, 317.
53. See, e.g., Müller, *Brief*, 27.
54. As will be clear from the above; see however also, Briggs Kittredge, *Community*, 73–74, as well as Hooker, "Philippians," 153.
55. For the traditional character of Phil. 2.5-11 from the perspective of its use, see also, e.g., Best, *Paul*, 80. See also the general considerations of Lieu, *Identity*, 27–61.
56. For similar considerations, see, e.g., Walter, "Brief," 57–59.

and his exaltation) and linguistic characteristics[57] also suggest non-Pauline authorship.[58] While pre-Pauline authorship becomes a distinct possibility for that reason, para-Pauline authorship may be considered an attractive option as well,[59] even if Pauline authorship continues to be proposed.[60]

In general, therefore, the use of the *enkomion* as an *exemplum* suggests not only that it was more widely known (at least to Paul and the Philippians), but also that it is of pre- or at least para-Pauline origin. This view is supported by further linguistic observations and striking aspects of the text's content.

In order to position this study within the field of research of Phil. 2.5-11, some further aspects of the provenance and character of Phil. 2.5-11 also need to be considered. In view of the amount of scholarly effort put into the interpretation of Phil. 2.5-11, with regard to both its provenance and its literary character, any discussion of these aspects which is less than a monograph runs the danger of remaining superficial. Given the limited importance of both issues for this study, however, the limited character of the discussion presented here is justified.

As far as the form-critical classification is concerned, here a relatively general classification, taken from Hellenistic rhetoric, is used—in other words, *enkomion*—which avoids, in particular, speculation about a liturgical setting.[61]

---

57.   On its "non-Pauline character" see, e.g., Schenk, *Philipperbriefe*, 185–186. For a different view, see Bockmuehl, *Philippians*, 118.

58.   See, e.g., Barth, *Brief*, 41; this quite in spite of the list of arguments to the contrary listed by, e.g., Park, *Submission*, 15–16.

59.   See, e.g., Walter, "Brief," 57, as well as O'Brien, *Epistle*, 198–202. The possibility offered by Schenk, *Philipperbriefe*, 173–175, that the text was composed by Philippian Christians, sent to Paul in the hope of his approval and then returned to them by Paul in an edited and reinterpreted form, is an interesting speculation, but beyond verification otherwise.

60.   For this option, see, e.g., Reumann, *Philippians*, 362–363; Brucker, *Christushymnen*, 312–314.

61.   As Vollenweider notes rightly, the decisive question behind all form-critical classifications is the question of the "Sitz-im-Leben" of the text: was it used in worship and chanted? It is possible, but not necessary. Vollenweider himself prefers the rather neutral term "Christuslob." See Samuel Vollenweider, "Der 'Raub' der Gottgleichheit: Ein religionsgeschichtlicher Vorschlag zu Phil 2.6(–11)," *NTS* 45 (1999), 413–433, esp. 413–415. Vollenweider has repeated this argument at greater length in idem, "Hymnus," noting especially that both *enkomion* and *hymnos* as classifications taken from their first-century usage do not fit fully; the lesser evil seems to be to stick to *enkomion*, rather than to introduce a non-contemporary term. For a more extensive terminological discussion, see, e.g., Brucker, *Christushymnen*. Decisive input for this discussion came from H. Riesenfeld, "Unpoetische Hymnen im Neuen Testament," in Jarmo Kiilunen (ed.), *Glaube und Gerechtigkeit. In Memoriam R. Gyllenberg*, SESJ 38 (Helsinki: Finnische exegetische Gesellschaft, 1983), 155–168. See further, Adele Yarbro Collins, "The Worship of Jesus and the Imperial Cult," in Carey C. Newman (ed.), *The Jewish Roots of Christological Monotheism: Papers from the St. Andrews Conference on the Historical Origins of the Worship of Jesus*, SJSJ 63 (Leiden: Brill, 1999), 234–257, esp. 240–251; idem, "Psalms, Phil 2.6–11, and the Origins of Christology," *BibInt* 11 (2003), 361–372; Alex Hardie, *Statius and the Silvae: Poets, Patrons, and Epideixis in the Graeco-Roman World* (Liverpool: Francis Cairns, 1983), esp. 97–99; similarly also, e.g., Reumann, *Philippians*, 361–362. See also, Michael Lattke, *Hymnus. Materialien zu einer Geschichte der antiken Hymnologie*, NTOA 19 (Fribourg i.Ue.: Universitätsverlag, 1991),

Furthermore, given that the term *hymnos* was, at least in the classical period, typically used in texts addressed to gods that included prayer,[62] *enkomion* seems to be the preferable form-critical classification, especially as the text does precisely what *enkomia* usually did: describing (and lauding) someone by recounting one's origins, deeds (*res gestae*) and end.[63] Also, further aspects of the text, especially its apparent use of rhythm and parallelism as well as its beginning with a relative clause in Phil. 2.5-11, agree well with those typical of *enkomia*.[64]

The question of the history of religions background cannot remain entirely untouched upon either, as it concerns the way in which the *enkomion* is read in its context in Philippians as well. The primary point of reference

---

and Gunter Kennel, *Frühchristliche Hymnen? Gattungskritische Studien zur Frage nach den Liedern der frühen Christenheit*, WMANT 71 (Neukirchen-Vluyn: Neukirchener Verlag, 1995). For an example of an interpretation in the setting of early Christian worship, see, e.g., Ralph P. Martin, "Some Reflections on New Testament Hymns," in Harold H. Rowdon (ed.), *Christ the Lord: Studies in Christology Presented to Donald Guthrie* (Leicester: InterVarsity, 1982), 37–49, and also Martin Hengel, "Hymn and Christology," in E. A. Livingstone (ed.), *Studia Biblica 1978 III: Papers on Paul and Other New Testament Authors*, JSNTSup 3 (Sheffield: JSOT Press, 1980), 173–197. Walter, "Brief," 50, 56–57, calls theses verses a "Lehrgedicht" ("catechetical poem"). This avoids question of genre as well and focuses on the function that Phil. 2.5-11 has in its present context. For the discussion in the older form-critical literature, see, e.g., Eduard Norden, *Agnostos Theos. Untersuchungen zur Formengeschichte religiöser Rede* (Leipzig: Teubner, 1913); Lohmeyer, *Kyrios*; Martin Dibelius, "Zur Formgeschichte des Neuen Testaments (außerhalb der Evangelien)," *ThR.NF* 3 (1931), 207–242; Günther Bornkamm, "Zum Verständnis des Christushymnus Phil 2,6–11," in idem, *Studien zu Antike und Urchristentum*, BEvTh 28 (München: Kaiser, 1959), 177–187; Käsemann, "Analyse"; Gottfried Schille, *Frühchristliche Hymnen* (Berlin: Evangelische Verlagsanstalt, 1965); Reinhard Deichgräber, *Gotteshymnus und Christushymnus in der frühen Christenheit: Untersuchungen zu Form, Sprache und Stil der frühchristlichen Hymnen*, StUNT 5 (Göttingen: Vandenhoeck & Ruprecht, 1967); Klaus Wengst, *Christologische Formeln und Lieder des Urchristentums*, StNT 7 (Gütersloh: Mohn, 1972). Questions about whether it is "poetic" or "rhetoric" may depend on more than just the presence or absence of a clearly discernible meter, given the mixing of genres in the Hellenistic period; see, e.g., Kennel, *Frühchristliche Hymnen?*, 359–361. It is very possible to arrive at such conclusions without launching into such a ridiculization of other scholars as presented by Michael Peppard, "'Poetry', 'Hymns' and 'Traditional Material' in New Testament Epistles or How to Do Things with Indentations," *JSNT* 30 (2008), 319–342 (especially as he misses out on important aspects of the history of research that he attacks; Berger, for example, had already used the category of *enkomion* instead of "hymn" to describe texts like Phil. 2.5-11, no less than 24 years before Peppard published his paper).

62. The absence of petitionary prayer in Phil. 2.5-11 is probably more important than the question of the divine or human status of the addressee; boundaries between human and divine persons could be fluid in the Hellenistic world, and specifically Heracles (associated with the Macedonian royal family after which Philippi was named) as well as emperors such as Caligula and Nero, as well as other, less notorious ones, not least Augustus, who crossed such boundaries, were associated with Philippi. For a brief overview, see, e.g., Reumann, *Philippians*, 337, 363–364.

63. See, e.g., Berger, *Formgeschichte*, 345, and further also, e.g., Reumann, *Philippians*, 369–370.

64. See, e.g., Berger, *Formgeschichte*, 344–346, as well as idem, *Formen*, 297–305, 401–403.

remains the last edition of Martin's monograph on the (more recent) history of interpretation of the *enkomion*, which discusses at considerable length the most significant interpretative proposals of the *enkomion* put forward in recent research. These are the following: servant of the Lord (see Isa. 52–53), the Righteous One, the Gnostic Redeemer, the Servant and Wisdom, and the First and Last Adam.[65] Here, it will be preferred to return to the earlier proposal of Eduard Schweizer, who suggested a more general background in a common early Jewish pattern of the obedient humiliation and subsequent exaltation of (God's) righteous ones.[66] As Schweizer does not illustrate this all that thoroughly, Byron has offered an elaborate comparison with the Testament of Joseph, but other examples may be given as well.[67] The advantage of

---

65. See Martin, *Hymn*, discerning a "dogmatic view" (63–66), a "kenotic theory" (66–68), an "ethical example interpretation" (68–74, 84–93), a "background in heterodox Judaism" (74–75), a Hellenistic background (76–78), a specific Old Testament background (78)—for a concise critique of two different brands of the "Adam-Christology" of J. D. G. Dunn and N. T. Wright, see Park, *Submission*, 17–23—specific Hellenistic examples (78–80), "historical allusions" (80–81), "a baptismal setting" (81–82), and a "eucharistic setting" (94–95); see also the concise overview offered by Byron, *Metaphors*, 150–155, whose terminology is followed here. See further, Fowl, *Story*, esp. 64–75; Williams, *Enemies*, 64–68; Barth, *Brief*, 45–48; and O'Brien, *Epistle*, 193–198. James D. G. Dunn, *The Theology of Paul the Apostle* (Edinburgh: T&T Clark, 1998), 286, argues that Phil. 2.5-11 is, after Heb. 2.5-9, the fullest expression of Adam-Christology in the New Testament; still, such an interpretation is not necessary and the differences in "fullness" between Heb. 2.5-9 and Phil. 2.5-11 in this respect are sizeable.

66. Schweizer has put forward his proposal in three stages: the first is the first edition of *Erniedrigung und Erhöhung bei Jesus und seinen Nachfolgern* of 1955, followed by a revised English edition in 1960, which was in turn followed by a revised second edition in German: *Erniedrigung und Erhöhung bei Jesus und seinen Nachfolgern*, AThANT 28 (Zürich: Zwingli, 1962); see here 71–76, 93–102, esp. 97. See also the proposal of Dieter Georgi, "Der vorpaulinische Hymnus Phil 2,6–11," in Erich Dinkler (ed.), *Zeit und Geschichte. Dankesgabe an Rudolf Bultmann zum 80. Geburtstag* (Tübingen: Mohr Siebeck, 1964), 264–293, who firmly argues (against Käsemann's proposal that the hymn originated in early Gnosticism) that the origins of the hymn should be seen in early Judaism. An interpretation such as that of Thomas H. Tobin, "The World of Thought in the Philippian Hymn (Philippians 2:6–11)," in John Fotopoulos (ed.), *The New Testament and Early Christian Literature in Greco-Roman Context*, NTSup 122 (FS David E. Aune; Leiden: Brill, 2006), 91–104, which focuses virtually exclusively on the question of pre-existence and leaves the descent and exaltation largely out of consideration, is for the reason just stated not convincing. Schweizer's proposal does not exclude the possibility noted by Vollenweider that the religious historical background of Phil. 2.6-8 is to be found in angelophanies. See Samuel Vollenweider, "Die Metamorphose des Gottessohnes. Zum epiphanialen Motivfeld in Phil 2,6–8," in Mell and Müller (eds.), *Urchristentum*, 107–131.

67. See for this, esp., Joost Holleman, *Resurrection and Parousia*, NTSup 84 (Leiden: Brill, 1996), 144–157, who follows the same line of thought as has been taken here. Most relevant texts from Hellenistic, early Jewish, early Christian, and rabbinic traditions have been collected and edited by Jan Willem van Henten and Friedrich Avemarie (eds.), *Martyrdom and Noble Death: Selected Texts from Graeco-Roman, Jewish and Christian Antiquity* (London: Routledge, 2002). In this volume both authors give a concise overview of the importance of the concepts of martyrdom in antiquity in the introduction (1–8). See also Bert-Jan Lietaert Peerbolte, "The Name Above All Names (Philippians 2:9)," in George H. van Kooten (ed.), *The Revelation of the Name YHWH to Moses: Perspectives from Judaism, the Pagan Graeco-Roman World, and Early Christianity*, TBN 9 (Leiden: Brill, 2006), 187–206, esp. 205.

this broader approach is that one is not limited to the grid of one particular reference text as would be the case of an interpretation in terms of Isa. 52–53 or wisdom texts, while elements of both can still be drawn upon, and that the problems of the use of an "Adam-Christ" Christology as a projection screen are also avoided.

3.1.3.2 Christ in the Enkomion

When considering the presentation of Christ in the *enkomion*, its introduction in Phil. 2.5 deserves attention first, given that the interpretation of this verse determines to some extent one's interpretation of Paul's use of the *enkomion*. Here, the problem of the so-called "ethical" interpretation of the *enkomion* immediately arises as well. This problem often takes the form of the question of what should be added as a verb in the elliptic Phil. 2.5b: a form of φρονέω or a form of εἶναι? In the first case, the result would be an interpretation that proceeds from Christ's lordship that determines how one has to think "in Christ," and in the second case it would lead to a "bloß paradigmatische [merely paradigmatic] Interpretation,"[68] in which only Christ and his "Gesinnung" [attitude] would be in view.[69] Given that in the first case the form of being in Christ still depends on the shape of Christ's "career" as depicted in the *enkomion*,[70] and that in the second case the *exemplum* can only be effective if Christ has been accorded a substantial degree of lordship over the Philippian community, one may well have to do with an overstated issue here. In fact, both exegetical strategies largely amount to the same thing: both imply Christ's lordship over the Philippians, either as a point of departure or as a precondition, and both assume the exemplary function of Christ (as presented by the *enkomion*), either as a starting point or as a consequence.[71]

---

68. Müller, *Brief*, 80. As Hurtado, "Jesus," 124–125, rightly points out, one can hardly deny the exemplary character of Jesus in the *enkomion* if one moves beyond a view of *exempla* that is broader than the view related to a "naïve ethical idealism." Different, e.g., is Larsson, *Christus*, 233, and Deichgräber, *Gotteshymnus*, 192.

69. Müller, *Brief*, 90, following the lead of Dibelius, *Philipper*, 72, Barth, *Erklärung*, 57, and Käsemann, "Analyse," 91.

70. For this emphasis, see, e.g., Bruce N. Fisk, "The Odyssey of Christ: A Novel Context for Philippians 2:6–11," in C. Stephen Evans (ed.), *Exploring Kenotic Christology: The Self-Emptying of God* (Oxford: Oxford University Press, 2006), 45–73, esp. 72–73, noting the surprising character for Greco-Roman ears of Christ's *self*-humiliation in Phil. 2.6-8. See further, e.g., Walter, "Brief," 59, and Reumann, *Philippians*, 376.

71. This largely agrees with the view taken by Barth, *Brief*, 40–41: "Was Jesus getan hat, hat uns die Möglichkeit eröffnet, uns selbst loszulassen und für andere da zu sein. Sein Verhalten ist damit zunächst einmal der Grund, aber dann auch Norm und Maßstab christlichen Seins. Insofern ist also der Vorbildgedanke durchaus eingeschlossen—wie sich der Vorbildgedanke ja auch sonst bei Paulus findet (vgl. Röm. 15,7; 1 Kor. 11,1)—aber Jesus ist dabei nicht einfach das Ideal, dem die Christen nachstreben sollen, sondern zugleich der, der das neue Denken und Handeln der Glaubenden begründet und ermöglicht hat." It may be added that "was Jesus getan hat" must be presupposed by Barth and other readers of the hymn, given that it famously lacks *any* notion of something done or achieved by Jesus "pro nobis." This is probably the strongest argument against taking one's point of departure for the interpretation of Phil. 2.5-11 in the topic of Christ's redeeming work. For an interpretation similar to that of Barth, see, e.g., Park, *Submission*, 33–34.

Therefore, the alternative as it is sometimes presented seems to be a false one, as the following example will show:

> "In Christus Jesus" [ist] bei Paulus eine feste formelhafte Wendung zur Bezeichnung des mit Christus gegebenen Heilsbereiches ... es also nicht um die Gesinnung geht, die Jesus auch hatte, sondern um die Gesinnung, die "in Christus Jesus" gilt, die durch das Heilsgeschehen begründet ist, die im Bereich des Christus angemessen ist. Was Jesus getan hat, hat uns die Möglichkeit eröffnet, uns selbst loszulassen und für andere da zu sein. Sein Verhalten ist damit zunächst mal der Grund, aber dann auch Norm und Maßstab christlichen Seins. Insofern ist also der Vorbildgedanke durchaus eingeschlossen ... aber Jesus ist dabei nicht einfach das Ideal, dem die Christen nachstreben sollen, sondern zugleich der, der das neue Denken und Handeln der Glaubenden begründet und ermöglicht hat.[72]

To this should be added that arguments against reading the *enkomion* in terms of an *exemplum* often use expressions such as "a mere example,"[73] which does not give the impression that the first-century use of *exempla* (implying authority and some sort of relationship to the *maiores* of a community) has been sufficiently taken into account. Therefore, the position taken here is that it is not so much backing away from reading the *enkomion* in terms of an *exemplum* that solves problems here, but much rather reading it in terms of an *exemplum* properly. In fact, as the example of Spartan national identity given above (1.3) or the examples of the use of the Roman *mos maiorum* show,[74] having a particular identity included behaving according to the patterns determined by those having lived or who are living this identity in an exemplary way.[75] On the basis of these considerations, it may be argued that Christ is to be imitated *because*

---

72. Barth, *Brief*, 40–41: "'In Christus Jesus' is in Paul's letters a fixed formula to indicate the realm of salvation established through Christ ... the focus is therefore not on the attitude that Jesus had, but on the attitude that applies 'in Christus Jesus,' which is grounded in salvation and which is appropriate in the realm of Christ. That is what Jesus has done, he has given us the opportunity to let go of ourselves and to be there for others. His behavior is therefore, first of all, the foundation, but subsequently also the norm and measuring rod for Christian existence. To this extent, the notion of an example is certainly there ... but in this context, Jesus is not just the ideal that needs to emulated by Christians, but he is at the same time the one who has laid the foundation for this new thinking and acting, and who has made it possible" (author's translation). See along similar lines also Park's critique of Martin (*Submission*, 23–26). Hooker, "Philippians," 389, rightly emphasizes that "the function of the so-called 'hymn' is both kerygmatic *and* ethical" (emphasis in original). See also the earlier view of Gnilka, *Philipperbrief*, 109, who does not accept Phil. 2.5-11 as a reference to the earthly "Gesinnung" ("disposition") of Jesus, but views it as a description of the Christ-event according to which the Philippians now have to behave.

73. See, e.g., Müller, *Brief*, 90 (who on 113 proceeds to interpret the *enkomion* as an *exemplum* nevertheless), and Barth, *Brief* 41. See for critical remarks also Gräbe, "Citizens," 290–292.

74. See above, 1.3.

75. For an emphasis on identity, also, see, e.g., Park, *Submission*, 35–36.

he is the Lord (Phil. 2.9-11).[76] At the same time, it seems to be questionable, however, to argue that Christ has to be imitated because he is the redeemer, since the *enkomion* lacks any explicit soteriology.[77]

When turning to the remainder of Phil. 2.5-11,[78] that is, verses 6-11, it may be assumed that the quotation of the *enkomion* proper begins in Phil. 2.6. At its beginning, the *enkomion* states very briefly Christ's (divine) status before his "incarnation."[79] This description of Christ's status at the outset of the enfolding drama is a necessary preparation for the *enkomion*'s descent-ascent movement. This pattern continues by stating the option Christ did not choose—in other words, greedily remaining where he was (as would be "common sense" for someone with his status)[80]—and then, in explicit opposition to this (see verse 7: ἀλλά), the option he did choose: to empty himself (2.7), which is explicated in terms of his becoming human, i.e. his taking the "form" of a human being. This is all expressed by means of three coordinated participles: μορφὴν δούλου λαβών, ἐν ὁμοιώματι ἀνθρώπων γενόμενος· καὶ σχήματι εὑρεθεὶς ὡς ἄνθρωπος. As the three participles expressing this are coordinated, the three statements they make must be taken together: somehow becoming a slave amounts to becoming human. The most straightforward interpretation of this is to view it in terms of a not-uncommon description of the *condition humaine* as being not much better than that of a slave. Whose slave a human being is, is, in this case,

---

76. See, e.g., Dahl, "Euodia," 11; see also Scroggs, "Paul," 198–199 ("The Difference a Lord Makes").

77. So, however, Dahl, "Euodia," 11. E.g. Ware, *Mission*, 233, sees Christ's universal rule as the soteriological content of the *enkomion*, but even that does not seem to be necessary. From the point of view of intertextuality, the notions used in the *enkomion*, such as the cross, may within a Pauline context well echo other texts where they are filled with soteriological content. See also, e.g., Dahl, "Euodia," 12. A more promising, but yet to be tested, proposal is put forward by Susan Grove Eastman, "Philippians 2:6–11: Incarnation as Mimetic Participation," *Journal for the Study of Paul and His Letters* 1 (2010), 1–22, who suggests against the background of (Greco-)Roman theatrical conventions that because Christ has mimicked humans by assuming human "form," humans are drawn to mimicking him, thus eventually assuming his "form" and being saved.

78. The following is largely in agreement with Reumann, *Philippians*, 366–374.

79. See, e.g., Fowl, *Story*, 49–54, for a brief and well-informed discussion of the linguistic aspects of the description of Christ's exalted status in Phil. 2.6 prior to his self-emptying; the fact that Christ has such an exalted position is probably more important than the question of its precise character. See along similar lines, George H. van Kooten, "Image, Form and Transformation: A Semantic Taxonomy of Paul's 'Morphic' Language," in Buitenwerf, Hollander, and Tromp (eds.), *Jesus*, 213–242, esp. 222–224. As Barth, *Brief*, 42, rightly notes, Phil. 2.6b points to the significance of Phil. 2.6a: Christ was equal to God; similarly, Müller, *Brief*, 93–96, Walter, "Brief," 59, and Reumann, *Philippians*, 367.

80. The discussion about the precise meaning and accurate translation of οὐχ ἁρπαγμὸν ἡγήσατο τὸ εἶναι ἴσα θεῷ cannot be taken up here. It can be assumed, however, that it is opposed to what Christ *has* done, and that is to give up his being ἐν μορφῇ θεοῦ and taking up the μορφὴ δούλου. The classical meaning of the expression just mentioned is, however, "to grasp as spoil," "to take advantage"; see, e.g., Dibelius, *Philipper*, 75–76; see also, e.g., Müller, *Brief*, 95–96, Walter, "Brief," 59–60, O'Brien, *Epistle*, 211–216, as well as Samuel Vollenweider, "'Raub'."

probably of lesser importance.[81] Subsequently, the active[82] self-emptying and "incarnation" of Christ are further interpreted in terms of his self-humiliation, a process that begins in verses 6-7 and reaches its climax in Christ's obedience until the point of death,[83] specifically, death on a cross (verse 8).[84] This kind of death agrees well with Christ's status of slave, given that crucifixion was a means of execution often used for slaves. The whole of this, then, constitutes the basis (see διὸ, verse 9) for God's "hyper-exaltation" of Christ in verses 9-10,[85] truly the turning point of the *enkomion*,[86] as κύριος Ἰησοῦς Χριστὸς,[87] which, given the worship that it involves, probably implies the reception of the divine name.[88] Because of this, i.e. the bestowal of the divine name, this

---

81. Nevertheless, for Phil. 2.5-11, a plausible option would be that Christ is God's slave, given that Christ is obedient to God. The focus is more on Christ's obedient embrace of a lowly status as an expression of his submission to God's intention than on whose slave he is precisely. See, e.g., Hurtado, "Jesus," 122–123, and O'Brien, *Epistle*, 216–224. Other options include: enslavement to death, to sin, to the powers of the cosmos, etc. See, e.g., Walter, "Brief," 60, as well as, for a well-documented consideration of various options with this conclusion, Müller, Brief, 96–102, and further also, Fowl, *Story*, 57–61, and Barth, *Brief*, 42–43.

82. For this emphasis, see, e.g., O'Brien, *Epistle*, 228, noting the difference with the "Suffering Servant" in Isa. 53.8.

83. Implying his full identification with the *condition humaine*. See, e.g., Müller, *Brief*, 105–106, and Barth, *Brief*, 43.

84. See, e.g., Williams, *Enemies*, 132–133. It is often argued that the notion that Christ died on a cross has been added redactionally by Paul (see, e.g., Barth, *Brief*, 41). With this view, however, there are two substantial problems. First, from a formal point of view, the argument that Paul has added the clause θανάτου δὲ σταυροῦ in Phil. 2.8 depends on notions about the structure of the *enkomion* that are not necessarily compelling. Second, from the point of view of content, it is hard to see from the immediate context in which Paul uses the *enkomion* what he would have gained by adding it. Christ's cross only returns in Phil. 3.18, which seems to be too far removed from Phil. 2.8 to be the reason why Paul would have added this reference to the hymn. Brucker, *Christushymnen*, 309–311, identifies the clause θανάτου δὲ σταυροῦ as an anadiplosis, a characteristic of epideictic style; therefore it is not necessarily a theologically informed Pauline addition.

85. With regard to the causality, see, e.g., Barth, *Brief*, 43, "Die Erhöhung ist Gottes Antwort auf die gehorsame Erniedrigung." The terminology of "hyperexaltation" is used by, e.g., Müller, *Brief*, 106, with respect to ὑπερύψωσεν in Phil. 2.9. See also the analogous view of Reumann, *Philippians*, 372.

86. This turning point is also the safest starting point for any proposal as to the structure of the hymn, i.e. as a bipartite text with a subdivision in verse 9 based on the change in subject that occurs there. See, e.g., Williams, *Enemies*, 61–64; see also, e.g., O'Brien, *Epistle*, 188–193, and Schenk, *Philipperbriefe*, 185–190. See also the attempt by Charles J. Robbins, "Rhetorical Structure of Philippians 2:6–11," *CBQ* 42 (1980), 73–82, to structure Phil. 2.6-11 according to rhetorical principles. For an exhaustive syntactic and linguistic analysis of the hymn, see Kennel, *Frühchristliche Hymnen?*, 185–224. On the importance of the change of subject in verse 9, see, e.g., Brucker, *Christushymnen*, 309; Walter, "Brief," 57; Müller, *Brief*, 106; Barth, *Brief*, 41, 43.

87. This is in all likelihood the name Jesus receives in verse 9, with κύριος being a new addition. See also Hellerman, *Honor*, 150: for honor to be "effective" it needed to be proclaimed publicly, which is precisely what takes place here. For an argument about the identity of the name, see, e.g., Lietaert Peerbolte, "Name," esp. 201–202.

88. See Müller, *Brief*, 106–107, 109–111, but without referring to the worship as a reason for this interpretation. The use of the wording of Isa. 45.23LXX is another pointer in this direction; see Lietaert Peerbolte, "Name," 203–204, and further, e.g., Walter, "Brief," 62–63.

final position of Christ may well be superior to the one that he started out with in Phil. 2.6.[89] This is the main movement of the Christ *enkomion* and also provides the scope of its contents. It should serve as a basis for what follows in this and the following sections, which will offer not so much an interpretation of the *enkomion* itself, as of Paul's use of it. While the relationship between the *enkomion* and Phil. 2.12-18 will be discussed below,[90] here some attention should be given to the way in which the *enkomion* substantiates what has been said before.

First, a connection between 2.1 and 2.5 may be noted. Both verses refer to something taking place or existing ἐν Χριστῷ. Second, the call τοῦτο φρονεῖτε ἐν ὑμῖν in verse 5 echoes what Paul had stated in verse 2: ἵνα τὸ αὐτὸ φρονῆτε … τὸ ἓν φρονοῦντες.[91] Third, ταπεινοφροσύνη, as it occurs in verse 3, returns in verse 8, where Christ humiliates himself (ἐταπείνωσεν ἑαυτόν).[92] Fourth, in 2.4, Paul places much emphasis on not pursuing one's own interest (see also verse 3): μὴ τὰ ἑαυτῶν ἕκαστος σκοποῦντες ἀλλὰ [καὶ] τὰ ἑτέρων ἕκαστοι. This has a direct echo in 2.6: οὐχ ἁρπαγμὸν ἡγήσατο τὸ εἶναι ἴσα θεῷ. Fifth, in 1.29 Paul makes reference to the fact that the Philippians may also suffer for Christ, while the suffering of Christ is outlined in 2.7-8. Sixth, and finally, the κενοδοξία mentioned in verse 3 may be seen to return in the formulation εἰς δόξαν θεοῦ πατρός in 2.11.

Even though these observations are relatively brief, they nevertheless demonstrate how Paul's appeals in Phil. 1.27–2.4, especially those in 2.1-4, are supported by the presentation of the one normative embodiment of these attitudes, i.e. Christ Jesus. In particular, the humility of Christ backs up Paul's calls to humility on the part of the Philippians, while Paul also provides a single point of orientation (i.e. the *enkomion*), which can be seen as a means to help the Philippians to think alike. The basis for this line of thought that connects the behavior of the Philippians to that of Christ may well be found in the idea that the Philippians are "in Christ" (see also the address of the Philippians in

---

89. See, e.g., Barth, *Erklärung*, 55; Barth, *Brief* 43; Dibelius, *Philipper*, 79. Therefore, this name is certainly not a human name as Bittasi, *Esempi*, 66–67, argues. Given that Bittasi's argument about the chiastic structure of the hymn (A: 2.6-7a: Christ as God, B: 2.7bc-8: Christ as human being, B': 2.9: Christ as human being receiving the historical human name Jesus, A': universal recognition of Jesus Christ as God) hinges on an interpretation of verse 9 in terms of a reference to Christ's reception of the name Jesus as τὸ ὄνομα τὸ ὑπὲρ πᾶν ὄνομα, discarding, as is done here, his exegesis of Phil. 2.9, means to discard his chiastic structure for the *enkomion*.

90. See below, 3.1.4–5.

91. See, e.g., Fowl, *Story*, 89–90, and Walter, "Brief," 52–53.

92. See Müller, *Brief*, 113: "Nicht Eigennutz noch Geltungsbedürfnis sind Verhaltensweisen, die der Christusgemeinschaft entsprechen, sondern Bereitschaft zur Demut (2,1–4). Das Kreuz verweist den Christen in neuer Weise in die Existenz irdischer Geschichte. Das scheint schon in 1,27–30 anvisiert zu sein, wenn als neue erst zu akzeptierende Lebensform der Philipper das Leiden für Christus ins Blickfeld tritt. In der ausdrücklichen Erwähnung des Kreuzes in 2,8 ist dieser Gedanke wohl fortgeführt. Wenn die Philipper in ihrer Leidensexistenz seinem Leidensweg konform werden, realisieren sie die Christusgemeinschaft, die Paulus ihnen mit der Formel ἐν Χριστῷ vor Augen hält (2,5)."

1.1 and compare 2.1, 5), that is, incorporated into Christ's sphere of influence. Life within this sphere is determined by the shape of the life of Christ, who has established this "sphere" to begin with.[93] As Collange puts it, "Imiter Christ n'est donc pas autre chose que être 'en Christ'."[94]

Having considered this, it will also be clear that not all parts of the *enkomion* are linked to an aspect of Paul's exhortation. This will be considered next, specifically with regard to Christ's origins.

3.1.4 A Misfit? The Problem of Christ's Origins

When considering the relationship between Phil. 2.1-4 and 2.5-11 further, it is also useful to draw attention to an element of the *enkomion* that is not taken up by Paul in his argument based on the *enkomion*: Christ's exalted position at the beginning of the *enkomion* (and to some extent also his lordship at the end of the poem). In fact, this "pre-existence" is the only element from the *enkomion* which cannot be found back in any part of Paul's preceding or subsequent arguments, at least in as far as the Philippians are concerned (there is a connection between Christ in Phil. 2 and Paul in Phil. 3 with regard to self-emptying and loss of status, to be sure).[95] This, however, does not at all speak against the use of the *enkomion* as an *exemplum*. The reason for this is that the conventional use of *exempla* in the first century CE did not require a one-to-one agreement between all parts of the *exemplum* and the argument that was supported by means of it. Of course, the elements of the *exemplum* that are being used to support an argument should provide a fit, but even then not only agreement in terms of content is of importance, but also the proximity of the *exemplum* to the intended audience, and the authority that the *exemplum* has. Therefore, for the analysis of Paul's use of Phil. 2.5-11 in order to support what he has said in 1.27–2.4 and what he will say in 2.12-18, it is of more importance to look at the elements of the *enkomion* in 2.5-11 that he does use, rather than at those that he does not use.[96] For the issue of Christ's origins (Phil. 2.6), this means that they are simply not used by Paul in his argument, without this having any consequences for the functioning of Phil. 2.5-11 as an *exemplum*. However, Christ's self-emptying and specifically his self-humiliation and obedience are used by him. In this context, Christ's origins only provide a necessary and logical precondition for this process of self-emptying, nothing more. Beyond

---

93. This would also amount to the view of Käsemann; see, e.g., Fowl, *Story*, 81, 89–90.
94. "Imitating Christ is therefore nothing else but being 'in Christ'" (author's translation). Jean-François Collange, *De Jésus à Paul: L'éthique du Nouveau Testament* (Genève: Labor et Fides, 1980), 201. See also, e.g., Heil, *Philippians*, 93.
95. See below, 3.4.3.2.
96. See above, esp. 1.3. This also agrees well with the fact that Paul probably uses the *enkomion* in a new and "secondary" context; see, e.g., Briggs Kittredge, *Community*, 86. Witherington, *Friendship*, 64–65, reaches a similar conclusion as the present study, albeit on a different theoretical basis.

this, Christ's origins may add to the authority of the *exemplum*, even if it seems likely that this authority derives from Christ's (eventual) lordship primarily.

This way of operating makes also other strategies of interpretation superfluous. This applies, for example, to a popular interpretative strategy that seeks to include Christ's origins into Paul's argument by arguing that Paul operates on the basis of a "New-Adam Christology." When thinking along these lines, the analogy between Christ's self-emptying and the Philippians would be provided by Adam's fall (see also, e.g., Rom. 5.14). It is questionable, however, that this strategy is indeed necessary. In fact, as was outlined already, the Christology of the *enkomion* does not present Christ explicitly (or even implicitly) as a new Adam. Furthermore, if the *enkomion* would indeed imply a "New-Adam Christology," with Christ's self-emptying as the way in which the new Adam acquired the same status as the old one *post lapsum*, it would have been counterproductive to Paul's argument to emphasize this: from Phil. 2.12 onwards, he will refer to Christ's obedience (2.8), not Adam's disobedience to make his point (Phil. 2.12). Christ's obedient self-emptying and self-humiliation leads to his glorification, whereas the disobedient self-humiliation of Adam results in quite the opposite of this. Rather, Paul suggests that, for the Philippians, behavior similar to Christ's is necessary, both by following Christ in his obedience (Phil. 2.12-18) and by adopting a meek attitude (see Phil. 2.1-4). Having considered this, it is now possible to turn to some of the elements of the *enkomion* that Paul *does* use in Phil. 2.12-18.

3.1.5 Obedience and the Glorification of the Faithful (2.12-18)

In the *enkomion*, kenosis, "incarnation," self-humiliation, and obedience up to the point of death are mentioned as parts of the process because of which Christ is exalted by God (see Phil. 2.6-9). While this dynamic serves to support Paul's argument and appeal in Phil. 1.27–2.4, it is also taken up by Phil. 2.12-18.[97] At the beginning of Phil. 2.12, ὥστε indicates that what follows is based on what has just been said (i.e. Phil. 2.5-11).[98] Apart from this, also other connections between what preceded the enkomion, what follows it, and the *enkomion* itself point in this direction, i.e. that Phil. 2.12-18 has its basis in Phil. 2.5-11 and is prepared by Phil. 1.27–2.1-4. The latter is indicated, for example, by Paul's return to the topic of deliverance (Phil. 1.28, 2.12) and of his own absence and presence (Phil. 1.30, 2.12).[99] With this, it is possible to turn to the first element that Paul emphasizes after the *enkomion*: obedience.

---

97. See, e.g., Williams, *Enemies*, 135; see also Witherington, *Friendship*, 71.
98. See, e.g., Williams, *Enemies*, 136, and O'Brien, "Gospel," 277; similarly, Bockmuehl, *Philippians*, 149. Arguments that there is no such connection are not convincing; see, however, e.g., Barth, *Brief*, 49. Verse 12 also does not refer back to Phil. 2.4, as, e.g., Dibelius, *Philipper*, 82, and Müller, *Brief*, 114, suggest: Paul will have inserted the *enkomion* for a reason.
99. See, e.g., Müller, *Brief*, 114–115.

3.1.5.1 Obedience

The first element of the *enkomion* that Paul takes up in Phil. 2.12-18 is that of obedience (see Phil. 2.8: γενόμενος ὑπήκοος and Phil. 2.12: πάντοτε ὑπηκούσατε).[100] Obedience is a central characteristic of the description of Christ in the *enkomion*. Also, it suits the description of Christ as a slave very well: a slave is obedient *per se*.[101] Placing some emphasis on the connection between Phil. 2.8 and 2.12, as was just proposed, is also supported by a semantic observation: Paul's use of the notion of "obedience" is striking, given that he seems to use it instead of the more common concept of servanthood here.[102] The concept of obedience to God is much less common; in fact, it is only referred to by forms based on the root ὑπήκο- seven more times in the New Testament.[103]

Thus, by referring to obedience, Paul first returns to the first part of the *enkomion*.[104] The Philippians are to be faithful to this paradigm provided by Christ, both in Paul's (equally paradigmatic) presence and in his absence, even with fear and trembling, in order to achieve their eschatological salvation (2.12).[105] It is not clearly stated to whom the Philippians should be obedient;[106] options are certainly God,[107] Christ, and Paul. The option that obedience is due to God is attractive because it would constitute a parallel to Christ's obedience in the *enkomion*; obedience to Christ can be argued for by pointing to the necessity of obedience to the "way of life" that he paradigmatically displayed in the *enkomion*; and obedience to Paul is plausible because Paul is the one making the argument and because he emphasizes obedience regardless

---

100. See, e.g., Fowl, *Story*, 96; O'Brien, "Gospel," 277; Fee, *Philippians*, 229–240; also and emphatically, J. Ross Wagner, "Working Out Salvation: Holiness and Community in Philippians," in Kent E. Brower and Andy Johnson (eds.), *Holiness and Ecclesiology in the New Testament* (Grand Rapids: Eerdmans, 2007), 257–274, esp. 259, as well as Gnilka, *Philipperbrief*, 147–148. Why it should be unclear that Phil. 2.12 refers back to Phil. 2.8, as is suggested by, e.g., Walter, "Brief," 64, is not perspicuous, especially as obedience plays such a pivotal role in the *enkomion*. Also, why this agreement should be a coincidence, as Müller, *Brief*, 115, claims (but does not argue), is not immediately obvious.

101. See Byron, *Metaphors*, 29: "[T]he imagery of subordination and obedience is the most basic premise of slavery and would have easily lent itself to relationships involving kings, deities and any other similarly constructed relationship." See for his overview, idem, *op. cit.*, 22–28.

102. Forms of the root δουλ- occur 34 times in the Pauline letters.

103. Forms of the root ὑπηκ- are only used in 2 Cor. 2.9; Phil. 2.8 (adjective), 2.12; and Rom. 6.13, 16-17; 10.16.

104. See, e.g., Briggs Kittredge, *Community*, 83–84.

105. Σωτήρια is for Paul, even when it is not entirely otherworldly, clearly eschatologically oriented and refers in many instances to the state to be granted to Christians after the (soon to come) arrival (i.e. return) of the Lord. See, e.g., Ekkehard W. Stegemann,"'Auf Hoffnung sind wir gerettet'. Heilserwartung im frühen Christentum zwischen Apokalyptik und realisierter Eschatologie," in idem, *Paulus und die Welt. Aufsätze* (ed. Christina Tuor and Peter Wick; Zürich: TVZ, 2005), 113–124, and in the same volume, "'Das ängstliche Harren der Kreatur'. Angst und Hoffnung im apokalyptischen Weltentwurf des Paulus," 251–258.

106. With emphasis on this; see Reumann, *Philippians*, 409.

107. See, e.g., Bittasi, *Esempi*, 76.

of his presence and absence (Phil. 2.12; see also Phil. 2.16).¹⁰⁸ One may well ask, however, whether these three alternatives are mutually exclusive. In fact, it seems that obedience to God on the part of the Philippians would imply obedience to the authentic preaching of the gospel (by Paul) in obedience to the pattern set by Christ (as outlined in the *enkomion*).¹⁰⁹ It seems likely that such a multi-faceted kind of obedience is in view rather than obedience to Paul as such, or to God or Christ without reference to Paul, God, and/or Christ. Obedience may well have been a concept with considerable affinity for many Philippians: many had a military background and even more a background in slavery;¹¹⁰ hence, they will have been able to relate to obedience as a matter of fact, given that it was typical for soldiers and slaves.¹¹¹ Reading the *enkomion* from this perspective also has the consequence that the thesis defended by, for instance, Otfried Hofius and Martin Hengel, that Christ's (salvific) death on the cross is the main focus of the *enkomion*, appears to be beside the point: in Phil. 2, Christ's death on the cross is the climax of his obedience to God, but it has no soteriological function of its own.¹¹² With regard to this, one may well agree with Byron's observation that "[i]n the light of the way the hymn functions as a governing metaphor in the epistle and the fact that the Greco-Roman 'friendly letter of exhortation' routinely used examples of model behaviour, it seems best to understand the use of slave language in light of the hymn and not vice-versa."¹¹³ This observation both prevents one from reading foreign soteriological concepts into the *enkomion* and facilitates a retrospective association of the image of Christ as a slave in *enkomion* and the surrounding exhortations concerning obedience with the self-description of Paul and Timothy as slaves in Phil. 1.1.¹¹⁴

With regard to the flow of Philippians, it must now be asked what purpose this emphasis on obedience serves. The answer seems to be twofold. First, it may link back to the text that led into the *enkomion*, Phil. 1.17–2.4, where Paul

---

108.   See also, e.g., Fowl, *Story*, 96.
109.   See, e.g., Gerber, *Paulus*, 246, who notes with regard to Phil. 2.12 and the missing object of ὑπηκούσατε: "Gehorsam zu Gott und zu Paulus scheinen äquivalent." See also Briggs Kittredge, *Community*, 84–85.
110.   See, e.g., Reumann, *Philippians*, 55; if Philippi had a population similar to that of a city like Corinth, about 33 percent of the population would have been slaves and another 33 percent ex-slaves.
111.   See, e.g., Byron, *Metaphors*, 36. From the New Testament itself, the attention may be drawn to Mt. 8.5-13, especially to verse 9: καὶ γὰρ ἐγὼ ἄνθρωπός εἰμι ὑπὸ ἐξουσίαν, ἔχων ὑπ' ἐμαυτὸν στρατιώτας, καὶ λέγω τούτῳ· πορεύθητι, καὶ πορεύεται, καὶ ἄλλῳ· ἔρχου, καὶ ἔρχεται, καὶ τῷ δούλῳ μου· ποίησον τοῦτο, καὶ ποιεῖ. The centurion addressing Jesus refers to obedience in terms of being ὑπὸ ἐξουσίαν in two respects: with reference to the military and with reference to the life of slaves.
112.   For justified caution against reading a Pauline theology of the cross in this statement, which is often seen as Pauline redaction, see, e.g., Schenk, *Philipperbriefe*, 191–192.
113.   Byron, *Metaphors*, 174; see also Watson, "Integration," 410–411, and Williams, *Enemies*, 107; see esp. the use of "slave language" in 1.2, 2.7, 27 (δοῦλος), 2.22 (δουλεύω).
114.   As can be readily recognized; see, e.g., Heil, *Philippians*, 88–89.

pleads with the Philippians to remain faithful and steadfast, which implies a strong call to obedience to the faith. Second, this same theme occurs in Phil. 2.12-18, which is focused on the Philippians' obedience with regard to their salvation. This leads to the exhortation πάντα ποιεῖτε χωρὶς γογγυσμῶν καὶ διαλογισμῶν in Phil. 2.14 in combination with the notion of holding fast to the word of life (or proclaiming it)[115] in Phil. 2.16 and the image of shining like stars among a perverse generation in Phil. 2.15. All of this taken together can be plausibly interpreted as a restatement of Phil. 2.1-4, but now with a focus on eschatological salvation, rather than on group coherence. The notion of eschatological salvation, which is absent from Phil. 2.1-4, comes from the final section of the *enkomion*, where, from verse 9 onwards, the "hyper-exaltation" of Christ is recounted. In this way, obedience has two aspects: it points back to the faithfulness demanded by Paul in Phil. 1.27–2.4, which was mainly concerned with the unity of the community, and it points forward to a further effect of the obedience: eschatological salvation. As the (implicit) reference to struggles in Phil. 2.14 suggests, this obedience probably includes embracing the suffering that comes with being in Christ, while standing together and looking forward to full redemption,[116] in analogy to Christ's eventual fate.[117] This may also be the sense of Phil. 2.12b, in the context of which Phil. 2.13 appears as a comforting and reassuring comment.[118] These verses will be considered in more detail in the next section.

3.1.5.2 Suffering and the Eschaton
Distributed over four imperatives, Phil. 2.12-18 continues the exhortation begun in Phil. 1.27-30.[119] On the *enkomion*, together with Phil. 2.12, Phil. 2.13 follows somewhat like an afterthought, supporting the call for obedience issued in verse 12 with the statement that it is God who works both the willing and the doing among the Philippians, according to his good pleasure. Even this is not generally agreed upon; the last three words of Phil. 2.13, ὑπὲρ τῆς εὐδοκίας, can be interpreted both as "according to his (i.e. God's) good pleasure" and as

---

115. Thus Ware, *Paul*, 256–270.
116. As Fowl has it: "If the Philippians will unite in a steadfast adherence to the gospel (which will entail the practice of the virtues in 2.2–4), even in the face of suffering, then God will save them in the same way he saved the obedient, humiliated and suffering Christ in vv. 6–11" (Fowl, *Story*, 92). For a similar position, see, e.g., Peterlin, *Letter*, 67. See, e.g., also, Bittasi, *Esempi*, 71, Müller, *Brief*, 28, and esp. Fowl, *Story*, 61–64.
117. With, e.g., Fowl, *Story*, 83.
118. Similarly, e.g., Müller, *Brief*, 117; μετὰ φόβου καὶ τρόμου in Phil. 2.12 can be seen as expressing awe *vis-à-vis* God's workings. See also, Reumann, *Philippians*, 410–411, and Ross Wagner, "Working," 259–260. Reading these verses with late medieval and early modern debates about free will and grace in mind constitutes in any case an anachronism; see however, e.g., Barth, *Brief*, 49. See also Müller, *Brief*, 115–117, rightly noting the problem of theological tradition(s) and exegesis. See for a lengthy consideration also, Ware, *Mission*, 238–248, arguing that Phil. 2.12 constitutes a call to suffer with Christ.
119. See Reumann, *Philippians*, 407.

referring to a positive or benign human attitude. The word εὐδοκία can carry both nuances,[120] and indeed does refer to a positive human attitude in Phil. 1.15.[121] This, however, by no means implies that it has to mean precisely the same in Phil. 2.13; rather, the meaning best suiting the rest of the verse has to be chosen and that is "according to God's good pleasure." This may come as a surprise, as Paul seems to be at pains to emphasize the activity of the Philippians on the basis of the *exemplum* on Christ. Nevertheless, the note on the activity of God in Phil. 2.13 seems to make good sense in the context of the *enkomion*: Phil. 2.9 also contains an emphatic reference to God's activity with regard to Christ. Earlier, Phil. 1.28 also contained a similar appendix-like reference to God's agency. The statement of Phil. 2.13 then turns out to be consoling and exhortative at the same time: consoling in that it assures the Philippians of God's working in them, and exhortative in that it seems to assure the Philippians that they will also be able to do what they are supposed to do (Phil. 2.12).

In Phil. 2.14, the reference to "doing everything" without murmuring, itself possibly echoing Israel's murmuring in the wilderness, which would make it a very brief negative *exemplum* here,[122] may well constitute a further elaboration of the concept of obedience, as obedience may well be thought of as taking place without protest. In any case, the result of this behavior is receiving divine parentage (Phil. 2.15), apparently already on earth, where the faithful will shine like stars among a generation walking in darkness,[123] which positions the Philippians in society by taking up Deut. 32.5.[124] This, in turn, is probably in line with the actual tension that this community experiences with its social environment.[125] After further developing the description of these faithful Christians as those who hold forth the word of life,[126] which secures their "shiny" position in the world, Paul describes this (ideal) situation as a cause

---

120. See, e.g., Reumann, *Philippians*, 389.
121. This seems to be undisputed; see, e.g., Reumann, *Philippians*, 178–179.
122. See, e.g., Witherington, *Friendship*, 72–73; Williams, *Enemies*, 104; Müller, *Brief*, 117–118; Barth, *Brief*, 49–50; O'Brien, "Gospel," 278; and compare 1 Cor. 10.10; Ex. 16.2, 17.3; and Num. 11.1, 14.27. Müller, *op. cit.*, 118, considers the possibility that the use of this expression speaks to the situation in Philippi, where suffering might cause the questioning of God's ways in a way analogous to Israel's in the wilderness. See further, also, Williams, *Enemies*, 138: The remark could play a role in Paul's argument against the "radical Jewish Christians," but can just as well be a manner of speech.
123. Echoing texts about the eschatological Israel such as Dan. 12.3LXX; see, e.g., Müller, *Brief*, 118–119.
124. See, e.g., Barth, *Brief*, 50, and Müller, *Brief*, 118.
125. See, e.g., Barth, *Brief*, 50.
126. See for detailed considerations as to the meaning of ἐπέχω in Phil. 2.16, Ware, *Mission*, 256–270, esp. 269; the missionary denotation that Ware establishes suits the accompanying image of the shining stars well. See also Brucker, "*Christushymnen*," 320, with reference to the missionary connotation of κατεργάζομαι on the basis of the semantic field that it belongs to (compare Phil. 3.2 and 2 Cor. 11.13). Witherington, *Friendship*, 73, argues against this interpretation, stating that cohesion not proclamation is in view in this passage; proclamation seems to imply cohesion, however.

for his boasting on the day of Christ,[127] thus reintroducing the eschatological perspective (Phil. 2.16-17). He then reinforces these statements by stating that even if his activities on behalf of the Philippians would cost him his life,[128] he rejoices wholeheartedly and calls on the Philippians to rejoice wholeheartedly with him.[129] All of this should probably be seen in the context of Paul's eschatological outlook in Philippians that was already mentioned earlier (see verses 9-11, 12).[130] In fact, this outlook of Phil. 2.12, which is restated in terms of the day of Christ (εἰς ἡμέραν Χριστοῦ) in Phil. 2.16, is related to a web of other eschatological references in Philippians[131] that indicate the position of the Philippian community with regard to the "end" (see, e.g., Phil. 1.6, 10, and also and esp. 3.20-21).[132] Also Phil. 2.9-11, the description of Christ's "hyper-exaltation," may be mentioned in this context again, even if the connection between this text and Phil. 3.20-21 is probably tighter than between this text and Phil. 2.16.

When turning to Phil. 2.16, it may be noted that in its second part Paul uses an agonistic metaphor, indicating his hope that he has not run and labored in vain (ὅτι οὐκ εἰς κενὸν ἔδραμον οὐδὲ εἰς κενὸν ἐκοπίασα).[133] With respect to this, it is significant that in Phil. 2.16 eschatological glory, earthly toiling, and obedience are placed into the same kind of relationship to each other as is the case in Phil. 2.12, albeit with a different terminology and with reference to a struggle that is on the part of Paul, not of the Philippians.

Thus, with regard to both the question of obedience and the double issue of suffering and glorification, Phil. 2.5-11 has a paradigmatic function for what follows in Phil. 2.12-18, while simultaneously substantiating what has been said in Phil. 2.1-4.

127. The background to this is probably that Paul operates on the assumption that he will need to account for his ministry at the Last Day; see, e.g., Müller, *Brief*, 119–120.
128. See for this interpretation, Gerber, *Paulus*, 166–168.
129. See, e.g., Müller, *Brief*, 120–121.
130. With, e.g., Müller, the joy that Paul calls for in Phil. 2.18 may also be interpreted in terms of an eschatological orientation: "Es ist die Freude über die siegreich bestandene Bewährung des Glaubens, die jetzt schon die innere Haltung der Gemeinde bestimmt und einen Vorgriff auf den eschatologischen Jubel darstellt." See Müller, *Brief*, 28. For further references to joy that are related both to the community and to the eschaton, see, e.g., Rom. 14.17; 2 Cor. 7.13, 8.2-3; Gal. 5.22; 1 Thess. 1.6, 3.9-10.
131. See, e.g., also Schenk, *Philipperbriefe*, 223–224, and Müller, *Brief*, 28. On the "eschatological framework" see, e.g., Fee, *Philippians*, 50–52.
132. Therefore, it may well be maintained with Giesen that part of the purpose of Philippians in general is to remind the Philippian Christians of their orientation towards the eschaton: Heinz Giesen, "Eschatology in Philippians," in Stanley E. Porter (ed.), *Paul and His Theology*, Pauline Studies 3 (Leiden: Brill, 2006), 217–282.
133. Byron relates this to two earlier indications of "emptiness": vainglory (κενοδοξία, 2.3) and Christ's self-emptying (Phil. 2.7), which would therefore have a paradigmatic function for the statement in Phil. 2.16. Whereas this seems likely in the case of the vainglory in 2.3, it is unlikely in the case of Christ's self-emptying: hardly the same kind of emptiness is in view. See Byron, *Metaphors*, 174.

3.1.5.3 Excursus: What Sort of Exemplum?

Based on the earlier consideration of *exempla* in rhetorical theory,[134] it might be worthwhile considering whether the *exempla* in Philippians can also be analyzed following the standards of Aristotelian logic, thus viewing them as logical proofs. This will be attempted now for Phil. 2. What is needed for this is the assumption that the *exemplum* presented in Phil. 2.5-11 can be reduced to a valid first (major) premise in order to begin to construct a syllogism. Furthermore, Paul's ensuing argument in Phil. 2.12-18 should also be reduced to a valid second (minor) premise.[135] In fact, it seems that it could be argued that what Paul argues, is one of the following three, depending on what one thinks he is trying to show with his paradigm (in fact, Paul could be demonstrating all three).

Model A:
First premise: All those who are in Christ are obedient (CaO)
Second premise: All Christians in Philippi are in Christ (PaC)
Conclusion: All Christians in Philippi are obedient (PaO)

Model B:
First premise: All who are in Christ suffer and will be glorified (CaSG)
Second premise: All Christians in Philippi are in Christ (PaC)
Conclusion: All Christians in Philippi suffer and will be glorified (PaSG)

Model C:
First premise: All who are in Christ are giving up on their prerogatives (CaGP)
Second premise: All Christians in Philippi are in Christ (PaC)
Conclusion: All Christians in Philippi give up their prerogatives (PaGP)

Or, when following the narrative example of an Aristotelian παράδειγμα given above, with its requirements about comparability of the various parties involved,[136] one can restate the above narratively (for all cases, but only one will be spelled out here): in order to prove that it is fitting for those in Christ (A) to suffer and to be glorified (B), one can appeal to the *enkomion* that demonstrates that Christ suffered and was glorified (C) as well as to the generally accepted fact that the Philippians are in Christ (D). Given that A applies to D and C, as they are both examples of being (in) Christ, and B to C, it can be proven by means of C that A applies to B. This also applies to the two further models given above.

134. See above, 1.3.
135. For the following I am indebted to Prof. Dr. Moisés Mayordomo-Marín, Bern.
136. See above, 1.3.

Thus, it is theoretically possible to present what can be found in Phil. 2 as a valid *exemplum* following Aristotelian criteria. The main problem that needed to be solved in this case,[137] namely whether the *exemplum* and the ensuing argument can be reduced to valid (and useful) first and second premises, can be considered solved, given that the options presented above are all being propagated in the exegetical literature as points that Paul intends to make in this part of Philippians.

However, even if this is all possible, two problems remain. The first is contextual: as has been outlined above, *exempla* were by the first century CE not usually employed along strictly (Aristotelian) logical lines. The second problem, however, which is also contextual, but in the literary sense of the word, is that Paul would not have reached his rhetorical aim with a logical *exemplum* in this context. Even though he would have been able to prove that the Philippians in Christ are obedient, or are suffering and will be glorified, or are giving up on prerogatives, he could not have used the *exemplum* directly to argue that the Philippians *should* be obedient, or that they should be content to suffer with the prospect of being glorified, given that that belongs to being in Christ. This is something that a logical demonstration of proof cannot achieve; it can only show that something is the case or not.

Therefore, a more plausible way of interpreting the *exemplum* in Phil. 2 would be to read it in terms of an *exemplum* functioning as a "cultural symbol," as has been described above. This, in turn, would be well in line with the general deliberative character of Philippians.

3.1.5.4 The Relationship between the Philippians and Christ as the Basis of the Argument

As was already illustrated above[138] when discussing the subject of the so-called symbolic *exempla*, one significant aspect of this kind of *exempla* is that the *exemplum* used is accessible and acceptable to the audience to which it is presented. If not, the *exemplum* will fall flat. Therefore, it is worthwhile to ask how the Philippians relate to the *exemplum* that Paul presents. In order to do this it is necessary to focus on Phil. 2.5 again.

Phil. 2.5 constitutes the bridge between the preceding paraenesis (Phil. 1.27–2.4) and the subsequent *enkomion*. Linking the *enkomion* with his preceding statements,[139] Paul states: τοῦτο φρονεῖτε ἐν ὑμῖν ὃ καὶ ἐν Χριστῷ Ἰησοῦ. A call for both comparable behavior and like-mindedness results from this. That Paul is able to call for this at all is probably closely related to the latter part of Phil. 2.5: ἐν Χριστῷ Ἰησοῦ, which is the way the Philippians (and Paul) relate to Christ,[140] the most prominent of their *maiores*. On this basis the "story of

---

137. See, e.g., Mayordomo-Marín, *Paulus*, esp. 70–71; further also, 135, 137, for considerations about this.
138. See above, 1.3, 1.3.1.
139. Dahl, "Euodia," 11, is right in pointing out that this aspect of Phil. 2.5 should not be forgotten.
140. In Philippians this has been indicated in 1.1; see also 1.26, 2.1, 3.3, and 4.2, 7, 21.

Christ" is an *exemplum* valid for the Philippians who,[141] just like Paul, have the source of their (ethically binding) communal identity in their incorporation into Christ (their "participation" in him), a community that is determined by the "Christ-tradition," specifically by traditions about the shared *maior*, Christ. Shared identity on the basis of a shared incorporation into Christ and a shared tradition issuing from the Christ-event leads to the possibility of using precisely the (*encomiastic*) narrative of this (normative) event as an *exemplum*.

3.1.5.5 Excursus: Participation in Philippians

As part of the above argument hinges on the notion that the Philippian Christians are incorporated into Christ and participate in his "career," here attention should be drawn to Baumert's recent critique of mainstream interpretations of such language of participation.[142] Concerning Philippians, the question involves six verses: Phil. 1.5, 7, 2.1, 3.10, and 4.14-15.[143] Given the thoroughness of Baumert's research and its justifiable suspicion concerning reading too much theology into everyday language, its conclusions as far as Philippians is concerned should be considered here.

A first pair of texts that Baumert argues to have a common meaning in as far as the supposed language of participation is concerned, consists of Phil. 1.5 and 4.15. Baumert interprets both texts in relation to business transactions. In the first text he translates κοινωνία ὑμῶν εἰς τὸ εὐαγγέλιον as "eure (*mir gegebene*) *Unterstützung für das Evangelium*";[144] in the second text he renders ἐκοινώνησεν εἰς λόγον δόσεως καὶ λήμψεως as "(Geschäfts-)Beziehung haben *in* Verrechnung."[145] Concerning the latter text, the rendering "business partnership" makes excellent sense given the context of the discussion of a gift and the accountancy terminology used in the same verse. A reference to the same gift (as part of a continuous support for Paul by the Philippians) also makes sense in the opening section of Philippians, i.e. in 1.5.

In Phil. 1.7, Baumert translates συγκοινωνούς μου τῆς χάριτος as "(mir) Gefährten in/hinsichtlich meiner Gnade."[146] Whether or not one may wish to debate the grammatical and syntactical moves that Baumert makes to arrive at this translation (esp. not taking μου with the preceding noun), the result is interesting. The Philippians are Paul's associates with respect to his grace. This "grace" Baumert interprets as the prayerful support that Paul receives from Philippi, which would be an unusual, but nevertheless possible, interpretation of the Pauline χάρις. Another option would be to argue that the grace that

---

141. See for the "story of Christ," esp. Fowl, *Story*. For emphasis on the narrative character of the "drama" of Phil. 2.5-11, see also Robert J. Karris, *A Symphony of New Testament Hymns* (Collegeville: Liturgical Press, 1996), 42–62.
142. Norbert Baumert, *Koinonein und Metechein—synonym? Eine umfassende semantische Untersuchung*, SBS 51 (Stuttgart: Verlag Katholisches Bibelwerk, 2003).
143. See, e.g., the table provided by Baumert, *Koinonein*, 501–502.
144. See for a more extensive justification, Baumert, *Koinonein*, 200–205. An interpretation along the lines of material support is rejected by Dibelius, *Philipper*, 62.
145. See Baumert, *Koinonein*, 50–56, 273–274.
146. See Baumert, *Koinonein*, 108–111.

Paul experiences is not necessarily the commitment of the Philippians to him, but may also consist of his imprisonment and suffering, which would suit the rest of the letter very well. In this case, the Philippians would be partakers of Paul's grace because of the relationship between them and Paul. Compared to the previous cases considered (Phil. 1.5 and 4.15), in the case of Phil. 1.7 Baumert's argument is much more complicated and needs to choose, at least twice, less plausible interpretative options (concerning the person that μου refers to and concerning the meaning of χάρις), while in addition the meaning that he eventually gives to the verse is not immediately obvious, when considering the larger context of Philippians.

For Phil. 2.1, which represents a *crux interpretum* even without Baumert's monograph, Baumert rightly draws attention to the fact that it is the most plausible that all four clauses of the verse have something to do with an attitude or action on the part of the Philippians towards Paul. Translating κοινωνία πνεύματος as "fellowship of the Spirit" or "participation in the Spirit" is therefore problematic from a syntactical point of view. Baumert follows an interpretative course that aligns Phil. 2.1 with texts such as Heb. 13.16, in which κοινωνία is habitually translated as "generosity," even if he prefers the less exuberant "Mitteilung" and sees Phil. 2.1 as a parallel in terms of meaning to, for instance, Clement of Alexandria, *Paed.* 2.12.[147]

The use of συγκοινωνέω in Phil. 4.14 Baumert interprets as "sich verbinden/ befassen,"[148] which makes sense again in terms of the sentence as well as of the entirety of Philippians: the one thing that the Philippians are concerned with is the suffering of Paul, for which Paul seems to try to give an explanation. Rendering the verse in a way that expresses their concern rather than their participation may suit the general tendency of Philippians well.

Probably the most interesting case is the following occurrence of a word of the κοινον-root: [τὴν] κοινωνίαν [τῶν] παθημάτων αὐτοῦ (Phil. 3.10). As Baumert points out,[149] translating κοινωνία as "participation" here creates a tautology with the verb γνῶναι, which itself already indicates knowledge through participation. Therefore, it is preferable to take the noun in a meaning analogous to that of the preceding δύναμις, which is also associated with Christ's gift of something (namely the resurrection); thus, the κοινωνία [τῶν] παθημάτων indicates here the "Mitteilung" of his (i.e. Christ's) sufferings (a consequence of which is sharing them, but this is not what κοινωνία itself indicates here).

By way of conclusion it may maintained here that, following Baumert's considerations, words built upon the κοινον-root do not necessarily indicate communion through participation in Philippians, even if participation in something may well be the consequence of whatever *is* indicated by these

---

147. See Baumert, *Koinonein*, 214–219.
148. See Baumert, *Koinonein*, 65.
149. See Baumert, *Koinonein*, 210–211; see also the considerations of Josef Hainz, *Koinonia: "Kirche" als Gemeinschaft bei Paulus*, BU 16 (Regensburg: Pustet, 1982), 95–98.

various expressions.[150] For example, in Phil. 3.10 the result of the "Mitteilung" of Christ's sufferings is probably that Paul shares them, just as in Phil. 4.14 the Philippians' concern about Paul's travails certainly leads to (strengthened) communion between them and him, just as in Phil. 2.1 κοινωνία πνεύματος is an expression of the communion between Paul and the Philippians; *mutatis mutandis* this also applies to Phil. 1.5, 7 and 4.15.

3.1.6 Paul's Appeal in the Context of Philippi

At this point the question of the addressees of Phil. 1.27–2.18 has to be taken up again in order to contextualize the text further. With regard to its social context, Hellerman's study in particular provides a helpful tool for analyzing its significance. Comparing the contents of the *enkomion* with conventional values of the surrounding Greco-Roman world, especially with its *cursus honorum*,[151] Hellerman comes to the following conclusion: "The presentation ... was intended by Paul ... to encourage persons in the church who possessed some degree of honor or status in the broader social world of the colony to utilize their status, after the analogy of Jesus, in the service of others."[152]

This can only be agreed with partially: in Philippians there are no unambiguous indications that class or honor differences played a role in causing disunity in the community. Apart from the issue of "orthopraxis," raised only later in the letter (Phil. 3), nothing specific is said about the strife's origins, even though Paul had in general no trouble in addressing specific causes, including social ones (see, e.g., Gal. 3.27-28 and 1 Cor. 11.17-34). There could be a hint of singling out the leaders of the Philippian community in the epistolary prescript with its emphasis on the "bishops and deacons." However, all this is fairly speculative and it has to be noted that social or religious class differences play no explicit role of significance in the outline of the problems presented in Phil. 1.27–2.18, nor do office bearers who are identified by their title play a role of importance in the rest of Philippians. Hellerman's insights remain valuable, however, in order to gain a better understanding of the kind of society that Philippians addresses; e.g. paying attention to its *cursus honorum* is very helpful, as through it the controversial character of the letter's ecclesiology and ethics now becomes fully clear: it entails obedience to God's working in the Philippians, which turns them into slaves/servants of God, just like Christ, Paul, and Timothy. This kind of position is at odds with what may be considered the conventional Greco-Roman *cursus honorum* as it has been outlined by

---

150. See also the considerations of Baumert, *Koinonein*, 522–524, though it is hard to see why he separates his section "Zu persönlichen Beziehungen in der Kirche" from his section on "Ekklesiologische Aspekte," as the Church is made up both of its external and its internal relationships.
151. See in general, Hellerman, *Honor*; Hellerman refers to Christ's "cursus honorum" as a "cursus pudorum" ("course of ignominies").
152. Hellerman, *Honor*, 2.

Hellerman. In first-century Philippi, this message would have stood out, given the Philippians' apparent preoccupation with honor.[153]

3.1.7 Concluding Observations

On the basis of the above, the following may be maintained by way of conclusions about the function of Phil. 2.5-11 as an *exemplum* in the context of Phil. 1.27–2.18.

First, as could be shown, the *enkomion* on Christ can well be seen to substantiate Paul's argument in Phil. 1.27–2.18. The call for humility and disregard for one's own interests in Phil. 2.3-4 could well be seen to be supported by Christ's *kenosis* and his resulting humiliation (Phil. 2.6-7). The theme of obedience and faithfulness that comprises the background of Phil. 1.27–2.4 (see esp. Phil. 1.27) is equally substantiated by Christ's obedience until death in Phil. 2.8, while the subject of obedience is taken up again explicitly in Phil. 2.12. Similarly, the theme of arriving at glorification through suffering, as it occurs in the verses leading into the *exemplum* (Phil. 1.28-30), receives an authoritative basis in the *enkomion*, and is then elaborated upon against the background of the (*exemplum* of the) people of Israel in Phil. 2.13-18, where again Paul's suffering is related to that of the Philippians (compare Phil. 1.30 with Phil. 2.17). In sum, the *enkomion* is both a paradigmatic confirmation of Paul's preceding argument and a (paradigmatic) point of departure for that which comes in 2.12-18;[154] like the entirety of Paul's argument, his use of Phil. 2.5-11[155] is finally deliberative and (hence) ecclesiological.[156]

Second, as far as the character of Phil. 2.5-11 as an *exemplum* is concerned, it could be shown, operating on the basis of observations about the false alternative of a "soteriological" and "exemplary" interpretation of Phil. 2.5-11,[157] that it can be understood best as an authoritative and paradigmatic text against the background, not so much of logic, even if this would be a theoretical possibility, but rather of the relationship between the Philippians

---

153. See the general argument of Hellerman, *Honor*; see also above, 2.2.4.

154. Thus, with respect to the function of the hymn one may well follow Dahl, who stated that "In the context of the main hortatory part of the letter (1:12–2:18), the function of the inserted "hymn" is to undergird the preceding and following exhortations by means of a hymnic commemoration of Christ" (Dahl, "Euodia," 11).

155. On which see also the remarks of Dibelius, *Philipper*, 72: "Der Hinweis auf Christus hat zunächst innerhalb dieser Paränese keine andere Bedeutung als der entsprechende Hinweis Rm 15 3 und 15 7. Nur unterscheidet er sich von der ersten Stelle durch seine Ausführlichkeit und von beiden durch seine Selbständigkeit." Kennel, *Frühchristliche Hymnen?*, 221–221, notes the communicative openness of this text, which makes it applicable to other communicative situations.

156. See also the translation that Beare gives of Phil. 2.5: "Let this be the disposition that governs in your common life, as is fitting in Christ Jesus"; F. W. Beare, *A Commentary on the Epistle to the Philippians* (New York: Harper, 1959), 73. See also Ascough, *Associations*, 143.

157. See above, 1.3.3.1; see also 3.1.

Models of Identity in Philippians 107

and Christ. Taking this into account, the precise significance of the *enkomion* as an *exemplum* can be learned from its relationship to its current literary context, and not from reconstructions of its place in the history of religions or from exegeses of the *enkomion* in isolation from its immediate literary context. For interpretations of the *enkomion* that view, for example, the cross of Christ as its centerpiece, this has the consequence that the cross of Christ in Phil. 2.8, which as such is not taken up directly by either Phil. 1.27–2.4 or Phil. 2.12-18, cannot be seen as the soteriological heart of the text, especially not in the broader context of Phil. 2 where the cross hardly plays any role at all, but only appears as part of the overall "career" of Christ and as something that indicates the extent (and radicality) of Christ's obedience to God, which is now the normative pattern for life in Christ, to which the Philippian Christians are asked to conform.[158]

Having thus considered a first *exemplum* in Philippians, it is now possible to turn to the next section of Philippians in which *exempla* may be identified: Phil. 2.19-30.

3.2 Timothy and Epaphroditus as **Exempla***?*

3.2.1 Introduction

It would be an exaggeration to argue that Timothy (Phil. 2.18-24) and Epaphroditus (Phil. 2.25-30) are introduced as explicit paradigms of ideal-typical identity in Philippians.[159] They are mentioned in the letter first of all because Paul deems it necessary to notify the Philippian community about the plans he has concerning the two men.[160] He intends to send Timothy as quickly as circumstances allow (Phil. 2.19a), apparently as a messenger, returning to Paul later on (Phil. 2.19b). Paul also indicates why he wants to send Epaphroditus back to Philippi, probably immediately and possibly carrying the letter.[161] The main reason that Paul gives for this is the rejoicing of the Philippians over his return (Phil. 2.28) and Paul's removal of a burden from his own shoulders (Phil. 2.28). Taking into account that Epaphroditus has been nearly mortally ill recently (Phil. 2.27, 30), it may well be that Paul is sending back a companion who has become more a burden than a help and who is in need of recovery. Throughout this section of Philippians, Paul refers twice to the common frame of reference of the Philippians and himself (i.e. the Lord Jesus, Phil. 2.19, 24)

---

158.   With Hurtado, "Jesus," 125, and Nils A. Dahl, *Jesus in the Memory of the Early Church* (Minneapolis: Augsburg, 1976), 34. See for a similar line of argument, also Gräbe, "'Citizens'," in Van der Watt and Malan (eds.), *Identity*, as well as Ross Wagner, "Working," 264–267.
159.   See, e.g., the cautionary remarks of Reumann, *Philippians*, 439–440.
160.   See, e.g., Reumann, *Philippians*, 442. It could be argued, however, on the basis of Paul's use of παιδεία that the two men appear as model pupils. See Lietaert Peerbolte, "Paul."
161.   See, e.g., Barth, *Brief*, 53.

and underlines in the same verses that he himself intends to come as quickly as possible. Thus, the relationship between Paul and the Philippians is also addressed here and this section of Philippians appears to be much more than just a "dry" bit of information about sending messengers. That there is more at stake than just this is also indicated by the somewhat surprising fact of Timothy's recommendation—he must have been well known and (presumably) well respected by the Philippian community (see Phil. 2.22 and cf. Acts 16), which certainly also applies to Epaphroditus.[162] These observations also support the inquiry into further functions of Phil. 2.19-30 beyond the provision of information. Specifically, and for two reasons especially, it should be seriously considered whether Timothy and Epaphroditus do not also function as *exempla* in this context.

First, the unusual placement of the information about the two men in the letter—generally, one would have expected this much further towards the end of the letter—draws attention to its possible functions. Given that the content and structure of the body of a letter could be fluid and that an author could fairly freely compose it,[163] one should wonder about reasons for the placement of this information at this spot. One option would be to consider the section as functioning as a *digressio* in relation to the preceding argument and appeal,[164] because the presentation of both Timothy and Epaphroditus is characterized by epideictic elements typical of the *digressio* and their description can be seen to restate part of Paul's concerns outlined in Phil. 1.27–2.18.[165] Two voices from the first century illustrate the then-understanding of the *digressio* well. Quintilian (*Or.* 3, *passim*) argues, among other things, that such "digressions" are particularly helpful to develop a main point after it has been stated and argued. Furthermore, he underlines the illustrative nature of digressions, which makes them suitable to move the audience (see *Or.* 9.1). Cicero takes a very similar approach to the *digressio*, largely following the lead of Hermagoras (see *De Inv.* 97). All of this would suit Phil. 2.19-30 well. Alternatively, this section of Philippians could also be seen as fulfilling the function of a further part of the *probatio* of the thesis stated in Phil. 1.27-30.[166] Both of these options would also open up the possibility of Timothy and Epaphroditus being presented as further *exempla* in order to back up Paul's argument, in

---

162. See, e.g., Müller, *Brief*, 122–123, and Reumann, *Philippians*, 440–441. See for this and the following also: Paul A. Holloway, "Alius Paulus: Paul's Promise to Send Timothy at Philippians 2.19-24," *NTS* 54 (2008) 542–556, esp. 543, and R. Alan Culpepper, "Co-workers in Suffering: Philippians 2:19–30,", *RevExp* 77 (1980), 349–58.

163. See, e.g., the argument of Alexander, "Letter-Forms."

164. See, e.g., Watson, "Integration," 419, followed by Williams, *Enemies*, 140–141, but see the caution expressed by Reed, *Discourse*, 228.

165. On which, see Brucker, *Christushymnen*, 321–325. This way of reading differs subtly from that proposed by Briggs Kittredge, *Community*, 87, who views Phil. 2.19-30 as a rhetorically intentionally composed continuation of the "proof" provided in Phil. 2.6-11.

166. See, e.g., Witherington, *Friendship*, 75–76; the material difference between the two options seems to be limited.

addition, of course, to the function of Phil. 2.19-30 as providing practical information.[167]

Second, the context in which the information about Timothy and Epaphroditus appears is dominated by *exempla*; the argument using the Christ *enkomion* has just preceded this and Paul's argument using a *periautological exemplum* is about to come in Phil. 3. This fact alone already invites one to consider reading the characterizations of Paul's two companions along similar lines.

3.2.2 Timothy

3.2.2.1 Elements of Identity

Paul recommends Timothy to the Philippians by characterizing him in a number of ways, especially in verses 20-22.[168] Central to his identity is that he is being sent to the Philippians as a messenger, albeit not immediately (see Phil. 2.19, 23).[169] In this way, he becomes a (physical) tie between Paul and the Philippians. Paul's aim in sending him, however, is also to be reassured about the Philippians. As has become clear from the contents of the letter so far, Paul is worried about this community,[170] and, even though he would like to visit them (verse 24), he is not in the position to come himself in the foreseeable future. Having said this, it is now possible to consider in somewhat more detail the description of Timothy in Phil. 2.19-24, which, as was already noted, is all the more striking because it introduces someone to the Philippians whom they should really know already (if the account of Acts 16 is to be trusted—apart from that, Phil. 1.1 also suggests a position of prominence for Timothy).

First, Timothy's attitude towards the Philippians is described: he will be genuinely concerned about them and not only about his own interests, as all others are (Phil. 2.20-21, and compare 1.27 and 2.2).[171] From the beginning of the introduction of Timothy onwards, Paul also emphasizes Timothy's trustworthiness and sincerity as well as his preciousness (see Phil. 2.20). This is probably not meant to pass a negative judgment on others (at least not on the Philippians; see Phil. 1.17), but rather to praise Timothy hyperbolically.[172] The earlier reference to Paul and Timothy as two

---

167. See, e.g., Williams, *Enemies*, 143.
168. See, e.g., Dibelius, *Philipper*, 84, and Schenk, *Philipperbriefe*, 230–232. On Paul's policies of recommendation in their Greco-Roman context in general, see, e.g., Efrain Agosto, "Paul and Commendation," in Sampley (ed.), *Paul*, 101–133.
169. See, e.g., Barth, *Brief*, 52: Paul wishes only to part with Timothy as soon as he knows what his own situation amounts to, this presumably both for the benefit of Timothy's presence as well as with an eye to the information that Timothy can convey to the Philippians.
170. See, e.g., Barth, *Brief*, 52.
171. See for emphasis on the singular character of this recommendation, Müller, *Brief*, 123–124.
172. See, e.g., Barth, *Brief*, 52–53.

(apparently) coequal servants of God in Phil. 1.1 may well have paved the way for this recommendation.[173] By stressing that he gives the best he has, which is also the best for the Philippians (verse 20), Paul again emphasizes his personal and friendly ties with the Philippian community and presents Timothy as favorably as possible. Even at this point, much is to be said for Bloomquist's observation that, as Paul's *viva vox* and *vivum exemplum*, Timothy can be regarded as "Paul's surrogate,"[174] a living letter of sorts.

Second, from Phil. 2.21 onwards, which itself presents Timothy in harsh contrast with "all others" around Paul (see Phil. 1.17), the focus is not primarily on Timothy as a tie between the Philippians and Paul, but rather on the relationship of Timothy to Paul, while elaborating on Timothy's qualities (Phil. 2.22). In this part of the description, two elements can be singled out. First, Paul underlines Timothy's relationship to him as that of a son to a father (Phil. 2.22), which indicates both the closeness of their association, as well as Timothy's subordination to Paul;[175] as such it presents a further differentiation compared to Phil. 1.1 where Paul and Timothy appear on a par. Second, Timothy's service to Paul is further characterized by together serving the gospel (Phil. 2.22), which brings out the common orientation of Paul and his companion. Having outlined this, Phil. 2.23 paraphrases what has gone before by pointing out emphatically that *this one* (τοῦτον μὲν οὖν) is the one Paul hopes to be able to send to Philippi.

3.2.2.2 The Paradigmatic Quality of Timothy
Having surveyed the characterization of Timothy, it may be asked now whether, and, if so, how, elements of it can plausibly be considered to fulfill a paradigmatic function, keeping in mind especially what has preceded Phil. 2.19-24, namely Phil. 1.27–2.18.

First, Paul's recommendation of Timothy as someone who is of one mind with Paul (ἰσόψυχος, Phil. 2.20) should be mentioned;[176] it may well recall Paul's appeal to the Philippians to be of one mind, using a very similar term (πληρώσατέ μου τὴν χαρὰν ἵνα τὸ αὐτὸ φρονῆτε, τὴν αὐτὴν ἀγάπην ἔχοντες, σύμψυχοι, τὸ ἓν φρονοῦντες, Phil. 2.2).[177] For this reason, Timothy may be seen as representing (*vis-à-vis* Paul) the attitude that Paul longs to see among the Philippians.

---

173. See, e.g., Byron, *Metaphors*, 174: This is indeed the only occurrence of such equality between Paul and a co-author of a letter among the letters generally assumed to be authentically Pauline. See further, only in Col. 1.13, 4.7.
174. Holloway, *Consolation*, 126; see also, idem, "*Alius Paulus*." For a similar role of Timothy, see, e.g., 1 Cor. 4.17, 16.10; 1 Thess. 3.2, 6; see, e.g., Barth, *Brief*, 52.
175. Peter Balla, *The Child–Parent Relationship in the New Testament and its Environment*, WUNT 1.155 (Tübingen: Mohr Siebeck, 2003), 63–64, 86–92, 117–130 (on the fifth commandment). See further, esp., also, Gerber, *Paulus*, 208.
176. For this and the following, see also, e.g., Brucker, *Christushymnen*, 322–323, as well as Engberg-Pedersen, *Paul*, 129.
177. See Byron, *Metaphors*, 174.

Second, Timothy is presented as someone who has a selfless attitude; he will be truly concerned about the Philippians' welfare (Phil. 2.20).[178] Together with the subsequent verse 21, Paul can here be taken to praise Timothy as an embodiment of what he has presented as ideals of life in the Philippian community in Phil. 1.27–2.4, especially in Phil. 2.3: μηδὲν κατ' ἐριθείαν μηδὲ κατὰ κενοδοξίαν ἀλλὰ τῇ ταπεινοφροσύνῃ ἀλλήλους ἡγούμενοι ὑπερέχοντας ἑαυτῶν.[179]

Third, in Phil. 2.22, while noting that the Philippians know Timothy's worth, Paul not only outlines the relationship between himself and Timothy as that of a father and a(n obedient) son, but he also explicitly presents Timothy again in terms of servanthood (ἐδούλευσεν), which links the verses back both to Phil. 1.1, strengthening Timothy's identity as a(n obedient) slave like Paul, and, more importantly, to Phil. 2.7, where Christ is presented as μορφὴν δούλου λαβών.

Therefore, even if the recommendation of Timothy to the Philippian community might seem the most important issue in Phil. 2.19-24 at first sight,[180] Paul chooses to make this recommendation using a vocabulary that echoes other parts of Philippians. This invites one to view Paul's laudatory presentation of Timothy as not only of Timothy as such, but also of Timothy as an *exemplum* of identity "in Christ," given that Timothy embodies aspects of what Paul deems to be of importance for the Philippians: standing united and keeping the welfare of other members of the community in mind. Taking into account that Paul also indicates that he wishes to be reassured about the Philippians, the presentation of Timothy may well be geared towards assuring that Timothy will indeed have positive news for Paul upon his return, both by presenting Timothy as a model for the Philippians' attitude, and by describing him in a way that underscores the value the Philippians have for Paul, thus increasing the likelihood of a positive response by the Philippians to Paul's concerns and calls.[181] When asking the question of whether Timothy is here intentionally and explicitly presented as an *exemplum*, the answer has to be cautious, given that introductions or conclusions, such as those in Phil. 2.5, 12, or direct statements about something being an *exemplum* or an analogy (see Phil. 1.30, 3.17, 4.9), are lacking. However, it certainly seems to be the case that aspects of Paul's presentation of Timothy take on a paradigmatic quality due to the context in which they appear, especially because of what has gone before in Phil. 1.27–2.18.[182] In any case, themes that

---

178. Furthermore, Phil. 2.20b-21 may also be seen as echoing Phil. 1.15, reflecting Paul's situation in prison.
179. See Holloway, *Consolation*, 127, and Hooker, "Philippians," 390.
180. See, e.g., Dibelius, *Philipper*, 65; Gnilka, *Philipperbrief*, 157; Jean-François Collange, *L'épître de Saint Paul aux Philippiens*, CNT 10a (Neuchâtel: Delachaux et Niestlé, 1973), 103; Holloway, *Consolation*, 127.
181. See Müller, *Brief*, 123.
182. See, e.g., Byron, *Metaphors*, 174.

were of particular importance to Paul in the previous section are echoed in Phil. 2.19-24 in such a way that it is possible to regard it as (part of) a *digressio* that in epideictic language not only provides information about and an introduction for Timothy, but also gives him a paradigmatic quality.

3.2.3 Epaphroditus

3.2.3.1 Elements of Identity

Having noted the probable reasons for the note on Epaphroditus above,[183] here some elements of his recommendation and characterization by Paul can be considered further. Four elements of his characterization appear already in Phil. 2.25: Epaphroditus is ἀδελφός, συνεργός, and συστρατιώτης to Paul, ἀπόστολος to the Philippians and λειτουργός τῆς χρείας μου to Paul. This terminology is worth some further consideration.

First, it is noticeable that, like Timothy, Epaphroditus is characterized both in relation to Paul and in relation to the Philippians, though with a notable emphasis on the former. Epaphroditus is called the "brother," "co-worker," and "fellow soldier" of Paul first, before he is, with these qualities, called an "apostle" to the Philippians.

Second, one of the reasons given by Paul for his returning of Epaphroditus consists of Epaphroditus' longing for the Philippians (Phil. 2.26). In this context, Epaphroditus' concern for the Philippians is illustrated by the remark about Epaphroditus' distress over the Philippians' knowledge of his illness and their ensuing worries. Expressions of longing for those who are far away are an epistolary commonplace;[184] however, they are also a means of underlining the good relations of Epaphroditus with the (other) Philippians. The remark about Epaphroditus' illness leads to a brief elaboration on it, in which Paul notes that Epaphroditus nearly died because of it (Phil. 2.27), though due to God's mercy he did not. Now, Epaphroditus is being sent home, possibly for further recovery, so that the Philippians can rejoice about him and Paul will not have to worry about him (Phil. 2.28; see also, however, Epaphroditus' longing for the Philippians in Phil. 2.26).[185]

Third, after the account of Epaphroditus' illness follows a recommendation of him,[186] as Paul calls upon the Philippians to receive him joyfully in the Lord

---

183. See above, 3.2.1.
184. See, e.g., White, *Light*, 202, and Klauck, *Briefliteratur*, 45–46, 50.
185. This speaks against suggestions such as that made by Culpepper, "Co-Workers," 355–356, that Epaphroditus was being sent home as a "respected leader in the church who could help the church to ward off the threats of misguided perfectionism and legalism" (Williams, *Enemies*, 219).
186. See, e.g., Schenk, *Philipperbriefe*, 239–240. Paul seems to feel the need to justify or rehabilitate Epaphroditus in some way. For a different view, see Barth, *Brief*, 54.

and to honor people like him. The reason for this is, as becomes clear only now, that Epaphroditus' illness was διὰ τὸ ἔργον Χριστοῦ. For Paul, this means that Epaphroditus supported Paul in ways that the other Philippians could not (Phil. 2.30).

3.2.3.2 The Paradigmatic Significance of Epaphroditus
With the same caveats in mind as for Timothy in terms of the presentation of Epaphroditus as an *exemplum*, here possible paradigmatic aspects of Paul's presentation of Epaphroditus should be considered.

First, the description of Epaphroditus in Phil. 2.25 as brother, co-worker and fellow soldier,[187] as apostle to the Philippians, and as their minister to Paul,[188] emphasizes unity and communion, both between Paul and Epaphroditus and between Paul and the Philippians through the ministry of Epaphroditus, while the feelings of Epaphroditus towards the Philippians are emphasized in verse 26. The latter makes Epaphroditus similar to Paul in sentiment and attitude towards the Philippians (see Phil. 1.8), which also applies to the rest of the description of Epaphroditus, who appears to be on the one hand a representative of the Philippians to Paul and, like Timothy (see Phil. 2.22), a representative of Paul to the Philippians on the other. Furthermore, in verse 28, Paul also indicates why he sends back Epaphroditus, namely in order for the Philippians to rejoice at seeing him again. While these verses doubtless, and probably primarily, serve to underline the ties between the three parties involved, thus preparing the way for Paul's appeal to the Philippians to warmly welcome Epaphroditus (verse 29), they also paint a picture of unity and strong relationships, which can be seen as an illustration of the support for Paul's appeals for unity in Phil. 1.27–2.4.

Second, when reading the description of Epaphroditus with the Christ *enkomion* in mind, it is striking that Epaphroditus and Christ share the movement from death to life, be it that Christ did indeed die and Epaphroditus did not. With regard to this point, it should be underlined that the language that Paul uses to describe Epaphroditus' near-death in Phil. 2.30 is similar to the language used for Christ's obedience until death in Phil. 2.8, using a formulation that does not otherwise occur in the New Testament (and otherwise only a few times in 2–4 Macc.).[189] The difference between Christ's death and

---

187. A term that may well have spoken to the Philippians, given Philippi's background as a military colony.
188. Λειτουργός has here a "non-cultic" meaning (e.g. Reumann, *Philippians*, 443–444) only if cult is understood as liturgy *sensu stricto*; as a "public servant" (so Reumann, ibid.) of the commonwealth of Christ, Epaphroditus does very much indeed embark on a "liturgical" ministry here. It is likely that Epaphroditus brought the gift of the Philippians to Paul and served him in other ways as well; see, e.g., Barth, *Brief*, 53.
189. See Byron, *Metaphors*, 175. The similar construction with μέχρι both in Phil. 2.8 and 2.30 may well point in this direction as well. It is indeed striking that the string μέχρι θανάτου occurs exceptionally frequently within the martyriological contexts of 2 Macc. 13.14; 3 Macc. 7.16; and 4

Epaphroditus' near-death may well be accounted for in terms of the place at which Epaphroditus stands in his incorporation into the "career" of Christ: Christ has completed the "course" already, whereas Epaphroditus, like the Philippians to whom he is being sent, and like Paul who sends him, is yet at a different stage: he is being incorporated into the suffering of Christ (Phil. 3.10), but not yet into his death and resurrection. In this way, Epaphroditus embodies a Christ-like identity. In fact, besides being Paul's brother, co-worker, and fellow soldier, Epaphroditus is also like Paul in terms of his suffering for Christ, an aspect of being in Christ that he seems to have embraced, unlike the Philippians (see also Phil. 2.30). The fact that Epaphroditus does not show a one-to-one agreement with Christ (e.g. divine provenance, dying completely, and being glorified), as for example Dodd notes in his objections to viewing Epaphroditus as an *exemplum Christi*,[190] does not have to be a problem in the light of first-century conventions about the use and functioning of *exempla*. In the light of said conventions, one may also note that Epaphroditus (as well as Timothy and to a lesser extent also Paul), as a living person who is directly in touch with the Philippians, provides a directly accessible *exemplum*.

Third, it should be noted that the formulation of the recommendation of Epaphroditus in verse 29 transcends his individual case and turns him into an example of a whole class of people who should be received by the Philippians as Epaphroditus should, as he has risked his life διὰ τὸ ἔργον Χριστοῦ (Phil. 2.30). Whether it is also an implicit self-recommendation of Paul remains to be seen, but it is certain that Epaphroditus is directly presented as an example of a particular kind of people.

Therefore, Paul's announcement of Epaphroditus' upcoming return and his recommendation of him may also be regarded as fulfilling a paradigmatic function in Philippians. Specifically, Epaphroditus appears as someone who is an embodiment of the fellowship between Paul and the Philippians—even more so if he is indeed the carrier of the letter—and may as such be reminiscent of Paul's injunctions to stand together in the faith. Furthermore, as Paul's brother, co-worker, fellow soldier, and his emissary to the Philippians, and especially as someone who, like Paul and in accordance with the pattern provided by Christ in Phil. 2.5-11, has suffered and come close to death because of this,

---

Macc. 5.37, 6.21, 7.8, 16, 13.1, 27, 15.10, 16.1, 17.7, 10. See Holloway, *Consolation*, 129; O'Brien, "Gospel," 278; Schenk, *Philipperbriefe*, 239–240. Dodd, *Paul's Paradigmatic "I"*, 190, disagrees in as far as the claim is concerned that Epaphroditus is presented as an example because of the description of his near-death. Specifically, Dodd rejects the notion that there is anything hortatory about Epaphroditus; nevertheless, the link with Christ's fate through the repeated use of μέχρι θανάτου certainly shows Epaphroditus in a favorable light, which, even if it is not an explicitly hortatory *exemplum*, certainly presents him as someone who embodies existence "in Christ" in an authentic way (with predictable hortatory consequences). Dodd agrees with that (see *op. cit.*, 190); see also Kim, "'Imitators'," 161–162.

190. Dodd, *Paul's Paradigmatic "I"*, 190.
191. See above, 2.2.2.

Epaphroditus also exemplifies the sort of identity in Christ that Paul wishes to draw the Philippians to and in terms of which he interprets his own life as well (see Phil. 1 and 3). Furthermore, because of his relationship to the Philippians and the fact that he will actually go to them, Epaphroditus constitutes a directly accessible *exemplum* of the way of life that Paul wishes to convince the Philippians of—even more so than Christ, Paul, and Timothy, who, for the time being, are not there yet.

3.2.4 Timothy and Epaphroditus as Paradigms: Their Relationship to the Philippians

When reflecting on the above considerations, the following may be concluded. The notes on Timothy and Epaphroditus appear both as pieces of information Paul had to convey anyway, even if one would have expected them closer to the end of his letter,[191] and as examples that support Paul's argument. They can function so well in this way because Paul not only mentions both men, but also describes them in the recommendations that he gives them, in which elements occur that tie Epaphroditus and Timothy to Paul's argument in Phil. 1.27–2.18 and in particular also to the *exemplum* of Christ in 2.5-11. Thus, the sections about Timothy and Epaphroditus have a triple role: conveying information, recommending the two men, and providing support for what has been said before by Paul. Hence, Paul's two co-workers appear as living embodiments of the values that Paul cherishes and recommends, which suits the demand from rhetorical theory that *exempla* should be as close to the audience as possible. While Paul's two companions are certainly less authoritative *exempla* than Christ in Phil. 2 (or probably Paul in Phil. 3), given that neither of them is part of the foundational story of the Philippians (as is Christ) and that only Timothy can be considered as one of the *maiores* of the Philippians community, provided that the account in Acts 16 is correct in noting Timothy's involvement in the founding of the community, they are much more accessible *exempla*, given that both Christ and Paul are not in Philippi (at least not in the sense required to establish an *exemplum* in the way Epaphroditus and Timothy can upon their respective arrivals).[192]

---

192. As Holloway (*Consolation*, 129) suggested that, as an *exemplum*, Timothy is mainly associated with Paul's exhortation to behave in ways that enable and sustain communion, and Epaphroditus with Paul's exhortation to obedience, this needs to be considered here as well. In the end, Hollaway's proposal seems to be unconvincing. There are two principal reasons for this. First, Timothy is also associated with obedience (as a son to a father); second, Epaphroditus is presented as someone who enables and even embodies communion between Paul and the Philippians. Paul's different ways of phrasing the associations between himself and Timothy (father–son in Phil. 2.22, as well as fellow slaves in Phil. 1.1) and himself and Epaphroditus ("brother," "coworker," "fellow soldier," all in Phil. 2.25) may indicate more subordination in the case of Timothy than in the case of Epaphroditus (see Briggs Kittredge, *Community*, 88).

Having so far discussed the merits of the presentations of Timothy and Epaphroditus on their own, it is useful at this point to move beyond the pericopes that mention them explicitly and to draw attention to Paul's exhortation in Phil. 3.17: συμμιμηταί μου γίνεσθε, ἀδελφοί, καὶ σκοπεῖτε τοὺς οὕτω περιπατοῦντας καθὼς ἔχετε τύπον ἡμᾶς. Even though one might suspect that Paul's statement συμμιμηταί μου γίνεσθε, refers principally to the *imitatio Pauli* and not to the imitation of Paul, Timothy, and Epaphroditus, the final part of this call, καὶ σκοπεῖτε τοὺς οὕτω περιπατοῦντας καθὼς ἔχετε τύπον ἡμᾶς, explicitly refers to a larger number of persons whom the Philippians possess as types, in other words, examples.[193] Possibly, Paul oscillates between a plurality of examples and the example that he himself constitutes, as both in the larger biographical sections and in Phil. 4.9 he refers only to himself as an example (see 1.30, as well as 3.2ff.). Another option is that Paul uses a *pluralis modestiae* of sorts. Should this not be the case, then it is likely that Timothy and Epaphroditus are at least part of the larger group of people that Paul has in view in Phil. 3.17, or are even the entire group of examples that Paul has in mind.

At this point, Bittasi's thesis about the central position (and function) of Phil. 2.19-30 can be evaluated further as well. Given that it has become clear that Timothy and Epaphroditus are not introduced as *exempla* explicitly, and that their description only appears as paradigmatic because of the preceding Christ *enkomion*, on which they therefore depend, as well as the shaky foundation of the assumption that Philippians is constructed as a large chiasm around Phil. 2.19-30, Bittasi's thesis cannot be accepted. Rather, Timothy and Epaphroditus should be seen as (also) constituting exhortative *exempla* for what has preceded, recapitulating and restating Paul's earlier substantiation of his argument through fresh and different *exempla*. In other words: they have supporting, not main roles.

Finally, here a point that has already been made repeatedly should be taken up once more, given that Dodd in his discussion of Paul, Timothy, and Epaphroditus as "godly examples to the Philippians of how to live the gospel worthily"[194] drives a wedge between these three men and Christ by arguing that as "Paul, his co-workers and the Philippians are to live worthily of the gospel and even suffer for it, the depiction of Christ in Phil. 2.6-11 *is* the very gospel of which the Philippians are to live worthily."[195] For Dodd, this constitutes a "significant difference between their life-patterns."[196] Still, while Paul and other believers, such as Timothy and Epaphroditus, probably do not set up examples equal to Christ, it will be hard to deny that they have exemplary character, because they pursue the same course that Christ pursued (and completed), which is the form of being in Christ. Being "in Christ," it seems, is an embodied affair in Philippians, which involves pursuing the same "career" as Christ. The

---

193. See Byron, *Metaphors*, 176.
194. Dodd, *Paul's Paradigmatic "I"*, 190. See also the concise observations of Ware, *Paul*, 232.
195. Dodd, *Paul's Paradigmatic "I"*, 190–191.
196. Dodd, *Paul's Paradigmatic "I"*, 190.

difference between Christ and the other examples in Philippians may be smaller than Dodd thinks it is.

At this point, it may also be restated briefly that, from a rhetorical point of view, this part of Philippians in its presentation of both Timothy and Epaphroditus has a double function: (1) announcing the advent of the two men and recommending them, and (2) backing up Paul's argument in the way of a *digressio*.[197] A *digressio* exemplifies what has been said before by briefly dwelling on a related subject, which may well be the case in Phil. 2.19-30. Its framing by exhortations to rejoice (Phil. 2.18, 3.1) might also support an interpretation that gives Phil. 2.19-30 a function of its own within the letter.

Having thus considered the second set of *exempla* in Philippians, it is now possible to turn to Phil. 3 and Paul's self-presentation as an *exemplum*.

3.3 The Paradigm of "Paul in Christ" (Phil. 3.1–4.1)

3.3.1 Introduction

Phil. 3.1–4.1 is clearly marked off from the preceding pericope on Epaphroditus by the introductory τὸ λοιπόν.[198] At the other end of the pericope, Phil. 4.1 is a transitory verse, which is connected to both what has preceded and what comes next.[199] Phil. 3.1-21 itself may be structured as follows. Phil. 3.1 is an introductory verse, commenting upon Paul's writing, followed by the "header" of what follows, or rather, the attitude that Paul is going to deal with in Phil. 3.3-21: Βλέπετε τοὺς κύνας, βλέπετε τοὺς κακοὺς ἐργάτας, βλέπετε τὴν κατατομήν (Phil. 3.2).[200] Subsequently, Phil. 3.3 constitutes Paul's core statement *vis-à-vis* the group referred to as κύνες. From Phil. 3.4 onwards, Paul presents himself as the embodiment of the truth of Phil. 3.3, first by outlining his autobiography and his present status (Phil. 3.4-14), and then by calling upon the Philippians to follow this example (Phil. 3.15-17), in order that they may be saved (Phil. 3.20-21). In between he uses the example of his opponents as those who are on their way to their own destruction (Phil. 3.18-19). The use of *exempla*, both positive and negative in this text, seems to be obvious. Especially, Paul's use of himself as an example stands out. As this was not entirely unproblematic, some attention will have to be paid to the background of this rhetorical ploy, before proceeding to an analysis of Phil. 3.1-21.

---

197. See also, e.g., Brucker, *Christushymnen*, 321: "Exkurs." The same will be argued below for Phil. 3.1-21.
198. See, e.g., Strecker, *Heidenapostel*, 79–81.
199. See, e.g., Strecker, *Heidenapostel*, 79: Ὥστε ... οὕτως refers back to what had been said in Phil. 3 (see, e.g., Schenk, *Philipperbriefe*, 256, and Gnilka, *Philipperbrief*, 219; for a different view, see, for example, Lohmeyer, *Philipperbrief*, 163), the two imperatives in Phil. 3.1 (χαίρετε ἐν κυρίῳ) and 4.1 (στήκετε ἐν κυρίῳ) together with the address ἀδελφοί μου form an *inclusio* (see, e.g., Schenk, *Philipperbriefe*, 334), and τὸ λοιπόν (Phil. 3.1) is connected with the retrospective ὥστε in Phil. 4.1.
200. On the identity of the dogs, see above, 2.3.2.3.

3.3.2 Setting an Example Oneself: Periautologia

Self-praise, or, more pejoratively, boasting, constituted a not-insignificant problem for ancient rhetoric, just as it does for (contemporary and early) exegesis of the Pauline epistles, as the apostle seems to have a considerable amount of self-esteem at his disposal and repeatedly uses his own experiences and his own achievements as a rhetorical trump. Reactions to this have been varied.[201] Here, the issue will be approached from the contemporary discourse on so-called *periautologia*, in other words, on self-praise.[202] This approach enables one to shed light both on the possible rhetorical function that Paul's self-praise might have,[203] and on its appreciation by his audience/intended readership. From the start it is sensible to be open to a positive evaluation of this self-praise, as it is necessary to ask: why would Paul repeatedly opt for a rhetorical strategy which would qualify him as an inflated boaster,[204] and gain him anything but the sympathy and even less the agreement of those he sought to convince?[205]

---

201. See, e.g., the overview provided by Mitchell, *Paul*, 53–60, as well as the earlier contribution by Carl R. Holladay, "1 Corinthians 13: Paul as Apostolic Paradigm," in David L. Balch, Everett Ferguson, and Wayne A. Meeks (eds.), *Greeks, Romans, and Christians* (FS Abraham J. Malherbe; Minneapolis: Fortress, 1990), 80–98, esp. 85–88, with reference to Plutarch, Epictetus, and Seneca. Krister Stendahl, *The Final Account: Paul's Letter to the Romans* (Minneapolis: Fortress, 1995), 3, offers an outspoken evaluation: "Paul was arrogant. But he was so blatantly arrogant that one can somehow cope with it. He was always the greatest: the greatest of sinners, the greatest of apostles, the greatest when it came to speaking in tongues, the greatest at having been persecuted. That is because he wasn't married. Or perhaps that is *why* he wasn't married. Nobody could stand him – but he was great, and that makes his battle with his weakness so moving on quite a personal level." With a sense for understatement Williams, *Enemies*, 166, paraphrases Terrence Callan's findings ("Competition and Boasting: Towards a Psychological Portrait of Paul," *ST* 40 [1986], 137–156) by stating that "Paul was quite a competitor."

202. For an overview of the function of autobiography in general, see George Lyons, *Pauline Autobiography: Toward a New Understanding*, SBL.MS 73 (Atlanta: Scholars Press, 1985), 1–69. Schenk, *Philipperbriefe*, 274–276, refers to the self-recommendation of a teacher of wisdom; this background, however, seems to be much less relevant for a study of the communication between Paul and the (Roman, not Jewish) Philippians than the background that is considered here.

203. These texts can also be seen as Paul's *enkomia* on himself. For this form-critical classification, see, e.g., Bianchini, *L'Elegio*, 42, drawing on the work of Brucker, *Christushymnen*, 334–335, and George A. Kennedy, *New Testament Interpretation through Rhetorical Criticism* (Chapel Hill: University of North Carolina Press, 1984), 73–74.

204. A realistic possibility, given the following sentiments of Plutarch, *De laude ipsius* (= *Mor.*) 540A: "For just as those who can find no other food are compelled to feed unnaturally on their own persons, and this is the extremity of famine, so when those who hunger for praise cannot find others to praise them, they give the appearance of seeking sustenance and succour for their vainglorious appetite from themselves, a graceless spectacle" (*Mor.* 540A).

205. The recent suggestion of Standhartinger, "'Join'," that Phil. 3.1-21 represents parts of Paul's testamentary statement (either conceived as a speech or as a letter), "smuggled out of prison" (431) and subsequently integrated into what is now the canonical Philippians, has the advantage that it links Phil. 3 more closely to Hellenistic Judaism, but also the major disadvantage that it not only introduces many additional hypotheses, but also seems to be superfluous when considering Phil. 3 in the light of the possibilities that Hellenistic rhetoric offered in general.

Not too long ago, Mitchell provided a history of research on the relationship of Paul's boasting with Hellenistic rhetorical theory,[206] beginning with Windisch's 1924 commentary on 2 Corinthians.[207] Windisch's positive judgment on Paul's command of the limits that contemporary rhetorical customs set to self-praise was followed by others, for example by Betz, who stated the following: "Paulus hält sich strikt an die Vorschriften, wie sie die Rhetorik für die 'περιαυτολογία' aufgestellt hat."[208] Mitchell also moved beyond comparing Plutarch (and other Hellenistic authors)[209] and Paul by drawing on the early Christian interpretation of Paul. In doing this, she convincingly shows two things. First, the rules applying to περιαυτολογία remained remarkably stable.[210] Second, the apostle to the Gentiles remains, according to these authors, within the boundaries set by these rules. Indeed, the fit is so close that one would be tempted to think that Plutarch's *De laude ipsius* was the model on which Paul constructed his argument in Phil. 3.[211] As Betz presents it, Plutarch argues that self-praise may be used in the following instances:

a. if self-glorification is not done for personal glory or pleasure, but because the moment or circumstances demand the person to speak about himself; b. if self-praise consists of listing achievements and good deeds which may inspire others to achieve similar good deeds; c. if self-praise does not lead to reward for past achievement, but to new opportunities for further good achievements; d. if self-praise creates a climate of confidence in which useful things can be done easily. (See *Mor.* 539E–F)[212]

In *Mor.* 540C–534A, Plutarch continues to outline more specifically the circumstances that demand one to speak about oneself, such as when clearing one's name. Again, Betz's presentation is helpful, in particular by listing the following situations that legitimate self-praise:[213]

a. when one clears one's good name against a charge
b. when the unfortunate praises him
c. when it is part of παρρησία in a case of affront

206. Margaret M. Mitchell, "A Patristic Perspective on Pauline περιαυτολογία," *NTS* 46 (2001), 354–371. See further, also, e.g., Bianchini, *L'Elegio*, 58–61.
207. See Hans Windisch, *Der zweite Korintherbrief*, KEK (ed. Georg Strecker; Göttingen: Vandenhoeck & Ruprecht, ⁹1970 [1924]), esp. his judgment on the matter (in view of 2 Cor. 11–12) on p. 345: "Paulus teilt durchaus die Anschauungen Plutarchs und des Griechentums, in dessen Namen Plutarch spricht." See also Mitchell, "Perspective," 355.
208. Betz, *Apostel*, 75: "Paul strictly keeps to the rules with regard to περιαυτολογία as they had been established by the rhetorical tradition" (author's translation). See also Mitchell, "Perspective," 355.
209. See the text from Plutarch given above (1.4.2.5). See also Mitchell, "Perspective," 358–363.
210. Mitchell, "Perspective," 358: "In speaking about Paul's self-praise Chrysostom employs a cultural stock of terms and *topoi* about boasting which are completely familiar from Plutarch."
211. See for the following, esp. Hans Dieter Betz, "De laude ipsius," in idem (ed.), *Plutarch's Ethical Writings and Early Christian Literature*, SCHNT 4 (Leiden: Brill, 1978), 367–393.
212. Betz, "Laude," 369.
213. See the summary offered by Betz, "Laude," 370.

d. when a defendant employs the tactic of reversing the charges against him and calling them triumphs instead
e. when the device of antithesis is used, i.e., when one implicitly admits past action, but shows the opposite of what one has done would have been shameful
f. if the self-praise is blended with praise of the audience
g. when one praises others whose aims and deeds are the same as one's own
h. when in praising oneself not everything is claimed but part of the success is attributed to 'chance' or 'god.'

Furthermore, Plutarch outlines how noting imperfections on the part of the speaker may help the latter to avoid appearing as perfect (*Mor.* 534F–544C); how hardships and costs on the part of the speaker may be underlined as a way of mitigating self-praise's offensiveness (*Mor.* 544C–D); and how a speaker may also use self-praise to indicate that a challenge can be mastered (*Mor.* 544E). That *periautological exempla* would often have an exhortative character, especially when used in a deliberative argument, is natural and was already indicated by the quotation from Plutarch's *Moralia* given earlier.[214]

To these observations about self-praise may be added that in the rhetorical mode of deliberation, examples, specifically the example of the *rhetor* himself, were of paramount importance and would have suited the audience's expectations.[215] This also applies to letter writers and their self-presentation, as is indicated, for example, by Paul's near-contemporary Seneca in his *Epistolum ad Lucillum* 106.[216] The presentation of a speaker him- or herself as an example should be seen in the broader context of authoritative examples, as the same rules seem to apply: only an orator that fulfilled particular criteria (i.e. possessed an appropriate *ethos*) could present himself effectively as an example to be followed (or not).[217]

In this context, it should also be maintained that it is possible to find in Philippians all the elements that made up the positive "moral character" (ἦθος) that was necessary to evoke confidence in a speaker (or writer) that s/he needed in order to be able to be heard sympathetically.[218] As Marshall has it:

> Ethos is the relationship built up within the speech between the rhetor and the auditor which induces the auditor to believe the person speaking. Such a relationship is built up by means of identification between the rhetor and auditor, through participation in the world that exists between them. The persuasive power of this relationship increases as certainty about the subject matter decreases.[219]

---

214. See above, 1.4.2.5. Further examples can be found in, e.g., Malherbe, *Exhortation*, 135–136.
215. See, e.g., Williams, *Enemies*, 169, and Witherington, *Friendship*, 56.
216. For Stowers, "Friends," 108, even the "classic case."
217. See, e.g., Williams, *Enemies*, 103–104.
218. See esp. Aristotle, *Rhet.* 1.2:3–4; Cicero, *De Or.* 2.42:84; Quintilian, *Inst.* 3.8:48; and the discussion by John W. Marshall, "Paul's Ethical Appeal in Philippians," in Porter and Olbricht (eds.), *Rhetoric*, 357–374, esp. 358–359.
219. Marshall, "Appeal," 360, as well as Witherington, *Friendship*, 35–36.

As will become clear from the discussion of *exempla* in this study, and as Marshall already indicated, Paul can be seen as using a double set of identifications (with God/Christ and with the Philippians) in order to establish a relationship of confidence in Philippians, which provides the basis for his argument.[220] If one places Philippians in this category, this also means to say that the letter is a tool for the reaffirming, strengthening, and navigating and defining of the ties between Paul and the Philippians.[221]

Finally, as the above considerations indicate, the main condition for a legitimate use of boasting/self-praise was a certain necessity. In Phil. 3, it is possible to see such a situation: Paul's teaching is endangered (Phil. 3.2-3), his reputation is threatened because of this and his simultaneous imprisonment, and so is (in his view) the salvation of the Philippians (see Phil. 3.18-21).[222] Precisely the self-defense of the speaker and the benefit of the audience were regarded as two valid reasons to use the "paradigmatic I."

3.4 The Exempla *and their Aims in Phil. 3*

3.4.1 The Starting Point: "Dogs" in Philippi

As becomes clear from Phil. 3.2, the issue at stake in Phil. 3.2-21 is the fact that the early Christian community in Philippi is threatened by teachings that differ from Paul's, probably coming from outside missionaries, and that constitute a considerable threat to both the "orthodoxy" and the "orthopraxis" of the community (naturally from Paul's view) and also to Paul's relationship to this community (and probably vice versa). Even though this is hard to deduce from the initial statement in Phil. 3.2, it may well be that the alternative teaching threatening the community in Philippi is aimed directly at Paul as well,[223] undermining his reputation and authority, which would agree with his choice of *periautologia* in order to defend himself, or to convince the Philippians to adhere to the faith they received through him.[224] The (probable) identity of Paul's opponents in this section has already been discussed above; in other words, a kind of "radically Jewish Christianity," which Paul, the former zealous Pharisee, now addresses, taking as his starting point his own biography.

---

220. See further, Marshall, "Appeal."
221. See Alexander, "Letter-Forms," 95.
222. See, e.g., Gnilka, *Philipperbrief*, 189, and Wolfgang Harnisch, "Die paulinische Selbstempfehlung als Plädoyer für den Gekreuzigten. Rhetorisch-hermeneutische Erwägungen zu Phil 3," in Mell and Müller (eds.), *Urchristentum*, 133–154, esp. 135.
223. This would be all the more plausible if the question of Paul's suffering plays into Phil. 3.2-21 as well.
224. The situation seems to be more urgent than one in which the Philippians require reassurance as to the character of true righteousness only, as Andries H. Snyman, "A Rhetorical Analysis of Philippians 3:1–11," *Neotest* 40 (2006), 259–283, argues.

3.4.1.1 Paul the "Superdog" (3.1-6)[225]

Paul begins his exhortation in Phil. 3 in verse 2, prefacing it with the refrain-like "rejoice in the Lord"[226] and a remark that states the purpose of what will follow,[227] namely to provide a safeguard for the Philippians, in Phil. 3.1.[228] Between Paul's concern for the ἀσφάλεια (security, safety) of the Philippians (Phil. 3.1) and other parts of Philippians, there might be a specific connection, given that the *topos* of the safety of a *polis* was a topic frequented by political, or in other words, deliberative, rhetoric.[229] Citizenship occurs a few more times in Philippians and might therefore be related to Paul's remark about safety here.[230] The safety at stake is probably related to the salvation of the Philippians.[231]

Upon this introductory statement, Paul makes an emphatic statement about the "dogs" in Phil. 3.2,[232] before turning to the congregation once more (after Phil. 3.1), now not addressing them as ἀδελφοί, but rather in the first person plural (*pluralis sociativus*) as the (true) circumcised, clearly in separation from the "dogs" mentioned in the previous verse,[233] who are singled out as his target and simultaneously as a negative example for the Philippians.[234] That one has to

---

225. Unlike in Bianchini, *L'Elogio, passim*, here Phil. 3.1-4.1 will be treated as one continuous unit, thus enabling a more integrated discussion of the pericope rather than opting for a (somewhat artificial) subdivision into two *exempla*, one consisting of the verses 4b-6, 15-16, the other of the verses 2-4a, 17-21.

226. On the preparatory character of Phil. 3.1b, see Dodd, *Paul's Paradigmatic "I"*, 181. If Phil. 3.1 has a relation to epistolary hesitation formulas, as Reed, "Philippians," has argued, then it represents a brief pause before Paul launches into the rest of Phil. 3.1; given the substantial content of that chapter, a brief hesitation may well have been in place—as such hesitation formulas were also used.

227. From a rhetorical perspective this would be the statement of a *causa*; see, e.g., Williams, *Enemies*, 149, following Watson, "Integration," 421. Thus, Phil. 3.1 has a preparatory and transitory function; τὰ αὐτὰ can both be related to the reason for Paul's joy and constitute a reference to what follows (diff.: Schoon-Janssen, *"Apologien"*, 126-127. For the introductory function of Phil. 3.1, see also, e.g., Niebuhr, *Heidenapostel*, 83.

228. On the problems posed by this verse in terms of the letter's unity and structure, see above, 2.2.2.

229. See, e.g., Williams, Enemies, 150, following Timothy C. Geoffrion, *The Rhetorical Purpose and the Political and Military Character of Philippians: A Call to Stand Firm* (Lewiston: Mellen, 1993), 151-152.

230. See the discussion by Williams, *Enemies*, 150, and compare Phil. 1.27, 3.20.

231. For a more detailed proposal, see, e.g., Williams, *Enemies*, 151-153.

232. The emphasis derives to a considerable extent from the threefold repetition of βλέπετε; see, e.g., Dodd, *Paul's Paradigmatic "I"*, 181; O'Brien, *Epistle*, 352-354. With G. D. Kilpatrick, "BLEPETE, Philippians 3:2," in Matthew Black and Georg Fohrer (eds.), *In Memoriam Paul Kahle*, BZAW 103 (Berlin: Töpelmann, 1968), 146-148, and, e.g., Schoon-Janssen, *"Apologien"*, here the meaning "behold" is chosen, not "beware." What Kilpatrick rediscovered in the late 1960s had already been noted by Bernard Weiss in 1897—see also the critique of Reed, "Philippians," 85-86. A telling text in this respect is also the way in which the calling of the Church is introduced in 1 Cor. 1.26: Βλέπετε γὰρ τὴν κλῆσιν ὑμῶν. See further, also, Witherington, *Friendship*, 88, and Bockmuehl, *Philippians*, 185.

233. See, e.g., Dodd, *Paul's Paradigmatic "I"*, 181; see the position of ἡμεῖς in Phil. 3.3.

234. See Dodd, *Paul's Paradigmatic "I"*, 181, and Williams, *Enemies*, 153-154.

do with a negative example is indicated by the verb that Paul uses in Phil. 3.2: βλέπειν. This designates seeing something or looking at something, rather than "being aware of" or "watching out for" something.[235] Such an interpretation is also suggested by the similar introduction of Paul (and unidentified others) as a positive *exemplum* in Phil. 3.17.[236] Thus, Paul positions the Philippian community together with himself *vis-à-vis* the "dogs."[237] In holding up the "dogs" as a negative example—and in doing so strongly advising against following it—Paul spares neither invectives nor stylistic tools, phrasing his concerns in a tripartite, asyndectic sentence that expresses urgency.[238] One effect of the language Paul has chosen in these verses (and which goes widely beyond an "objective" description of his opponents) is to characterize those who advocated adherence to (more of) the ritual precepts of the Torah (than Paul) as being outside of the covenant.[239] Paul achieves this specifically by calling his opponents dogs, implying ritual impurity by Jewish standards, and by referring to them as part of the κατατομή (a play on words with περιτομή, circumcision).[240] This, as should be obvious, constitutes a contrast with the claims that Paul makes for himself and those in agreement with him.[241] Paul backs up his starting point in Phil. 3.2 with what may well be his main thesis in Phil. 3.3: ἡμεῖς γάρ ἐσμεν ἡ περιτομή, οἱ πνεύματι θεοῦ λατρεύοντες καὶ καυχώμενοι ἐν Χριστῷ Ἰησοῦ καὶ οὐκ ἐν σαρκὶ πεποιθότες.[242] The first part of this statement is positive; the second, however, is negative, and points to the controversy at stake.[243] The core of this controversy is probably not circumcision as such, but rather the value of being ἐν Χριστῷ Ἰησοῦ and the shape and consequences this has, specifically with regard to (ethnic and religious) identity (and status) markers such as circumcision,[244] which can be summarized as "the law" (see verse 6). The circumcision—understood as a way of referring to belonging to (the people of) God—that matters for

235. See, e.g., Schoon-Janssen, *"Apologien"*, 124 and esp., also, Kilpatrick, "BLEPETE." Diff., e.g., Barth, *Brief*, 55–56, and O'Brien, *Epistle*, 351–352.
236. See, e.g., Williams, *Enemies*, 212.
237. See, e.g., Williams, *Enemies*, 104.
238. See, e.g., Williams, *Enemies*, 154, and further also, e.g., Dodd, *Paul's Paradigmatic "I"*, 181, and Harnisch, "Selbstempfehlung," 138–139.
239. It should be taken into account that Paul may well have held a very similar position earlier on in his career; see, e.g., Douglas A. Campbell, "Galatians 5.11: Evidence of Early Law-observant Mission by Paul?", *NTS* 57 (2011), 325–347.
240. See, e.g., the argument of Williams, *Enemies*, 156–159.
241. It should be maintained here as well that the use of the description "workers of evil" (3.2) has a(n inverse) counterpart in Paul's description of Epaphroditus as συνεργός (Phil. 2.25) and that of Clement and others as συνεργοί in Phil. 4.3.
242. One might liken Phil. 3.2 to a *propositio* therefore; see, e.g., Bianchini, *L'Elogio*, 146. However, it seems preferable to consider Phil. 3.3 as the actual thesis statement here, as, e.g., Williams, *Enemies*, 159, argues; see also Dodd, *Paul's Paradigmatic "I"*, 181.
243. See, e.g., Williams, *Enemies*, 159, and Dodd, *Paul's Paradigmatic "I"*, 181.
244. For this interpretation of circumcision with respect to Phil. 3.2, see, e.g., Reumann, *Philippians*, 473–474. See also, e.g., Williams, *Enemies*, 160, Fee, *Philippians*, 295, and Niebuhr, *Heidenapostel*, 105–109.

124 *Paradigms of Being in Christ*

Paul is being adopted by God and worshipping in the Spirit (Phil. 3.3), not circumcision in the literal sense of the word as a physical identity marker associated with belonging to the people of the covenant.[245] In this way, Paul claims the promises of salvation of Israel for his community.[246]

The first thing Paul does in this counter-argument from Phil. 3.4 onwards, aiming to support the claim made in Phil. 3.3,[247] is to underline his familiarity with his opponents' point of view,[248] even to the extent that he once followed an according way of life in a superior way compared to them;[249] in this respect his credentials are even more convincing than his opponents'.[250] Taking up the language used at the end of Phil. 3.3,[251] Paul, beginning what amounts to an argument *a minore ad maius*,[252] claims to have been superior "in the flesh"— in other words, (in this case) in terms of Israelite identity[253]—to any of his opponents, irrespective of what they may think.[254] He is of the circumcision, from the Israelite tribe of Benjamin—this may be aimed at Gentile Christians who were circumcised: Paul is a circumcised Israelite—and he was even a Pharisee in terms of his adherence to the law, according to righteousness of which he was blameless. His zeal for the law was also evidenced by his

---

245. As Niebuhr, *Heidenapostel*, 84, notes, Paul "kann also die gegenwärtige Heilsteilhabe der Christen mit dem Stichwort und dem Bedeutungsgehalt von Beschneidung identifizieren." Paul places much emphasis on the identity of himself and the Philippians; note the position of ἡμεῖς in Phil. 3.3, as underlined by, e.g., Schenk, *Philipperbriefe*, 254; see also Walter, "Brief," 75–76. The "we" that are in view are probably more than just Paul and his companions, as Reumann, *Philippians*, 474, suggests; rather, the Philippians themselves are meant too.
246. See, e.g., Niebuhr, *Heidenapostel*, 98.
247. See, e.g., Williams, *Enemies*, 169.
248. Paul's extensive treatment of his own background in Pharisaism is unusual and most likely inspired by the situation that he addresses. See, e.g., Pilhofer, *Philippi*, 123, and esp. also, Niebuhr, *Heidenapostel*, 103.
249. See Dodd, *Paul's Paradigmatic "I"*, 183, noting that the turn to the first person singular in Phil. 3.4 already suggests a contrastive characterization of himself and the "dogs." For the following, see also, e.g., Holloway, *Consolation*, 136–142, and Walter, "Brief," 77–78.
250. For the heuristically helpful term "credentials," see Dodd, *Paul's Paradigmatic "I"*, 181. The expression trust(ing) in the flesh only occurs in Phil. 3.3-4; the use of πείθω with ἐν generally indicates trusting in; see, e.g., Gal. 5.10; Phil. 1.14, 2.24; 2 Thess. 3.4. See, e.g., Bianchini, *L'Elogio*, 66, and further, e.g., Harnisch, "Selbstempfehlung," 140–141.
251. See, e.g., Williams, *Enemies*, 165.
252. See, e.g., Bianchini, *L'Elogio*, 65.
253. The interpretation of ἐν σαρκὶ is debated: it could either be a reference to material things in general, human nature (e.g. Gerald F. Hawthorne, *Philippians*, WBC 43 [Waco: Word, 1983], 127–128), everything (but God) that human beings can put their trust in (e.g. O'Brien, *Epistle*, 363–364; Barth, *Brief*, 57; Walter, "Brief," 76), or ethnic-religious identity (e.g. Dunn, *Theology*, 69–70. With, e.g., Bianchini, *L'Elogio*, 67–68, here Dunn's line of thought is followed for this passage in Philippians, which is perspicuous, given that all that follows in Phil. 3.5-6 is related to precisely Paul's (former) ethnic-religious identity.
254. In Phil. 3.4, δοκέω carries the meaning "to opine"; see for similar occurrences, Mt. 3.9; Lk. 24.37; 1 Cor. 7.40; see O'Brien, *Epistle*, 368, and Bianchini, *L'Elogio*, 66.

persecution of the Church. Whatever his adversaries might claim, seems to be the bottom line of Phil. 3.4-6, Paul can claim the same and more than that.[255]

When analyzing Paul's "credentials" further, one may observe that half of them are related to his descent (those listed in Phil. 3.5) and half are related to his personal achievements (Phil. 3.6).[256] Thus, Paul covers two significant aspects of his biography (and with that, of his character and status): descent and achievements. What Paul presents in Phil. 3.5-6 (in fact, it continues with a twist in the subsequent verses) corresponds well to elements common to *enkomia* (i.e. descent and *res gestae*).[257] Fittingly, the two topics addressed by Paul in his *res gestae*, which can be captured by the keywords εὐσέβεια and δικαιοσύνη, were standard themes in *enkomia* of various sorts.[258] In this context, while taking into account what was said earlier about the character of Philippi as a city,[259] one may well consider Pilhofer's line of thought as at least illustrative. Pilhofer, noting the importance attached to the association of the (Roman) citizens of Philippi of their πολίτευμα with the Roman *tribus Voltinia*,[260] proceeds to compare Phil. 3.4-5 to a generic description of Philippian civil and ethnic identity in the following manner:[261]

Table 3.1: **Philippian Civic Identity and Paul's Self-Presentation**

Identification of Philippian Civil Identity	**Philippians 3.5-6**
Civis Romanus	ἐκ γένους ’Ισραήλ
Tribus Voltinia	φυλῆς Βενιαμίν
Cai filius	Ἑβραῖος ἐξ Ἑβραίων

---

255. See, e.g., Williams, *Enemies*, 172.
256. See, e.g., Williams, *Enemies*, 170–171.
257. See, e.g., Bianchini, *L'Elegio*, 72–73.
258. See, e.g., Bianchini, *L'Elogio*, 79–80; see also Berger, *Formen*, 401–402.
259. See above, 2.2.4.
260. As Pilhofer, *Philippi*, 122, notes with Friedrich Vittinghoff, *Römische Kolonisation und Bürgerrechtspolitik unter Caesar und Augustus*, Akademie der Wissenschaften und der Literatur. Abhandlungen der Geistes-und Sozialwissenschaftlichen Klasse 1951: 14 (Steiner: Wiesbaden, 1952), 23, "Kolonien wurden bei ihrer Gründung 'geschlossen einer der römischen Tribus zugeteilt, blieben also untrennbare Glieder der Stadt Rom, deren Bürger [die Kolonisten] ... waren, ohne in ihr zu wohnen, ja meist ohne sie überhaupt je gesehen zu haben."
261. See Pilhofer, *Philippi*, 126–127. See also Hellerman, *Reconstructing*, 121–127, as well as Bianchini, *L'Elogio*, 73–74. For an interpretation that emphasizes ethnic aspects, see, e.g., Dennis C. Duling, "'Whatever Gain I Had ...' Ethnicity and Paul's Self-Identification in Philippians 3:5–6," in David B. Gowler, L. Gregory Bloomquist, and Duane F. Watson (eds.), *Fabrics of Discourse* (FS Vernon K. Robbins; Harrisburg: Trinity, 2003), 222–241.

The listing of both his descent and his *res gestae* suits Paul's *periautological* rhetoric in Phil. 3.[262] By presenting them, Paul forcefully substantiates the claim made in Phil. 3.4, namely that if anyone has reason for boasting in the flesh, then this is him. In sum, as far as the question of *periautologia* in relation to Phil. 3 is concerned, it may be maintained that the first part of the entire *exemplum* in Phil. 3.4-11, that is, Phil. 3.4b-6, can well be seen as a *periautological exemplum* used in order to defend a speaker under attack by defensively establishing the speaker's own credentials, as it was explicitly sanctioned by contemporary rhetorical theorists.

3.4.1.2 Paul's Kenotic Christian Identity (3.7-14)

After what may be termed his self-praise in 3.4-6, which for Paul represents an example of "boasting in the flesh,"[263] he creates a turning point in Phil 3.7.[264] Here, he subverts all that has been said before[265] in a chiastic σύγκρισις (Phil. 3.7-8)[266] by arguing that there is something which is even greater than all of this. This statement implies a double claim *vis-à-vis* Paul's adversaries: not only do they not live up to the standards Paul himself once represented, but they also have not understood that there is something even more important than this.[267] Precisely the latter is Paul's pivot.[268] His statement about this indicates a reversal of values. What he once valued, he now despises, and what he once persecuted, he now labors for.[269] All this stands out exceedingly clearly through the contrast that Paul creates between this and his previous status.[270]

Paul's (new) *summum bonum*, compared to which everything else is a loss (verse 7) or rubbish (verse 8)—Paul's language grows stronger here[271]—is

---

262. So also, e.g., Bianchini, *L'Elogio*, 74–75.
263. See, e.g., Williams, *Enemies*, 169.
264. See Dodd, *Paul's Paradigmatic "I"*, 181; Gnilka, *Philipperbrief*, 187–191; Martin, *Philippians*, 126–129.
265. In Phil. 3.7, ἅτινα should be taken as a reference to all that has been said before in Phil. 3.4-6; see, e.g., Bianchini, *L'Elogio*, 82–83.
266. A: Phil. 3.7a; B: Phil. 3.7b; B': Phil. 3.8a; A': Phil. 3.8b. For the identification of this pattern as a σύγκρισις, see, e.g., Bianchini, *L'Elogio*, 82–83. The more extensive tripartite parallelism proposed by Byrnes, *Conformation*, 184, is not followed; it seems that the clause δι' ὅν (Phil. 3.8) is too small to constitute one half of a parallelism equivalent to διὰ τὸ ὑπερέχον τῆς γνώσεως Χριστοῦ Ἰησοῦ τοῦ κυρίου μου.
267. See Egger, *Philipperbrief*, 65. Similarly, Dodd, *Paul's Paradigmatic "I"*, 180: "Paul presents himself both as a paradigm for the Philippians and as part of his polemic against those whose teaching he wants them to reject."
268. So rightly, Dodd, *Paul's Paradigmatic "I"*, 184, with Hawthorne, *Philippians*, 149. Paul's point is not to show that there is something wrong with other kinds of Judaism as such, but that knowing Christ goes beyond it; see, e.g., Niebuhr, *Heidenapostel*, 100.
269. See, e.g., Williams, *Enemies*, 172–174.
270. See, e.g., Harnisch, "Selbstempfehlung," 141, identifying Paul's self-description as a *simulatio* that is designed to give the subsequent argument more relief and force.
271. See, e.g., Dodd, *Paul's Paradigmatic "I"*, 184; Bianchini, *L'Elogio*, 86; Barth, *Brief*, 60.

Christ (verse 7), specifically, knowing Christ (verse 8).²⁷² The statement of Phil. 3.7, using language that is related to bookkeeping,²⁷³ as well as what follows in Phil. 3.8-11, aims at pointing to the more advantageous option, as is common in deliberative rhetoric.²⁷⁴ Paul may also be seen to supplement information here with regard to the knowledge that the Philippians were told to strive for in Phil. 1.9.²⁷⁵

The initial and foundational statement of Phil. 3.7 is unpacked and emphasized in one long sentence,²⁷⁶ running through Phil. 3.8-11.²⁷⁷ Introduced with the augmentative ἀλλὰ μενοῦνγε (verse 8), Paul further describes the significance of Christ in terms of τὸ ὑπερέχον τῆς γνώσεως Χριστοῦ ᾽Ιησοῦ τοῦ κυρίου μου, which indicates both his own position *vis-à-vis* Christ²⁷⁸ and the mode of their relationship: "knowing" Christ, which must be interpreted in an encompassing, existential sense here.²⁷⁹ It goes widely beyond conveying information only. The remainder of 3.8 reiterates the consequences of knowing Christ: in view of Christ not only do Paul's Pharisaic—in other words, religious and social—credentials become worthless,²⁸⁰ but he is even led to give up everything and to regard it as refuse, in order to gain Christ

---

272. As Paul presents himself as someone who has gone through a learning process, he offers himself as a model of identification for the Philippians. See, e.g., Bianchini, *L'Elogio*, 40–43. For considerations about the structural analogy between Paul's "reinvention" of himself because of his knowledge of Christ and the Stoic idea of acquiring a new identity because of knowledge of the supreme good, see Engberg-Pedersen, *Paul*, 93.

273. See, e.g., Williams, *Enemies*, 174, as well as Walter, "Brief," 79.

274. See, e.g., Williams, *Enemies*, 174, following Mitchell, *Paul*, 203–206.

275. See, e.g., Holloway, *Consolation*, 130.

276. See, e.g., the increase in scope of Paul's statements: in verse 7 ἅτινα and ταῦτα are used to refer to what Paul regards as loss, in verse 8 it has become "πάντα." A similar creation of emphasis through progression can be observed regarding Paul's use of ζημία and ζημιόω (Phil. 3.7-8). See, e.g., Williams, *Enemies*, 175–176.

277. Dodd, *Paul's Paradigmatic "I"*, 184, sees the expression of Paul's gospel in terms of a paradigmatic "I" only in verses 9-10. It is difficult to see why only these verses and not the rest of Paul's self-description here should have paradigmatic value.

278. I.e. Christ is κύριος, hence Paul is δοῦλος. See, e.g., Williams, *Enemies*, 177.

279. See, e.g., Bockmuehl, *Philippians*, 205; Walter, "Brief," 80–81; Bianchini, *L'Elogio*, 86–87; and Koperski, *Knowledge, passim*, but esp. 237, quoting in (her own) translation Pierre Biard, *La puissance de Dieu*, TICP 7 (Paris: Bloud & Gay, 1960), 147: "The knowledge of Christ leads to a renovation, a transformation of being by conformity and communion with the one who is known. This knowledge is not an adventitious element of Christian life, but is Christian life itself, not simply an intellectual act, but a transforming union." See also, Dibelius, *Philipper*, 89.

280. Dodd, *Paul's Paradigmatic "I"*, 184, is probably right in seeing an exaggeration in Paul's generalization here, though it would also be possible to view the "everything" as referring back to Paul's former credentials. In the latter case the significance of these credentials is underlined in order to make an even more powerful statement about the significance of Christ in view of whom they count as rubbish.

and to be found in him.²⁸¹ The sentence begun in verse 8 continues in verse 9. From this verse onwards, however, Paul concentrates on the positive side of the matter,²⁸² the side to which he wishes to draw the Philippians and which is the one with the most advantages attached to it. The combination of Phil. 3.8 and 3.9 may seem to be problematic in terms of the coordination of the verbs κερδήσω and εὑρεθῶ, the one connoting the future realization of knowing Christ, the other a more realized state already.²⁸³ However, this problem disappears when the two verses are read as mutually explaining each other (the aorist εὑρεθῶ describes the event to which the future tense of κερδήσω points). This has as the implication that the whole of Phil. 3.10-11 and all of Phil. 3.9 after αὐτῷ become a long explanatory clause, outlining further what gaining Christ and being found in him entails. This explanatory clause, then, outlines the significance of what has been said before, using the concept of righteousness, stating that what Paul adheres to is not righteousness based on the law, but righteousness based on faith in Christ.²⁸⁴ Right status and identity, or righteousness, no longer derive from the law, but from God through faith in Christ.²⁸⁵ Boasting (καυχάομαι) in the flesh is, accordingly, replaced by having faith (πίστις) in Christ.

---

281. Regarding Paul's religious biography, one may maintain with Koperski, *Knowledge*, 236, that Paul does not so much reject his religious heritage, as mainly views it in a new light: "Paul ... repudiates all things, Jewish or otherwise, that seem to give him a claim to privileged status before God ... The contrast between *my own righteousness* and *that which is through faith in Jesus Christ* is not a contrast between human effort and divine grace, but rather an opposition between two human attitudes, two kinds of human perception, one of which is characterized by ignorance that in Christ the messianic age has dawned, and another which consists in *the knowledge of Christ Jesus my Lord*" (emphasis in original). As, e.g., Harnisch rightly notes, Paul is passive with regard to the "knowing of Christ" ("Selbstempfehlung," 143).
282. See, e.g., Williams, *Enemies*, 177.
283. See, e.g., Harnisch, "Selbstempfehlung," 144.
284. Phil. 3.9 can be regarded as a key text for the so-called "πίστις Χριστοῦ-debate." Here, the view is taken that the contrast drawn between righteousness through the law and faith in Christ read in the light of Paul's previous reflections in 3.6 (about his achieving "a perfect score" in terms of righteousness by keeping the law) points to interpreting the clause about faith as an objective, not a subjective genitive. For recent considerations of this question, see, e.g., Martinus C. de Boer, "Paul's Use and Interpretation of a Justification Tradition in Galatians 2.15–21," *JSNT* 28 (2005), 189–216; David L. Stubbs, "The Shape of Soteriology and the Pistis Christou Debate," *Scottish Journal of Theology* 61 (2008), 137–157; R. Barry Matlock, "The Rhetoric of Πίστις in Paul: Galatians 2:16, 3:22, Romans 3:22, and Philippians 3:9," *JSNT* 30 (2007), 173–203; idem, "Detheologizing the Pistis Christou Debate: Remarks from a Lexical Semantic Perspective," *NovT* 42 (2000), 1–23; and esp. the extensive study by Karl Friedrich Ulrichs, *Christusglaube: Studien zum Syntagma Pistis Christou und zum paulinischen Verständnis von Glaube und Rechtfertigung*, WUNT 2.227 (Tübingen: Mohr Siebeck, 2007), *passim*, and esp. 251–252. Ulrichs argues in favor of an "objective" genitive, but notes that the real question at stake is how this faith shapes the believers' relationship to Christ.
285. See, e.g., Williams, *Enemies*, 180. As Niebuhr, *Heidenapostel*, 100–101, rightly notes, the source, not the content of the righteousness, is at stake here.

The last part of Paul's long sentence deals no longer with the form, but with the content, of this righteousness:[286] Knowing Christ and (probably an explanatory καί)[287] the power of his resurrection as well as the fellowship of his suffering (verse 10),[288] all of which is repeated in reverse order: conforming to Christ's death (verse 10),[289] in view of sharing in Christ's resurrection (verse 11), about which Paul expresses himself rather reluctantly here.[290] In his awareness of the "already/not-yet" situation he is in, Paul may well also function in a paradigmatic way.[291] Phil. 3.10-11 thus constitutes the climax of Paul's *periautological* self-presentation and states that the *summum bonum* to be gained is to know Christ existentially in an encompassing way, that is, to be taken up in the dynamics of the suffering, death, and resurrection and exaltation of Christ.[292] At stake is a metamorphosis of those who are in Christ: Paul and the Philippians too.[293] The current experience of the power of the resurrection is connected to sharing in Christ's suffering[294] and to the future hope of participating in

---

286. See, e.g., Williams, *Enemies*, 183.

287. The reason for reading this καί as an epexegetical καί and the next καί as not is that all that follows the first use of καί in this verse must be an explanation of "knowing him," otherwise nothing would be added to the previous statement about knowing Christ.

288. For considerations about κοινωνία in Philippians, see 3.1.5.5; there also on Phil. 3.10. Here, it should mainly be maintained that the noun expresses something that is part of the (participatory) knowing to which Paul refers and that Baumert's suggestion of "Mitteilung" ("communication," "gift") fits well into this context. For a reading in terms of participation, see, e.g., Koperski, *Knowledge*, 248–256. The nature of this suffering is, again with Koperski, *op. cit.*, 256–260, to be seen as suffering that is related to being "in Christ," irrespective of whether it is of an "interior" (spiritual, psychological) or "exterior" (physical) kind.

289. Phil. 2.6-7 may well form the background to the use of συμμορφιζόμενος here as well as of σύμμορφον in Phil. 3.21. See Koperski, *Knowledge*, 270–271. Whether the participle needs to be taken in a passive sense, as, e.g., Marvin R. Vincent, *A Critical and Exegetical Commentary on the Epistles to the Philippians and to Philemon*, ICC (Edinburgh: T&T Clark, 1922), 105, and O'Brien, *Epistle*, 409–411, argue, in a medial sense (see, e.g., Hawthorne, *Philippians*, 129, 145), resp. a reflexive sense (e.g., Beare, *Philippians*, 123–124), or in an active sense (see, e.g., Robert C. Tannehill, *Dying and Rising with Christ: A Study in Pauline Theology*, BZNW 32 [Berlin: Töpelmann, 1967], 38–121), cannot be decided here, even though it seems that the fact that Paul is taken up in a dynamic initiated by Christ certainly suggests that he is being transformed as least as much as he actively supports this transformation. The notion of transformation may suggest a baptismal context; see, e.g., Rom. 6.1-11; 2 Cor. 4.7-15; Col. 2.12, 20, 3.1; 2 Tim. 2.11.

290. Dodd, *Paul's Paradigmatic "I"*, 184.

291. See Dodd, *Paul's Paradigmatic "I"*, 185: "If Paul must wait to receive the full blessings of the kingdom, then so must the Philippians."

292. See, e.g., Williams, *Enemies*, 183–184.

293. See, e.g., Van Kooten, "Image," 225–226.

294. See, e.g., Williams, *Enemies*, 187–189; also Koperski, *Knowledge*, 260–265, argues rightly that the experience of Christ's sufferings and that of the power of his resurrection balance each other, while the power of the resurrection will eventually gain the upper hand (see, e.g., Rom. 8.17-18; 2 Cor. 1.4-10, also 4.7-15).

Christ's resurrection.²⁹⁵ In this context, it should be noted that all the things mentioned in Phil. 3.10-11 are related to Christ in the first place: the once-humbled Christ is now the source of power for the (equally humbled) Paul *cum suis*.²⁹⁶ All this is expressed in a chiastic pattern that lends additional emphasis to the statement and may be described as a *reversio*:²⁹⁷

a: τοῦ γνῶναι αὐτὸν καὶ τὴν δύναμιν τῆς ἀναστάσεως αὐτοῦ
b: καὶ [τὴν] κοινωνίαν [τῶν] παθημάτων αὐτοῦ,
b': συμμορφιζόμενος τῷ θανάτῳ αὐτοῦ,
a': εἴ πως καταντήσω εἰς τὴν ἐξανάστασιν τὴν ἐκ νεκρῶν.

The forceful statement of Phil. 3.7-11 that has its climax in the latter two verses with their references to the death of Christ and the resurrection of the dead is nuanced in Phil. 3.12-13, which is already prepared by the somewhat reticent tone of Phil. 3.11.²⁹⁸ This nuancing, however, takes place in such a way as to prepare for the final point Paul has to make in this section, before turning to the Philippians to tell them the consequences of all this. That is to

---

295. See, e.g., Williams, *Enemies*, 191–192. The pattern described is clearly progressive and its development may well have been captured accurately by Koperski, *Knowledge*, 271: "the power of Christ's resurrection provides the courage for the believer to share in Christ's sufferings (10c), and, by means of this, become conformed to his death (10d)." The main problem with this view seems to be the lack of reference to "courage" in the text of Phil. 3. On the fundamental importance of participation and transformation in Paul's theology, see, e.g., Udo Schnelle, "Transformation und Partizipation als Grundgedanken paulinischer Theologie," *NTS* 47 (2001), 58–75, who on 64 also notes the close relationship between Phil. 2 and 3; see for related considerations also, idem, *Paulus. Leben und Denken* (Berlin: De Gruyter, 2003), 463–465, 545–554. The use of the unusual ἐξανάστασις has given rise to much interpretative effort; however, its precise meaning remains unclear. In this light, it is possibly prudent to adopt Plummer's view that the use of a double compound is common in first-century Greek and does not (necessarily) add anything to the meaning of a word. See Alfred Plummer, *A Commentary on St. Paul's Epistle to the Philippians* (London: Scott, 1912), 76, as well as for an overview of interpretative options, e.g., Koperski, *Knowledge*, 277–279.
296. See, e.g., the considerations of Koperski, *Knowledge*, 239–245.
297. See, e.g., Bianchini, *L'Elogio*, 90; see further, Barth, *Brief*, 61; Gnilka, *Philipperbrief*, 195–196; Schenk, *Philipperbriefe*, 320; Tannehill, *Dying*, 120. Critical are Koperski, *Knowledge*, 266, with Florence Morgan Gillman, *A Study of Romans 6: 5a: United to a Death like Christ's* (San Francisco: Mellen, 1992), 236–237; however, exact equivalence between all parts of a chiasm, as seems to be demanded by the latter two authors, is not a necessity.
298. See, e.g., Williams, *Enemies*, 195. For an overview of various interpretative options, see, e.g., Koperski, *Knowledge*, 275–276; a certain reluctance on the part of Paul, given the fact that he has not yet attained the goal and that it lies in the (unsure) future, may well be the principal reason for the construction with εἴ πως here. Also providing an extensive overview of the various interpretative options, Randall E. Otto, "'If Possible I May Attain the Resurrection from the Dead' (Philippians 3:11)," *CBQ* 57 (1995), 324–340, argues not implausibly that Paul's reluctance had to do with his own uncertainty as to whether he would remain faithful to the end.

say, in both Phil. 3.12 and 3.13, Paul states that he has not yet fully grasped,[299] but that he leaves that which lies behind him where it is and presses on to what lies before him. This and the (hope of) consummation of his communion with Christ are constitutive for this experience.[300] In Phil. 3.13, Paul's relative apprehension is contrasted with the one thing that he has apprehended already: that he has to leave what is past and press on. Continuing the metaphor introduced in Phil. 3.12, Paul then states the goal of this pressing on in Phil. 3.14 in agonistic terminology: τὸ βραβεῖον τῆς ἄνω κλήσεως. Running this course (and winning the prize) is certainly also what Paul has in mind for the Philippians. In this respect, Paul is as much a model for the Philippians as in other respects.[301] In fact, precisely by underlining that he has not achieved the goal yet, Paul puts himself on a par with the Philippians and offers himself as a model of identification (see also his reticent self-presentation in verse 11), which suits his earlier *periautological* self-presentation well.[302]

In view of this agonistic metaphor, Paul also models the movement from what lies behind towards Christ (see Phil. 3.13-14).[303] The point that Paul makes is that those who are the true circumcision, like himself, know Christ by sharing in Christ's suffering and experiencing the power of the resurrection, but have not risen from the dead yet, which is (to be hoped for as) an eschatological event.[304] The model that Paul outlines here places the resolution of (the faithful's) suffering in the eschaton, while earthly existence in agreement with "knowing Christ" is characterized by suffering and a partial experience of the power of the resurrection already.[305]

3.4.1.3 Consequences Resulting from Paul the Paradigm (3.15–4.1)

From Phil. 3.15 onwards, Paul addresses his readership directly, building on what he had said before.[306] He does so as follows.

---

299. The object of this clause must be the resurrection that was mentioned in Phil. 3.11; see, e.g., Williams, *Enemies*, 196–197. Paul knows the power of the resurrection as well as the participation in Christ's suffering, but not yet the resurrection as such; this will be the consummation of "knowing" Christ. See also, Barth, *Brief*, 61.

300. See, e.g., Niebuhr, *Heidenapostel*, 85.

301. Rightly so, e.g., *Paul's Paradigmatic "I"*, 185.

302. See, e.g., Barth, *Brief*, 63.

303. See, e.g., Dodd, *Paul's Paradigmatic "I"*, 185–186.

304. See, e.g., Williams, *Enemies*, 197–199.

305. See, e.g., Williams, *Enemies*, 199, 205, and Dodd, *Paul's Paradigmatic "I"*, 181–182; the supposition of a group advocating "legalistic perfectionism" in Philippians is not necessary to understand Paul's argument here, nor is it necessary to assume a group that posited a fully realized eschatology (including the resurrection), as Reumann, *Philippians*, 522–523, argues—even though his emphasis that one cannot have the one (resurrection) without the other (suffering) is entirely to the point.

306. See, e.g., Williams, *Enemies*, 206; τοῦτο, occurring twice in Phil. 3.15, makes this connection to the preceding verses clear. In the same verse, the use of οὖν also points to a connection with the preceding. See also the description by Harnisch, "Selbstempfehlung," 136: "Schlussappell."

First, Paul exhorts the "mature" or "perfected"[307] to "think this" (Phil. 3.15), which most likely refers to "the example of self-renunciation of confidence in the flesh, christocentrism and eschatological reserve that he has portrayed for them in 3.3-14"[308] with himself as its embodiment. The use of φρονέω is reminiscent of Phil. 2.5, where it introduces the *enkomion* in Phil. 2.6-11. Because Paul addresses his readership in the first person plural in Phil. 3.16-17,[309] the same effect develops as in Phil. 3.3: Paul and the Philippians stand together facing the potential threat to the community, which will be described a second time and even more drastically in Phil. 3.18-19.

Next, there is in Phil. 3.17 the explicit call to become, all together, imitators of Paul,[310] whose example the Philippians have as well—as a contrast to the example of the "dogs" (see verse 18).[311] Here, in a further *exemplum*, consisting again of himself, but introduced afresh, Paul develops a further argument for his thesis stated in Phil. 3.3-4. It is less elaborate than the first *exemplum* and more direct.[312] It can also be read as a brief restatement of the first *exemplum* and the accompanying appeals.[313] Using the language of examples explicitly,[314] Paul urges the Philippians to behold the example—in

---

307. With Niebuhr, *Heidenapostel*, 85, there is no reason to view the reference to the τέλειοι as a reference to only part of the community in terms of its quality or in terms of a particular faction. Diff., e.g., Barth, *Brief*, 65, even if his suggestion is followed to supplement Phil. 3.15 as "wir die Vollkommene (sein wollen)!" Dibelius, *Philipper*, 92, also assumes that there is a group that calls itself "perfected" in Philippi and that Paul takes up this self-designation to argue that they should behave accordingly. See for the latter also, Oakes, *Philippians*, 119–121.

308. Dodd, *Paul's Paradigmatic "I"*, 181–182. See further, e.g., Williams, *Enemies*, 207, and Niebuhr, *Heidenapostel*, 86.

309. See, e.g., Niebuhr, *Heidenapostel*, 81.

310. The precise meaning of συμμιμηταί is debated; see, e.g., Bianchini, *L'Elegio*, 30–32; with Bianchini, *op. cit.*, 37–38, here the interpretation is followed that emphasizes that the Philippians should together become imitators of Paul (not together with other Christians or together with Paul or Christ—even if the latter is Paul's ultimate interest); this interpretation of συμμιμηταί agrees best with the general theme of unity in the Philippian community that pervades Philippians. See also, e.g., Reumann, *Philippians*, 588; diff., e.g., Heil, *Philippians*, 132, 134. Also, given the reference to ἡμᾶς at the end of verse 17, and unless Paul is using a *pluralis majestatis* or *modestiae*, a multiplicity of persons is in view that serve together with Paul as an *exemplum* for the Philippians; see, e.g., Niebuhr, *Heidenapostel*, 86. This verse is sometimes for theological reasons excised from the letter. E.g. Harnisch ("Selbstempfehlung," 150) cannot see how Paul could be an example for other Christians. Rather, Paul should, in his weakness, be the place where Christ's grace works triumphantly; hence Phil. 3.17 must be a deutero-Pauline addition. This view is not taken here.

311. See, e.g., Niebuhr, *Heidenapostel*, 86.

312. See, e.g., Williams, *Enemies*, 210–211.

313. For the following, see esp., also, De Vos, *Church*, 281–286.

314. See συμμιμηταί and τύπος in Phil. 3.17, as well as the discussion by Dodd, *Paul's Paradigmatic "I"*, 182, and esp. Kurz, "Imitation," 114, and the extensive considerations of Reumann, *Philippians*, 584–589, with a good overview of literature and contemporary analogies.

thought and deed—³¹⁵ that he and others constitute (see also Phil. 4.9).³¹⁶ In all likelihood, reading what follows in Phil. 3.18-19 as a direct anti-type³¹⁷ (and hence as a negative *exemplum*),³¹⁸ this means adhering to and sharing in the "trajectory of salvation" outlined earlier: sharing in Christ's sufferings and experiencing the power of his resurrection on earth,³¹⁹ while awaiting future glorification through transformation (3.21)³²⁰ and disregarding ethnic/ cultural identity markers such as circumcision.³²¹ Phil. 3.20-21, where Paul again uses the first person plural (*pluralis sociativus*), aligning himself with the Philippians against the threat posed by the "dogs,"³²² functions in this respect as a paraphrase of the future of the Philippians that also takes into account their present experience of suffering and contrasts it with the sort of honor that others in Philippi presumably value.³²³ If it is, at least in part,³²⁴ a further *enkomion*, presumably known to both Paul and the Philippians, this would suit its function in Phil. 3 excellently; in that case, Paul concludes his argument by means of a text probably known and accepted by all and places himself and the Philippians on shared ground; just like he had done in Phil. 2 already.

In this context, the imagery used by Paul in Phil. 3.20, specifically of τὸ πολίτευμα ἐν οὐρανοῖς, deserves some consideration as well, especially in the light of what has been said before about the political background of Paul's *periautological exemplum* that he develops using the language of Philippian (Roman) citizenship. The recourse to the same semantic field in Phil. 3.20

---

315. See, e.g., Dodd, *Paul's Paradigmatic "I"*, 182: περιπατέω has a meaning encompassing both word and deed, i.e. one's "walk" of life.

316. For who these others might be, see also below, 3.4.5. For an overview of interpretative options, see, e.g., Gerald F. Hawthorne and Ralph P. Martin, *Philippians*, WBC 43 (rev. edn.; Waco: Word, 2004), 217.

317. Literally, see the use of τύπος in Phil. 3.17; see, e.g., Niebuhr, *Heidenapostel*, 86.

318. See, e.g., Williams, *Enemies*, 104; that Phil. 3.2, 3, 17b-19 constitutes a negative *exemplum* is also suggested by the fact that these verses do not address anyone directly, but only lift up a particular situation or attitude, quite unlike what happens *vis-à-vis* a very similar issue in Galatians or 2 Corinthians. See, e.g., Standhartinger, "'Join'," 427.

319. See also, e.g., Harnisch, "Selbstempfehlung," 151.

320. See regarding the use of σύμμορφον, also Phil. 2.6-7 and 3.10, as well as the discussion by Koperski, *Knowledge*, 270–271. See also, Peter Doble, "'Vile Bodies' or Transformed Persons? Philippians 3.21 in Context," *JSNT* 86 (2002), 3–27.

321. Following the caution expressed by Williams, *Enemies*, 218–228, with regard to knowing the agenda of Paul's opponents.

322. See, e.g., Niebuhr, *Heidenapostel*, 81.

323. See, e.g., Reumann, *Philippians*, 599.

324. This could well be argued on the basis of the passage's vocabulary and style, as is done by, e.g., Jürgen Becker, "Erwägungen zu Phil. 3, 20–21," *ThZ* 27 (1971), 16–29; still, while the beginning of Phil. 3.20 seems to be tailored for the situation in Philippi and may therefore be an occasional composition of Paul, the structure "N.N., who ..." of the final two words of Phil. 3.20 and the whole of Phil. 3.21 fit the structure of an *enkomion* very well. The parallelisms in these verses as well as the unusual vocabulary also make one think of a piece of tradition, presumably encomiastic in character; see, e.g., Barth, *Brief*, 68.

is probably no coincidence (see also 1.27).³²⁵ While the precise reasons—possibilities range from religious and theological considerations to the wish for juridical protection³²⁶—for the wish to adopt with circumcision a sign of belonging to a Jewish πολίτευμα can only be guessed at,³²⁷ it should be maintained that Paul's argument makes clear that the believers' πολίτευμα is located in heaven and that their savior will come from there. This creates a contrast both with membership of a possible Jewish πολίτευμα and with Roman citizenship.³²⁸ In fact, the phrasing of Phil. 3.20 might suggest that "Christian Philippi" is not so much a colony of Rome, but much more a colony of heaven.³²⁹ The occurrence of a further politically connoted concept in Phil. 3.20, σωτήρ, which could well be used to describe the operations of political (and military) leaders bringing well-being (σωτήρια) to town, city, region or country, is also of significance. For example, Roman emperors were regularly lauded with this epithet.³³⁰ If the Philippian community has indeed to endure suffering because of its social and political position,³³¹ Phil. 3.20 gives both an explanation of this fact (the Philippians' πολίτευμα is in heaven) and a consolation for it (i.e. the eschatological perspective). Thus, in Phil. 3 one has two *exempla*: Paul's own positive example in Phil. 3.4-14 (and, together with this, the example of Paul and others in 3.17),³³² and the negative example of Paul's competitors (Phil. 3.2, 18-19).

Before turning to the final sections of Philippians, here again an attempt will be made to read Paul's *periautological exemplum* in Phil. 3 along the lines of a logical Aristotelian *exemplum*.

3.4.2 Excursus: Paul the Paradigm: Logical and/or Illustrative?

The *exempla* as they occur in Phil. 3 can be formalized logically as well.³³³ Again, much depends on the way in which one reduces Paul's argument to

325. For a consideration of alternative directions of interpretation, see, e.g., Pilhofer, *Philippi*, 128–130.
326. So, e.g., Pilhofer, *Philippi*, 133–134.
327. Even if there was only a small Jewish community in Philippi, adopting the signs of belonging to a *religio licita* that was (elsewhere) organized as a πολίτευμα might still be an attractive option for the Philippians, possibly suggested to them by the "dogs"; see Pilhofer, *Philippi*, 130–134.
328. See, e.g., Pilhofer, *Philippi*, 130–134.
329. For the background of this imagery in early Judaism and esp. in its apocalyptic literature, see, e.g., Anna Maria Schwemer, "Himmlische Stadt und himmlisches Bürgerrecht bei Paulus (Gal 4,26 und Phil 3,20)," in Martin Hengel, Siegfried Mittmann, and Anna Maria Schwemer (eds.), *La Cité de Dieu/Die Stadt Gottes*, WUNT 1.129 (Tübingen: Mohr Siebeck, 2000), 194–243; for Philippians the notion of citizenship is probably primarily related to its Roman background, given the character of the city.
330. See, e.g., Standhartinger, "Theologie."
331. See above, 2.3.2.1; see also Pilhofer, *Philippi*, 135–136.
332. See, e.g., Dodd, *Paul's Paradigmatic "I"*, 182; Williams, *Enemies*, 104; and esp. Kurz, "Imitation," 114.
333. For this section, I am indebted to Prof. Dr. Moisés Mayordomo-Marín, Bern.

valid premises. Possible solutions include the following two. One solution (A) is that it has to be shown that the right attitude towards earthly prerogatives, specifically those of an ethnic and religious sort, is to count them for nothing with regard to Christ (3.7). A second possibility (B) is that it has to be shown that to trust in Christ is the proper attitude for those "in Christ." Both of these possibilities can be formalized:

Model A:
All those being in Christ count earthly prerogatives as nothing. (CaN)
All Philippians are in Christ. (PaC)
All Philippians count earthly prerogatives as nothing. (PaN)

Model B:
All those being in Christ put their faith in Christ alone. (CaA)
All Philippians are in Christ. (PaC)
All Philippians put their faith in Christ alone. (PaA)

Again, the problem of the reduction of both the *exemplum* and the accompanying argument to the first and second premise may be regarded as solved, given that all options presented here are also proposed in the exegetical literature and can be argued with some plausibility. However, even if it is possible to reformulate Phil. 3 as a logically valid syllogism, the same two problems remain as in the case of Phil. 2. First, the historical context makes it less likely that Paul indeed used such a logically valid *exemplum* in his argument. Second, the fit with the ensuing argument is not very neat. The syllogisms just presented may prove that something is the case, but they do not show directly that something ought to be the case, which sits uneasily with Paul's obvious attempt to convince the Philippians of what he considers the right attitude. Furthermore, the language of illustration that Paul uses (e.g. βλέπετε in Phil. 3.2, σκοπεῖτε in Phil. 3.17) also points in the direction of an illustrative, not a logical, *exemplum* here.

For the reasons just given, the more attractive option would be to consider Phil. 3.2-21 from the perspective of the later Greco-Roman *exemplum*, in which the authority of the adduced example derived not so much from its inherent quality or suitability, but rather from the authoritative character of the example as such for the audience that it was used for. This will be argued more extensively in the next section.

3.4.3 Paul the Christian and Identity "in Christ"

3.4.3.1 Paul's Paradigmatic Significance
Having surveyed the *exempla* in Phil. 3, it is now appropriate to turn to the question of Paul's paradigmatic significance and to the question of how the *exemplum* (or *exempla*) in Phil. 3 work(s).

A starting point for these considerations is the observation that in Phil. 3, Paul's argument rests largely on his own reliability as a person and as a speaker, not on logical proof.³³⁴ For this reason, it becomes attractive to consider Phil. 3.2-21 from the perspective of the later Greco-Roman *exemplum*, in which the authority of the adduced example was of such pre-eminent importance. Generally speaking, this meant that the adduced example needed to have something to do with a recognized *maior* of the audience at stake. Now, *vis-à-vis* the Philippian community, Paul certainly fulfills such a role: he is (one of) the founder(s) of the community and can therefore claim a special relationship with it. Furthermore, one may imagine that the Philippians were acquainted with Paul's biography. In fact, because it is the biography of one of its *maiores*, it may well be seen as part of the tradition of the Philippian community, just as the Christ *enkomion* is part of this tradition. By presenting himself as an example, Paul in fact appeals to a shared tradition of which he happens to be a living part.³³⁵ Furthermore, as was noted earlier, the closer an *exemplum* is to the audience, the more effective it is. Thus, by arguing *periautologically*, Paul uses an *exemplum* that is particularly close to the Philippians, possibly even closer than the Christ *enkomion*; namely, himself. To this may be added that Paul's emphasis in Phil. 3.12-14 on the fact that he is still running a course as well, just as the Philippians are (or should be), increases the extent to which he is an accessible model for the Philippians.³³⁶ In the context of Phil. 3, all of this might make Paul a more suitable *exemplum* than Christ.

Two more observations may be added to the above, again with regard to Paul's choice to use himself as an example. First, the appropriateness of this course of action should be briefly commented upon. One of the aims that Paul seems to have in mind when writing Philippians is to vindicate both his person and his teaching, both of which seem to be under pressure—if not under outright attack. To begin with, Paul's teaching, which is closely connected to the reliability of his person (*ethos*) and identity as an apostle, is threatened by the "dogs" that he addresses in chapter 3. Furthermore, even when this attack on his teaching already implies an attack on his person, Paul's person and his standing may well be under pressure due to his imprisonment and the suffering that he has been subjected to. According to first-century rhetorical conventions, precisely situations in which one's own position is under attack permit the use of *periautological* arguments. Second, besides the observation made above that Paul represents obvious "material" for an *exemplum* in his

---

334. See, e.g., Williams, *Enemies*, 172–173. The use of a paradigm does not require formal logic either; see above, 1.3. All of this agrees well with Philippians' probable character as a piece of deliberative rhetoric; see, e.g., Witherington, *Friendship*, 43; compare Quintilian, *Inst.* 3.8:12–13.

335. In agreement with, e.g., Lohmeyer, *Brief*, 151, and Niebuhr, *Heidenapostel*, 178, who states the following: "Die Person des Apostels und der Inhalt seiner Verkündigung sind bei Paulus unlösbar miteinander verknüpft."

336. For this emphasis, see, e.g., Frederick W. Weidmann, "An (Un)Accomplished Model: Paul and the Rhetorical Strategy of Philippians 3:3–17," in Virginia Wiles, Alexandra Brown, and Graydon F. Synder (eds.), *Putting Body & Soul Together* (FS Robin Scroggs; Valley Forge: Trinity, 1997), 245–263, esp. 255–256.

letter to the Philippians because of his relationship with them and his position *vis-à-vis* them, it should also be emphasized again that a speaker or a letter writer would always be part of his (or her) own message and contribute, as a person with a particular standing and reputation (*ethos*), to its reliability in the eyes of the audience. Paul is no exception in this respect and in dwelling on himself he uses the credit he has with the Philippians (i.e. a positively connoted *ethos*) to make his point: if he, as a reliable witness and spokesperson, sees things in a particular way, this must constitute an attractive perspective on the matter at hand.

Thus, in Phil. 3, Paul may be seen as reasserting his authority and his character as an *exemplum* for the Philippians by recalling forcefully why he is one of the *maiores* of the community.[337] Building on this status and his longstanding relationship with the Philippians, he can both clear his name and present his version of identity in Christ as a convincing one by offering the example of his own identity in Christ.[338] These considerations largely explain why it is appropriate for Paul to present himself as an *exemplum* in Phil. 3.

At this point, it is also time to return to Dodd's observations about the parts of Paul's identity that "hinder full identification of Paul's model for imitation."[339] Dodd is one of the more outspoken critics of viewing Paul as a model in Phil. 3.[340] His reservations are the following. First, there is the problem of Paul's own biography and his ("hyper-")Jewish identity, which obviously cannot be imitated by everyone, given the individual nature of biographies. Second, Dodd argues that Paul's model is hard to imitate by all because it is not equally accessible to all, given Paul's references to things outside of the text.[341] Third, Paul refers to further persons and models to which a non-Philippian reader has no access (anymore), which again limits the extent to which the Pauline *exemplum* can be identified with fully. With regard to the third point, one may maintain that this is a problem for secondary readers of Paul, but not for his readership (or audience) in Philippi and hence it says little about the exemplary character of Paul's self-presentation in Phil. 3. With regard to the second point: if the observation that Paul draws heavily on the relationship that is already in place between

---

337. Quite naturally, this implies that Paul presents himself as a figure of authority and in a hierarchical way (with esp. Castelli, *Imitating, passim*). However, all that is said and implied about hierarchy and authority in Philippians depends on the paradoxical *exemplum* of Christ, which makes structures of power and their quality less obvious than they might seem—at least, Paul seems to attempt to teach the Philippians precisely about what makes up true authority, which is not at all the same as earthly honor.

338. See also Soham Al-Suadi, *Essen als Christgläubige*, TANZ 55 (Tübingen: Francke, 2011), 182: the imitation of Christ is transmitted to the early Christian communities by way of the imitation of Paul. See also Al-Suadi, who follows Merk, "Nachahmung," 230, with regard to the interpretation of Phil. 3.17.

339. Dodd, *Paul's Paradigmatic "I"*, 182.

340. For a concise critique, see Park, *Submission*, 57–62.

341. Dodd, *Paul's Paradigmatic "I"*, 182–183.

himself and the Philippians is taken into account, as well as the assumption that the Philippians are familiar with Paul and his biography is plausible, then the fact that Paul refers to things outside of the text, specifically aspects of his own biography, ceases to be as problematic as Dodd sees it. With regard to Dodd's first point, it should be maintained that the point that Paul makes through his example is not at all that all Philippians should be able to identify with his entire biography—this is simply not demanded by the rhetorical theory governing the use of *exempla*; furthermore, it is the *Ernstbedeutung* that counts for an *exemplum*, not the *Eigenbedeutung*. On the contrary, he argues that the Philippians should identify with his current position rather than with his past, or, analogously, with the "radical Jewish Christian" position.

Finally, it may be added from the perspective of the history of research, in which the imitation to which Paul calls in Phil. 3 has been interpreted variously,[342] that the opposition between two main interpretative strategies can be shown to be a false one. These two strategies are the following. First, it has been argued that the example calls for imitating Paul in terms of (i.e. through) obedience to his preaching.[343] Second, it has been argued that Phil. 3.17 refers to following the model of life that Paul embodies.[344] While obedience is doubtless involved, in Phil. 3 it seems to be obedience to the example that Paul presents, in other words, imitation of his attitude (φρονεῖν, see Phil. 3.15),[345] not least *vis-à-vis* suffering,[346] and walk of life. Messenger and message are too closely intertwined here to be able to separate them.

3.4.3.2 Paul's Identity and the Paradigm of Christ

Besides the question of the paradigmatic qualities of Christ and Paul on their own, there is the question of the extent to which Paul provides an embodied representation of Christ to the Philippian community. While the question of Christ's paradigmatic character is a theologically sensitive one because of its (possible or at least supposed) consequences for Pauline soteriology, Paul's possible paradigmatic character, especially in as far as it "mediates" Christ to the Philippian congregation, is a sensitive question in particular for reasons of ecclesiology, specifically with regard to questions of ecclesial ministry and of sacramentality. Here, first the position taken in this study will be outlined, after which a number of objections will be considered. A good starting point is the following table, provided by Strecker, who reads both Phil. 2.6-11 and Phil. 3.2-21 as describing

---

342. For the following, see, e.g. Bianchini, *L'Elogio*, 47–48.
343. See influentially, e.g., Michaelis, "μιμέομαι," esp. 670; see also Castelli, *Imitating*, 96.
344. See, e.g., De Boer, *Imitation*, 186.
345. See, e.g., Bockmuehl, *Philippians*, 224.
346. See, e.g., Oakes, *Philippians*, 106, 121; Bianchini, *L'Elogio*, 48.

processes of transition from one status to another, in other words, as two analogous processes.[347]

Table 3.2: **A Comparison of Christ and Paul in Philippians 2 and 3**

	Christ (Phil 2.6-11)	Paul/Philippians (Phil 3.2-21)
Status A	Divine μορφή	(Jewish) social status
Separation[348]	Kenosis	Regarding the past as something harmful/dirt → διὰ τὸν Χριστὸν
Liminality[349]	Kenosis/death	Suffering/death → κοινωνία παθημάτων αὐτοῦ
Aggregation	Exaltation	Upward call/metamorphosis of the body → ἄνω κλήσεως ... ἐν Χριστῷ Ἰησοῦ.
Status B[350]	Kyrios	Body of glory → σύμμορφον τῷ σώματι τῆς δόξης αὐτοῦ

---

347. See Christian Strecker, *Die liminale Theologie des Paulus. Zugänge zur paulinischen Theologie aus kulturanthropologischer Perspektive*, FRLANT 185 (Göttingen: Vandenhoeck & Ruprecht, 1999), 176; see also, idem, *op. cit.*, 176, n. 86, for further linguistic support for this thesis. See also, e.g., Williams, *Enemies*, 231, 237–239, for similar graphics and, e.g., O'Brien, "Gospel," 276–277, for a concurring position. Reumann, *Philippians*, 528, is critical of this position and considers the agreements between Phil. 2.5-11 and 3.4-11 limited. Also, e.g., Müller, *Brief*, 29, argues that themes that play a role in Phil. 2 hardly play a role in Phil. 3.
348. The following verbal parallels can be observed: μορφή (Phil. 2.7, 3.10), εὑρίσκω (2.7, 3.9). The use of δοῦλος in Phil. 1.1 and the reference to Christ taking the form of a slave in Phil. 2.7 can also be seen as constituting an agreement between Paul and Christ, as, e.g., Dodd, *Paul's Paradigmatic "I"*, 189, notes. In line with his general argument, Dodd disagrees with this position, arguing that Paul still remains a slave over against Christ the exalted Lord (Phil. 2.11). While this is obviously the case, Dodd ignores that Christ's slaves will also share in Christ's glory (Phil. 3.21). This largely undoes Dodd's objection: the trajectories that will be covered by Christ and the Christians are largely the same, albeit that, unlike Christ, Christians are not "trailblazers," and that they currently occupy a different position on the trajectory (namely that of being humbled) than Christ, who has already completed the course (unlike Paul; see, e.g., Phil. 3.13).
349. See, e.g., Dodd, *Paul's Paradigmatic "I"*, 187–188. In addition Dodd, *op. cit.*, 188–189, notes his disagreement with the view that there is an agreement between Christ and Paul in terms of their humiliation (Phil. 2.8 for Christ, Phil. 4.12 for Paul; see further, 2.3, 3.21) given that Christ humbled himself as part of his self-renunciation, while for Paul humiliation is not related to his renunciation of his Jewish past (in fact, one should say, his social and religious status) and Paul also knows times of abundance (Phil. 4.12). While the latter is certainly true (even if the remark about this serves a different purpose in Philippians), the former is the case despite Dodd's argument: Paul's humiliation, i.e. his humbled state, is certainly also a result of renouncing his prominent social and religious status.
350. See for agreements between Phil. 2.5-11 and Phil. 3.20-21 further below.

To this may be added that, when regarding Phil. 3.15-16 as a transitory passage between Paul's autobiographical statements and what follows, a striking resemblance to Phil. 2.5 can be noted.[351] As was already indicated above, the *enkomion* in Phil. 2 is introduced with τοῦτο φρονεῖτε ἐν ὑμῖν, and in Phil. 3.15 Paul prepares his call to imitation in Phil. 3.17 by stating exhortatively ὅσοι οὖν τέλειοι, τοῦτο φρονῶμεν.[352] Furthermore, Phil. 2.5-11 and Phil. 3.20-21 share a certain poetic (or "hymnic") quality. While the agreements between Paul's and Christ's "careers," in terms of both trajectory and linguistic description, may be obvious from the table presented above, the question of the differences between the two must also be addressed. The three most significant differences are the following. First, Christ starts out from a divine status, but Paul starts out from a Pharisaic Jewish identity. Second, Christ suffers and dies, but Paul only comes close to this. Third, Christ is glorified by God and exalted to a position of supreme lordship, but Paul still toils on earth.[353] Objections against viewing Paul as a model of Christ that are based on these differences are valid, but only to a certain extent. They invite one to consider the differences between Christ and Paul in Philippians as well.[354] To begin with, it should be taken into consideration that Paul himself is clearly aware of substantial differences between himself and Christ, given that he can describe their position *vis-à-vis* each other in terms of a slave–master relationship (Phil. 1.1), which indicates both hierarchy and submission. The latter also gives a reason to think that Paul viewed himself as someone who was aligned with Christ. Therefore, while keeping in mind the various differences between Christ and Paul, especially the difference in status that Paul indicates himself, it is expedient to look for agreements at the level of processes and structures, rather than demanding a one-to-one agreement between all aspects of Paul's and Christ's (current) identities. When doing this, the differences between Paul and Christ in terms of their starting points and, though probably to a more limited extent (as a substantial assimilation to Christ takes place in the believers' eschaton), in terms of their ends, burden Paul's agreement in identity with Christ less: from the start it is clear that it will be an agreement in the context of an (overarching) disagreement. Furthermore, when thinking in terms of processes (or "careers") that are not synchronous, while the latter one of the two is shaped according to the earlier one, the fact that Paul is still toiling and suffering on earth while Christ is exalted becomes less problematic. Not only is Christ primary in terms of status, but he

---

351. With Byron, *Metaphors*, 175; see also, Fee, *Letter*, 199.
352. See Byron, *Metaphors*, 176.
353. For this and a similar critique, see, e.g., Dodd, *Paul's Paradigmatic "I"*, 187–194.
354. This nuances the thesis of Reumann, *Philippians*, 589, that the paradigm set forth in this verse remains that of Paul and does not become one of Christ; Paul's paradigm is only valid in as far as it is based on Christ's.

is also first in terms of chronology.[357] The fact that Paul emphasizes that those in Christ are looking forward or should be looking forward to becoming similar to Christ agrees well with this. Paul (Phil. 3.10) and the Philippians (Phil. 3.21) will be σύμμορφος to Christ in his exaltation through becoming σύμμορφος to him in the course of their earthly lives (see the agreement in "form" language with Phil. 2.6-7).[358] What has to happen specifically in the eschaton is that the humble or humiliated bodies of Paul and the Philippians (τὸ σῶμα τῆς ταπεινώσεως ἡμῶν—Paul's inclusion of himself aligns him with the Philippians) will be made similar to Christ's glorified body. Especially in this part of Phil. 3, i.e. verses 20-21, similarities can be observed with Phil. 2.6-11, which may well have to do with the fact that both texts probably share a similar genre (and are both probably para-Pauline).[359] Specifically, the movement from humiliation to glory is striking.[360] The various words that echo each other can be found in the following table:[361]

---

355. These observations agree largely with those of Christian Strecker, "Leben als liminale Existenz. Kulturanthropologische Betrachtungen zum frühchristlichen Existenzverständnis am Beispiel von Phil 3," *EvTh* 68 (2008), 460–472, who argues that the process of being integrated into Christ consists of three phrases, namely initial integration into the Christian community, the (continuously challenged) life in it, and eschatological glorification with Christ (e.g. 467); Christians live, unlike Christ, in the second of these phases. These considerations are plausible, even if Strecker's reconstruction of the religious-historical background to the hymn can be disputed; see idem, *Theologie*, 159–177.

356. See, e.g., Williams, *Enemies*, 187.

357. On which see, e.g., Reumann, *Philippians*, 583–584, and esp., idem, "Philippians 3:20–21 – a Hymnic Fragment," *NTS* 30 (1984), 593–609.

358. See Robert Jewett, *Paul's Anthropological Terms: A Study of Their Use in Conflict Settings*, AGJU 10 (Leiden: Brill, 1971), 252: "The interplay of the terms ταπείνωσις and δόξα makes it clear that an *imitatio Dei* scheme underlies the argument in Phil. 3:21. Just as in Phil. 2:6-11 where Christ's ταπείνωσις was followed by δόξα, so the destiny of the individual Christian will be transformed from lowliness to glory." See further, Byron, *Metaphors*, 173, and Fowl, *Story*, 95, and Hellerman, *Honor*, 152, 161–163, who rightly notes that what one has in these verses is a reconstructed *cursus honorum*, now including Christ's (and Paul's and the Philippian Christians') suffering (and death) as well.

359. See Williams, *Enemies*, 231, 242–243. To this one might add that there is a parallel in terms of content between the description of Jesus' exaltation in Phil. 2.9-11 and the description of Jesus' subjection of all things in Phil. 3.21 (ὑποτάξαι αὐτῷ τὰ πάντα). Some of the agreements are clearer than others, but what is the most important is the general picture of linguistic agreement between Phil. 2.5-11 and 3.20-21. See also Byrnes, *Conformation*, 229–230, 235, and Oakes, *Philippians*, 201–202.

Table 3.3: **A Comparison of the Exaltation of Christ and Paul's Eschatological Hope**

Phil 2.6-11	Phil. 3.20-21
⁶ ὃς ἐν μορφῇ θεοῦ *ὑπάρχων* οὐχ ἁρπαγμὸν ἡγήσατο τὸ εἶναι ἴσα θεῷ, ⁷ ἀλλὰ ἑαυτὸν ἐκένωσεν *μορφὴν* δούλου λαβών, ἐν ὁμοιώματι ἀνθρώπων γενόμενος· καὶ *σχήματι* εὑρεθεὶς ὡς ἄνθρωπος ⁸ *ἐταπείνωσεν* ἑαυτὸν γενόμενος ὑπήκοος μέχρι θανάτου, θανάτου δὲ σταυροῦ. ⁹ διὸ καὶ ὁ θεὸς αὐτὸν ὑπερύψωσεν καὶ ἐχαρίσατο αὐτῷ τὸ ὄνομα τὸ ὑπὲρ πᾶν ὄνομα, ¹⁰ ἵνα ἐν τῷ ὀνόματι Ἰησοῦ πᾶν γόνυ κάμψῃ *ἐπουρανίων* καὶ ἐπιγείων καὶ καταχθονίων ¹¹ καὶ πᾶσα γλῶσσα ἐξομολογήσηται ὅτι *κύριος Ἰησοῦς Χριστὸς* εἰς *δόξαν* θεοῦ πατρός.	²⁰ ἡμῶν γὰρ τὸ πολίτευμα ἐν *οὐρανοῖς* ὑπάρχει, ἐξ οὗ καὶ σωτῆρα ἀπεκδεχόμεθα κύριον Ἰησοῦν Χριστόν, ²¹ ὃς *μετασχηματίσει* τὸ σῶμα τῆς *ταπεινώσεως* ἡμῶν *σύμμορφον* τῷ σώματι *τῆς δόξης* αὐτοῦ κατὰ τὴν ἐνέργειαν τοῦ δύνασθαι αὐτὸν καὶ ὑποτάξαι αὐτῷ τὰ πάντα.

Thus, Paul, who in Phil. 3 underlines his authority and presents himself as a model at the same time, also indicates why he can claim this position and this function, namely not only because he is (one of) the founding father(s), but also because he represents the faith by being fully integrated into the dynamics of Christ's life. It is not possible therefore, as is sometimes done, to play out against each other the notions of "being incorporated in Christ" and "imitating Christ," both of which are, in the view taken here, clearly present in Philippians. In sum, therefore, Paul represents Christ, or at least Christ in terms of living according to the mind of Christ: that is, in accord with Christ as he has been presented in the *enkomion* in Phil. 2. This identity, Paul also recommends strongly to the Philippians. Thus, in a differentiated way, it is possible to view Paul as an "ideal-typical Christian."[360] Against this background, the *auctoritas* of Paul's *exemplum* grounds not only in his position of *maior* vis-à-vis the Philippian community, but also in his relationship to the one who is a *maior* to both the Philippians and Paul: Christ. The *auctoritas* of the *exemplum* of Paul grounds in his following an even more authoritative *exemplum*: Christ, whom the Philippians are called upon to imitate directly in Phil. 2.

At this point, it should also be asked again how this section of Philippians fits into the overall plan of the letter. These considerations elaborate on what has been said before about Phil. 3 and the unity of Philippians, where it was mainly argued that it is possible to view Phil. 3 as part of the letter. However, there the function of this section in the letter was not yet considered fully. This will be done now, especially with regard to the rhetorical aspects of the

---

360. See Koperski, *Knowledge*, 273–275; the notion "typical Christian" is found on 273. See also Hooker's statement that Paul is patterned after Christ: Hooker, "Philippians," 393.

letter. One attractive proposal is to view Phil. 3.2-21 as a *digressio* (not unlike 2.19-30),[361] in other words, as a "digressing" and illustrative discussion of a matter that is of use for the actual topic at stake.[362] That Paul probably uses a tradition common to him and the Philippians at the very end of this, in Phil. 3.20-21, suits this well, as he thus indicates that they are on shared ground. All of this would agree well with Phil. 3 in the context of Philippians. Viewed as a *digressio*, the epideictic language of Phil. 3 would serve the overarching deliberative goal that Paul seems to be pursuing in his letter, that is, his attempt to move the Philippians towards the right attitude *vis-à-vis* the challenges they face. Beyond this, two further aspects of Phil. 3 can be highlighted with regard to its possible character as a *digressio*.

First, one may note with regard to the illustrative character of a *digressio* that this suits the above interpretation of the "dogs" in Philippians as a negative *exemplum* and the illustrative character of Paul's self-presentation very well. The question remains what exactly is being illustrated. This question leads to the next point.

Second, when studying the *exempla* presented in Phil. 3, one discovers that the theme running through the passage is akin to what Paul had already argued in Phil. 1.27–2.18, namely the question of identity in Christ, specifically as it is related to the suffering of Paul and of the Philippian community. Behind the question of suffering stands the question of the unity of the Philippian community. This may be clearer in Phil. 2 than in Phil. 3, but also in the latter chapter this topic is of importance. At the very least, Paul attempts to uphold the fellowship between himself and the Philippians, but by attempting to keep the "dogs" out he also attempts to counter divisions in the community and to address the issue of suffering in relation to identity "in Christ."

These two considerations make it possible to view Phil. 3 as functioning as a *digressio* in Philippians. This *digressio*, however, does not elaborate on a merely illustrative topic, but on one that is of actual importance for the

---

361. See D. E. Garland, "The Composition and Unity of Philippians: Some Neglected Literary Factors," *NovT* 27 (1985), 141–173, esp. 164–165, drawing on the general insights of W. Wuellner, "Greek Rhetoric and Pauline Argumentation," in W. R. Schoedel and R. L. Wilken (eds.), *Early Christian Literature and the Classical Intellectual Tradition: In Honorem Robert M. Grant*, Theologie Historique 54 (Paris: Beauchesne, 1979), 177–188, and J. J. Collins, "Chiasmus, the ABA Pattern and the Text of Paul," in s.a., *Studiorum Paulinorum Congressus Internationalis Catholicus, 1961*, I–II AnBib 17–18 (Rome: Pontificio Istituto Biblico, 1963), II, 575–583. This suggestion differs from the much more strongly voiced proposal by Briggs Kittredge, *Community*, 88–89, that this section of Philippians constitutes the third stage of Paul's rhetorical *probatio*; the structure that Briggs Kittredge proposes for Philippians seems to be somewhat in contradiction to contemporary epistolary conventions. This does not mean, however, that the functions of parts of letters could not be described with the help of rhetorical terminology, without simultaneously implying letter-writing after the model of speech-writing.

362. So, e.g., the definitions of Lausberg, *Handbuch*, para. 340, and idem, *Elemente*, paras. 434, 441, as well as the older definition of R. Volkmann, *Die Rhetorik der Griechen und Römer in systematischer Übersicht* (repr. Hildesheim, 1963 [Leipzig, 1885]), para. 14.

Philippians as well (given that the "dogs" pose an actual threat to the integrity of their faith—this is at least how Paul sees it) and thus illustrates one issue by addressing another, related one. Thus, this section has both an "epistolary" and a "rhetorical" function, quite like Phil. 2.19-30.

3.4.4 Excursus: Paul as a Paradigmatic Man?

3.4.4.1 Introduction

The author of a letter, such as Paul, as well as the authorities that he appeals to (in Paul's case, Christ) and the people that he recommends (in Philippians, Timothy and Epaphroditus) all need to be credible (i.e. have an appropriate "ethos"). Part of the credibility of an author (or rhetor) is provided by his masculinity:[363] Only a "real man" had, at least generally speaking, the right to speak (in public) in the Greco-Roman world. As Paul presents himself and Timothy from the first verse of Philippians onwards as embodying highly unmasculine identities[364]—as slaves of Christ (Phil. 1.1), who, as a crucified slave, is not an example of ideal-typical masculinity either—and refers to Christ and himself as *exempla* throughout Philippians, asking the question about masculinity in Philippians is justified. The question at stake is therefore: How is the identity of Paul constructed from the perspective of "typical" Greco-Roman masculinity?[365] Answering this question will further the understanding of the construction of early Christian identity "at the foot of the cross." Even though Christ, Timothy, and Epaphroditus could also be analyzed, here only Paul is considered, given that he is the most prominent man in Philippians, which itself is also an expression of himself and his identity; furthermore, it seems that what can be said about him can also be said about the other three men.

---

363. See, e.g., Amy Richlin, "Gender and Rhetoric: Producing Manhood in the Schools," in William J. Dominik (ed.), *Roman Eloquence: Rhetoric in Society and Literature* (London: Routledge, 1997), 90–110. For a still helpful overview of the masculinity studies and the New Testament, see Stephen D. Moore, "'O Man, Who Art Thou ...?' Masculinity Studies and New Testament Studies," in idem and Janice Capel Anderson (eds.), *New Testament Masculinities*, Semeia Studies 45 (Atlanta: SBL, 2003), 1–22, as well as in the same volume, Janice Capel Anderson, Stephen D. Moore, and Seong Hee Kim, "Masculinity Studies: A Classified Bibliography," 23–42; for an overview in German, see Martin Leutzsch, "Konstruktionen von Männlichkeit im Urchristentum," in Frank Crüsemann, Claudia Janssen, Rainer Kessler, and Beate Wehn (eds.), *Dem Tod nicht glauben: Sozialgeschichte der Bibel* (FS Luise Schottroff; Gütersloh: Gütersloher Verlagshaus, 2004), 600–618.

364. On the importance of gender and embodiment in the creation and expression of identity, see, e.g., Lieu, *Identity*, 178–210.

365. See, e.g., Halvor Moxnes, "Conventional Values in the Hellenistic World: Masculinity," in Per Bilde, Troels Engberg-Pedersen, Lise Hannestad, and Jan Zahle (eds.), *Conventional Values of the Hellenistic Greeks*, Studies in Hellenistic Civilization 8 (Aarhus: Aarhus University Press, 1997), 263–284.

3.4.4.2 Masculinity in the Greco-Roman World

The table of contents of Goodman's *The Roman World* provides an interesting starting point for a discussion of masculinity and related questions of gender ideals in the early imperial world.[366] This table of contents indicates that the book also discusses the organization of the city of Rome, listing its constituent parts as follows: imperial court,[367] senators, *equites*, *plebs*, women, and slaves.[368] This not only gives a good impression of a heavily stratified society, but also offers an illustration of a highly hierarchical concept of masculinity, in which women also have their place. In the Greco-Roman world, a "monosexual" model was current,[369] in which a person can only be more or less masculine and is not man or woman and hence not masculine or feminine in any essential sense of the word.[370] Such a concept of sex and gender may also be assumed for the world in which Paul and the Philippians lived. This hierarchy of masculinity can be described as a hierarchy of penetration.[371]

---

366. Martin Goodman, *The Roman World 44 BC – AD 180* (New York: Routledge, 1997), ix. The view presented here should be nuanced somewhat by taking into consideration that indulging in "feminine" luxury could also be seen as a symbol of power; see on this, e.g., Emma Dench, "Austerity, Excess, Success and Failure in Hellenistic and Early Imperial Italy," in Maria Wyke (ed.), *Parchments of Gender: Deciphering the Bodies of Antiquity* (Oxford: Clarendon Press, 1998), 121–146.

367. On the imperial court from the perspective of gender studies, see, e.g., Susan Fischer, "Imperial Cult: Engendering the Cosmos," in Foxhall and Salmon, *Men*, 165–183, esp. 169; see in the same volume, also, Jim Roy, "The Masculinity of the Hellenistic King," 111–135.

368. Goodman, *World*, ix.

369. See, e.g., Sandra Hack Polaski, *A Feminist Introduction to Paul* (St. Louis: Chalice, 2005), 17–23.

370. With obvious consequences for the interpretation of texts such as Rom. 1.26-27, which cannot be read in a "heterosexual–homosexual" framework; see on this, e.g., Diana M. Swancutt, "'The Disease of Effemination': The Charge of Effeminacy and the Verdict of God (Romans 1:18–2:16)," in Moore and Capel Anderson (eds.), *Masculinities*, 193–233, esp. 194–205. See further, e.g., H. Herter, "Effeminatus," *RAC* 4 (1959), 620–650.

371. The title and content of Eckhard Meyer-Zwiffelhoffer, *Im Zeichen des Phallus. Die Ordnung des Geschlechtsleben im antiken Rom* (Frankfurt: Campus, 1995) express this eloquently. A statement like "Greek culture was bisexual" (Daniel H. Garrison, *Sexual Culture in Ancient Greece* [Norman: University of Oklahoma Press, 2000], 108) is potentially misleading: Greek culture was not so much bisexual as "monosexual" and more focused on the question of "penetration" (understood both physically and symbolically) than on that of biological "sex" in order to answer the question whether someone was male/masculine or female/feminine. See, e.g., James Davidson, "Dover, Foucault and Greek Homosexuality," *Past and Present* 170 (2001), 3–51, and also, e.g., Jorunn Økland, "Sex, Gender and Ancient Greek: A Case-Study in Theoretical Misfit," *StTh* 57:2 (2003), 1–19. The (critical) account given by Bruce S. Thornton, *Eros: The Myth of Ancient Greek Sexuality* (Boulder: Westview, 1997), 106–110, entitled "The Heterosexual Paradigm" is convincing. See further, also, Hans van Wees, "A Brief History of Tears: Gender Differentiation in Archaic Greece," in Foxhall and Salmon (eds.) *Men*, 10–53, and Alan H. Sommerstein, "Rape and Young Manhood in Athenian Comedy," in Lin Foxhall and John Salmon (eds.), *Thinking Men: Masculinity and Self-Representation in the Classical Tradition* (London: Routledge, 1998), 100–114, as well as Jonathan Walters, "Juvenal, *Satire* 2: Putting Male Sexual Deviants on Show," in Foxhall and Salmon (eds.), *Thinking*, 148–157. Other insightful contributions include, notably, Thomas Laqueur, *Making Sex: Body and*

This is shorthand for a situation in which one's degree of masculinity is determined by the extent to which one penetrates others and vice versa. Even though much of the background of this image is sexual, it is of importance to note that it could be applied to all aspects of life.[372] In this context, concepts such as autarky and the control over one's own passions became closely associated with the ideal of masculinity.[373] Larson describes the state of affairs as follows:

> Elite males were highly conscious of the fact that each of these groups (i.e. slaves, clients, women; *pbs*) was subject to their sexual demands; their right to sexually penetrate members of these groups was a reflection of their political and social dominance. According to a celebrated saying of the advocate Haterius, "Loss of sexual virtue (*impudicitia*) is a crime in a free man, a necessity for a slave, and a duty (*officium*) for a freed-man." What was most appalling about free, elite males who played a passive role in intercourse was that they willingly surrendered the masculine prerogative, thus allying themselves with lower-status groups who were expected to conciliate, flatter, and provide pleasure to their superiors.[374]

Gender from the Greeks to Freud (Cambridge, MA: Harvard University Press, 1990), 1–62. On Roman views of sexuality, see further, Jonathan Walters, "Invading the Roman Body: Manliness and Impenetrability in Roman Thought," in Judith P. Hallett and Marilyn B. Skinner (eds.), *Roman Sexualities* (Princeton: Princeton University Press, 1997); in the same volume also, the discussion of the masculinisation of "lesbian" women is of importance; see Pamela Gordon, "The Lover's Voice in *Heroides* 15: Or, Why is Sappho a Man?", 274–291, as well as Judith P. Hallett, "Female Homoeroticism and the Denial of Roman Reality in Latin Literature," 255–273. From the Hellenistic-Jewish tradition, for example, the description of the mother of the seven Maccabean martyrs is of interest, given that she is said to have had the "soul of Abraham" (4 Macc. 14.20); see Robin Darling Young, "The 'Woman with the Soul of Abraham': Traditions about the Mother of the Maccabean Martyrs," in Amy–Jill Levine, *"Women Like This": New Perspectives on Jewish Women in the Greco-Roman World*, SBL Early Judaism and Its Literature 1 (Atlanta: Scholars Press, 1991), 67–81. This mother is very clearly presented as a masculine woman.

372. Including, even *par excellence*, the field of rhetoric; see Jennifer Larson, "Paul's Masculinity," *JBL* 123 (2004), 85–97, esp. 87–91 on 2 Cor. 10.10. See also, Moisés Mayordomo-Marín, "Construction of Masculinity in Antiquity and Early Christianity," *Lectio Difficilior* 2, 2006.

373. See Colleen M. Conway, "'Behold the Man!' Masculine Christology and the Fourth Gospel," in Moore and Capel Anderson (eds.), *Masculinities*, 163–180, esp. 166–170, concerning self-control as an aspect of masculinity. Conway's observations agree well with the outline provided by Ivarsson: masculinity was defined positively as dominance and self-mastery, negatively as the opposite of effeminacy, and depended on corporal and sexual integrity. See Fredrik Ivarsson, "Christian Identity as True Masculinity," in Bengt Holmberg (ed.), *Exploring Early Christian Identity*, WUNT 1.226 (Tübingen: Mohr Siebeck, 2008), 159–171, esp. 160–161.

374. Larson, "Masculinity," 93. The quotation of Haterius stems from Seneca, *Contr.* 4, pref. 10. In Petronius, *Sat.* 75:11, a similar concept surfaces: Trimalchio, a freedman, argues that nothing that is commanded by the master is immoral. See further, e.g., Moses I. Finley, *Ancient Slavery and Modern Ideology* (London: Chatto & Windus, 1980), 95–96, and Maud W. Gleason, *Making Men: Sophists and Self-Presentation in Ancient Rome* (Princeton: Princeton University Press, 1995).

A further illustration of this state of affairs concerning gender and the construction of masculinity, with women and slaves (typically) at the bottom of the hierarchy, is the high frequency of themes such as the "clever slave" or the "dominant woman" in contemporary comedy,[375] addressing the perpetually vulnerable masculinity of husbands and masters.[376] Larson again helpfully summarizes the situation:

> Masculinity was viewed as an attribute only partially related to an individual's anatomical sex ... Because masculinity was all but identified with social and political dominance, there was no assumption that all males must be masculine. The masculinity of slaves, for example, was by definition impaired. Personal dignity, bodily integrity, and specific details of one's appearance were all factors in individual self-assessment and in men's evaluation of one another's masculinity. Elite men of the day were constantly concerned with the maintenance of their masculinity, because it both displayed and justified their positions of power. Unlike noble birth, which was immutable, masculinity was a matter of perception. While elites always represented their masculinity to outsiders as innate, among insiders it was implicitly recognized that masculinity was a performance requiring constant practice and vigilance.[377]

---

375. This reflects a social dynamic; see, e.g., Beate Wagner-Hasel, "Das Diktum der Philosophen: Der Ausschluss der Frauen aus der Politik und die Sorge vor der Frauenherrschaft," in Thomas Späth and Beate Wagner-Hasel (eds.), *Frauenwelten in der Antike. Geschlechterordnung und weibliche Lebenspraxis* (Darmstadt: Wissenschaftliche Buchgesellschaft, 2000), 198–217. See also the excursus about Amazons, "Amazons: Women in Control," in Elaine Fantham, Helene Peet Foley, Natalie Boymel Kampen, Sarah B. Pomeroy, and H. A. Shapiro, *Women in the Classical World: Image and Text* (Oxford: Oxford University Press, 1994), 128–135; the negative portrayal of Amazons by ancient authors has to do with the problem of control as well.

376. See Annalisa Rei, "Villains, Wives and Slaves in the Comedies of Plautus," in Sandra R. Joshel and Sheila Murnaghan (eds.), *Women and Slaves in Greco-Roman Culture* (New York: Routledge, 1998), 92–108; see further also, Walters, "Juvenal," and Karen F. Pierce, "Ideals of Masculinity in New Comedy," in Foxhall and Salmon (eds.), *Thinking*, 130–147. Love and being in love was (naturally) seen as a destabilizing factor that threatened (self-)control; see Kathleen McCarthy, "Servitium Amoris: Amor Servitii," in Joshel and Murnaghan (eds.), *Women*, 174–192. In times that were perceived as ideological crises, themes such as the faithful wife and, ditto, slave were more frequent in the arts; see Holt Parker, "Loyal Slaves and Loyal Wives: This Crisis of the Outsider-Within and Roman *Exemplum* Literature," in Joshel and Murnaghan (eds.), *Women*, 152–173. On the question of social control, see further, e.g., Keith R. Bradley, *Slaves and Masters in the Roman Empire: A Study in Social Control*, Collection Latomus 185 (Bruxelles: Latomus, 1984), esp. 113–137. Thornton, *Eros*, 166–169, refers with regard to this question to the chaste and faithful wife as a man's "most important possession" (166). On the relation between gender and power in Rome in general, see, e.g., Amy Richlin, *The Garden of Priapus: Sexuality and Aggression in Roman Humor* (rev. edn.; Oxford: Oxford University Press, 1992), xiii–xxxiii, and Sandra Joshel, "The Body Female and the Body Politic: Livy's Lucretia and Virginia," in Amy Richlin (ed.), *Pornography and Representation in Greece and Rome* (Oxford: Oxford University Press, 1992), 120–126.

377. Larson, "Masculinity," 86.

On this basis, some aspects of Paul's masculinity in Philippians may now be considered.[378]

3.4.4.3 Outstanding Aspects of Paul's Masculinity in Philippians

Beginning with the epistolary introduction (Phil. 1.1-2), the following striking aspects of Paul's masculinity may be noted.

First, the description of Paul (and Timothy) as "slaves of Christ" in Phil 1.1 should be addressed. Even though it is, in the tradition of the LXX,[379] well possible to describe devotees of YHWH as "slaves," being a slave, which implies loss of control (literally "ownership") over one's own life,[380] is highly problematic from the perspective of contemporary ideals of masculinity.[381] To quote Larson again: "The essence of the Greco-Roman concept of masculinity was that a 'real' man does not cede power or control to another, as slaves and women do. As traditionally constructed, masculinity was closely tied to the concepts of personal freedom and power over others and was incompatible with Paul's concept of 'willing slavery' in Christ."[382] Because of the expression used in Phil. 1.1, Christ appears as the lord ("master") of Paul and Timothy. This is not without problems either, as will be considered below with regard to Christ's shameful death on the cross and Christ's own identity as a slave.

Second, Paul's imprisonment is relevant. It is first mentioned in Phil. 1.7. Incarceration is the opposite of a situation in which the masculine ideals of autonomy and autarky can be realized.[383] The fact that Paul addresses his

---

378. See also David J. A. Clines, "Paul, the Invisible Man," in Moore and Capel Anderson (eds.), *Masculinities*, 181–192, who lists "strength," "violence," "powerful and persuasive speech," "male bonding," and "the womanless man" as typical aspects of a real man in the early empire; Clines' contribution suffers from a lack of interaction with the actual state of affairs in the first century; most of his observations could well be fitted in the model of the "hierarchy of penetration" just described and his conclusion that Paul was a fairly common male should also be reconsidered with reference to the same body of theory and literature.

379. The importance of the LXX for Philippians may have been limited, given their largely Gentile background and the fact that there was only a small Jewish presence in their city.

380. On slaves, masters and control, subjects closely related to the question of autarky. see, e.g., Bradley, *Slaves*, esp. 21–45 on obedience and faithfulness, and 113–137 on fear, with an epilogue on control (139–143).

381. This also applies to someone who takes the part of a slave voluntarily, as Paul does in 1 Cor. 9.19. See, e.g., Mayordomo-Marín, "Construction"; apart from losing one's masculine status (or honor) due to loss of control over oneself, someone that behaves in this way could also be seen as a flatterer. Nevertheless, Paul aims at strengthening his own position through his usage of this image. See Dale Martin, *Slavery as Salvation: The Metaphor of Slavery in Pauline Christianity* (New Haven: Yale University Press, 1990), 117–118, 124–126; see further, Erik Gunderson, *Staging Masculinity: The Rhetoric of Performance in the Roman World* (Ann Arbor: University of Michigan Press, 2000), 87–110.

382. Larson, "Masculinity," 91. See on this, also, Michel Foucault, *The Use of Pleasure* (trans. R. Hurley; New York: Pantheon Books, 1985), 78–86. Such self-control was related to all aspects of life; see, e.g., Alfred R. Mele, *Irrationality: An Essay on Akrasia, Self-Deception, and Self-Control* (Oxford: Oxford University Press, 1987).

383. Different from 2 Cor. 11, Paul does not mention the humiliating and unmasculine punishment of flagellation, on which see, e.g., Larson, "Masculinity," 93–94.

imprisonment and its consequences so extensively at the very beginning of his letter has its background most likely not only in the circumstance that an "epistolary self-disclosure" would be expected at this point, but also in the fact that Paul, as a prisoner, has to justify himself and establish his masculine right to speak. This latter point needs to be elaborated somewhat further.

Letters to some extent made up for the absence of the letter writer from the recipient and, for that reason, could also provide the sender a place at the table in a debate during his absence. As will be clear from, for example, the various attempts to regulate public speech in the New Testament,[384] it was by no means granted to all to speak in the public arena. In analogy to this, it may well be surmised that having one's letter received and read in public, as was probably the case with Paul's letters upon their first arrival in a community, thereby making the apostle's voice heard to distant communities, was not at all a matter of course.[385] Furthermore, it may be regarded as commonplace that the weight that one's voice was given depended not only to a considerable extent on a speaker's reputation and status, but also on his delivery, or "performance."[386] Paul's defense of his rhetorical performance in 2 Cor. 10.10 is an interesting pointer with regard to this.[387] Even clearer are texts like the following portion from Tacitus' *Dialogus* 18.5, especially as it refers to letters; the same conventions seem to apply to letters as to speeches:

> You have read, of course, the letters of Calvus and Brutus to Cicero, from which it is easy to gather that, as for Calvus, Cicero thought him bloodless and attenuated, just as he thought Brutus spiritless and disjointed; while Cicero was in his turn criticized by Calvus as flabby and pithless, and by Brutus, to use his own expression as "feeble and emasculate."[388]

---

384. See, e.g., 1 Cor. 14.27-30, 34-35; 1 Tim. 2.11-15; Tit. 1.11; Jas. 3.1; note that two of these texts are related to questions of gender.
385. See below on the example of 2 Cor. 10.10.
386. See, e.g., Mayordomo-Marín, "Construction," 9.
387. On this passage and the background in Greco-Roman rhetoric, see, e.g., Margareth E. Thrall, *2 Corinthians* 2, ICC (Edinburgh: T&T Clark, 2000), 630–631, and esp. J. Albert Harrill, "Invective against Paul (2 Cor 10:10), the Physiognomics of the Ancient Slave Body, and the Greco-Roman Rhetoric of Manhood," in Adela Yarbro Collins and Margaret M. Mitchell (eds.), *Antiquity and Humanity: Essays on Ancient Religion and Philosophy* (FS Hans Dieter Betz; Tübingen: Mohr Siebeck, 2001), 189–213; Clines, "Paul," 186–188, manages to push the relevance of this passage to the margins by arguing that what really counts is that Paul is persuasive in his letters; however, this ignores the importance of the performance of masculinity precisely in the arena of public speech, not letter-writing.
388. W. Peterson and M. Winterbottom, "Dialogus," in Tacitus, *Agricola, Germania, Dialogus*, LCL 35 (Cambridge, MA: Harvard University Press, 1980), 279. For the Latin text, see Roland Mayer (ed.), *Tacitus: Dialogus de Oratoribus* (Cambridge, UK: Cambridge University Press, 2001), 66: "legistis utique et Calvi et Bruti ad Ciceronem missas epistulas, ex quibus facile est deprehendere Calvum quidem Ciceroni visum exsanguem et aridum, Brutum autem otiosum atque diiunctum; rursusque Ciceronem a Calvo quidem male audisse tamquam solutum et enervem, a Bruto autem, ut ipsius verbis utar, tamquam 'fractum atque elumbem'."

In particular, the question to what extent a speaker could truly be regarded as virtuous, quite literally in the sense of being a proper *vir* and hence worthy of performing in the arena of public speech, was a topic of much interest among speakers,[389] as the following examples from the fourth century BCE and the first century CE show:

> In the case of Demosthenes' nickname, he is called Batalos, not wrongly, by report, not by his nurse; he has brought the name on himself for his effeminacy and his deviance. If someone were to take off you those fancy little cloaks and those delicate little tunics, which you wear when you are writing your speeches against your friends, and were to pass them around and give them to the jurymen, I think that they would be quite uncertain, if someone had not told them in advance when doing this, whether they were handling the clothes of a man or of a woman.[390]

> If you wish to distress the man who hates you, do not revile him as lewd, effeminate, licentious, vulgar, or illiberal, but be a man yourself, show self-control, be truthful, and treat with kindness and justice those who have to deal with you. And if you are led into reviling, remove yourself as far as possible from the things for which you revile him. (Plutarch, *Mor.* 88C–D)[391]

Both Aeschines[392] and Plutarch[393] refer to situations of public debate. Finally, a text from Seneca the Elder may be quoted, in which he presents a(n admittedly contested) Roman ruling:

> An unchaste man shall be barred from speaking in public.
> A handsome youth betted he would go out in public in women's clothes. He did so, and got raped by ten youths. He accused them of violence, and had them convicted.

---

389. See, e.g., Larson, "Masculinity," esp. 89–90, and also Mayordomo-Marín, "Construction," 5, 9–10, as well as, esp., Gunderson, *Staging*, particularly 29–110.

390. Aeschines, *Against Timarchos* 131, quoted from Nick Fisher, *Aeschines: Against Timarchos*, Clarendon Ancient History Series (Oxford: Oxford University Press, 2001), 101–102; Batalos, who is mentioned here, was a particularly feminine flute-player, also featuring in a play; see idem, *op. cit.*, 271–272. For the Greek text, see Mervin R. Dilts (ed.), *Aeschines: Orationes*, Bibliotheca Scriptorum Graecorum et Romanorum Teubneriana (Stuttgart: Teubner, 1997), 65.

391. Text and translation: Frank Cole Babbitt (ed. and trans.), *Plutarch: Moralia*, II LCL 222 (Cambridge, MA: Harvard University Press, 1928), *ad loc.*

392. As an orator Aeschines often accused his opponents and their associates of being κίναιδοι, or pathetics, as a way of delegitimizing their right to bring suits and to speak in public (Aeschines, *Fais. leg.* 88:6, 99:5, 151:4; *Tim.* 131:4, 181:10). See also John Winkler, "Laying Down the Law: The Oversight of Men's Sexual Behavior in Classical Athens," in D. Halperin, J. Winkler, and F. Zeitlin (eds.), *Before Sexuality: The Construction of Erotic Experience in the Ancient Greek World* (Princeton: Princeton University Press, 1990), 171–209.

393. Plutarch is apparently familiar with the tradition of verbal abuse in which Aeschines also stands. See further, also, the overview offered by Jane F. Gardner, "Sexing a Roman: Imperfect Men in Roman Law," in Foxhall and Salmon (eds.), *Men*, 136–152.

Forbidden by a magistrate to speak to the people [i.e. because of his loss of virility; *pbs*], he accuses the magistrate of injuring him.[394]

As will be apparent from these texts, the opposite of what may be termed "virility," with which the ideal of autarky was closely associated, namely "weakness," was something that indeed diminished a speaker's credibility, or even his right to speak at all in the somewhat extreme case cited above. From these examples, it will also be clear that a man's reputation was constantly challenged and called into question.[395]

As has been illustrated now, virility was a precondition for speaking in the public arena and imprisonment did not enhance a man's standing in terms of his masculinity. Paul overcomes this obvious problem by presenting his imprisonment as a tool for his apostolic ministry. In this way, he (re-)establishes himself as a potent man and thus establishes his right to speak in the public arena.

Third, it should be stressed that Paul is preoccupied with honor (δόξα; opposite: αἰσχύνη, shame), a concept of central importance for the early imperial discourse about masculinity.[396] "Honor" occurs in Philippians in 1.11, 2.11, 3.19, 21, and 4.19-20. In Phil. 1.11, the honor (or glory or splendor) of God is mentioned. In Phil. 2.11, Christ's lordship is to the honor (glory) of God. As these two texts, together with Phil. 4.19-20, are concerned with the honor of God, they are not of primary importance for the topic at stake here. In Phil. 3.19-21, however, two kinds of honor are contrasted with one another that have directly to do with the question of earthly status and hence have a bearing on the topic of masculinity. In Phil. 3.19, Paul refers pejoratively (and presumably hyperbolically) to people whose god is their belly and whose honor is in their shame (ὧν ὁ θεὸς ἡ κοιλία καὶ ἡ δόξα ἐν τῇ αἰσχύνῃ αὐτῶν). Whatever the precise meaning of the reference to the belly and the shame, Paul's point is that these people seek honor where it cannot really be found, namely by focusing on earthly things.[397] The earthly status and honor of these people may well have been considerable, but it is vainglory (see 2.3) in the truest sense of the word as it leads to destruction

---

394. Text and translation: Michael Winterbottom (trans. and ed.), *The Elder Seneca I: Controversiae I–VI*, LCL 463 (Cambridge, MA: Harvard University Press, 1974), 488–489. Parallels to this law from Greek and Roman circles can be found in S. F. Bonner, *Roman Declamation in the Late Republic and Early Empire* (Liverpool: Liverpool University Press, 1969 [1949]), 105, For other examples of attacks on masculinity in Roman rhetoric, see Richlin, *Garden*, 81–104; see also the discussion by Fisher, *Aeschines*, 36–53.

395. See also Larson, "Masculinity," 86.

396. See Witherington, *Friendship*, 63; Williams, *Enemies*, 125; Walter, "Brief," 53–54. In the tradition of the Hebrew Bible/Old Testament, humility was seen as a virtue; however, see, e.g., Pss. 10.17-18, 25.18, 31.7; Prov. 3.34, 11.2, 15.33; Job 5.11. Humility or meekness could also be associated with flattery, on which, see, e.g., Larson, "Masculinity," 92, and esp. Peter Marshall, *Enmity in Corinth: Social Conventions in Paul's Relations with the Corinthians*, WUNT 2.23 (Tübingen: Mohr Siebeck, 1987), 323–325.

397. See, e.g., Reumann, *Philippians*, 595.

(verse 19), not to lasting honor. This misguided (earthly) glory stands in contrast with the heavenly (or eschatological) honor that is due to those who seemed to be without honor on earth because they were humiliated because of Christ (see 3.21: τὸ σῶμα τῆς ταπεινώσεως ἡμῶν). Earthly glory leads to annihilation, earthly humiliation because of Christ leads, in analogy to Christ (3.21, see Phil. 2.5-11), to glorification. The resulting paradox is that for those in Christ, true masculinity is not necessarily the kind of masculinity that is generally recognizable as such on earth, but rather the kind of masculinity that only becomes realized through God's intervention. Paul's ultimate aims, avoiding dishonor and gaining honor, are well in line with those of the society in which he lived, but the road towards it is controversial, just as Christ's lordship is controversial, as it is the result of glorification following his humiliation on the cross.

Fourth, in his laudatory recommendation of Timothy, who is to be sent to Philippi soon, Paul no longer presents himself as Timothy's fellow slave, but as his father (Phil. 2.22), which positions Paul as a figure with literally patriarchal status, which agrees well with the self-presentation of first-century patrons in general.[398]

Fifth, the climax of Paul's self-presentation, also in terms of masculinity, comes in Phil. 3, where Paul, arguing against the "dogs" that present a threat to the faithful in Philippi, presents himself first as a kind of "superdog" by recounting his pedigree and *res gestae* before his encounter with Christ (Phil. 3.4-6). Paul's descent and *res gestae* are immaculate with all sorts of (positive) consequences for his status as a man. Paul's giving up all this in order to gain Christ (Phil. 3.8) means also the giving up of his status as a (typical) man in the eyes of contemporary society. Not all is said with this, however: Paul defends his giving up of all his achievements and his former status with a reference to gaining Christ (Phil. 3.7-8). The choice for the most advantageous option, as that is how Paul presents his opting for Christ, would be easily understandable as such, though it is not immediately obvious why the choice for Christ is so much more attractive than Paul's glorious career up until that point. This, however, becomes clear in subsequent parts of Phil. 3. In terms of Paul's self-presentation, the climax of this chapter comes in Phil. 3.9-14. Here, Paul recounts his reorientation towards Christ. In terms of masculinity, the most controversial part of this is Paul's wish to share in Christ's suffering and to be conformed to his death (Phil. 3.10)[399] in order to participate in his resurrection as well (Phil. 3.11). These wishes of Paul serve his overarching goal of being justified, not through the works of the law, but through faith in Christ (Phil. 3.9),[400]

---

398. On which, see Larson, "Masculinity," 95–96; see esp. 1 Cor. 4.21, and further, e.g., 1 Cor. 4.14-15; 2 Cor. 11.2-3, 12.14.

399. The form that is used in Phil. 3.10, συμμορφιζόμενος, is reminiscent of Phil. 2.7 where Christ takes the μορφή of a slave (instead of the μορφή of God; see Phil. 2.6).

400. Phil. 3.9 is a text of central importance for the interpretation of the expression πίστις Χριστοῦ; see on this, above, 3.4.1.2.

and hence achieving eschatological glorification. That Paul's masculinity is controversial and ambiguous becomes in this context especially clear in Phil. 3.8-11, where Paul pursues a highly controversial course of action: moving away from the status that he had acquired during his previous life and embracing suffering and death as the consequence and outward shape of following Christ as κύριος. In doing this, he succeeds in achieving an (even more) honorable status again. Paul addresses this apparent paradox again in Phil. 3.12-14, now using the image of the ἀγών with the help of which he is able to combine the notions of (shameful) suffering (and even death) with reaching an honorable goal, and to conceptualize all of this in a way that was accessible to a first-century audience.[401] The image of the ἀγών itself stems from two of the fields (besides the political arena) in which achieving or losing masculinity was the most prominent: the military, and athletics.[402] In this way, something that would have been rather controversial, especially also in terms of masculinity, is cast in the mode of a model that no one in the first century could have objected to and that could also serve well as a model for the church in Philippi (see also Phil. 3.17).

A final text in which Paul's masculinity, specifically his autarky or self-sufficiency, plays a role is Phil. 4.10-20 (see Phil. 1.5), where Paul addresses the material support that he has received from the Philippians. In Phil. 4.10, Paul expresses his joy over the Philippians' attention, but underlines immediately afterwards that he is really autarkic (Phil. 4.11-13, see esp. verse 11: αὐτάρκης) under all circumstances.[403] That the source of Paul's autarky is Christ is mentioned as little more than an aside (verse 13). While autarky is a masculine attribute in general, in Phil. 4.10-20 it is not just this that is at stake, but also Paul's attempt to retain his "patronal" status *vis-à-vis* the Philippian church. If Paul were to become financially dependent on the Philippians, this would change his status from patron to that of client, with all sorts of consequences for his status as a man. In order to avoid this, Paul on the one hand emphasizes his autarky (and, with that, traditional masculinity) and on the other hand he reinterprets the support of the Philippians in such a way that it turns out to be his support for the Philippians rather than vice versa.[404] In this way, Paul establishes both his autarky and his position as a patron of the Philippian church, and, with that, his masculinity.

---

401. See, e.g., Scroggs, "Paul," 198.

402. On this topic, see, e.g., Onno van Nijf, "Athletics, *Andreia* and the *Askêsis*-Culture," in Ralph M. Rosen and Ineke Sluiter (eds.), *Andreia: Studies in Manliness and Courage in Classical Antiquity* (Leiden: Brill, 2002), 263–286. With regard to athletics, James R. Harrison, "Paul and the Athletic Ideal in Antiquity: A Case Study in Wrestling with Word and Image," in Stanley E. Porter (ed.), *Paul's World*, Pauline Studies 4 (Leiden: Brill, 2008), 81–109, should especially be noted, which innovatively takes into account visual representations of athletes.

403. Having to endure difficult circumstances as such is not a mark of masculinity; however, see, e.g., Larson, "Masculinity," 93.

404. See above, 2.3.4.

Thus, "Paul the man" is ambiguous. At first sight, Paul is a highly unusual man, both in terms of his orientation towards Christ (Paul is the slave of a crucified slave) and in terms of the performance of his masculinity. As becomes clear from Phil. 3, the consequence of encountering Christ is to renounce all (social and religious) status (symbols) and to embrace even suffering and death because of Christ. Paul's imprisonment fits into this picture. This all equals giving up masculinity as such, it seems. All of this is but one side of the coin, however, given that Paul presents himself (and Christ) as hypermasculine figures simultaneously. As he indicates, his own imprisonment is really an effective evangelistic tool, Christ who died a slave's death on the cross eventually becomes ruler of all, and the acceptance of suffering and death because of Christ that Paul has embraced and that he recommends to the Philippians aims at the eventual glorification with Christ. In between, Paul also appears as a father in relation to Timothy and he makes sure that he is the Philippians' patron and not their client with regard to their material support. Therefore, things are not the way they seem: in his unmasculine appearance Paul is very much the man—or at least hopes to be this in the future. Paul does not so much question contemporary ideals of masculinity, as have his own view of the road towards it, which he sees in terms of the ἀγών, a concept that enables him to combine unmasculine appearance and activities with striving to achieve hypermasculinity.

3.4.4.4 Conclusions
In view of the above, it may be proposed that Paul is a good Greco-Roman man at the meta-level of some of his interests, though he is less so in terms of some of the contents of his preaching and lifestyle; his encounter with and subsequent following of Christ leads him to redefine what is truly honorable and truly authoritative, at least during one's earthly existence.[405]

In the end, Paul does not so much question conventional Greco-Roman masculinity, as redefine it in the light of the traditions he received about Christ, which are the most authoritative criteria that he has.[406] The motif of the ἀγών is

---

405. In this way, Ivarsson's suggestive title "Christian Identity as True Masculinity" also applies to Philippians; see Ivarsson, "Identity."
406. This agrees with the history of reception of the New Testament discourse on masculinity; as Gillian Clark, "The Old Adam: The Father and the Unmaking of Masculinity," in Foxhall and Salmon (eds.) *Thinking*, 170–181, quoting here from 180–181, has noted, the answer to the question "what difference did Christianity make to the discourse of masculinity" is "for most people, very little; for a few, an immense difference. ... Patriarchy was maintained in the family ... and in the male church hierarchy. Change occurred in attempts to restrict male sexual freedom, and in willingness to support women who opted for celibacy, but women were still excluded from any position of authority, including teaching, and were still harangued about their vanity, their extravagance, and their provocation of desire. Women who renounced all female vice were praised for being male. Yet Christianity supplied a new tool-kit, if that is not too loaded an expression, for the deconstruction of masculinity." While Clark's statements may not accurately represent early Christianity in all its diversity, her observation seems to hold true as a very broad picture.

a tool that Paul uses in this context to communicate his view of masculinity in a way that would have been accessible for his contemporaries.

3.4.5 Ensuing Exhortations: Euodia and Syntyche (Phil. 4.2-3) as (Negative) Paradigms?

Returning to the flow of Philippians, the beginning of chapter 4 of the letter now needs to be addressed. If so many persons appearing in Philippians can be read as *exempla* and if Paul's depiction of his adversaries in Phil. 3 also has paradigmatic features, it becomes inviting to attempt a similar reading of Euodia and Syntyche, even if the fact that they are nowhere explicitly identified as *exempla* should make one cautious in doing so.

In order to move to his strongly voiced appeal to both women in Phil. 4.2,[407] Paul makes a transition from Phil. 3.2-21 in 4.1 by stating rather generally that the faithful should stand firm in the Lord (see also 2.1-4, and 1.27). As the latter expression is part of the agonistic vocabulary at Paul's disposal, it is also related to the metaphor drawn from the same field in Phil. 4.3.[408] Phil. 4.4 seems to provide a similar kind of transition as Phil. 4.1, by taking up a "refrain" (i.e. "joy") from the whole of Philippians in a more general way,[409] in order to turn to a different subject again, in this case the general exhortations in Phil. 4.4-7, 8-9, which end upon yet another note with Paul as a paradigm in verse 9 (compare 1.30 and 3.17). Given that the section on Euodia and Syntyche lacks explicit ties with the parts of Philippians surrounding it, it may be noted here that it has, on the basis of the structure of family letters as outlined by Alexander, "its natural place toward the end of the letter, and the somewhat loose combination of various injunctions and other items in a concluding section is not without analogy in other Pauline letters."[410]

If Euodia and Syntyche should indeed be read as (negative) examples of a particular kind of behavior, or inverse mirrors of what Paul recommends, the obvious starting point for looking at what they are to embody lies in what they are called upon to do: to think the same in the Lord (τὸ αὐτὸ φρονεῖν ἐν κυρίῳ, 4.2), which was precisely also one of the main concerns addressed in Phil. 1.27-30 and 2.1-5 (esp. 1.27, 2.2),[411] supported by the subsequent *exemplum*

---

407. See the verbs used in Phil. 4.2-3: παρακαλέω indicates a "polite yet urgent request" (Dahl, "Euodia," 5), which Paul also uses in Phlm. 9 as an alternative to the stronger ἐπιτάσσω (Phlm. 8). Apparently it calls for a more voluntary response. The σύζυγος in Phil. 4.3 is addressed with the much more neutral ἐρωτάω. This careful choice of words and the fact that Paul calls upon three individuals personally within the scope of two verses (while mentioning Clement as a fourth person), suggests that this is not a routine matter (see also, e.g., Dahl, "Euodia," 5).
408. See Dahl, "Euodia," 5.
409. See on this above, 2.2.2.1.
410. See esp. 1 Cor. 16.1-23; 1 Thess. 5.12-28: Dahl, "Euodia," 7.
411. See also, e.g., Reumann, *Philippians*, 631.

of Christ.⁴¹² This indeed suggests "correspondence between the initial, general exhortations in Phil 1:27–2:5 and the special appeal to Euodia and Syntyche in the context of 3:20–4:3."⁴¹³ Still, all this does not prove that Paul wrote the entire letter with the two influential women in mind.⁴¹⁴ Rather, it seems likely that what Paul had outlined earlier on in his letter, *also* applies to the two disagreeing women, without turning them into the main cause of Paul's displeasure with and worries about the Philippians as such.⁴¹⁵ The connection between the appeal to Euodia and Syntyche on the one hand and the preceding paraenetical sections on the other is established in a number of ways.

To begin with, the first thing the two women are called upon to do is to be of one mind (4.2; see Phil. 2.2), presumably with each other first of all, but probably also with the community and Paul. The unnamed σύζυγος is called upon to assist them in achieving this.⁴¹⁶ The significance of this concept of unanimity has already been discussed.⁴¹⁷

Second, there is a striking agreement between the description of Paul's past cooperation (and implied good relationship) with these women and both his appeal to them and earlier appeals in Philippians. Paul's past cooperation with the two women is described in an agonistic vocabulary (Phil. 4.3: συνήθλησάν μοι; see also 4.1: στήκετε ἐν κυρίῳ). This is highly reminiscent of similar descriptions in Phil. 1.27 (στήκετε, συναθλοῦντες).⁴¹⁸ Cooperation is also a key notion in Paul's reference to Clement's relationship with the two (συλλαμβάνου αὐταῖς, 4.3). These references to cooperation and like-mindedness are the context of Paul's call to the two women to "τὸ αὐτὸ φρονεῖν ἐν κυρίῳ" (which is also reminiscent of Phil. 2.5, φρονεῖτε). In view of this agreement one might suggest that Euodia and Syntyche are called upon to follow the example of their own past, given that this is described in terms of their former cooperation with Paul and Clement. Like-mindedness is a topic that has occurred more

---

412. See, e.g., Dahl, "Euodia," 9; Holloway, *Consolation*, 147.
413. Dahl, "Euodia," 9.
414. So, however, Dahl, "Euodia," 10; Briggs Kittredge, *Community*, esp. 108–110, comes to a concurring interpretation. Peterlin, *Letter*, 101–132, both turns the two women into a central issue of the letter and also regards them as deacons—both with little basis in Philippians, it seems.
415. This implies turning Dahl's proposal—that everything in Philippians has been formulated with Euodia and Syntyche in mind—on its head: Philippians has not so much been formulated with these verses in mind; rather, these verses have been formulated with the other sections of Philippians in mind. See Dahl, "Euodia," 10. See also Black, "Discourse," 16.
416. See, e.g., Reumann, *Philippians*, 608–609, 628–630: there is probably no further co-worker called "Syzygos" in view, given lack of onomastic evidence for such a name. The question remains of who is addressed here; see, e.g., Briggs Kittredge, *Community*, 107; Dibelius, *Philipper*, 94. Reumann's educated guess that it might be Epaphroditus is attractive in view of partial parallels in letters of friendship—see Reumann, Philippians, 629–630, as well as Malherbe, *Theorists*, 33—but his proposal is too conjectural to serve as a basis for the exegesis of this pericope. Furthermore, if Epaphroditus is the letter carrier, it would have been odd to instruct him by means of this same letter.
417. See above, e.g. 2.3.2.2.
418. See, e.g., Dahl, "Euodia," 10. See further, Reumann, *Philippians*, 632.

than once in Philippians already (see esp. Phil. 2.1-4) and it seems to be a subject of continuous concern to Paul. He has also highlighted it in his earlier recommendation of Timothy and Epaphroditus; the following instances stand out: Phil. 2.20 (ἰσόψυχος), 2.22 (σὺν ἐμοὶ ἐδούλευσεν), and 2.25 (συνεργὸν καὶ συστρατιώτην μου). When reading Phil. 4.2-3 in the context of Philippians as a whole, Euodia and Syntyche appear to be requested to change their behavior in a way that also leads to recalling other persons that appear in the letter, who already embody what they should behave like.

Third, the specification ἐν κυρίῳ in Phil. 4.2, used already in the preceding Phil. 4.1, might well be reminiscent of Phil. 2.5, where all the Philippians are called upon to think ὃ καὶ ἐν Χριστῷ Ἰησοῦ. The "realm of Christ," i.e. being "in Christ," also has a bearing on the behavior expected from the two women. Again, it seems to be the case that being incorporated into Christ determines what is an appropriate walk of life.

When drawing conclusions from this discussion of Euodia and Syntyche from the perspective of this study, it is helpful to recall that it was argued, in the case of Timothy and Epaphroditus, not so much that they are explicitly presented as *exempla ad imitandum*, but that the reader of Philippians is invited rather to read the recommendations of the two in a paradigmatic light because of the context in which they are found (most notably the texts concerned with Christ and Paul as *exempla* in Phil. 2 and 3). Because of this, the most convincing approach seems to be to read Euodia and Syntyche not so much as explicit (and negative) παραδείγματα, but as people that are addressed as two embodiments of the "evil" that Paul is writing against in Philippians as a whole and therefore also have a paradigmatic quality.

Chapter 4

CONCLUSIONS

On the basis of the above research, the following conclusions may be drawn about the role that *exempla* play in Philippians as a whole. These conclusions pertain to the character of the *exempla*, the light they shed on Paul's self-understanding, the relationship between him and the early Christian community in Philippi, and—with that—further aspects of his theology.

4.1 **Exempla** *in Philippians: Concluding Overview*

In the course of this study, a number of elements of Philippians were identified as *exempla*, with various functions and with both negative and positive aspects. Throughout, the *exempla* identified were discussed within the framework of first-century considerations about and conventions with regard to *exempla*. In doing so, this study has moved beyond philological observations and arguments about analogies in Philippians based on keyword connections and thematic agreements between parts of the letter. The following *exempla* could be identified.

First, Phil. 1.30 should be mentioned. Here, Paul draws an analogy between his own situation, which he has outlined at length in Phil. 1.12-26, and that of the Philippians, and encourages them on the basis of it. More precisely, he places his own struggle before the eyes of the Philippians as a means of bonding with them, which then serves to encourage the Philippians and also provides a vantage point for admonishing them. In this context, 1.12-26 also can be seen to fulfill a paradigmatic function, given that Paul's own behavior in prison as well as that of the people around him (except for those preaching the gospel out of envy, of course) is exemplary and can be seen as providing part of the content of Paul's statement in Phil. 1.30. Beyond this, Paul might refer to another *exemplum* in 1.19. There, he quotes *verbatim* from Job 13.16LXX. Therefore, Job may well serve as an *exemplum* that helps to interpret Paul's imprisonment by associating it with the suffering of Job, the paradigmatic suffering righteous.

Second, Phil. 2.5-11 was identified as an *exemplum*, thus aligning this study with a longer tradition of scholarship that has done so. However, the main difference is that, here, Phil. 2.5-11 was argued to be an *exemplum* because its usage agrees with first-century CE rhetorical conventions and not only because of literary connections between the passages surrounding the text, that is, Phil. 2.1-4 and 2.12-18. It was also shown that Phil. 2.5-11 can even be formalized as a παράδειγμα in the Aristotelian sense of the word. However, from an historical perspective, it is more likely that Paul utilized the *exemplum* in the way that was most common in first-century writing. The slavery language of Phil. 2.5-11 also lets Paul's introduction of himself and Timothy in Phil. 1.1 appear in an "exemplary" light, at least retrospectively.

Third, Phil. 2.19-30, the section concerning Timothy and Epaphroditus, was considered. Even though in some scholarly literature the exemplary character of these two individuals is emphasized to the extent that they are even seen as the true center of the letter, a more cautious stance was taken here. This has to do with considerations concerning the structure of Philippians—it is not seen as consisting of a macro-chiasm with Phil. 2.19-30 at the center—as well as with the epistolary function that Phil. 2.19-30 has in terms of providing information about the traveling plans of Paul himself and those of his companions. At the same time, it was recognized that Timothy and Epaphroditus are presented in ways that echo central themes from the preceding paraenetical section, Phil. 2.1-18, in such a way that they also appear as exemplary characters. Paul thus uses the sharing of information that he needed to convey anyway to further an underlying aim of exhortation and instruction.

The fourth section of Philippians that was considered as an *exemplum* is Paul's lengthy argument in Phil. 3 where, on the one hand, he vindicates himself, and, on the other hand, he outlines the superiority of his position compared to that of his competitors. Paul holds himself up as a positive example here, employing the rhetorical technique of *periautologia*, which was to be used in situations precisely like the one addressed in Phil. 3. At the same time, Paul holds up his competitors as negative examples in Phil. 3.2 and points to others who constitute a positive example together with him in Phil. 3.17.

Next, Phil. 4.2-3 was considered and conclusions were drawn that were akin to those drawn concerning Phil. 2.19-30: the section has a primary aim that is different from that of an *exemplum*, but the language that is used to describe the main actors, that is, Euodia, Syntyche and (to some extent) Clement, also makes it possible to view them as negative and positive examples at the same time, given that their descriptions echo themes from earlier paraenetical sections in Philippians.

Finally, Phil. 4.9 (ἃ καὶ ἐμάθετε καὶ παρελάβετε καὶ ἠκούσατε καὶ εἴδετε ἐν ἐμοί) also was identified as an *exemplum*. Here, Paul places before their eyes what the Philippians have received from, heard from (and about), and seen in Paul and his walk of life, thus exhorting them once again. This *exemplum*, brief as it is, is similar to the other brief *exempla* in 1.30 and 3.17, where Paul also routinely refers to himself (and others) to visualize and support what he is communicating to the Philippians.

Thus, there are two large sections of Philippians, namely 2.5-11 and 3.2-21, that function clearly as *exempla*, while in Phil. 1.30 (giving much of the preceding the character of an *exemplum*), 3.17, and 4.9 *exempla* are explicitly mentioned, each time involving at least Paul himself. In 1.19, Paul refers to Job 13.16LXX as an example. Other sections have an "exemplary" character because they echo themes and notions that are prominent in the two large sections just mentioned in relation to persons that embody them (or not): in Phil. 2.19-30, 4.2-3, and possibly (retrospectively) also 1.1.

4.1.1 Exempla *and the Structure of Philippians*

The study of the use of *exempla* in Philippians also has a bearing on the literary structure of the letter. Specifically, the various observations with regard to the structure of Philippians and the role of examples in the letter that have been made throughout this study render the hypothesis that Paul's letter to the Philippians is governed by an overarching chiasm unlikely and unnecessary.[1] The main reasons for this are the following. First, and on this the initial skepticism was based, a chiastic structure is certainly not very common for first-century letters in general. Second, it turned out that it is not conceivable that the two sections on Timothy and Epaphroditus should make up the core of Philippians given the theological content and communicative aims of the two large *exempla* in Phil. 2.1-18 and 3.2-21. This does not deny the interrelationships between the two *exempla* nor the paradigmatic character of the descriptions of Paul's co-workers, but merely indicates that the idea of Philippians as a chiasm is misleading as it directs one away from Paul's main concerns to less substantial matters. Thus, in Philippians, *exempla* are of rhetorical importance, but not of such structural significance that they govern the structure of the letter. At the same time, it should be noted that the occurrence of a series of *exempla* in Philippians does contribute to the epistle's coherence and might therefore provide an argument for its unity in addition to arguments that take their point of departure in more general thematic and linguistic observations.[2]

4.2 The Point of the Paradigms

When noticing the substantial place that smaller and larger *exempla* occupy in Philippians, one must ask what the point of their use is. The answer moves in three directions.

First, it should be maintained that for most kinds of rhetoric, especially for the deliberative *genus* that Paul seems to use in Philippians, *exempla* were a highly effective tool in general, and *periautological exempla*, as they are used by the somewhat cornered Paul in Philippians, were likewise effective, in particular for people in dire straits.

Second, it may be noted that Paul seeks to communicate a coherent pattern of behavior, or a consistently patterned attitude in a situation of duress, such as those that he and the Philippians were experiencing. Given the character of *exempla*

---

1. See also Reumann, *Philippians*, 10–11, n. 3, and above, 2.2.2.
2. See above, 2.2.2.

as cultural symbols, the use of precisely this tool enabled Paul to communicate a particular pattern of identity "in Christ" highly effectively. By placing a shared and accessible normative tradition before the eyes of the Philippians, Paul also aims at preserving the unity of the Philippian community—even in the face of hardship. Furthermore, by using normative *exempla* (notably of Christ, but also of himself), he can also call upon the Philippians to be obedient to their Lord and to be faithful to their identity "in Christ."

Third, the content of the pattern of identity that Paul seeks to promote throughout Philippians, both in the sections that have a primary exhortative character and by means of the language used in sections of Philippians that have other primary purposes, can be formulated as follows. On the one hand, Paul promotes a pattern of a meek and humble attitude on earth—including deference to other community members, the giving up of social (and religious) status, and the acceptance of suffering. This is understood as life according to the pattern provided by Christ, given that this pattern includes the willing acceptance of suffering and death. On the other hand, this pattern also includes an orientation towards eschatological salvation and glorification. During the earthly part of this way of life, this leads to a certain reversal of values. Given that the future glorification with Christ is dependent on identification with Christ's suffering and meekness, conventional earthly honor and glory must be regarded as vainglory, while earthly suffering and humiliation become the preparation for acquiring true honor and glory with Christ.[3] Paul communicates this way of life to the Philippians by means of a number of interacting and interlocking *exempla*, all depending on the *exemplum* of Christ and making Christ and the pattern of life in Christ present to the community.[4] With Hays, for the Philippians this means indeed that "the right action must be *discerned* on the basis of a Christological paradigm."[5] (See Phil. 1.9.)

---

3. Thus, in general, scholars such as Park are right in their emphasis on the importance of submission in Philippians, as this is largely what is to be imitated. See esp. Park, *Submission*, 117–170.

4. Byron, *Metaphors*, 177, must be agreed with: "Finally, at the conclusion of all the examples and patterns, one may ask what it was that Paul ultimately wanted the Philippians to imitate? In view of the prominence of the language and the imagery of the hymn, the answer is undoubtedly the pattern displayed by Christ. The emphasis on Christ's obedience in the hymn is paradigmatic for the whole epistle. Just as Christ displayed the pattern of *Humility-Obedience-Exaltation*, the Philippians should conduct their lives in the same way by placing an emphasis on the need to be obedient to God. Paul's exhortation is that they humble themselves (2.3), remain obedient (1.10; 2.12-16; 3.16; 4.1), and wait in anticipation for their exaltation on the day of Christ when they will participate in the eschatological resurrection (1.6, 10; 2.15; 3.10-12, 20-21). True Paul has offered himself and others as examples to follow, but Paul and his companions were modeling behavior they imitated from Christ. Thus Paul's exhortation that he be imitated is not centered on him, but on Christ's behavior that he in turn models for the Philippians."

5. Richard B. Hays, "Ecclesiology and Ethics in 1 Corinthians," *Ex Auditu* 10 (1994), 31–43, esp. 38 (emphasis in original); see also Burridge, *Imitating*, 104.

4.3 Embodied Identity and Relational Ecclesiology

On the basis of the above considerations, it will be clear that identity "in Christ" (see, e.g., Phil. 1.1, 2.5; see also 4.1-2) appears in Philippians primarily in embodied form; in other words, as represented by the *exempla* of Christ and Paul in the first place—whereby the *exemplum* of Paul is patterned after that of Christ—and those of Timothy, Epaphroditus, unnamed others, and, possibly, Clement; while Syntyche and Euodia, and the "dogs" provide negative examples.[6] This leads to the conclusions both that, for Paul, identity in Christ is an embodied affair, that is, a question of patterning one's life in a particular way under particular circumstances, and that the communication of "the faith," to use a deutero-Pauline term, takes place very much through embodying this Christ-patterned identity *vis-à-vis* others. In Philippians, Paul bases his entire authority on embodying this particular pattern of identity.[7] In placing so much emphasis on his own authenticity in relation to the way of life patterned by the *maiores*—or by the one *maior*, Christ—he follows contemporary rhetorical conventions, even if the particular *maior* who is for him the source of true identity is one who provides a highly unusual kind of (earthly) identity. Paul's emphasis on embodied identity, inherent in the use of *exempla*, draws the attention to the relational character of this brand of early Christian identity. The relational and participatory character of identity "in Christ" stands out in two ways. First, the use of the *exempla* of Christ and Paul presupposes that the Philippians can see both Paul and Christ as standing in the line of their *maiores*, or figures of authority, whose "way of life" provides a normative pattern for the audience that Paul addresses. Thus, being part of the body of Christ—without doubt a central Pauline concept,[8] even if it is one that does not occur in Philippians—is characterized by "embodying" the shape of this belonging to it *vis-à-vis* others, as well as by experiencing it bodily, not least through suffering. Second, it ought to be remembered that Paul applies the pattern of identity "in Christ" that he finds in Phil. 2.5-11 to the relationships of the Philippian community *ad extra* and *ad intra*; in other words, the kind of identity that Paul encourages the Philippians to embrace is relational in its enactment too.[9]

---

6. See also, e.g., the argument of Kim, "'Imitators'."
7. See also, e.g., Heil, *Philippians*, 157.
8. See, e.g., Dunn, *Paul*, 548–552.
9. All this agrees well with Engberg-Pedersen's argument that, for Paul, building up the community in Philippi through his letter is his primary aim in writing it. See Engberg-Pedersen, *Paul*, 126–130.

4.4 The Traditional Character of Paul's Relational Ecclesiology

Another result of Paul's extensive use of *exempla* to make his point is that he draws heavily on a shared tradition,[10] on the memory of the Philippian community, and on shared relationships. As was discussed, the fact that Paul uses Phil. 2.5-11 suggests that the text is a pre- or para-Pauline creation, or at the very least a text with which the Philippians and Paul were both familiar. Probably, this also applies to Phil. 3.20-21. Paul presents himself therefore as a representative of "traditional" values, at least *vis-à-vis* the Philippian community. This also clarifies the relationship between himself and Christ: Christ is the original, Paul is a kind of copy. Accordingly, the Philippians are "in Christ," not "in Paul" or the like. The men that represent and embody the values of the "Christ-tradition"—in other words, Paul, Timothy, Epaphroditus, unnamed others (likely including women), and (to some extent) Clement— have authority because they embody this tradition, as is outlined in Phil. 2.5-11 in particular.

4.5 Paul's Authority in its Ecclesiological Context

Paul's use of *exempla* in Philippians also sheds light on his understanding of "apostolic" authority. His *modus operandi* and even his formal understanding of authority does not seem to differ substantially from models of authority in the Greco-Roman world. Like others, Paul derives his authority from the agreement of the shape of his life, including both words and deeds, with that of the *maiores* of the community that he and the Philippians are part of. In the case of Paul and the Philippians there is only one such *maior*, however: Christ. The common recognition of the normativity of Christ, specifically as he is presented in Phil. 2.5-11, is the basis of Paul's arguments in Phil. 2 and 3. Even though Paul also recounts in Phil. 3 the way in which he came to recognize the normativity of Christ for the shaping of his own life, his way of arguing also builds on the underlying assumption that both he and the Philippians regard the same lord as Lord. Being "in Christ" and living a commensurate life is fundamental to Paul's reasoning, and his (tacit) claim that, in his case, being "in Christ" agrees with the shape of his life makes it possible for him to present himself as an *exemplum* to the Philippians. Even though the authority of a speaker always depended on his authenticity and credibility, statements by an author or speaker on his own life were seen to be particularly appropriate when someone's credibility was at stake, when the occasion at hand was particularly close to that of the person speaking, and when others could profit from the example of oneself. Paul's argument in Philippians, especially in Phil. 3, agrees with both of these conventions. Thus, for Paul, at least in Philippians, true authority is based on an authentic

---

10. See also Eriksson, *Tradition*.

"being in Christ" and it is enacted through the embodiment of this "Christian identity" *vis-à-vis* others.[11] This, at least, is the way in which he operates in Philippians. In other words, the community "in Christ" is for Paul characterized by structured relationships, which are in turn qualified by their relationship to Christ (in Philippians as presented in Phil. 2.5-11).[12] For Paul, ecclesiology is ultimately shaped by Christology; Christology is, conversely, expressed through his ecclesiology, more specifically even through the concrete shape of the life of the *ekklesia*, which is precisely what Paul considers to be endangered in Philippians; a deficient ecclesiology would imply a deficient Christology, given that a deficient Christology would lead to a deficient ecclesial life. These considerations agree well with the observation that Paul's goal in Philippians is ultimately an ecclesiological one; he wishes to guide the community in a way of life that befits it as a community "in Christ."

---

11. This agrees with the view that Hans Urs von Balthasar had of Paul; see the following quotation: "Paulus [empfiehlt] bei jeder Gelegenheit ..., ihn nachzuahmen, weil er das konkreteste Bild des Herrn für die Kirche ist, das Bild auch des Apostels katexochen [*sic*], der mehr gearbeitet hat als alle anderen, das Bild der personifizierten Sendung, der somit befugt ist, seine Existenz zur Schau zu stellen, mit seiner Existenz zu exemplifizieren, an seiner Existenz die Lehre zu demonstrieren, und das volle Licht der Gnade Gottes auf seine Existenz fallen zu lassen. Nicht nur seine Lehre, nicht seine Taten sind der Inhalt einer Sendung, sondern ausdrücklich er selbst, sein Leben und sein Benehmen, seine Schicksale und die Begegnungen mit ihm." From *Schwestern im Geist. Thérése von Lisieux und Elisabeth von Dijon* (Einsiedeln: Johannes, 1973), 53–54; quoted by Bianchini, *L'Elogio*, 51.

12. This, however, does not mean that Paul has no place for formal structures of authority. On the contrary, in Phil. 1.1 Paul addresses the leaders of the Philippian community and does not seem to question their authority on the basis of his qualitative understanding of what is truly authoritative. As always in Paul's remarks on offices and ministries in the Church, charism and order belong together.

BIBLIOGRAPHY

Agosto, Efrain, "Paul and Commendation," in Sampley (ed.), *Paul*, 101–133.
Alexander, Loveday, "Hellenistic Letter-Forms and the Structure of Philippians," *JSNT* 37 (1989), 87–101.
Alexeev, Anatoly A., Christos Karakolis, and Ulrich Luz (eds.), *Einheit der Kirche im Neuen Testament*, WUNT 1.218 (Tübingen: Mohr Siebeck, 2008).
Alston, Richard, "Arms and the Man: Soldiers, Masculinity and Power in Republican and Imperial Rome," in Foxhall and Salmon (eds.), *Men*, 205–223.
Al-Suadi, Soham, *Essen als Christgläubige*, TANZ 55 (Tübingen: Francke, 2011).
Anderson, H., "4 Maccabees," in James H. Charlesworth (ed.), *The Old Testament Pseudepigrapha* II (London: Darton Longman and Todd, 1985), 531–564.
Anderson, Jr., R. Dean, *Ancient Rhetorical Theory and Paul*, CBETh 18 (Kampen: Kok, 1996).
Ascough, Richard S., Review of Wick, *Philipperbrief*, *JBL* 114 (1995), 750–752.
Ascough, Richard S., *Paul's Macedonian Associations*, WUNT 2.161 (Tübingen: Mohr Siebeck, 2003).
Assmann, Jan, *Das kulturelle Gedächtnis. Schrift, Erinnerung und politische Identität in frühen Hochkulturen* (München: Beck, [4]2002).
Babbitt, Frank Cole (ed. and trans.), *Plutarch. Moralia* II LCL 222 (Cambridge, MA: Harvard University Press, 1928).
Badian, E., "Amicitia," *DNP* 1 (1996), 590–591.
Bakirtzis, Charalambos and Helmut Koester (eds.), *Philippi at the Time of Paul and after his Death* (Harrisburg: Trinity, 1998).
Balla, Peter, *The Child–Parent Relationship in the New Testament and its Environment*, WUNT 1.155 (Tübingen: Mohr Siebeck, 2003).
Balthasar, Hans Urs von, *Schwestern im Geist. Thérése von Lisieux und Elisabeth von Dijon* (Einsiedeln: Johannes, 1973).
Balz, Horst, "Philipperbrief," *TRE* 26 (1996), 504–513.
Barclay, John M. G., "Mirror-Reading a Polemical Letter: Galatians as a Test Case," *JSNT* 31 (1987), 73–93.
Barth, Gerhard, *Der Brief an die Philipper*, Zürcher Bibelkommentare (Zürich: TVZ, 1979).
Barth, Karl, *Erklärung des Philipperbriefes* (München: Kaiser, [3]1936).

Bartlett, David L., *Ministry in the New Testament* (Minneapolis: Fortress, 1993).
Basevi, Claudio and Juan Chapa, "Philippians 2.6-11: The Rhetorical Function of a Pauline 'Hymn'," in Porter and Olbricht (eds.), *Rhetoric*, 338–356.
Baumert, Norbert, *Koinonein und Metechein—synonym? Eine umfassende semantische Untersuchung*, SBS 51 (Stuttgart: Verlag Katholisches Bibelwerk, 2003).
Beare, F. W., *A Commentary on the Epistle to the Philippians* (New York: Harper, 1959).
Becker, Eve-Marie, *Schreiben und Verstehen: paulinische Briefhermeneutik im Zweiten Korintherbrief*, NET 4 (Tübingen: Francke, 2002).
Becker, J., "Erwägungen zu Phil. 3, 20–21," *ThZ* 27 (1971), 16–29.
Benoit, P., J. T. Milik, and R. de Vaux, *Les grottes de Murabba'at*, DJD II (Oxford: Clarendon, 1961).
Berger, Klaus, "Die impliziten Gegner. Zur Methode der Erschließung von 'Gegnern' in neutestamentlichen Texten," in Dieter Lührmann and Georg Strecker (eds.), *Kirche* (FS Günther Bornkamm; Tübingen: Mohr, 1980), 373–400.
Berger, Klaus, *Formgeschichte des Neuen Testaments* (Heidelberg: Quelle und Meyer, 1984).
Berger, Klaus, *Formen und Gattungen im Neuen Testament* (Tübingen: Francke, 2005).
Berger, Peter L. and Thomas Luckmann, *Die gesellschaftliche Konstruktion der Wirklichkeit. Eine Theorie der Wissenssoziologie* (Frankfurt: Fischer, ⁵1997).
Berry, D. H. and Malcolm Heath, "Oratory and Declamation," in Porter (ed.), *Handbook*, 394–420.
Berry, Ken L., "Friendship Language in Philippians 4:10-20," in Fitzgerald (ed.) *Friendship*, 107–124.
Best, Ernest, *Paul and His Converts* (Edinburgh: T&T Clark, 1988).
Betz, Hans Dieter, *Nachfolge und Nachahmung Jesu Christi im Neuen Testament*, BHT 37 (Tübingen: Mohr, 1967).
Betz, Hans Dieter, *Der Apostel Paulus und die sokratische Tradition: Eine exegetische Untersuchung zu seiner "Apologie" 2 Korinth 10–13*, BHT 45 (Tübingen: Mohr Siebeck, 1972).
Betz, Hans Dieter, "De laude ipsius," in idem (ed.), *Plutarch's Ethical Writings and Early Christian Literature*, SCHNT 4 (Leiden: Brill, 1978), 367–393.
Bianchini, Francesco, *L'Elogio di sé in Cristo. L'utilizzo della περιαυτολογία nel contexto di Filippesi 3,1–4,1*, AnBib 164 (Rome: Pontificio Istituto Biblico, 2006).
Biard, Pierre, *La puissance de Dieu*, TICP 7 (Paris: Bloud & Gay, 1960).
Bittasi, Stefano, *Gli esempi necessari per discernere: il significato argomentativo della struttura della lettera di Paolo ai Filippesi*, AnBib 153 (Rome: Pontificio Istituto Biblico, 2003).
Black, David Alan, "The Discourse Structure of Philippians: A Study in Textlinguistics," *NovT* 37 (1995), 16–49.

Bloch, René, *Antike Vorstellungen vom Judentum: Der Judenexkurs des Tacitus im Rhmen der griechisch-römischen Ethnographie, Hist.E* 160 (Franz Steiner: Stuttgart, 2002).
Bloomquist, L. Gregory, *The Function of Suffering in Philippians*, JSNTSup 78 (Sheffield: JSOT, 1993).
Bockmuehl, Markus, *The Epistle to the Philippians* (London: Black, 1997).
Bonner, S. F., *Roman Declamation in the Late Republic and Early Empire* (Liverpool: Liverpool University Press, 1969 [1949]).
Bormann, Lukas, "Reflexionen über Sterben und Tod bei Paulus," in Friedrich Wilhelm Horn (ed.), *Das Ende des Paulus: Historische, theologische und literaturgeschichtliche Aspekte*, BZNW 106 (Berlin: De Gruyter, 2001), 307–330.
Bormann, Lukas, *Philippi: Stadt und Christengemeinde zur Zeit des Paulus*, NovTSup 78 (Leiden: Brill, 1995).
Bornkamm, Günther, "Zum Verständnis des Christushymnus Phil 2,6–11," in idem, *Studien zu Antike und Urchristentum*, BEvTh 28 (München: Kaiser, 1959), 177–187.
Böttrich, Christfried, "Verkündigung aus Neid und Rivalität? Beobachtungen zu Phil 1,1," *ZNW* 95 (2006), 84–101.
Bradley, Keith R., *Slaves and Masters in the Roman Empire: A Study in Social Control*, CollLat 185 (Bruxelles: Latomus, 1984).
Brändl, Martin, *Der Agon bei Paulus: Herkunft und Profil paulinischer Agonmetaphorik*, WUNT 2.222 (Tübingen: Mohr Siebeck, 2006).
Brenk, Frederick E., "Setting a Good Exemplum: Case Studies in the Moralia, the Lives as Case Studies," in A. G. Nikolaidis (ed.), *The Unity of Plutarch's Work: "Moralia" Themes in the "Lives", Features of the "Lives" in the "Moralia"* (Berlin: De Gruyter, 2008), 237–254.
Briggs Kittredge, Cynthia, *Community and Authority: The Rhetoric of Obedience in the Pauline Tradition* (Harrisburg: Trinity, 1998).
Brown, Colin, "Ernst Lohmeyer's *Kyrios Jesus*," in Martin and Dodd (eds.), *Christology*, 6–42.
Brown, Raymond E., *An Introduction to the New Testament* (New York: Doubleday, 1997).
Bruce, F. F., *Philippians*, NIBCNT (Peabody, MA: Hendrickson, 1983).
Brucker, Ralph, *Christushymnen oder epideiktische Passagen? Studien zum Stilwechsel im Neuen Testament und seiner Umwelt*, FRLANT 176 (Göttingen: Vandenhoeck & Ruprecht, 1997).
Bultmann, Rudolf, *Der Stil der paulinischen Predigt und die kynisch-stoische Predigt*, FRLANT 13 (Göttingen: Vandenhoeck & Ruprecht, 1984 [1910]).
Bürgel, Peter, "Der Privatbrief. Entwurf eines heuristischen Modells," *DVfLG* 50 (1976), 281–297.
Burridge, Richard A., *Imitating Jesus: An Inclusive Approach to New Testament Ethics* (Grand Rapids: Eerdmans, 2007).
Byrnes, Michael, *Conformation to the Death of Christ and the Hope of Resurrection: An Exegetico-Theological Study of 2 Corinthians 4,7-15 and Philippians 3,7-11* TGr.T (Roma: Pontificia Università Gregoriana, 2003).

Byron, John, *Slavery Metaphors in Early Judaism and Pauline Christianity*, WUNT 2.162 (Tübingen: Mohr, 2003).

Byrskog, Samuel, "The Early Church as a Narrative Fellowship: An Exploratory Study of the Performance of the *Chreia*," *TTK* 78 (2007), 207–226.

Caird, George B., *Paul's Letters from Prison*, NClB (New York: Oxford University Press, 1976).

Callan, Terrence, "Competition and Boasting: Towards a Psychological Portrait of Paul," *ST* 40 (1986), 137–156.

Capel Anderson, Janice, Stephen D. Moore, and Seong Hee Kim, "Masculinity Studies: A Classified Bibliography," in Moore and Capel Anderson (eds.), *Masculinities*, 23–42.

Castelli, Elizabeth, *Imitating Paul: A Discourse of Power* (Louisville: Westminster/John Knox, 1991).

Clark, Gillian, "The Old Adam: The Father and the Unmaking of Masculinity," in Foxhall and Salmon (eds.) *Thinking*, 170–181.

Clarke, Andrew D., "'Be Imitators of Me': Paul's Model of Leadership," *TynBul* 49 (1998), 329–360.

Clarke, Andrew D., *Serve the Community of the Church* (Grand Rapids: Eerdmans, 2000).

Clarke, Andrew D., *A Pauline Theology of Church Leadership*, LNTS 362 (London: T&T Clark, 2008).

Classen, Carl Joachim, "St. Paul's Epistles and Ancient Greek and Roman Rhetoric," in Porter and Olbricht (eds.), *Rhetoric*, 264–291.

Classen, Carl Joachim, *Rhetorical Criticism of the New Testament*, WUNT 1.128 (Tübingen: Mohr Siebeck, 2000).

Claussen, Carsten, *Versammlung, Gemeinde, Synagoge: das hellenistisch-jüdische Umfeld der frühchristlichen Gemeinden*, StUNT 27 (Göttingen: Vandenhoeck und Ruprecht, 2002).

Clines, David J. A., "Paul, the Invisible Man," in Moore and Capel Anderson (eds.), *Masculinities*, 181–192.

Collange, Jean-François, *L'épître de Saint Paul aux Philippiens*, CNT 10a (Neuchâtel: Delachaux et Niestlé, 1973).

Collange, Jean-François, *De Jésus à Paul: L'éthique du Nouveau Testament* (Genève: Labor et Fides, 1980).

Collins, J. J., "Chiasmus, the ABA Pattern and the Text of Paul," in s.a., *Studiorum Paulinorum Congressus Internationalis Catholicus, 1961*, I-II AnBib 17–18 (Rome: Pontificio Istituto Biblico, 1963), II, 575–583.

Conway, Colleen M., "'Behold the Man!' Masculine Christology and the Fourth Gospel," in Moore and Capel Anderson (eds.), *Masculinities*, 163–180.

Cotter, Wendy J., "Our *Politeuma* is in Heaven: The Meaning of Philippians 3:17-21," in McLean (ed.), *Origins*, 92–104.

Cowley, Arthur E. (ed. and trans.), *Aramaic Papyri of the Fifth Century B.C.* (Oxford: Oxford University Press, 1923).

Croy, N. C., "'To Die is Gain' (Philippians 1:19-26): Does Paul Contemplate Suicide?", *JBL* 122 (2003), 517–531.

Culpepper, R. Alan, "Co-Workers in Suffering: Philippians 2.19-30," *RevExp* 77 (1980), 349–358.

Dahl, Nils A., *Jesus in the Memory of the Early Church* (Minneapolis: Augsburg, 1976).

Dahl, Nils A., "Euodia and Syntyche and Paul's Letter to the Philippians," in L. Michael White and O. Larry Yarbrough (eds.), *The Social World of the First Christians: Essays in Honor of Wayne A. Meeks* (Minneapolis: Fortress, 1995), 3–15.

Darling Young, Robin, "The 'Woman with the Soul of Abraham': Traditions about the Mother of the Maccabean Martyrs," in Amy-Jill Levine, *"Women Like This": New Perspectives on Jewish Women in the Greco-Roman World*, SBLEJL 1 (Atlanta: Scholars Press, 1991), 67–81.

David, Jean-Michel, "Majorum Exempla sequi: l'exemplum historique dans les discours judiciaires de Cicéron," in Jacques Berlioz and idem (eds.), *Rhétorique et histoire. L'exemplum et le modèle de comportement dans le discours antique et medieval*, MEFR 92:1 (Rome: École française, 1980), 67–86.

Davidson, James, "Dover, Foucault and Greek Homosexuality," *Past and Present* 170 (2001), 3–51.

Davis, Casey Wayne, *Oral Biblical Criticism: The Influence of the Principle of Orality on the Literary Structure of Paul's Epistle to the Philippians*, JSNTSup 172 (Sheffield: Sheffield Academic Press, 1999).

De Boer, Martinus C., "Paul's Use and Interpretation of a Justification Tradition in Galatians 2.15–21," *JSNT* 28 (2005), 189–216.

De Boer, Willis Peters, *The Imitation of Paul* (Kampen: Kok, 1962).

De Vos, Craig S., *Church and Community Conflicts: The Relationships of the Thessalonian, Corinthian, and Philippian Churches with Their Wider Civic Communities*, SBLDS 168 (Atlanta: SBL, 1999).

Debanné, Marc J., *Enthymemes in the Letters of Paul*, LNTS 303 (London: T&T Clark, 2006).

Deichgräber, Reinhard, *Gotteshymnus und Christushymnus in der frühen Christenheit: Untersuchungen zu Form, Sprache und Stil der frühchristlichen Hymnen*, StUNT 5 (Göttingen: Vandenhoeck & Ruprecht, 1967).

Deissmann, Adolf, "Zur ephesinischen Gefangenschaft des Apostels Paulus," in W. H. Buckler and W. M. Calder (eds.), *Anatolian Studies Presented to Sir William Mitchell Ramsay* (Manchester: Manchester University Press, 1923), 121–127.

Deissmann, Adolf, *Paul: A Study in Social and Religious History* (trans. W. E. Wilson; London: Hodder & Stoughton, ²1927).

Demoen, Kristoffel, *Pagan and Biblical Exempla in Gregory Nazianzen: A Study in Rhetoric and Hermeneutics*, CCLP 2 (Turnhout: Brepols, 1996).

Demoen, Kristoffel, "A Paradigm for the Analysis of Paradigms: The Rhetorical *Exemplum* in Ancient and Imperial Greek Theory," *Rhetorica* 15 (1997), 125–155.

Dench, Emma, "Austerity, Excess, Success and Failure in Hellenistic and Early Imperial Italy," in Maria Wyke (ed.), *Parchments of Gender: Deciphering the Bodies of Antiquity* (Oxford: Clarendon Press, 1998), 121–146.

Dibelius, Martin, "Zur Formgeschichte des Neuen Testaments (außerhalb der Evangelien)," *ThR.NF* 3 (1931), 207–242.

Dibelius, Martin, *An die Thessalonicher I II. An die Philipper*, HNT 11 (Tübingen: Mohr Siebeck, 1937).

Dibelius, Martin, *Die Formgeschichte des Evangeliums* (mit einem erweiterten Nachtrag von Gerhard Iber herausgegeben von Günter Bornkamm; Tübingen: Mohr Siebeck, 6[3]1971).

Dilts, Mervin R. (ed.), *Aeschines: Orationes*, BSGRT (Stuttgart: Teubner, 1997).

Doble, Peter, "'Vile Bodies' or Transformed Persons? Philippians 3.21 in Context," *JSNT* 86 (2002), 3–27.

Dodd, Brian, *Paul's Paradigmatic "I": Personal Example as Literary Strategy*, JSNTSup 177 (Sheffield: Sheffield Academic Press, 1999).

Donaldson, Amy M. and Timothy B. Sailors (eds.), *New Testament Greek and Exegesis: Essays in Honor of Gerald F. Hawthorne* (Grand Rapids: Eerdmans, 2003).

Doughty, Darrel J., "Citizens of Heaven: Philippians 3.2-21," *NTS* 41 (1995), 102–122.

Droge, Arthur J., "*Mori Lucrum*: Paul and Ancient Theories of Suicide," *NovT* 30 (1988), 263–286.

Duff, Tim, *Plutarch's Lives: Exploring Virtue and Vice* (Oxford: Clarendon, 1999).

Duling, Dennis C., "'Whatever Gain I Had …' Ethnicity and Paul's Self-Identification in Philippians 3:5-6," in David B. Gowler, L. Gregory Bloomquist, and Duane F. Watson (eds.), *Fabrics of Discourse* (FS Vernon K. Robbins; Harrisburg: Trinity, 2003), 222–241.

Dunn, James D. G., "One Church – Many Churches," in Alexeev, Karakolis, and Luz (eds.), *Einheit*, 3–33.

Dunn, James D. G., *The Theology of Paul the Apostle* (Edinburgh: T&T Clark, 1998).

Ebel, Eva, *Die Attraktivität früher christlicher Gemeinden: die Gemeinde von Korinth im Spiegel griechisch-römischer Vereine*, WUNT 2.178 (Tübingen: Mohr Siebeck, 2004).

Ebner, Martin, *Leidenslisten und Apostelbrief. Untersuchungen zu Form, Motivik und Funktion der Peristasenkataloge bei Paulus*, FzB 66 (Würzburg: Echter, 1991).

Egger, Wilhelm, *Galaterbrief. Philipperbrief. Philemonbrief*, NEB (Würzburg: Echter, 1985).

Egger, Wilhelm, *Methodenlehre zum Neuen Testament. Einführung in linguistische und historisch-kritische Methoden* (Freiburg: Herder, ³1993).

Ellington, Dustin W., "Imitating Paul's Relationship to the Gospel: 1 Corinthians 8.1–11.1," *JSNT* 33 (2011), 303–315.

Engberg-Pedersen, Troels, "Radical Altruism in Philippians 2:4," in Fitzgerald, Olbricht, and White (eds.), *Christianity*, 197–214.

Engberg-Pedersen, Troels, "The Concept of Paraenesis," in Starr and Engberg-Pedersen (eds.), *Paraenesis*, 47–71.

Engberg-Pedersen, Troels, *Paul and the Stoics* (Edinburgh: T&T Clark, 2000).

Eriksson, Anders, *Tradition as Rhetorical Proof: Pauline Argumentation in 1 Corinthians*, ConBNT 29 (Stockholm: Almqvist & Wiksell, 1998).

Exler, Francis Xavier J., *The Form of the Ancient Greek Letter: A Study in Greek Epistolography* (Washington, D.C.: Catholic University of America Press, 1923).

Fantham, Elaine, Helene Peet Foley, Natalie Boymel Kampen, Sarah B. Pomeroy, and H. A. Shapiro, *Women in the Classical World: Image and Text* (Oxford: Oxford University Press, 1994).

Fee, Gordon D., *Paul's Letter to the Philippians*, NIBCNT (Grand Rapids: Eerdmans, 1995).

Finley, Moses I., *Ancient Slavery and Modern Ideology* (London: Chatto & Windus, 1980).

Fiore, Benjamin, *The Function of the Personal Example in the Socratic and Pastoral Epistles*, AnBib 105 (Rome: Biblical Insitute, 1986).

Fiore, Benjamin, "Paul, Exemplification, and Imitation," in Sampley (ed.), *Paul*, 228–257.

Fischer, Susan, "Imperial Cult: Engendering the Cosmos," in Foxhall and Salmon, *Men*, 165–183.

Fisher, Nick, *Aeschines: Against Timarchos*, CAHS (Oxford: Oxford University Press, 2001).

Fisk, Bruce N., "The Odyssey of Christ: A Novel Context for Philippians 2:6-11," in C. Stephen Evans (ed.), *Exploring Kenotic Christology: The Self-Emptying of God* (Oxford: Oxford University Press, 2006), 45–73.

Fitzgerald, John T. (ed.), *Friendship, Flattery, and Frankness of Speech*, NTSup 82 (Leiden: Brill, 1996).

Fitzgerald, John T., "Philippians in the Light of Some Ancient Discussions of Friendship," in idem (ed.), *Friendship*, 141–160.

Fitzgerald, John T., Thomas H. Olbricht, and L. Michael White (eds.), *Early Christianity and Classical Culture: Comparative Studies in Honor of Abraham J. Malherbe*, NovTSup 110 (Leiden: Brill, 2003).

Foucault, Michel, *The Use of Pleasure* (trans. R. Hurley; New York: Pantheon Books, 1985).

Fowl, Stephen E., "Philippians 1:28b, One More Time," in Donaldson and Sailors (eds.), *Greek*, 167–179.

Fowl, Stephen E., *The Story of Christ in the Ethics of Paul: An Analysis of the Function of the Hymnic Material in the Pauline Corpus*, JSNTSup 36 (Sheffield: JSOT Press, 1990).

Fowl, Stephen E., *Philippians*, THNTC (Grand Rapids: Eerdmans, 2005).

Foxhall, Lin and John Salmon (eds.), *Thinking Men: Masculinity and its Self-Representation in the Classical Tradition*, LNSAS 7 (Routledge: London, 1998).

Frazier, Françoise, *Histoire et morale dans les* Vies Parallèles *de Plutarque*, CEA 124 (Paris: Les belles lettres, 1996).

Galitis, Georgios, Joachim Gnilka, Lars Hartman, Vasile Mihoc, Benoît Standaert, and Johan S. Vos, *Per me il vivere è Cristo (Filippesi 1,1–3,21)*, SMBen.BE 14 (Rome: Benedictina, 2001).

Galloway, Lincoln E., *Freedom in the Gospel: Paul's Exemplum in 1 Cor 9 in Conversation with the Discourses of Epictetus and Philo*, CBETh 38 (Leuven: Peeters, 2004).

Gardner, Jane F., "Sexing a Roman: Imperfect Men in Roman Law," in Foxhall and Salmon (eds.), *Men*, 136–152.

Garland, D. E., "The Composition and Unity of Philippians. Some Neglected Literary Factors," *NovT* 27 (1985), 141–173.

Garrison, Daniel H., *Sexual Culture in Ancient Greece* (Norman: University of Oklahoma Press, 2000).

Gehrke, H.-J. and B. von Reibnitz, "Freundschaft," *DNP* 4 (1998), 669–674.

Geoffrion, Timothy C., *The Rhetorical Purpose and the Political and Military Character of Philippians: A Call to Stand Firm* (Lewiston: Mellen, 1993).

Georgi, Dieter, "Der vorpaulinische Hymnus Phil 2,6–11," in Erich Dinkler (ed.), *Zeit und Geschichte. Dankesgabe an Rudolf Bultmann zum 80. Geburtstag* (Tübingen: Mohr Siebeck, 1964), 264–293.

Gerber, Christine, *Paulus und seine "Kinder". Studien zur Beziehungsmetaphorik der paulinischen Briefe*, BZNW 136 (Berlin: De Gruyter, 2005).

Gerhardsson, Birger, *Memory and Manuscript: Oral Tradition and Written Transmission in Rabbinic Judaism and Early Christianity*, ASNU 22 (Lund: Almquist & Wiksell, 1961).

Giesen, Heinz, "Eschatology in Philippians," in Stanley E. Porter (ed.), *Paul and His Theology*, Pauline Studies 3 (Leiden: Brill, 2006), 217–282.

Gleason, Maud W., *Making Men: Sophists and Self-Presentation in Ancient Rome* (Princeton: Princeton University Press, 1995).

Gnilka, Joachim, *Der Philipperbrief*, HTKNT (Freiburg: Herder, 1968).

Gooder, Paula, "In Search of the Early 'Church': The New Testament and the Development of Christian Communities," in Gerald Mannion and Lewis S. Mudge (eds.) *The Routledge Companion to the Christian Church* (New York: Routledge, 2008), 9–27.

Goodman, Martin, *The Roman World 44 BC – AD 180* (New York: Routledge, 1997).

Gordon, Pamela, "The Lover's Voice in *Heroides* 15: Or, Why is Sappho a Man?", in Hallett and Skinner (eds.), *Sexualities*, 274–291.

Gräbe, Petrus J., "'... as citizens of heaven live in a manner worthy of the gospel of Christ ...'," in Jan G. van der Watt and François S. Malan (eds.), *Identity, Ethics, and Ethos in the New Testament*, BZNW 141 (Berlin: De Gruyter, 2006), 289–302.

Grove Eastman, Susan, "Philippians 2:6–11: Incarnation as Mimetic Participation," *JSPL* 1 (2010), 1–22.

Gunderson, Erik, *Staging Masculinity: The Rhetoric of Performance in the Roman World* (Ann Arbor: University of Michigan Press, 2000).

Gunther, John J., *St. Paul's Opponents and Their Background: A Study of Apocalyptic and Jewish Sectarian Teachings*, NovTSup 35 (Leiden: Brill, 1973).

Gupta, Nijay K., "'I Will Not Be Put to Shame': Paul, the Philippians, and the Honourable Wish for Death," *Neot* 42 (2008), 253–267.

Hack Polaski, Sandra, *Paul and the Discourse of Power*, BiSe 62 (Sheffield: Sheffield Academic Press, 1999).

Hack Polaski, Sandra, *A Feminist Introduction to Paul* (St. Louis: Chalice, 2005).

Hainz, Josef, *Koinonia: "Kirche" als Gemeinschaft bei Paulus*, BU 16 (Regensburg: Pustet, 1982).

Hallett, Judith P., "Female Homoeroticism and the Denial of Roman Reality in Latin Literature," in Hallett and Skinner (eds.), *Roman Sexualities*, 255–273.

Hallett, Judith P. and Marilyn B. Skinner (eds.), *Roman Sexualities* (Princeton: Princeton University Press, 1997).

Haltenhoff, Andreas, "Institutionalisierte Geschichten. Wesen und Wirken des literarischen *Exemplum* im alten Rom," in Melville (ed.), *Institutionalität*, 213–217.

Hansen, G. Walter, "Transformation of Relationships: Partnership, Citizenship, and Friendship in Philippi," in Donaldson and Sailors (eds.), *Greek*, 181–204.

Hardie, Alex, *Statius and the Silvae: Poets, Patrons, and Epideixis in the Graeco-Roman World* (Liverpool: Francis Cairns, 1983).

Harnisch, Wolfgang, "Die paulinische Selbstempfehlung als Plädoyer für den Gekreuzigten. Rhetorisch-hermeneutische Erwägungen zu Phil 3," in Mell and Müller (eds.), *Urchristentum*, 133–154.

Harrill, J. Albert, "Invective against Paul (2 Cor 10:10), the Physiognomics of the Ancient Slave Body, and the Greco-Roman Rhetoric of Manhood," in Adela Yarbro Collins and Margaret M. Mitchell (eds.), *Antiquity and Humanity: Essays on Ancient Religion and Philosophy* (FS Hans Dieter Betz; Tübingen: Mohr Siebeck, 2001), 189–213.

Harrison, James R., "Paul and the Athletic Ideal in Antiquity: A Case Study in Wrestling with Word and Image," in Stanley E. Porter (ed.), *Paul's World*, Pauline Studies 4 (Leiden: Brill, 2008), 81–109.

Hartman, Lars, "Overseers and Servants – For What? Philippians 1:1–11 as Read with Regard to the Implied Readers of Philippians," in Galitis, Gnilka, Hartman, Mihoc, Standaert, and Vos, *Vivere*, 13–51.

Hawthorne, Gerald F., *Philippians*, WBC 43 (Waco: Word, 1983).

Hawthorne, Gerald F. and Ralph P. Martin, *Philippians*, WBC 43 (rev. edn.; Waco: Word, 2004).

Hays, Richard B., "Ecclesiology and Ethics in 1 Corinthians," *ExAud* 10 (1994), 31–43.

Heil, John Paul, *Philippians: Let Us Rejoice in Being Conformed to Christ*, SBLECL 3 (Atlanta: Society of Biblical Literature, 2010).

Hellerman, Joseph H., *Reconstructing Honor in Roman Philippi: Carmen Christi as Cursus Pudorum*, SNTSMS 132 (Cambridge, UK: Cambridge University Press, 2005).

Hengel, Martin, "Hymn and Christology," in E. A. Livingstone (ed.), *Studia Biblica 1978 III: Papers on Paul and Other New Testament Authors*, JSNTSup 3 (Sheffield: JSOT Press, 1980), 173–197.

Henten, Jan Willem van and Friedrich Avemarie (eds.), *Martyrdom and Noble Death: Selected Texts from Graeco-Roman, Jewish and Christian Antiquity* (London: Routledge, 2002).

Herter, H., "Effeminatus," *RAC* 4 (1959), 620–650.

Holloway, Paul A., *Consolation in Philippians: Philosophical Sources and Rhetorical Strategy*, SNTS.MS 112 (Cambridge, UK: Cambridge University Press, 2001).

Holloway, Paul A., "*Alius Paulus*: Paul's Promise to Send Timothy at Philippians 2.19–24," *NTS* 54 (2008), 542–556.

Holleman, Joost, *Resurrection and Parousia*, NovTSup 84 (Leiden: Brill, 1996).

Hölscher, Tonio, "Die Alten vor Augen. Politische Denkmäler und öffentliches Gedächtnis im republikanischen Rom," in Melville (ed.), *Institutionalität*, 183–211.

Hooker, Morna D., "Philippians 2:6–11," in idem, *From Adam to Christ: Essays on Paul* (Cambridge, UK: Cambridge University Press, 1990), 88–100.

Hooker, Morna D., "Philippians: Phantom Opponents and the Real Source of Conflict," in Ismo Dunderberg, Christopher Tuckett, and Kari Syreeni (eds.), *Fair Play: Diversity and Conflict in Early Christianity*, NovTSup 103 (Leiden: Brill, 2002), 377–395.

Horrell, David, "Pauline Churches or Early Christian Churches? Unity, Disagreement, and the Eucharist," in Alexeev, Karakolis, and Luz (eds.), *Einheit*, 185–203.

Hurtado, Larry W., "Jesus as Lordly Example in Philippians 2:5-11," in Richardson and Hurd (eds.), *Jesus*, 113–126.

Ivarsson, Fredrik, "Christian Identity as True Masculinity," in Bengt Holmberg (ed.), *Exploring Early Christian Identity*, WUNT 1.226 (Tübingen: Mohr Siebeck, 2008), 159–171.

Jaquette, J. L., "A Not-so-Noble Death: Figured Speech, Friendship and Suicide in Philippians 1:21–26," *Neot* 28 (1994), 177–192.

Jaquette, James L., "Life and Death, *Adiaphora*, and Paul's Rhetorical Strategies," *NovT* 38 (1996), 30–54.

Jewett, Robert, *Paul's Anthropological Terms: A Study of Their Use in Conflict Settings*, AGJU 10 (Leiden: Brill, 1971).

Johnson, Luke Timothy, "The Mind and Moral Discernment in Paul," in John T. Fitzgerald, Thomas H. Olbricht, and L. Michael White (eds.), *Early Christianity and Classical Culture: Comparative Studies in Honor of Abraham J. Malherbe*, NTSup 110 (Leiden: Brill, 2003), 215–236.

Joshel, Sandra, "The Body Female and the Body Politic: Livy's Lucretia and Virginia," in Amy Richlin (ed.), *Pornography and Representation in Greece and Rome* (Oxford: Oxford University Press, 1992), 120–126.

Joshel, Sandra R. and Sheila Murnaghan (eds.), *Women and Slaves in Greco-Roman Culture* (New York: Routledge, 1998).

Karris, Robert J., *A Symphony of New Testament Hymns* (Collegeville: Liturgical Press, 1996).
Käsemann, Ernst, "Kritische Analyse von Phil 2:5-11," *ZThK* 47 (1950), 313–360 (English: "Critical Analysis of Philippians 2:5-11," *JTC* 5 [1968], 45–88).
Kellbe, Mikael, "The Sociological Factors Behind Philippians 3.1–11 and the Conflict at Philippi," *JSNT* 55 (1994), 97–121.
Kellbe, Mikael, *Paul between Synagogue and State: Christians, Jews, and Civic Authorities in 1 Thessalonians, Romans, and Philippians* (Stockholm: Almqvist & Wiksell, 2001).
Kennedy, George A., *New Testament Interpretation through Rhetorical Criticism* (Chapel Hill: University of North Carolina Press, 1984).
Kennel, Gunter, *Frühchristliche Hymnen? Gattungskritische Studien zur Frage nach den Liedern der frühen Christenheit*, WMANT 71 (Neukirchen-Vluyn: Neukirchener Verlag, 1995).
Kilpatrick, G. D., "BLEPETE, Philippians 3:2," in Matthew Black and Georg Fohrer (eds.), *In Memoriam Paul Kahle*, BZAW 103 (Berlin: Töpelmann, 1968), 146–148.
Kim, Yung Suk, "'Imitators' (*Mimetai*) in 1 Cor. 4:16 and 11:1: A New Reading of Threefold Embodiment," *HBT* 33 (2011), 147–170.
Klauck, Hans-Josef, *Die antike Briefliteratur und das Neue Testament* (Paderborn: Schönigh, 1998).
Klauck, Hans-Josef, *Ancient Letters and the New Testament: A Guide to Context and Exegesis* (Waco: Baylor, 2006).
Klein, J., "Exemplum," *HWdR* 3 (1996), 60–70.
Klostergaard Petersen, Anders, "Paraenesis in Pauline Scholarship and in Paul – An Intricate Relationship," in Starr and Enberg-Pedersen (eds.), *Paraenesis*, 267–295.
Koester, Helmut, "The *Purpose* of the Polemic of a Pauline Fragment," *NTS* 8 (1962), 317–332.
Koller, Hermann, *Die Mimesis in der Antike. Nachahmung, Darstellung, Ausdruck* (Bern: Francke, 1954).
Konradt, Matthias, *Gericht und Gemeinde. Eine Studie zur Bedeutung und Funktion von Gerichtsaussagen im Rahmen der paulinischen Ekklesiologie und Ethik im 1 Thess und 1 Kor*, BZNW 117 (Berlin: De Gruyter, 2003).
Koperski, Veronica, "The Early History of the Dissection of Philippians," *JThS* 44 (1993), 599–603.
Koperski, Veronica, *The Knowledge of Christ Jesus My Lord: The High Christology of Philippians 3:7–11*, CBETh 16 (Kampen: Kok, 1996).
Koskenniemi, Heikki, *Studien zur Idee und Phraseologie des griechischen Briefes bis 400 n.Chr*, AASF B.102:2 (Helsinki: Finnish Academy, 1956).
Krentz, Edgar M., "Military Language and Metaphors in Philippians," in McLean (ed.), *Origins*, 105–127.
Kuhn, T. S., *The Structure of Scientific Revolutions* (Chicago: University of Chicago Press, ²1970).

Kurz, William S., "Kenotic Imitation of Paul and of Christ in Philippians 2 and 3," in Fernando F. Segovia (ed.), *Discipleship in the New Testament* (Philadelphia: Fortress, 1985), 103–126.
Kwon, Soon-Gu, *Christ as Example: The Imitatio Christ Motive in Biblical and Christian Ethics*, AUU (Uppsala: Uppsala University Press, 1998).
Lacy, Phillip H. de and Benedict Einarson (trans. and eds.), *Plutarch's Moralia* VII LCL 405 (Cambridge, MA: Harvard University Press, 1968).
Lampe, Peter, *Die stadtrömischen Christen in den ersten beiden Jahrhunderten: Untersuchungen zur Sozialgeschichte*, WUNT 2.18 (Tübingen: Mohr Siebeck, ²1989).
Laqueur, Thomas, *Making Sex: Body and Gender from the Greeks to Freud* (Cambridge, MA: Harvard University Press, 1990).
Larson, Jennifer, "Paul's Masculinity," *JBL* 123 (2004), 85–97.
Larsson, Edvin, *Christus als Vorbild: eine Untersuchung zu den paulinischen Tauf- und Eikontexten*, ASNU 23 (Uppsala: Gleerup, 1962).
Lattke, Michael, *Hymnus. Materialien zu einer Geschichte der antiken Hymnologie*, NTOA 19 (Fribourg i.Ue.: Universitätsverlag, 1991).
Lausberg, Heinrich, *Elemente der literarischen Rhetorik* (Ismaning: Hueber, ¹⁰1990).
Lausberg, Heinrich, *Handbuch der literarischen Rhetorik: eine Grundlegung der Literaturwissenschaft* (Stuttgart: Steiner, ⁴2008).
Leutzsch, Martin, "Konstruktionen von Männlichkeit im Urchristentum," in Frank Crüsemann, Claudia Janssen, Rainer Kessler, and Beate Wehn (eds.), *Dem Tod nicht glauben: Sozialgeschichte der Bibel* (FS Luise Schottroff; Gütersloh: Gütersloher Verlagshaus, 2004), 600–618.
Levine, Amy-Jill, *A Feminist Companion to Paul* (London: T&T Clark International, 2004).
Lietaert Peerbolte, Bert-Jan, "The Name Above All Names (Philippians 2:9)," in George H. van Kooten (ed.), *The Revelation of the Name YHWH to Moses: Perspectives from Judaism, the Pagan Graeco-Roman World, and Early Christianity*, TBN 9 (Leiden: Brill, 2006), 187–206.
Lietaert Peerbolte, Bert-Jan, "Paul and the Practice of παηδεία," in Rieuerd Buitenwerf, Harm W. Hollander, and Johannes Tromp (eds.), *Jesus, Paul, and Early Christianity*, NovTSup 130 (Leiden: Brill, 2008), 261–280.
Lieu, Judith M., *Christian Identity in the Jewish and Graeco-Roman World* (Oxford: Oxford University Press, 2004).
Lohmeyer, Ernst, *Kyrios Jesus. Eine Untersuchung zu Phil. 2,5–11*, SHAW. PH, 1927/28:4 (Heidelberg: Winter, 1928).
Luther, Boyd and Michelle V. Lee, "Philippians as Chiasmus: Key to the Structure, Unity and Theme Questions," *NTS* 41 (1995), 89–101.
Lyons, George, *Pauline Autobiography: Toward a New Understanding*, SBLMS 73 (Atlanta: Scholars Press, 1985).
Malherbe, Abraham J., "Hellenistic Moralists and the New Testament," *ANRW* II.26.1 (1992), 267–333.
Malherbe, Abraham J., *Moral Exhortation: A Greco-Roman Sourcebook*, LEC 4 (Philadelphia: Westminster, 1986).

Malherbe, Abraham J., *Paul and the Thessalonians: The Philosophic Tradition of Pastoral Care* (Philadelphia: Fortress, 1987).
Malherbe, Abraham J., *Ancient Epistolary Theorists* (Atlanta, Scholars Press, 1988).
Malherbe, Abraham J., *Paul and the Popular Philosophers* (Minneapolis: Fortress, 1989).
Marchal, Joseph A., *Hierarchy, Unity and Imitation: A Feminist Rhetorical Analysis of Power Dyna-mics in Paul's Letter to the Philippians*, AcBib 24 (Atlanta: Society of Biblical Literature, 2006).
Marshall, John W., "Paul's Ethical Appeal in Philippians," in Porter and Olbricht (eds.), *Rhetoric*, 357–374.
Marshall, Peter, *Enmity in Corinth: Social Conventions in Paul's Relations with the Corinthians*, WUNT 2.23 (Tübingen: Mohr Siebeck, 1987).
Martin, Dale, *Slavery as Salvation: The Metaphor of Slavery in Pauline Christianity* (New Haven: Yale University Press, 1990).
Martin, Ralph P., "Some Reflections on New Testament Hymns," in Harold H. Rowdon (ed.), *Christ the Lord: Studies in Christology Presented to Donald Guthrie* (Leicester: Inter-Varsity, 1982), 37–49.
Martin, Ralph P., *The Epistle of Paul to the Philippians* (Leicester: InterVarsity, ²1989).
Martin, Ralph P., *A Hymn of Christ: Philippians 2:5-11 in Recent Interpretation & in the Setting of Early Christian Worship* (Downers Grove: InterVarsity, ³1997).
Martin, Ralph P. and Brian J. Dodd (eds.), *Where Christology Began: Essays on Philippians 2* (Louisville: Westminster/John Knox, 1998).
Matlock, R. Barry, "Detheologizing the Pistis Christou Debate: Remarks from a Lexical Semantic Perspective," *NovT* 42 (2000), 1–23.
Matlock, R. Barry, "The Rhetoric of Πίστις in Paul: Galatians 2:16, 3:22, Romans 3:22, and Philippians 3:9," *JSNT* 30 (2007), 173–203.
Mayer, Roland (ed.), *Tacitus: Dialogus de Oratoribus* (Cambridge, UK: Cambridge University Press, 2001).
Mayordomo-Marín, Moisés, *Argumentiert Paulus logisch? Eine Analyse auf dem Hintergrund antiker Logik*, WUNT 1.188 (Tübingen: Mohr Siebeck, 2005).
Mayordomo Marin, Moisés, "Construction of Masculinity in Antiquity and Early Christianity," *Lectio Difficilior* 2006:2.
McCarthy, Kathleen, "Servitium Amoris: Amor Servitii," in Joshel and Murnaghan (eds.), *Women*, 174–192.
McLean, Bradley H. (ed.), *Origins and Method: Towards a New Understanding of Judaism and Christianity*, JSNTSup 86 (Sheffield: JSOT Press, 1993).
Mearns, Chris, "The Identity of Paul's Opponents at Philippi," *NTS* 33 (1987), 194–204.
Meeks, Wayne A., *The First Urban Christians: The Social World of the Apostle Paul* (New Haven: Yale University Press, ²2003).
Mele, Alfred R., *Irrationality: An Essay on Akrasia, Self-Deception, and Self-Control* (Oxford: Oxford University Press, 1987).

Mell, Ulrich and Ulrich B. Müller (eds.), *Das Urchristentum in seiner literarischen Geschichte*, BZNW 100 (FS Jürgen Becker; Berlin: De Gruyter, 1999).
Melville, Gert (ed.), *Institutionalität und Symbolisierung. Verstetigungen kultureller Ordnungsmuster in Vergangenheit und Gegenwart* (Cologne: Böhlau, 2001).
Merk, Otto, "Nachahmung Christi: zu ethischen Perspektiven in der paulinischen Theologie," in Helmut Merklein (ed.), *Neues Testament und Ethik* (FS Rudolf Schnackenburg; Freiburg: Herder, 1989), 172–206.
Metzner, Rainer, "Paulus und der Wettkampf: Die Rolle des Sports in Leben und Verkündigung des Apostels (1 Kor 9.24–7; Phil 3.12–16)," *NTS* 46 (2000), 565–583.
Meyer-Zwiffelhoffer, Eckhard, *Im Zeichen des Phallus. Die Ordnung des Geschlechtsleben im antiken Rom* (Frankfurt: Campus, 1995).
Michaelis, Wilhelm, "Die Gefangenschaftsbriefe des Paulus und antike Gefangenenbriefe," *NKZ* 36 (1925), 586–595.
Michaelis, Wilhelm, "μιμέομαι," *ThWNT* 4 (1942), 661–678.
Miller, Jr., Ernest C., "Πολιτεύεσθε in Philippians 1.27: Some Philological and Thematic Observations," *JSNT* 15 (1982), 86–96.
Mitchell, Alan C., "'Greet the Friends by Name': New Testament Evidence for the Greco-Roman *Topos* on Friendship," in John T. Fitzgerald (ed.), *Greco-Roman Perspectives on Friendship*, SBLRBS 34 (Atlanta: Scholars Press, 1997), 225–262.
Mitchell, Alan C., Review of Holloway, *Consolation*, in *Journal of Religion* 83 (2003), 435–436.
Mitchell, Margaret M., *Paul and the Rhetoric of Reconciliation: An Exegetical Investigation of the Language and Composition of 1 Corinthians*, HUT 28 (Tübingen: Mohr Siebeck, 1991).
Mitchell, Margaret M., Review of Anderson, *Theory*, *CBQ* 60 (1998), 356–358.
Mitchell, Margaret M., "A Patristic Perspective on Pauline περιαυτολογία," *NTS* 46 (2001), 354–371.
Moore, Stephen D., "'O Man, Who Art Thou …?' Masculinity Studies and New Testament Studies," in Moore and Capel Anderson (eds.), *Masculinities*, 1–22.
Moore, Stephen D. and Janice Capel Anderson (eds.), *New Testament Masculinities*, SemeiaSt 45 (Atlanta: SBL, 2003).
Moos, Peter von, *Geschichte als Topik. Das rhetorische Exemplum von der Antike zur Neuzeit und die* historiae *im "Policraticus" Johanns von Salisbury*, Ordo 2 (Hildesheim: Olms, 1988).
Morgan Gillman, Florence, *A Study of Romans 6:5a: United to a Death like Christ's* (San Francisco: Mellen, 1992).
Morgan, Robert, "Incarnation, Myth, and Theology: Ernst Käsemann's Interpretation of Philippians 2:5-11," in Martin and Dodd (eds.), *Christology*, 43–73.
Morgan, Teresa, *Literate Education in the Hellenistic and Roman Worlds* (Cambridge, UK: Cambridge University Press, 1998).

Morgan, Teresa, *Popular Morality in the Early Roman Empire* (Cambridge, UK: Cambridge University Press, 2007).
Mortara Garavelli, Bice, *Manuale di retorica* (Milano: Bompiani, ⁷2003).
Moss, Candida, *The Other Christs: Imitating Christ in Ancient Ideologies of Martyrdom* (Oxford: Oxford University Press, 2010).
Moxnes, Halvor, "Conventional Values in the Hellenistic World: Masculinity," in Per Bilde, Troels Engberg-Pedersen, Lise Hannestad, and Jan Zahle (eds.), *Conventional Values of the Hellenistic Greeks*, Studies in Hellenistic Civilization 8 (Aarhus: Aarhus University Press, 1997), 263–284.
Müller, Ulrich B., "Der Brief aus Ephesus. Zeitliche Plazierung und theologische Einordnung des Philipperbriefes im Rahmen der Paulusbriefe," in Mell and Müller (eds.), *Urchristentum*, 155–171.
Müller, Ulrich B., *Der Brief des Paulus an die Philipper*, THKNT 11.1 (Leipzig: Evangelische Verlagsanstalt, ²2002).
Nagler, Norbert, *Frühkatholizismus: zur Methodologie einer kritischen Debatte*, RST 43 (Bern: Lang, 1994).
Niebuhr, Karl-Wilhelm, "Der Jakobusbrief im Licht frühjüdischer Diasporabriefe," *NTS* 44 (1998), 420–443.
Niebuhr, Karl-Wilhelm, *Heidenapostel aus Israel. Die jüdische Identität des Paulus nach ihrer Darstellung in seinen Briefen*, WUNT 1.62 (Tübingen: Mohr Siebeck, 1992).
Nijf, Onno van, "Athletics, *Andreia* and the *Askêsis*-Culture," in Ralph M. Rosen and Ineke Sluiter (eds.), *Andreia: Studies in Manliness and Courage in Classical Antiquity* (Leiden: Brill, 2002), 263–286.
Norden, Eduard, *Agnostos Theos. Untersuchungen zur Formengeschichte religiöser Rede* (Leipzig: Teubner, 1913).
Nüßlein, Theodor (ed. and trans.), *Rhetorica ad Herennium* (Düsseldorf: Artemis & Winkler, ²1998).
O'Brien, Peter T., *The Epistle to the Philippians*, NIGTC (Grand Rapids: Eerdmans, 1991).
O'Brien, Peter T., "The Gospel and Godly Models in Philippians," in M. J. Wilins and T. Paige (eds.), *Worship, Theology and Ministry in the Early Church: Essays in Honor of Ralph P. Martin*, JSNTSup 87 (Sheffield: JSOT Press, 1992), 273–284.
Oakes, Peter, "Jason and Penelope Hear Philippians 1.1–11," in Christopher Rowland and Crispin H. T. Fletcher-Louis (eds.), *Understanding, Studying and Reading: New Testament Essays in Honour of John Ashton*, JSNTSup 153 (Sheffield: Sheffield Academic Press, 1998), 155–164.
Oakes, Peter, *Philippians: From People to Letter*, SNTSMS 110 (Cambridge, UK: Cambridge University Press, 2001).
Økland, Jorunn, "Sex, Gender and Ancient Greek: A Case-Study in Theoretical Misfit," *ST* 57:2 (2003), 1–19.
Otto, Randall E., "'If Possible I May Attain the Resurrection from the Dead' (Philippians 3:11)," *CBQ* 57 (1995), 324–340.
Park, M. Sydney, *Submission within the Godhead and the Church in the Epistle to the Philippians: An Exegetical and Theological Examination of*

the Concept of Submission in Philippians 2 and 3, LNTS 361 (London: T&T Clark, 2007).

Parker, Holt, "Loyal Slaves and Loyal Wives: This Crisis of the Outsider-Within and Roman *Exemplum* Literature," in Joshel and Murnaghan (eds.), *Women*, 152–173.

Patte, Daniel, *Paul's Faith and the Power of the Gospel: A Structural Introduction to the Pauline Letters* (Philadelphia: Fortress, 1983).

Peppard, Michael, "'Poetry', 'Hymns' and 'Traditional Material' in New Testament Epistles or How to Do Things with Indentations," *JSNT* 30 (2008), 319–342.

Peterlin, Davorin, *Paul's Letter to the Philippians in the Light of Disunity in the Church*, NovTSup 79 (Leiden: Brill, 1995).

Peterman, G. W., *Paul's Gift from Philippi: Conventions of Gift-Exchange and Christian Giving*, SNTSMS 92 (Cambridge, UK: Cambridge University Press, 1997).

Peterson, W. and M. Winterbottom, "Dialogus," in Tacitus, *Agricola, Germania, Dialogus*, LCL 35 (Cambridge, MA: Harvard University Press, 1980).

Pierce, Karen F., "Ideals of Masculinity in New Comedy," in Foxhall and Salmon (eds.), *Thinking*, 130–147.

Pilhofer, Peter, *Philippi. Band 1: Die erste christliche Gemeinde Europas*, WUNT 1.87 (Tübingen: Mohr Siebeck, 1995).

Pilhofer, Peter, "Philippi," *RGG*[4] 6 (2003), 1274–1275.

Plummer, Alfred, *A Commentary on St. Paul's Epistle to the Philippians* (London: Scott, 1912).

Popkes, Wiard, "Paraenesis in the New Testament: An Exercise in Conceptuality," in Starr and Enberg-Pedersen (eds.), *Paraenesis*, 13–45.

Poplutz, Uta, *Athlet des Evangeliums: eine motivgeschichtliche Studie zur Wettkampfmetaphorik bei Paulus*, HBS 43 (Freiburg: Herder, 2004).

Porter, Stanley E. (ed.), *Handbook of Classical Rhetoric in the Hellenistic Period 330 B.C. – A.D. 400* (Leiden: Brill, 1997).

Porter, Stanley E., "Paul as Epistolographer *and* Rhetorician?", in Stanley E. Porter and Dennis L. Stamps (eds.), *The Rhetorical Interpretation of Scripture: Essays from the 1996 Malibu Conference*, JSNTSup 180 (Sheffield: Sheffield Academic Press, 1999), 222–248.

Porter, Stanley E., "The Theoretical Justification for Application of Rhetorical Categories to Pauline Epistolary Literature," in Porter and Olbricht (eds.), *Rhetoric*, 100–122.

Porter, Stanley E. and Jeffrey T. Reed, "Philippians as a Macro-Chiasm and Its Exegetical Significance," *NTS* 44 (1998), 213–231.

Porter, Stanley E. and Thomas H. Olbricht (eds.), *Rhetoric and the New Testament: Essays from the 1992 Heidelberg Conference*, JSNTSup 90 (Sheffield: Sheffield Academic Press, 1993).

Probst, Hermann, *Paulus und der Brief: Die Rhetorik des antiken Briefes als Form der paulinischen Korintherkorrespondenz (1 Kor 8–10)*, WUNT 2.45 (Tübingen: Mohr Siebeck, 1991).

Rahner, Karl, *Spiritual Exercises* (New York: Herder & Herder, 1965).

Raymond, James C., "Enthymemes, Examples, and Rhetorical Method," in Robert J. Connors, Lisa S. Ede, and Andrea A. Lunsford (eds.), *Essays in Classical Rhetoric and Modern Discourse* (Carbondale: Southern Illinois University Press, 1984), 140–151.
Rebenich, Stefan, "Historical Prose," in Porter (ed.), *Handbook*, 265–337.
Reed, Jeffrey T., "Are Paul's Thanksgivings 'Epistolary'?", *JSNT* 61 (1996), 87–99.
Reed, Jeffrey T., "Philippians 3:1 and the Epistolary Hesitation Formulas: The Literary Integrity of Philippians, Again," *JBL* 115 (1996), 63–90.
Reed, Jeffrey T., "The Epistle," in Porter (ed.), *Handbook*, 171–193.
Reed, Jeffrey T., "Using Ancient Rhetorical Categories to Interpret Paul's Letters: A Question of Genre," in Porter and Olbricht (eds.), *Rhetoric*, 294–324.
Reed, Jeffrey T., *A Discourse Analysis of Philippians: Method and Rhetoric in the Debate over Literary Integrity*, JSNTSup 136 (Sheffield: Sheffield Academic Press, 1997).
Rei, Annalisa, "Villains, Wives and Slaves in the Comedies of Plautus," in Joshel and Murnaghan (eds.), *Women*, 92–108.
Reumann, John, "Philippians 3:20–21 – a Hymnic Fragment," *NTS* 30 (1984), 593–609.
Reumann, John, *Philippians*, AB 33B (New Haven: Yale University Press, 2008).
Richardson, P. and J. Hurd (eds.), *From Jesus to Paul* (Waterloo: Wilfrid Laurier University Press, 1984).
Richlin, Amy, *The Garden of Priapus: Sexuality and Aggression in Roman Humor* (rev. edn.; Oxford: Oxford University Press, 1992).
Richlin, Amy, "Gender and Rhetoric: Producing Manhood in the Schools," in William J. Dominik (ed.), *Roman Eloquence: Rhetoric in Society and Literature* (London: Routledge, 1997), 90–110.
Riesenfeld, H., "Unpoetische Hymnen im Neuen Testament," in Jarmo Kiilunen (ed.), *Glaube und Gerechtigkeit. In Memoriam R. Gyllenberg*, SESJ 38 (Helsinki: Finnische exetische Geselschaft, 1983), 155–168.
Robbins, Charles J., "Rhetorical Structure of Philippians 2:6–11," *CBQ* 42 (1980), 73–82.
Roller, Matthew B., "Exemplarity in Roman Culture: The Cases of Horatius Cocles and Cloelia," *CP* 99 (2004), 1–56.
Roloff, Jürgen, "Amt, Ämter, Amtsverständnis IV. Neues Testament," *TRE* 2 (1978), 508–533.
Roloff, Jürgen, *Die Kirche im Neuen Testament*, NTD.E 10 (Göttingen: Vandenhoeck & Ruprecht, 1993).
Ross Wagner, J., "Working Out Salvation: Holiness and Community in Philippians," in Kent E. Brower and Andy Johnson (eds.), *Holiness and Ecclesiology in the New Testament* (Grand Rapids: Eerdmans, 2007), 257–274.
Ross, W. D. (ed.), *Aristotle's Prior and Posterior Analytics* (Oxford: Clarendon, 1965).

Roy, Jim, "The Masculinity of the Hellenistic King," in Foxhall and Salmon, *Men*, 111–135.
Sampley, J. Paul (ed.), *Paul in the Greco-Roman World: A Handbook* (Harrisburg: Trinity, 2003).
Sandnes, Karl Olav, *Belly and Body in the Pauline Epistles*, SNTSMS 120 (Cambridge, UK: Cambridge University Press, 2002).
Schenk, Wolfgang, *Die Philipperbriefe des Paulus: Kommentar* (Stuttgart: Kohlhammer, 1984).
Schille, Gottfried, *Frühchristliche Hymnen* (Berlin: Evangelische Verlagsanstalt, 1965).
Schinkel, Dirk, "'Unsere Bürgerschaft befindet sich im Himmel' (Phil 3,20): ein biblisches Motiv und seine Entwicklung im frühen Christentum," *BN* 133 (2007), 79–97.
Schittko, Martin Paul, *Analogien als Argumentationstyp. Vom Paradeigma zur Similitudo*, Hyp 144 (Göttingen: Vandenhoeck & Ruprecht, 2003).
Schmithals, Walter, *Paul and the Gnostics* (Nashville: Abingdon, 1972).
Schnelle, Udo, "Transformation und Partizipation als Grundgedanken paulinischer Theologie," *NTS* 47 (2001), 58–75.
Schnelle, Udo, *Paulus. Leben und Denken* (Berlin: De Gruyter, 2003).
Schnelle, Udo, *Einleitung in das Neue Testament* (Göttingen: Vandenhoeck & Ruprecht, [6]2007).
Schoon-Janssen, Johannes, *Umstrittene "Apologien" in den Paulusbriefen. Studien zur rhetorischen Situation des 1. Thessalonicherbriefes, des Galaterbriefes und des Philipperbriefes*, GTA 45 (Göttingen: Vandenhoeck & Ruprecht, 1991).
Schreiber, Stefan, "Cavete Canes! Zur wachsenden Ausgrenzungsvalenz einer neutestamentlichen Metapher," *BZ* 45 (2001), 170–192.
Schreiber, Stefan, "Paulus im 'Zwischenzustand': Phil 1.23 und die Ambivalenz des Sterbens als Provokation," *NTS* 49 (2003), 336–359.
Schüssler Fiorenza, Elisabeth, *In Memory of Her: A Feminist Theological Reconstruction of Christian Origins* (New York: Crossroad, [10]1994).
Schüssler Fiorenza, Elisabeth, *The Power of the Word: Scripture and the Rhetoric of Empire* (Minneapolis: Fortress, 2007).
Schweizer, Eduard, *Erniedrigung und Erhöhung bei Jesus und seinen Nachfolgern*, AThANT 28 (Zürich: Zwingli, [2]1962).
Schwemer, Anna Maria, "Himmlische Stadt und himmlisches Bürgerrecht bei Paulus (Gal 4,26 und Phil 3,20)," in Martin Hengel, Siegfried Mittmann, and Anna Maria Schwemer (eds.), *La Cité de Dieu/Die Stadt Gottes*, WUNT 1.129 (Tübingen: Mohr Siebeck, 2000), 194–243.
Scroggs, Robin, "Paul the Prisoner: Political Asceticism in the Letter to the Philippians," in Leif E. Vaage and Vincent L. Wimbush (eds.), *Asceticism and the New Testament* (London: Routledge, 1999), 187–208.
Seeley, David, *Deconstructing the New Testament*, BIS 5 (Leiden: Brill, 1994).
Silva, Moisés, *Philippians*, BECNT (Grand Rapids: Baker, [2]2005).
Simmons, William A., "Sovereignty and Existential Anxiety in Paul: Soliloquy and Self-Disclosure in Philippians," in T. L. Cross and E. B. Powery (eds.),

The Spirit and the Mind (Lanham: University Press of America, 2000), 119–129.
Smallwood, E. Mary, *The Jews Under Roman Rule: From Pompey to Diocletian: A Study in Political Relations* (Leiden: Brill, 2001).
Smallwood, E. Mary, *The Reluctant Parting: How the New Testament's Jewish Writers Created a Christian Book* (San Francisco: HarperSanFrancisco, 2005).
Smith, James A., *Marks of an Apostle: Deconstruction, Philippians, and Problematizing Pauline Theology*, SemeiaSt 53 (Atlanta: Society of Biblical Literature, 2005).
Snyman, A. H., "Persuasion in Philippians 4.1–20," in Porter and Olbricht (eds.), *Rhetoric*, 325–337.
Snyman, Andries H., "A Rhetorical Analysis of Philippians 3:1–11," *Neot* 40 (2006), 259–283.
Söding, Thomas and Christian Münch, *Kleine Methodenlehre zum Neuen Testament* (Freiburg: Herder, 2005).
Sommerstein, Alan H., "Rape and Young Manhood in Athenian Comedy," in Foxhall and Salmon (eds.), *Thinking*, 100–114.
Späth, Thomas, "Männerfreundschaften—politische Freundschaften? Männerbeziehungen in der römischen Aristokratie," in Walter Erhart and Britta Herrmann (eds.), *Wann ist der Mann ein Mann? Zur Geschichte der Männlichkeit* (Stuttgart: Metzler, 1997), 192–211.
Standhartinger, Angela, "Die paulinische Theologie im Spannungsfeld römisch-imperialer Machtpolitik. Eine neue Perspektive auf Paulus, kritisch geprüft anhand des Philipperbriefs," in Friedrich Schweitzer (ed.), *Religion, Politik und Gewalt*, VWGT 29 (Gütersloh: Gütersloher Verlagshaus, 2006), 364–382.
Standhartinger, Angela, "'Join in imitating me' (Philippians 3.17): Towards an Interpretation of Philippians 3," *NTS* 54 (2008), 417–435.
Stanley, David M., "Imitation in Paul's Letters: Its Significance for His Relationship to Jesus and to His Own Christian Foundations," in Richardson and Hurd (eds.), *Jesus*, 127–141.
Starr, James and Troels Engberg-Pedersen (eds.), *Early Christian Paraenesis in Context*, BZNW 125 (Berlin: De Gruyter, 2004).
Stegemann, Ekkehard W., "'Auf Hoffnung sind wir gerettet'. Heilserwartung im frühen Christentum zwischen Apokalyptik und realisierter Eschatologie," in idem, *Paulus*, 113–124.
Stegemann, Ekkehard W., "'Das ängstliche Harren der Kreatur'. Angst und Hoffnung im apokalyptischen Weltentwurf des Paulus," in idem, *Paulus*, 251–258.
Stegemann, Ekkehard W., *Paulus und die Welt. Aufsätze* (ed. Christina Tuor and Peter Wick; Zürich: TVZ, 2005).
Stemmler, Michael, "*Auctoritas exempli*. Zur Wechselwirkung von kanonisierten Vergangen-heitsbildern und gesellschaftlicher Gegenwart in der spätrepublikanischen Rhetorik," in Bernhard Linke and Michael Stemmler (eds.), *Mos Maiorum. Untersuchung zu den Formen der Identitätsstiftung*

und Stabilisierung der römischen Republik, Historia-Einzelschriften 141 (Stuttgart: Steiner, 2000), 141–205.

Stemmler, Michael, "Institutionalisierte Geschichte. Zur Stabilisierungsleistung und Symbolizität historischer Beispiele in der Redekultur der römischen Republik," in Melville (ed.), *Institutionalität*, 219–240.

Stendahl, Krister, *The Final Account: Paul's Letter to the Romans* (Minneapolis: Fortress, 1995).

Sterling, Gregory E., "Hellenistic Philosophy and the New Testament," in Stanley E. Porter (ed.), *Handbook to the Exegesis of the New Testament* (Leiden: Brill, 2002), 313–358.

Still, Todd D. and David G. Horrell (eds.), *After the First Urban Christians: The Social-Scientific Study of Pauline Christianity* (London: T&T Clark, 2009).

Stowers, Stanley K., *Letter Writing in Greco-Roman Antiquity*, LEC 5 (Philadelphia: Westminster, 1986).

Stowers, Stanley K., "Social Typification and the Classification of Ancient Letters," in Jacob Neusner, Peder Borgen, Ernest S. Frerichs, and Richard A. Horsley (eds.), *The Social World of Formative Christianity and Judaism: Essays in Tribute to Howark Clark Kee* (Philadelphia: Fortress, 1988), 78–90.

Stowers, Stanley K., "Friends and Enemies in the Politics of Heaven," in Jouette M. Bassler (ed.), *Pauline Theology. Vol. 1: Thessalonians, Philippians, Galatians, Philemon* (Minneapolis: Fortress, 1991), 105–121.

Strecker, Christian, *Die liminale Theologie des Paulus. Zugänge zur paulinischen Theologie aus kulturanthropologischer Perspektive*, FRLANT 185 (Göttingen: Vandenhoeck & Ruprecht, 1999).

Strecker, Christian, "Leben als liminale Existenz. Kulturanthropologische Betrachtungen zum frühchristlichen Existenzverständnis am Beispiel von Phil 3," *EvTh* 68 (2008), 460–472.

Stubbs, David L., "The Shape of Soteriology and the Pistis Christou Debate," *SJT* 61 (2008), 137–157.

Swancutt, Diana M., "'The Disease of Effemination': The Charge of Effeminacy and the Verdict of God (Romans 1:18–2:16)," in Moore and Capel Anderson (eds.), *Masculinities*, 193–233.

Taatz, Irene, *Frühjüdische Briefe. Die paulinischen Brief im Rahmen der offiziellen religiösen Briefe des Frühjudentums*, NTOA 16 (Göttingen: Vandenhoeck & Ruprecht, 1991).

Tannehill, Robert C., *Dying and Rising with Christ: A Study in Pauline Theology*, BZNW 32 (Berlin: Töpelmann, 1967).

Tellbe, Mikael, *Paul between Synagogue and State: Christians, Jews, and Civic Authorities in 1 Thessalonians, Romans, and Philippians*, ConBNT 34 (Stockholm: Almqvist & Wiksell, 2001).

Theissen, Gerd, *Studien zur Soziologie des Urchristentums*, WUNT 1.19 (Tübingen: Mohr Siebeck, ³1989).

Theobald, M., "Freundschaft I. Griechisch-hellenistisch und NT," *LThK*³ 4 (1995), 132–133.

Thielman, Frank S., "Ephesus and the Literary Setting of Philippians," in Donaldson and Sailors (eds.), *Greek*, 205–223.
Thornton, Bruce S., *Eros: The Myth of Ancient Greek Sexuality* (Boulder: Westview, 1997).
Thraede, Klaus, *Grundzüge griechisch-römischer Brieftopik*, Zet 48 (München: Beck, 1970).
Thrall, Margareth E., *2 Corinthians*, ICC (Edinburgh: T&T Clark, 2000).
Tobin, Thomas H., "The World of Thought in the Philippian Hymn (Philippians 2:6–11)," in John Fotopoulos (ed.), *The New Testament and Early Christian Literature in Greco-Roman Context*, NovTSup 122 (FS David E. Aune; Leiden: Brill, 2006), 91–104.
Trapp, Michael (ed.), *Greek and Latin Letters: An Anthology with Translation* (Cambridge, UK: Cambridge University Press, 2003).
Tredennick, Hugh (ed. and trans.), *Aristotle: Prior Analytics*, LCL (London: Heinemann, 1938).
Tsjuji, Manabu, *Glaube zwischen Vollkommenheit und Verweltlichung. Eine Untersuchung zur literarischen Gestalt und inhaltlichen Kohärenz des Jakobusbriefes*, WUNT 2.93 (Tübingen: Mohr Siebeck, 1997).
Tunstead Burtchaell, James, *From Synagogue to Church: Public Services and Offices in the Earliest Christian Communities* (Cambridge, UK: Cambridge University Press, 1992).
Ulrichs, Karl Friedrich, *Christusglaube: Studien zum Syntagma Pistis Christou und zum paulinischen Verständnis von Glaube und Rechtfertigung*, WUNT 2.227 (Tübingen: Mohr Siebeck, 2007).
Van Kooten, George H. (ed.), *The Revelation of the Name YHWH to Moses: Perspectives from Judaism, the Pagan Graeco-Roman World, and Early Christianity*, TBN 9 (Leiden: Brill, 2006).
Verseput, Donald J., "Genre and Story: The Community Setting of the Epistle of James," *CBQ* 62 (2000), 96–110.
Vincent, Marvin R., *A Critical and Exegetical Commentary on the Epistles to the Philippians and to Philemon*, ICC (Edinburgh: T&T Clark, 1922).
Vischer, Lukas, Ulrich Luz, and Christian Link, *Ökumene im Neuen Testament und heute* (Göttingen: Vandenhoeck & Ruprecht, ²2009).
Vittinghoff, Friedrich, *Römische Kolonisation und Bürgerrechtspolitik unter Caesar und Augustus*, AbhMainz 1951: 14 (Steiner: Wiesbaden, 1952).
Volkmann, R., *Die Rhetorik der Griechen und Römer in systematischer Übersicht* (repr. Hildesheim, 1963 [Leipzig, 1885]).
Vollenweider, Samuel, "Die Waagschalen von Leben und Tod: Zum antiken Hintergrund von Phil 1,21–26," *ZNW* 85 (1994), 93–115.
Vollenweider, Samuel, "Der 'Raub' der Gottgleichheit: Ein religionsgeschichtlicher Vorschlag zu Phil 2.6(–11)," *NTS* 45 (1999), 413–433.
Vollenweider, Samuel, "Die Metamorphose des Gottessohnes. Zum epiphanialen Motivfeld in Phil 2,6–8," in Mell and Müller (eds.), *Urchristentum*, 107–131.
Vollenweider, Samuel, "Hymnus, Enkomion oder Psalm? Schattengefechte in der neutesta-mentlichen Wissenschaft," *NTS* 56 (2010), 208–231.

Vos, Johan S., "Phil 1,12–26 und die Rhetorik des Erfolges," in Galitis, Gnilka, Hartman, Mihoc, Standaert, and Vos, *Vivere*, 53–87.

Wagner-Hasel, Beate, "Das Diktum der Philosophen: Der Ausschluss der Frauen aus der Politik und die Sorge vor der Frauenherrschaft," in Thomas Späth and Beate Wagner-Hasel (eds.), *Frauenwelten in der Antike. Geschlechterordnung und weibliche Lebenspraxis* (Darmstadt: Wissenschaftliche Buchgesellschaft, 2000), 198–217.

Walter, Nikolaus, "Der Brief an die Philipper," in Nikolaus Walter, Eckhart Reinmuth, and Peter Lampe (eds.), *Die Briefe and die Philipper, Thessalonicher und an Philemon*, NTD 8.2 (Göttingen: Vandenhoeck & Ruprecht, 1998), 11–101.

Walters, Jonathan, "Invading the Roman Body: Manliness and Impenetrability in Roman Thought," in Hallett and Skinner (eds.), *Sexualities*, 29–43.

Walters, Jonathan, "Juvenal, *Satire* 2: Putting Male Sexual Deviants on Show," in Foxhall and Salmon (eds.), *Thinking*, 148–157.

Ware, James P., *The Mission of the Church in Paul's Letter to the Philippians in the Context of Ancient Judaism*, NovTSup 120 (Leiden: Brill, 2005).

Ware, James P., *Paul and the Mission of the Church: Philippians in Ancient Jewish Context* (Grand Rapids: Baker, 2011).

Watson, Duane F., "A Reexamination of the Epistolary Analysis Underpinning the Arguments for the Composite Nature of Philippians," in Fitzgerald, Olbricht, and White (eds.), *Christianity*, 157–177.

Watson, Duane F., "A Rhetorical Analysis of Philippians and its Implications for the Unity Question," *NovT* 30 (1988), 57–88.

Watson, Duane F., "The Integration of Epistolary and Rhetorical Analysis of Philippians," in Stanley E. Porter and Thomas H. Olbricht (eds.), *Rhetorical Analysis of Scripture*, JSNTSup 146 (Sheffield: Sheffield Academic Press, 1997), 398–426.

Webb, Ruth, "Poetry and Rhetoric," in Stanley Porter (ed.), *Handbook of Classical Rhetoric in the Hellenistic Period 330 B.C. – A.D. 400* (Leiden: Brill, 1997), 339–369.

Webster, John B., "Christology, Imitability and Ethics," *SJT* 39 (1986), 309–326.

Webster, John B., "The Imitation of Christ," *TynB* 37 (1986), 95–120.

Wees, Hans van, "A Brief History of Tears: Gender Differentiation in Archaic Greece," in Foxhall and Salmon (eds.) *Men*, 10–53.

Weidmann, Frederick W., "An (Un)Accomplished Model: Paul and the Rhetorical Strategy of Philippians 3:3–17," in Virginia Wiles, Alexandra Brown, and Graydon F. Synder (eds.), *Putting Body & Soul Together* (FS Robin Scroggs; Valley Forge: Trinity, 1997), 245–263.

Wendland, Ernst R., "Modeling the Message: The Christological Core of Philippians (2:5-11) and its Communicative Implications," *APB* 19 (2008), 350–378.

Wengst, Klaus, *Christologische Formeln und Lieder des Urchristentums*, StUNT 7 (Gütersloh: Mohn, 1972).

White, John L., "Saint Paul and the Apostolic Letter Tradition," *CBQ* 45 (1983), 433–444.

White, John L., *Light from Ancient Letters* (Philadelphia: Fortress, 1986).
Wick, Peter, *Der Philipperbrief: Der formale Aufbau des Briefs als Schlüssel zum Verständnis seines Inhalts*, BWANT 135 (Stuttgart: Kohlhammer, 1994).
Williams, Demetrius K., *Enemies of the Cross of Christ: The Terminology of the Cross and Conflict in Philippians*, JSNTSup 223 (Sheffield: Sheffield Academic Press, 2002).
Williams, Ritva H., *Stewards, Prophets, Keepers of the Word: Leadership in the Early Church* (Peabody: Hendrickson, 2006).
Windisch, Hans, *Der zweite Korintherbrief*, KEK (ed. Georg Strecker; Göttingen: Vandenhoeck & Ruprecht, ^{9}1970 [1924]).
Winkler, John, "Laying Down the Law: The Oversight of Men's Sexual Behavior in Classical Athens," in D. Halperin, J. Winkler, and F. Zeitlin (eds.), *Before Sexuality: The Construction of Erotic Experience in the Ancient Greek World* (Princeton: Princeton University Press, 1990), 171–209.
Winter, J. G., "In the Service of Rome: Letters from the Michigan Papyri," *CP* 22 (1927), 237–256.
Winterbottom, Michael (trans. and ed.), *The Elder Seneca I: Controversiae I-VI*, LCL 463 (Cambridge, MA: Harvard University Press, 1974).
Wire, Antoinette C., *The Corinthian Women Prophets* (Minneapolis: Fortress, 1990).
Witherington III, Ben, *Friendship and Finances in Philippi: The Letter of Paul to the Philippians* (Valley Forge: Trinity, 1994).
Wolter, Michael, "Der Apostel und seine Gemeinden als Teilhaber am Leidensgeschick Jesu Christi: Beobachtungen zur paulinischen Leidenstheologie," *NTS* 36 (1990), 535–557.
Wuellner, W., "Greek Rhetoric and Pauline Argumentation," in W. R. Schoedel and R. L. Wilken (eds.) *Early Christian Literature and the Classical Intellectual Tradition: In Honorem Robert M. Grant*, ThH 54 (Paris: Beauchesne, 1979), 177–188.
Yadin, Yigael, "Expedition D," *IEJ* 11 (1961), 36–52.
Yarbro Collins, Adele, "The Worship of Jesus and the Imperial Cult," in Carey C. Newman (ed.), *The Jewish Roots of Christological Monotheism: Papers from the St. Andrews Conference on the Historical Origins of the Worship of Jesus*, SJSup 63 (Leiden: Brill, 1999), 234–257.
Yarbro Collins, Adele, "Psalms, Phil 2.6–11, and the Origins of Christology," *BibInt* 11 (2003), 361–372.
Zimmermann, Ruben, "Urchristliche Parabeln im Horizont antiken Rhetorik. Der Beitrag von Aristoteles und Quintilian zur Formbestimmung der Gleichnisse," in Linda Hauser, Ferdinand R. Prostmeier, and Christa Georg-Zöller (eds.), *Jesus als Bote des Heils. Heilsverkündigung und Heilserfarhung in frühchristlicher Zeit*, SBS 60 (FS Detlev Dormeyer; Stuttgart: Verlag Katholisches Bibelwerk, 2008), 201–225.

INDEX OF AUTHORS

Aeschines 150
Agosto, Efrain 109
Al-Suadi, Soham 137
Alexander, Loveday 41–42, 44, 46, 49, 51, 56, 108, 121
Alston, Richard 66
Anderson, H. 30
Anderson, Jr., R. Dean 32
Andocides 34
Apsines 34
Aristides 34
Aristophanes 6
Aristotle 17–21, 24, 25, 29, 30, 33, 34, 35, 36, 120
Ascough, Richard S. 3, 40, 58, 77, 106
Assmann, Jan 23
Avemarie, Friedrich 88

Babbitt, Frank Cole 150
Badian, E. 48
Bakirtzis, Charalambos 55
Balla, Peter 110
Balthasar, Hans Urs von 164
Balz, Horst 43
Barclay, John M. G. 72
Barth, Gerhard 54, 57, 58, 59, 60, 63, 64, 65, 71, 72, 73, 75, 82, 83, 86, 88, 89, 90, 91, 92, 93, 95, 98, 99, 107, 109, 110, 112, 113, 123, 124, 126, 130, 131, 132
Barth, Karl 8, 47, 54, 58, 64, 89, 93
Bartlett, David L. 2
Basevi, Claudio 35
Baumert, Norbert 103–105
Beare, F. W. 106, 129
Becker, Eve-Marie 38
Becker, Jürgen 133
Berger, Klaus 6, 23, 29, 72, 87, 125
Berger, Peter L. 23

Berry, D. H. 27
Berry, Ken L. 48
Best, Ernest 1, 85
Betz, Hans Dieter 7, 84, 119–120
Bianchini, Francesco 14–15, 16, 72, 73, 118, 119, 122, 123, 124, 125, 126, 127, 130, 132, 138
Biard, Pierre 127
Bittasi, Stefano 15, 40, 79, 83, 93, 96, 98, 116
Black, David Alan 4, 11, 40, 61, 71, 79, 82, 156
Bloch, René 70
Bloomquist, L. Gregory 13, 68, 69, 110
Bockmuehl, Markus 11, 52, 54, 86, 95, 122, 127, 138
Bonner, S. F. 151
Bormann, Lukas 49, 55, 66, 77
Bornkamm, Günther 87
Böttrich, Christfried 54
Bradley, Keith R. 147, 148
Brändl, Martin 69
Brenk, Frederick E. 23
Briggs Kittredge, Cynthia 36, 49, 85, 94, 96, 97, 108, 115, 143, 156
Brown, Colin 8
Brown, Raymond E. 53
Bruce, F. F. 3, 10
Brucker, Ralph 31, 33, 40, 43, 61, 78, 80, 83, 84, 86, 92, 99, 108, 110, 117, 118
Bultmann, Rudolf 33
Bürgel, Peter 31
Burridge, Richard A. 6, 23, 161
Burtchaell, James Tunstead 3
Byrnes, Michael 43, 126, 141
Byron, John 10, 52, 57, 84, 88, 96, 97, 100, 110, 111, 113, 116, 140, 141, 161
Byrskog, Samuel 23

C. Iulius Victor 32
Callan, Terrence 118
Campbell, Douglas A. 123
Capel Anderson, Janice 144
Castelli, Elizabeth 2, 3, 12, 16, 137, 138
Chapa, Juan 35
Cicero 18, 20, 24, 34, 108, 120
Clark, Gillian 154
Clarke, Andrew D. 2, 3, 6, 16
Classen, Carl Joachim 30, 31, 32
Claussen, Carsten 3
Clement of Alexandria 104
Clines, David J. A. 148, 149
Collange, Jean-François 94, 111
Collins, J. J. 143
Conway, Colleen M. 146
Cotter, Wendy J. 81
Cowley, Arthur E. 50
Croy, N. Clayton 66
Culpepper, R. Alan 108, 112

Dahl, Nils A. 45, 71, 84, 91, 102, 106, 107, 155, 156
Darling Young, Robin 146
David, Jean-Michel 27
Davidson, James 145
Davis, Casey Wayne 40
De Boer, Martinus C. 128
De Boer, Willis Peters 6, 12, 138
De Lacy, Phillip H. 26, 28, 29
De Vaux, R. 50
De Vos, Craig S. 55, 70, 75, 81, 82, 132
Debanné, Marc J. 16, 19, 34
Deichgräber, Reinhard 87, 89
Deissmann, Adolf 40, 54
Demetrius 32
Democrites 34
Demoen, Kristoffel 25, 27
Demosthenes 26, 34, 35
Dench, Emma 145
Dibelius, Martin 7, 53, 58, 59, 65, 72, 74, 80, 83, 87, 89, 91, 93, 95, 103, 106, 109, 111, 127, 132, 156
Dilts, Mervin R. 150
Dio Cassius 34
Dio Chrysostomos 26

Doble, Peter 133
Dodd, Brian 6, 9, 12–13, 46, 65, 68, 69, 70, 71, 72, 73, 74, 75, 76, 114, 116–117, 122, 123, 124, 126, 127, 129, 131, 132, 133, 134, 137–138, 139, 140
Doughty, Darrel J. 72
Droge, Arthur J. 66
Duff, Tim 28
Duling, Dennis C. 125
Dunn, James D. G. 74, 88, 124, 162

Eastman, Susan Grove 16–17, 91
Ebel, Eva 3
Ebner, Martin 77
Egger, Wilhelm 4, 5, 62, 126
Ehrensperger, Kathy 35
Einarson, Benedict 26, 28, 29
Ellington, Dustin W. 6
Engberg-Pedersen, Troels 4, 10, 16, 52, 71, 77, 82, 110, 127, 162
Epictetus 118
Eriksson, Anders 23, 163
Exler, Francis Xavier J. 44

Fantham, Elaine 147
Fee, Gordon D. 11, 33, 52, 54, 84, 96, 100, 123, 140
Finley, Moses I. 146
Fiore, Benjamin 6, 17, 19, 20, 23
Fischer, Susan 145
Fisher, Nick 150, 151
Fisk, Bruce N. 89
Fitzgerald, John T. 48
Foley, Helene Peet 147
Foucault, Michel 148
Fowl, Stephen E. 11, 14, 39, 54, 60, 62, 72, 75, 79, 80, 82, 88, 91, 92, 93, 94, 96, 97, 98, 103, 141
Frazier, Françoise 24, 28

Galloway, Lincoln E. 6
Gardner, Jane F. 150
Garland, D. E. 143
Garrison, Daniel H. 145
Gehrke, H.-J. 48
Geoffrion, Timothy C. 122
Georgi, Dieter 88

Index of Authors

Gerber, Christine 30, 31, 37, 48, 49, 51, 58, 60, 62, 63, 67, 97, 100, 110
Gerhardsson, Birger 35
Giesen, Heinz 100
Gleason, Maud W. 146
Gnilka, Joachim 63, 75, 82, 90, 96, 111, 117, 121, 126, 130
Gooder, Paula 2
Goodman, Martin 145
Gordon, Pamela 146
Gräbe, Petrus J. 79, 90, 107
Gunderson, Erik 148, 150
Gunther, John J. 74
Gupta, Nijay K. 65

Hack Polaski, Sandra 2, 145
Hainz, Josef 104
Hallett, Judith P. 146
Haltenhoff, Andreas 23
Hansen, G. Walter 48, 60
Hardie, Alex 86
Harnisch, Wolfgang 121, 123, 124, 126, 128, 131, 132, 133
Harrill, J. Albert 149
Harrison, James R. 153
Hartman, Lars 59
Haterius 146
Hawthorne, Gerald F. 75, 124, 126, 129, 133
Hays, Richard B. 161
Heath, Malcolm 27
Heil, John Paul 40, 61, 84, 94, 97, 132, 162
Hellerman, Joseph H. 16, 55, 56, 92, 105–106, 125, 141
Hengel, Martin 87, 97
Hermagoras 108
Herter, H. 145
Hock, Ronald F. 23
Hofius, Otfried 97
Holladay, Carl R. 118
Holleman, Joost 88
Holloway, Paul A. 40, 43, 51, 53, 62, 63, 64, 72, 73, 77, 108, 110, 111, 114, 115, 124, 127, 156
Hölscher, Tonio 24
Hooker, Morna D. 10, 11, 64, 85, 90, 111, 142

Horrell, David G. 3, 72
Hurley, R. 148
Hurtado, Larry W. 9, 10, 89, 92, 107

Isocrates 6, 26, 34
Ivarsson, Fredrik 146, 154

Jaquette, James L. 66
Jewett, Robert 141
Johnson, Luke Timothy 11
Josephus 47, 57
Joshel, Sandra 147

Kampen, Natalie Boymel 147
Karris, Robert J. 103
Käsemann, Ernst 7, 8–11, 87, 88, 89, 94
Kellbe, Mikael 55, 56, 70, 75, 79, 81
Kennedy, George A. 118
Kennel, Gunter 87, 92, 106
Kilpatrick, G. D. 122, 123
Kim, Seong Hee 144
Kim, Yung Suk 2, 114, 162
Klauck, Hans-Josef 31, 32, 38, 39, 40, 41, 50, 54, 75, 112
Klostergaard Petersen, Anders 4
Koester, Helmut 55, 69–70, 74
Konradt, Matthias 65
Koperski, Veronica 43, 74, 127, 128, 129, 130, 133, 142
Koskenniemi, Heikki 38, 42, 45–46
Krentz, Edgar M. 82
Kuhn, T. S. 14
Kurz, William S. 11, 74, 132, 134
Kwon, Soon-Gu 7

Lampe, Peter 3
Laqueur, Thomas 145–146
Larson, Jennifer 146–147, 148, 150, 151, 152, 153
Larsson, Edvin 1, 7, 11, 89
Lattke, Michael 86
Lausberg, Heinrich 17, 27, 143
Lee, Michelle V. 40
Leutzsch, Martin 144
Levine, Amy-Jill 3
Libanius 38
Lietaert Peerbolte, Bert-Jan 16, 88, 92, 107

Lieu, Judith M. 24, 85, 144
Link, Christian 69
Lohmeyer, Ernst 7, 8, 87, 117, 136
Lucian 81
Luckmann, Thomas 23
Luther, Boyd 40
Luz, Ulrich 69
Lyons, George 118
Lysias 6

Malherbe, Abraham J. 6, 17, 35, 39, 51, 120, 156
Marchal, Joseph A. 2, 3, 48, 64
Marcion 43
Marshall, John W. 120–121
Marshall, Peter 151
Martin, Dale 148
Martin, Ralph P. 7, 9–10, 70, 74, 87, 88, 90, 126, 133
Matlock, R. Barry 128
Mayer, Roland 149
Mayordomo-Marín, Moisés 18, 19, 101, 102, 134, 146, 148, 149, 150
McCarthy, Kathleen 147
Mearns, Chris 74
Meeks, Wayne A. 3
Mele, Alfred R. 148
Merk, Otto 6, 7, 8, 137
Metzner, Rainer 69
Meyer-Zwiffelhoffer, Eckhard 145
Michaelis, Wilhelm 2, 60, 138
Milik, J. T. 50
Miller, Jr., Ernest C. 81
Mitchell, Alan C. 48, 51
Mitchell, Margaret M. 2, 21, 25, 26, 32, 33–34, 35, 36, 118, 119, 127
Moore, Stephen D. 144
Moos, Peter von 17
Morgan, Robert 8
Morgan, Teresa 17, 21, 23, 24, 27, 28
Morgan Gillman, Florence 130
Mortara Garavelli, Bice 17
Moss, Candida 1, 2
Moxnes, Halvor 144
Müller, Ulrich B. 44, 46, 48, 53, 54, 55, 57, 58, 59, 60, 61, 62, 63, 64, 65, 76, 79, 80, 81, 82, 83, 84, 85, 89, 90, 91, 92, 93, 95, 96, 98, 99, 100, 108, 109, 111, 139
Mullins, Terence Y. 46
Münch, Christian 5

Nagler, Norbert 2
Niebuhr, Karl-Wilhelm 34–35, 50, 52, 69, 70, 71, 72, 73, 74, 75, 122, 123, 124, 126, 128, 131, 132, 133, 136
Nijf, Onno van 153
Norden, Eduard 87
Nüßlein, Theodor 21

Oakes, Peter 9, 12, 55, 83, 132, 138, 141
O'Brien, Peter T. 11, 14, 43, 52, 54, 71, 73, 79, 86, 88, 91, 92, 95, 96, 99, 114, 122, 123, 124, 129, 139
Økland, Jorunn 145
O'Neil, Edward 23
Otto, Randall E. 130

Park, M. Sydney 11, 14, 16, 86, 88, 89, 90, 137, 161
Parker, Holt 147
Patte, Daniel 16
Peppard, Michael 87
Peterlin, Davorin 69, 73, 79, 98, 156
Peterman, G. W. 77
Peterson, W. 149
Petronius 146
Philo 6, 32, 57
Pierce, Karen F. 147
Pilhofer, Peter 54, 55, 56, 58, 71, 78, 80, 81, 124, 125, 134
Plato 17, 26
Plummer, Alfred 130
Plutarch 23, 26–30, 118, 119–120, 150
Polycarp 43
Pomeroy, Sarah B. 147
Popkes, Wiard 4
Poplutz, Uta 69
Porter, Stanley E. 17, 31, 40
Probst, Hermann 31
Proclus 38
Ps.-Philo 6
Pseudo-Demetrius 32, 38–39
Pseudo-Libanius 39, 49

Quintilian 18, 21, 25, 33, 34, 35, 36, 108, 120, 136

Ramsaran, Rolin A. 2, 82
Raymond, James C. 19
Rebenich, Stefan 23
Reed, Jeffrey T. 31, 32–33, 34, 35, 40, 41, 42, 43, 47, 50, 51, 52, 60, 79, 108, 122
Rei, Annalisa 147
Reibnitz, B. von 48
Reumann, John 10, 43, 44, 48, 49, 54, 55, 56, 57, 58, 62, 65, 66, 71, 72, 73, 77, 79, 80, 81, 82, 83, 84, 85, 86, 87, 89, 91, 92, 96, 97, 98, 99, 107, 108, 113, 123, 124, 131, 132
Richlin, Amy 144, 147, 151
Riesenfeld, H. 86
Robbins, Charles J. 92
Roller, Matthew B. 24
Roloff, Jürgen 2
Ross Wagner, J. 96, 98, 107
Roy, Jim 145
Russell, R. 52

Sanders, E. P. 17
Sandnes, Karl Olav 15–16, 74
Schenk, Wolfgang 4, 44, 48, 54, 59, 62, 65, 75, 82, 86, 92, 97, 100, 109, 112, 114, 117, 118, 124, 130
Schille, Gottfried 87
Schinkel, Dirk 81
Schittko, Martin Paul 17, 18, 19–22
Schmithals, Walter 74
Schnelle, Udo 53, 130
Schoon-Janssen, Johannes 33, 72, 122, 123
Schreiber, Stefan 65, 72
Schüssler Fiorenza, Elisabeth 2, 3
Schweizer, Eduard 88
Schwemer, Anna Maria 134
Scroggs, Robin 81, 91, 153
Seeley, David 3
Seneca 39, 51, 77, 81, 118, 120, 146, 151
Seneca the Elder 150, 151
Shapiro, H. A. 147
Silva, Moisés 10

Simmons, William A. 66
Smallwood, E. Mary 70
Smit, Peter-Ben 40, 66
Smith, James A. 64
Snyman, Andries H. 77, 121
Socrates 34
Söding, Thomas 5
Sommerstein, Alan H. 145
Späth, Thomas 48
Standhartinger, Angela 43, 81, 118, 133, 134
Stanley, David M. 1, 12
Stegemann, Ekkehard W. 96
Stemmler, Michael 23, 24, 25, 26, 27
Stendahl, Krister 118
Sterling, Gregory E. 49–50
Still, Todd D. 3, 40
Stowers, Stanley K. 38, 48, 52, 120
Strecker, Christian 117, 139, 141
Stubbs, David L. 128
Swancutt, Diana M. 145

Taatz, Irene 50–51, 57
Tacitus 70, 149
Tannehill, Robert C. 129, 130
Tellbe 70
Theissen, Gerd 3
Theobald, M. 48
Thielman, Frank S. 54
Thornton, Bruce S. 145, 147
Thraede, Klaus 38
Thrall, Margareth E. 149
Tobin, Thomas H. 47, 88
Trapp, Michael 37–38, 47
Tredennick, Hugh 18
Tsjuji, Manabu 50

Ulrichs, Karl Friedrich 128

van Henten, Jan Willem 88
Van Kooten, George H. 91, 129
Verseput, Donald J. 50
Vincent, Marvin R. 129
Vischer, Lukas 69
Vittinghoff, Friedrich 125
Volkmann, R. 143
Vollenweider, Samuel 65, 86, 88, 91
Vos, Johan S. 53, 64, 72

Wagner-Hasel, Beate 147
Walter, Nikolaus 48, 54, 55, 57, 60, 62, 63, 64, 65, 66, 70, 72, 73, 81, 82, 83, 85, 86, 87, 89, 91, 92, 93, 96, 124, 127, 151
Walters, Jonathan 145, 146, 147
Ware, James P. 7, 48, 60, 64, 65, 66, 67, 75, 81, 91, 98, 99, 116
Watson, Duane F. 32, 40, 42, 46, 80, 97, 108, 122
Webb, Ruth 23
Webster, John B. 9
Wees, Hans van 145
Weidmann, Frederick W. 136
Weiss, Bernard 122
Wendland, Ernst R. 10, 15
Wengst, Klaus 87
White, John L. 37, 38, 42, 44, 45, 46, 49, 50, 61, 63, 68, 112
Wick, Peter 40, 50
Williams, Demetrius K. 8, 21, 25, 32, 33, 34, 35, 36, 42–43, 47, 53, 61, 62, 63, 66, 68, 72, 73, 74, 79, 80, 81, 84, 88, 92, 95, 97, 99, 108, 109, 112, 118, 120, 122, 123, 124, 125, 126, 127, 128
Williams, Ritva H. 3
Windisch, Hans 119–120
Winkler, John 150
Winter, J. G. 44
Winterbottom, Michael 151
Wire, Antoinette C. 2
Witherington III, Ben 31, 32, 34, 36, 40, 57, 62, 66, 78, 83, 84, 94, 95, 99, 108, 120, 122, 136, 151
Wolter, Michael 68
Wright, N. T. 88

Yadin, Yigael 50
Yarbro Collins, Adele 86

Zimmermann, Ruben 7, 17, 32

INDEX OF REFERENCES

(Numbers in italics indicate a footnote reference)

Old Testament

Exodus
16.2 *99*
17.3 *99*

Numbers
11.1 *99*
14.27 *99*

Deuteronomy
26.5-9 *6*
32.5 *99*

2 Samuel
11.9, 11, 13 (LXX) *57*

1 Kings
1.33 (LXX) *57*

2 Kings 18.24 (LXX) *57*

Ezra
4.11b-16, 17b-22 *50*
5.7b-17 *50*
5.11 (LXX) *57*
7.12-26 *50*

Nehemiah
10.30 (LXX) *57*

Job
5.11 *151*
5.11-19 *84*
13.16 (LXX) *64, 158, 159*

Psalms
10.17-18 *84, 151*
21.6 (LXX) *65*
22.16, 20 *73*
24.2–3.20 (LXX) *65*
25.18 *84, 151*
31.7 *84, 151*
68.7 (LXX) *65*
95.7-9 *6*
118.31, 80, 116 (LXX) *65*

Proverbs
3.34 *84, 151*
11.2 *84, 151*
15.33 *84, 151*

Isaiah
4.3 *58*
42.19 (LXX) *57*
45.23 (LXX) *92*
50.10-11 *73*
52–53 *88–89*
53.8 *92*
62.12 *58*

Jeremiah
29 *50*

Ezekiel
37.28 *58*

Daniel
3.31–4.15 *50*
3.93 (LXX – Da$^{th.}$) *57*
6.21 (LXX– Da$^{th.}$) *57*
6.26-28 *50*
9.11 (LXX– Da$^{th.}$) *57*
12.3 (LXX) *99*

New Testament

Matthew
3.9 *124*
6.26, 28 *6*
8.5-13 *97*
9.37-38 *72*
10.10 *72*
12.11 *6*
15.21-28 par. *73*
26.36-46 *6*
27.27 *53*

Mark
2.25-26 *6*
3.24-25 *6*
15.16 *53*

Luke
4.25-27 *6*
10.2 *72*
10.7 *72*
10.13-14 *6*
10.29-37 *6*
10.39-42 *6*
12.6-7, 24, 27 *6*
12.54-55 *6*
13.15 *6*
13.27 *72*
14.5 *6*
14.32-42 *6*
22.40-46 *6*
24.37 *124*

John
18.28, 33 *53*
19.9 *53*

Acts
5.36-37 *6*
6.1-7 *58*
9.13, 32 *58*
16 *56, 108, 109, 115*
16.9-40 *62*
19 *54*
23.1 *80*

Romans *51, 57, 59*
1.1 *57*
1.7 *58*
1.8 *60*
1.8-9 *60*
1.9 *60*
1.9-10 *61*
5.14 *95*
6.1-11 *6, 129*
6.4 *80*
6.13, 16-17 *96*
6.16-17, 19-20 *57*
8.4 *80*
8.17-18 *129*
8.28-30 *6*
10.16 *96*
12.2 *75*
12.7 *58*
12.8 *59*
13.13 *80*
14.15 *80*
14.17 *100*
15.3 *106*
15.7 *89, 106*
15.28 *67*
16 *59*
16.22 *59*

1 Corinthians *36, 59, 61*
1.2 *58*
1.4 *60*
1.4-5 *60*
1.4-8 *60*
1.26 *122*
2.6 *75*

3.5 *58*
3.13 *80*
4.14-15 *152*
4.16 *6*
4.17 *110*
4.18-21 *67*
4.21 *152*
7.17 *80*
7.21-23 *57*
7.40 *124*
8–11 *6*
9.1-27 *6*
9.19 *148*
10.1-12 *6*
10.10 *99*
11.1 *6, 12, 89*
11.17-34 *105*
11.19-24 *59*
12.28 *59*
14.20 *75*
14.27-30, 34-35 *149*
15.32 *54*
15.44-49 *6*
15.52 *65*
16.1-23 *155*
16.5-8 *67*
16.10 *110*
16.21 *59*

2 Corinthians *61, 133*
1.1 *58*
1.3-6 *60*
1.4-10 *129*
2.4, 7, 8 *43*
2.9 *96*
3.8 *58*
3.18 *6*
4.2 *80*
4.4 *6*
4.5 *57*
4.7-15 *129*
5.7 *80*
6.4 *58*
6.5 *54*
7.13 *100*
8.2-3 *100*
10.2-3 *80*
10.10 *146, 149*

11 *148*
11–12 *119*
11.2-3 *152*
11.13 *72, 99*
11.23 *54, 58*
12.14 *67, 152*
12.18 *80*
13.12 *59*

Galatians *57, 58, 59, 60, 61, 72, 73, 133*
1.1 *47*
1.18 *59*
1.23 *80*
2.10 *80*
2.16 *73*
2.17 *73*
2.19 *73*
2.19-20 *6*
3.2 *80*
3.27-28 *105*
4.1-7 *57*
4.12 *6, 12*
5.5 *73*
5.10 *124*
5.12 *73*
5.13 *80*
5.15 *84*
5.16 *80*
5.22 *100*
5.25 *82*
6.11 *59*
6.12 *71*
6.13-14 *73*

Ephesians
6.5-6, 8 *57*
6.23 *59*

Philippians
1.1 *3–4, 7, 57, 58, 94, 97, 102, 109, 110, 111, 115, 139, 140, 144, 148, 159, 160, 162, 164*
1.1-2 *40, 41, 42, 60, 148*
1.1-6 *60*
1.1-11 *41*
1 *80, 115*

Index of References

1.2 59, 62, *97*
1.3 *60*, 61, *62*
1.3-4 62, 76
1.3, 7 *60*
1.3-8 60, *61*
1.3-11 40, 41, 42, 48, *60, 61*, 76
1.4, 8 61
1.4, 25 46
1.5 60, 62, 76, 104, 153
1.5, 7 103, 105
1.6, 10 100, *161*
1.7 *53*, 60, *61*, 76, 103–104, 148
1.7-8 *60*
1.7, 12-18 68
1.7, 12-18, 21-26 *69*
1.8 *33*, 113
1.9 *61*, 127, 161
1.9-11 60, 61, *62*
1.10 61, *161*
1.10, 28 34
1.10b-11 61
1.11 151
1.12 *9, 42, 53*, 63
1.12-16 64
1.12-18a 66
1.12-26 40, 42, 51, 63–67, 80, 83, 158
1.12–2.18 *106*
1.12–4.9 41
1.12–4.20 41
1.13 *53*
1.13-14 *53*
1.13-26 63
1.14 *64*, 66, *124*
1.15 66–67, 99, *111*
1.15a, 17 *64*
1.15, 17 74
1.15-18 *54*
1.15, 16-17, 21, 23-24, 29 *33*
1.16 67
1.17 *53, 64*, 67, 109, 110
1.17–2.4 97–98
1.18 *33*
1.18b-26 *64*, 66
1.19 158, 159

1.19-26 64
1.20 *63*
1.20-24 *53*
1.20-26 *53*
1.21 *65*
1.22 65
1.22-23 *65*
1.23 *65*
1.25 46
1.26 *102*
1.27 *33, 34*, 36, 48, 75, 79–81, 83, 106, 109, *122*, 134, 155, 156
1.27-28a 81
1.27-28 71, 82
1.27-29 82, 83
1.27-30 1, 79–80, 83, 85, *93*, 98, 108, 155
1.27–2.4 80–85, 93, 94, 95, 98, 102, 106, 107, 111, 113
1.27–2.5 156
1.27–2.18 42, 57, 61, *62*, 79–108, 110, 111, 115, 143
1.27–4.1 40
1.28 66, 75, 95, 99
1.28-30 106
1.28b-30 82
1.29 82, 93
1.29-30 65, 75, 82
1.30 6, 66, 75, 83, 95, 106, 111, 116, 155, 158, 159
1.30b *82*
1.39 48
2.1 83, 93, *102*, 103, 104
2.1-2 67
2.1-4 71, 80, 83–85, 93, 94, 95, 98, 100, 155, 157, 158
2.1-4, 12-18 35
2.1-5 155
2.1, 5 94
2.1-18 1, 15, *79*, 159, 160
2 7, 34, 94, 97, 101, 102, 107, 115, *130*, 133,

135, *139*, 140, 142, 143, 157, 163
2–3 1, 44
2.2a 83
2.2 46, *83*, 84, 93, 109, 110, 155, 156
2.2, 3, 12, 14, 18, 29 *33*
2.2-4 83, *98*
2.2-5, 12-18 *34*
2.2, 29 46
2.3 67, 71, 93, *100*, 111, *139*, 151, *161*
2.3-4 84, 106
2.4 71, 85, 93, *95*
2.5 *9*, 84, *88*, 89, 93, 102, *106*, 132, 140, 156, 157, 162
2.5-11 xiii, 6, 7–11, 14, *34, 35, 40*, 57, 71, 80, 84, 85–95, 100, 101, *103*, 106–107, 114, 115, *139*, 140, *141*, 152, 158–164
2.5, 12 111
2.5b 89
2.6a *91*
2.6 85, 93, 94, *152*
2.6b *91*
2.6-7a *93*
2.6-7 92, 106, *129, 133*, 141
2.6-8 *88, 89*
2.6-9 95
2.6-11 *9*, 91, *92, 98, 108*, 116, 132, 138–139, 141–142
2.7 91, *100*, 111, *139, 152*
2.7-8 93
2.7, 27 *97*
2.7bc-8 *93*
2.8 84, 92, 93, 95, 96, 106, 107, 113, *139*
2.8, 17, 25-30 *69*
2.8-9, 15, 17, 21, 27 *33*
2.9 92, *93*, 98, 99
2.9-10 92
2.9-11 *9*, 91, 100, *141*

2.9-11, 12 100
2.11 *139*, 151
2.12 *64*, 95, 97, 98, 99, 100, 106
2.12-16 *161*
2.12, 16 36
2.12-18 93, 94, 95–102, 106, 158
2.12b 98
2.13 67, 98–99
2.13-18 106
2.14 98, 99
2.15 98, 99, *161*
2.16 34, *83*, 97, 98, *99*, 100
2.16-17 100
2.17 14, *33*, 46, *63*, 106
2.18 46, *100*, 117
2.18-19 46
2.18-24 107
2.18-29 48
2.19a 107
2.19 *3*, 67
2.19b 107
2.19, 21 67
2.19-23 *53*
2.19, 23 109
2.19-24 *11*, *34*, 57, 109, 110, 111, 112
2.19, 24 107–108
2.19-30 14, 15, *40*, 42, 63, 67–68, 107–117, 143, 144, 159, 160
2.19-31 1
2.20 109–110, 111, 157
2.20-21 109
2.20-22 109
2.20, 22 67
2.20b-21 *111*
2.21 *111*
2.21f. 110
2.22 *33*, *97*, 108, 110, 111, 113, *115*, 152, 157
2.23 67, 110
2.24 *53*, 54, 109, *124*
2.25 67, 112, 113, *115*, *123*, 157

2.25-20 *53*
2.25-30 *11*, *34*, 107
2.26 68, 112, 113
2.26, 30 *53*, 68
2.27 112
2.27-30 67
2.27, 30 107
2.28 68, 107, 112, 113
2.29 46, 113, 114
2.30 113, 114
3.1 41, 43–44, 46, 117, 122
3.1-2 *44*
3.1-2, 17 *33*
3.1-6 122–126
3:1-16 *11*
3.1-21 *28*, 44, 117, *118*
3 7, 13, 28, *34*, 43, 69, 71, 72–74, 75, 94, 105, 109, 115, 117, *118*, 119, 121–144, 152, 154, 155, 157, 159, 163
3.1–4.1 14–15, 41, *52*, 117–121, *122*
3.1–4.9 43
3.1b 36, *122*
3.2 *33*, 43, 72–75, *99*, 117, 121, 122–123, 135, 159
3.2ff. 116
3.2-3 121
3.2-3, 7, 8, 9 *33*
3.2, 3, 17b-19 *133*
3.2-4a, 17-21 *122*
3.2-16 15
3.2, 18-19 134
3.2-21 1, *9*, 46, 54, 57, 61, *72*, *76*, 121, 135, 136, 138–139, 143, 155, 159, 160
3.3 *73*, *102*, *122*, 117, 123–124, 132
3.3-4 *124*, 132
3.3-14 132
3.3-21 117
3.4 126
3.4f. 117, 124
3.4-5 125

3.4-6 *33*, 125, 126, 152
3.4-11 126, *139*
3.4-14 117, 134
3.4b-6 13, 126
3.4b-6, 15-16 *122*
3.5 125
3.5-6 *124*, 125
3.6 123, 125, *128*
3.7a *126*
3.7 126, 127, 135
3.7b *126*
3.7-8 126–127, 152
3.7-11 130
3.7-14 126–131
3.8a *126*
3.8 126–128, 152
3.8-11 127, 153
3.8b *126*
3.9 *73*, 128, *139*, 152
3.9-10 *127*
3.9-14 152
3.10 *53*, 103, 104, 105, 114, 129, *133*, *139*, 141, 152
3.10-11 128, 129–130
3.10-12, 20-21 *161*
3.10, 18 *69*
3.11 *33*, 129, 130, 131, 152
3.12 75, 131
3.12-13 130–131
3.12-14 136, 153
3.12-14, 20-21 34
3.12-16 *83*
3.13 131, *139*
3.13-14 *33*, 131
3.14 131
3.15 75, 131–132, 138, 140
3.15-16 140
3.15-17 117
3.15–4.1 131–134
3.16 *161*
3.16-17 132
3.17 6, *12*, 13, 65, 111, 116, 123, 132, *133*, 134, 135, *137*, 138, 140, 153, 155, 159

3.17-18 *80*
3.17-20 35, 36
3.18 75, *92*, 132
3.18-19 117, 132, 133
3.18-21 121
3.19 151–152
3.19-21 151–152
3.20 *73*, 81, *122*, 133–134
3.20-21 100, 117, 133, *139*, 140, 141–143, 163
3.20–4.3 156
3.21 36, *129*, 133, *139*, 141, 152
3.25 *53*
4.1 46, 48, 117, 155, 156, 157, *161*
4.1-2 162
4.1-3 71
4.1, 4-6, 8-9 *33*
4.1-9 76
4.1-10 76
4 1
4.2 156, 157
4.2-3 1, 59, 155–157, 159, 160
4.2-3, 4-6, 8-9 *34*
4.2-7 76
4.2-9 40
4.2, 7, 21 *102*
4.3 *69*, *123*, 155, 156
4.4 46, 155
4.4-7, 8-9 155
4.8 67
4.8-9 76
4.9 6, 65, 111, 116, 133, 155, 159
4.10 45–46, 76, 153
4.10, 15 77
4.10-13, 16-17 *33*
4.10-20 41, 43, 44, 45, *49*, *53*, 60, 62, 76, *77*, 78, *79*, 153
4.11 153
4.11, 12 *33*
4.11-13 77, 153
4.11-14 *69*
4.12 *139*

4.13 *77*, 153
4.14 76, 78, 104, 105
4.14-15 103
4.15 *53*, 76, 103, 104, 105
4.16 *43*
4.17 45, 77
4.17-19 77
4.19-20 151
4.21 59
4.21-22 41, 42, *54*, 59
4.21-23 41
4.22 *53*, 59
4.23 41, 42, 62

Colossians
1.13 *110*
2.12, 20 *129*
3.1 *129*
4.7 *110*
4.16 *47*
4.18 *59*

1 Thessalonians *58*
1.2a *60*
1.2 *60*, *61*
1.3-4 *60*
1.6 6, *100*
1.6-7 *12*
2.4 *12*
2.14 6
2.24 6
3.2, 6 *110*
3.6-8 *81*
3.9-10 *100*
3.13 *60*
4.13-18 *65*
5.12 *59*
5.12-28 *155*
5.26 *59*

2 Thessalonians
3.4 *124*
3.17 *59*

1 Timothy
2.11-15 *149*

5.18 *72*
6.21 *59*

2 Timothy
2.11 *129*
2.15 *72*
4.19-21 *59*

Titus
1.11 *149*
3.14 *59*

Philemon 44, *51*, *52*, *58*, *59*, 77
v. 1 58
v. 4 *60, 61*
vv. 4-7 *60*
v. 5 *60*
v. 8 *155*
v. 9 *155*
vv. 23-24 59

Hebrews *31*, 39
2.5-9 *88*
3–4 *6*
11 *6*
13.16 104
13.24 *58, 59*

James 50, *59*
3.1 *149*
5.11, 17-18 *6*

1 Peter *31*
2.21-24 *6*
5.13 *59*

2 Peter *59*
2.4-7 *6*
2.15-22 *6*

1 John *31*, 39, *59*

2 John
1.13 *59*

3 John
v. 15 *59*

Jude *59*
vv. 5-7 *6*
v. 11 *6*

Revelation *39, 59*
1.11 *59*
14.12 *58*
22.21 *59*

Apocrypha

Epistle of Jeremiah *50*

Judith
11.4 (LXX) *57*

1 Maccabees
5.10-13 *50*
8.22-28 *50*
10.18-20, 25b-45 *50*
11.30-37 *50*
12.6-18, 20-23 *50*
13.36-40 *50*
14.20-23 *50*
15.2-9 *50*
16-21 *50*

2 Maccabees *57*
1.1–2.18 *50*
9.19-27 *50*
11.16-21, 22-26, 27, 33, 34-38 *50*
13.14 *83, 113*

2–4 Maccabees *113*

3 Maccabees
2.3-7 *6*
7.16 *113*

4 Maccabees *27, 32*
5.37 *113–114*
6.21 *113–114*
7.8, 16 *113–114*
11.20 *83*
13.1, 27 *113–114*
13.2 *57*
14.20 *146*

15.10 *113–114*
15.29 *83*
16.1 *113–114*
16.16, 19, 25 *83*
16.16-25 *29–30*
16.17 *30*
17.7, 10 *113–114*
17.11-16 *83*

Sirach
16.5-15 *6*
44–50 *6*

Other early Jewish texts

2 Baruch
78-86 *50*
78.2 *57*

4 Baruch
6.19-25 *50*

1 Enoch
89.41-50 *73*

Epistle of Aristeas
256 *57*

Testaments of the Twelve Patriarchs *57*
Testament of Asher
3.2 *57*

Testament of Joseph *88*
7.8 *57*

Testament of Judah
15.2 *57*
18.6 *57*

Test of Naftali
2.8–4.3 *6*

New Testament Apocrypha

Didache
13.2 *72*

Letter to the Laodiceans
v. 13 *43*

Qumran

1 QS 2.24 *84*
1 QS 4.3 *84*
1QS 5.24-25 *84*

CD 2.14–3.12 *6*

Patristic and Greek texts

Aeschines
Against Timarchos
131 *150*

Fais. leg.
88:6 *150*
99:5 *150*
151:4 *150*

Tim.
131:4 *150*
181:10 *150*

Andocides
Or.
3:2 *34*

Rhet. Al.
8:1 *16, 20*
8:1–2 *34*
32:1–2 *34*
32:1–5 *20*

Apsines
Ars Rhet.
1:373 *34*

Aristides
Or.
24:23 *34*

Aristotle
Prior Analytics
24 [= 68b.38–69a.19] *18*

Rhet.
1.2:3–4 *35, 120*
1.2:19 *24*
1.3:4 *34*
1.3:5 *33*
1.4:7 *36*
1.6:1 *35*
1.9:40 *34*
2.20:2 *24, 25*
3.1:5 *33*
3.13:2 *34*
3.17:5 *34, 35*

Rhet. Herr. 20
4:57 *25*

Rhetorica ad Alexandrum
  16, 18, 20

Rhetorica ad Herrenium
  18, 20
4.45:59 *21*

BGU III.846, line 10 *44*

C. Iulius Victor
Ars rhet.
26-27 *32*

Catalogus Sinaiticus 43

Cicero
De Inventione 20
97 *108*

De Or.
2.42:84 *120*
2:335 *34*

Clement of Alexandria
Paed.
2.12 *104*

Demetrius
De Eloq.
223–225 *32*

Democrites
Or.
3:23 *34*

Demosthenes
Ep.
1:10 *35*

Or.
15:35 *26*

Proemia
42:2 *34*

Dio Cassius
Hist. Rom.
52.9:4 *34*

Dio Chrysostomos
Or.
37:23 *26*
41:9-10 *26*

Isocrates
Antid.
231–235 *6*

Ep.
2:5 *26*

Or.
5:111, 113–114 *26*
5:113 *34*
6:82 *26*
7:84 *26*
8:36–37, 143 *26*

Josephus
Ant.
5:39 *57*
7:367 *57*
8:198 *57*
8:257 *57*
11:3 *47*
11:70, 101 *57*
11:90, 101 *57*

B.J.
3:354 *57*
7:323 *57*

P. Oxy.
1409 *47*

Vit.
245 *47*

"Letter of Claudius to the
  Alexandrians" *47*

Lucian
Nig.
6–7 *81*

Lysias
Or.
29 *6*

P. Mich. 191
line 8 *44*

Petronius
Sat.
75:11 *146*

Philo
Mut.
46:4 *57*

Post.
182 *57*

Praem.
13 *6*

Prob.
17 *57*

Sap. Sal.
11 *6*

Sobr.
126, 131 *57*

Somn.
2.51:5   *57*

Plato
Ep.
7:336C   *26*

Plutarch
De laude ipsius
(= Mor. 539A–547F)
  28–29
(= *Mor.* 540A)   *118*
(= Mor. 540C–E)   28
(= Mor. 544D–E)   29
(= Mor. 544E–F)   26

Moralia
88C–D   150
534F–544C   120
539E–F   119
540C–534A   119–120
544C–D   120
544E   120

Vitae Parallelae   28

POxy XII 1481   44, 45

Ps.-Philo
Ant. Bib.
20:3–4   *6*

Pseudo-Demetrius
τύποι ἐπιστολικοι   *32,*
  38–39

Pseudo-Libanius
ἐποστολιμαῖοι χαρακτῆρες
  32, 49
15:17–16:1   *39*
22:4–6   *39*

Quintilian
Inst.
3.8:6   *33*
3.8:10–11   *34*
3.8:12–13   *136*
3.8:13   *35*
3.8:24   *35*
3.8:34–35   *36*
3.8:36–66   *34*
3.8:48   *120*

Inst. Orat.
12.2:22   *25*

Or.
3 (*passim*)   108
9.1   108

Seneca
Ad Helviam matrem
1:3   51

Contr.
4, pref. 10   *146*

De benef.
2.24:2–3   *77*

Ep.
11:8–10   *81*
25:5–6   *81*

Epistolum ad Lucillum
106   120

Epistulae morales   39

Seneca the Elder
Controversiae
I–VI   150, *151*

Socrates
Ep.
5:21–22   *34*
28:10   *34*

Tacitus
Dialogus
18.5   149

His.
5:5   *70*